Message about zagat.com

We are inviting you to become a Charter Member of our zagat.com subscription service for a special introductory price of only $9.95 (a 33% discount off the normal membership charge).

The benefits of membership include:

- **Ratings and Reviews:** Our renowned restaurant ratings and reviews for over 70 major cities worldwide.

- **New Restaurants:** A look at important restaurants as they open throughout the year.

- **ZagatWire:** Our monthly e-mail newsletter covering the latest restaurant openings, closings, chef changes, special offers, events, promotions and lots more.

- **Advanced Search:** With 50+ search criteria, you can find the perfect place for any occasion.

- **Discounts:** Up to 25% off at our online Shop.

We also encourage you to visit zagat.com to vote or make reservations at your favorite restaurants.*

Given all these benefits, we believe that your zagat.com membership is sure to pay for itself many times over – each time you have a good meal or avoid a bad one.

To redeem these benefits, go to zagat.com and enter promotional code LA2004 when you subscribe.

Please join us.

Nina and Tim
Nina and Tim Zagat

*Voting at zagat.com requires independent registration but otherwise continues to be free of charge.

Y0-BBE-644

Offer expires 5/31/04. Cannot be combined with any other offer.

ZAGATSURVEY.

2004

LOS ANGELES SO. CALIFORNIA RESTAURANTS

L.A. Editor: Merrill Shindler

Orange County Editor: Gretchen Kurz

Coordinator: Nicole Prentice

**Editors: Yoji Yamaguchi
and Benjamin Schmerler**

Published and distributed by
ZAGAT SURVEY, LLC
4 Columbus Circle
New York, New York 10019
Tel: 212 977 6000
E-mail: losangeles@zagat.com
Web site: www.zagat.com

Acknowledgments

We'd like to thank Merri Howard, Bob and Marilyn Johnson, Eric Norman, Jayne Prentice, Judy Stabile, Robert Williams and especially Sarah Shindler for giving us the youthful point of view.

This guide would not have been possible without the hard work of our staff, especially Catherine Bigwood, Reni Chin, Schuyler Frazier, Jeff Freier, Shelley Gallagher, Katherine Harris, Natalie Lebert, Mike Liao, Dave Makulec, Jennifer Napuli, Rob Poole, Kelly Sinanis and Sharon Yates.

The reviews published in this guide are based on public opinion surveys, with numerical ratings reflecting the average scores given by all survey participants who voted on each establishment and text based on direct quotes from, or fair paraphrasings of, participants' comments. Phone numbers, addresses and other factual information were correct to the best of our knowledge when published in this guide; any subsequent changes may not be reflected.

© 2003 Zagat Survey, LLC
ISBN 1-57006-544-6
Printed in the United States of America

Contents

About This Survey	5
What's New	6
Ratings & Symbols	7

TOP RATINGS

Greater Los Angeles Area
- Most Popular Places 9
- Food; Cuisines, Features, Locations 10
- Decor; Outdoors, Romance, Stargazing and other Views 15
- Service 16
- Best Buys 17

DIRECTORY & TOP RATINGS BY AREA

Names, Addresses, Phone Numbers, Web Sites, Ratings and Reviews
- Los Angeles/Hollywood/West Hollywood .. 19
- The Westside 83
- South Bay and Long Beach........... 155
- San Fernando Valley and Burbank 177
- San Gabriel Valley/Pasadena/Glendale ... 207
- Orange County.................... 233

INDEXES

Cuisines 278
Locations 291

Special Features
- Breakfast........................... 308
- Brunch............................. 308
- Business Dining 309
- Entertainment....................... 310
- Garden Dining 311
- Historic Places 312
- Hotel Dining 312
- "In" Places 313
- Late Dining 314
- Noteworthy Newcomers 315
- People-Watching 315
- Power Scenes...................... 315

Romantic Places 316
Singles Scenes 317
Special Occasions. 317
Views. 318
Waterside 319
Winning Wine Lists. 319
Worth a Trip 320
Alphabetical Page Index. 321
Wine Chart 332

About This Survey

For 24 years, Zagat Survey has reported on the shared experiences of diners like you. Here are the results of our *2004 Los Angeles/So. California Restaurant Survey,* covering some 1,638 restaurants. This marks the 18th year we have covered restaurants in Los Angeles.

By regularly surveying large numbers of avid local restaurant-goers, we hope to have achieved a uniquely current and reliable guide. For this book, more than 6,000 people participated. Since they dined out an average of 3.7 times per week, this *Survey* is based on roughly 1.2 million meals annually. Of these people, 49% are women, 51% men; the breakdown by age is 17% in their 20s; 28%, 30s; 20%, 40s; 20%, 50s; and 15%, 60s or above. We sincerely thank each of these surveyors; this book is really "theirs."

Of course, we are especially grateful to our editors, Merrill Shindler, distinguished radio personality and restaurant critic, and Gretchen Kurz, a journalist and radio correspondent who covers restaurant, wine and travel topics, and our coordinator, Nicole Prentice, a columnist at *Coast Magazine* and writer/producer at Fox 11 News in LA.

To help guide our readers to LA's best meals and best buys, we have prepared a number of lists. See Top Ratings (pages 9–17), including Best Buys (page 17). In addition, we have provided a number of handy indexes and have tried to be concise. This year, for the first time, we have organized the book by neighborhood and included Top Ratings for each section. Finally, it should be noted that our editors have synopsized our surveyors' opinions, with their comments shown in quotation marks.

As companions to this guide, we also publish guides to restaurants in 70 other markets worldwide, plus nightlife, hotels, resorts, spas, shopping, movies, theater and music, as well as maps, including one to the LA region. Most of these guides are also available on mobile devices and at **zagat.com,** where you can vote and shop as well.

To join any of our upcoming *Surveys,* just register at **zagat.com.** Each participant will receive a free copy of the resulting guide when it is published.

Your comments and even criticisms of this guide are also solicited. There is always room for improvement with your help. You can contact us at losangeles@zagat.com or by mail at Zagat Survey, 4 Columbus Circle, New York, NY 10019. We look forward to hearing from you.

New York, NY
October 1, 2003

Nina and Tim Zagat

get updates at zagat.com

What's New

As this *Survey* goes to press, we're still awaiting the outcome of Total Recall 2003, starring Gray, Arnold and 134 others. In any event, the state's fiscal woes have caused little collateral damage to Angeleno appetites. LA leads the country in dining out, with an average of 3.7 restaurant meals per week, vs. the national figure of 3.2. Only 17% of our surveyors are dining out less than they did two years ago, while 37% are terminating more meals than before.

Your Struggling Actor Will Be With You Shortly: When it comes to crowded rooms or cell phones, our surveyors are a patient lot. Only 1% of them consider either issue a pet peeve. The biggest beef is over service. A whopping 75% of surveyor complaints address spotty treatment by restaurant staffs. Even so, the average tip in LA is a healthy 18%.

Westside Story: Surveyors overwhelmingly prefer the west for fine dining. Home to this *Survey*'s No. 1 for Food, Matsuhisa, Wolfgang Puck's flagship, Spago, and others, Beverly Hills is the not-surprising choice for LA's top dining locale. Not far behind is Santa Monica, where Mélisse and Josie set the standard for New American cuisine. West LA is the place to go for a taste of the East, with Hamasaku, Hide Sushi, Mori Sushi and Sushi Sasabune. West Hollywood is where you'll find two of LA's brightest newcomers, the Provençal specialist Bastide and New French Sona.

Bumper Crop: Even as standout Ginza Sushi-Ko departs for NYC, a wealth of dazzling arrivals is filling the void. These include the Third Street French-Med/wine bar A.O.C., Grace, a classy New American in Fairfax, and White Lotus, Hollywood's new Cal-Asian hot spot. This year's crop is arguably the best since the '80s, when Campanile, Matsuhisa, Patina and Spago turned this town into a major dining destination.

Parla Italiano? LA has long been one of the U.S.'s most diverse cities. The San Gabriel Valley is our answer to Kowloon, with scores of Cantonese seafooders in places like Alhambra, Monterey Park and Rosemead. Studio City's Ventura Boulevard is now known as Sushi Row. There are growing Indian communities in Artesia, Persian enclaves in Westwood and let's not forget East LA's massive Latino population. Yet, the most popular cuisine chosen by our surveyors was, hands down, good old Italian.

Money Matters: The average cost of a meal in LA remained flat at $29.61 (up 1% from last year). Dining here remains a bargain compared to NY ($36.95) or San Francisco ($34.07).

Los Angeles, CA Merrill Shindler
October 1, 2003

Ratings & Symbols

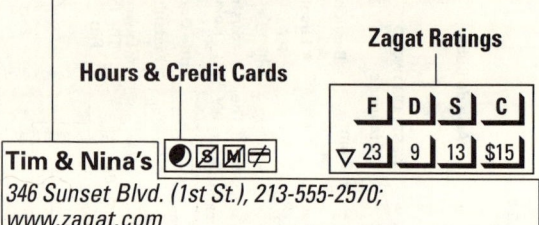

Name, Address, Phone Number & Web Site

Zagat Ratings

Hours & Credit Cards

F	D	S	C
▽ 23	9	13	$15

Tim & Nina's ◐ 🅢 🅜 ⊄

346 Sunset Blvd. (1st St.), 213-555-2570;
www.zagat.com

◪ "Legendary director Alan Smithee is a regular" at this "terrifyingly trendy" "industry hang", a "one-of-a-kind" Chinese-German where "an hour after you eat you're hungry for more sweet-and-sour schnitzel"; nostalgics put off by its severe "Bauhaus meets Mao's house" look and the staff's "yin-yang" uniforms (lederhosen for men, cheongsam for women) say "let's blow this popsicle stand and grab some flannel cakes at Musso's"; P.S. child star Sarah S., the now generation's Shirley Temple, has been seen here eating General Tso's Linzer torte.

Review, with surveyors' comments in quotes

Restaurants with the highest overall ratings and greatest popularity and importance are printed in CAPITAL LETTERS.

Before reviews a symbol indicates whether responses were uniform ■ or mixed ◪.

Hours: ◐ serves after 11 PM
🅢 closed Sunday
🅜 closed Monday

Credit Cards: ⊄ no credit cards accepted

Ratings: Food, Decor and Service are rated on a scale of **0** to **30**. The Cost (C) column reflects our surveyors' estimate of the price of dinner including one drink and tip.

F Food	D Decor	S Service	C Cost
23	9	13	$15

0–9 poor to fair   **20–25** very good to excellent
10–15 fair to good   **26–30** extraordinary to perfection
16–19 good to very good ▽ low response/less reliable

For places listed without ratings or a numerical cost estimate, such as an important newcomer or a popular write-in, the price range is indicated by the following symbols.

| **I** | $15 and below | **E** | $31 to $50 |
| **M** | $16 to $30 | **VE** | $51 or more |

get updates at zagat.com 7

Most Popular

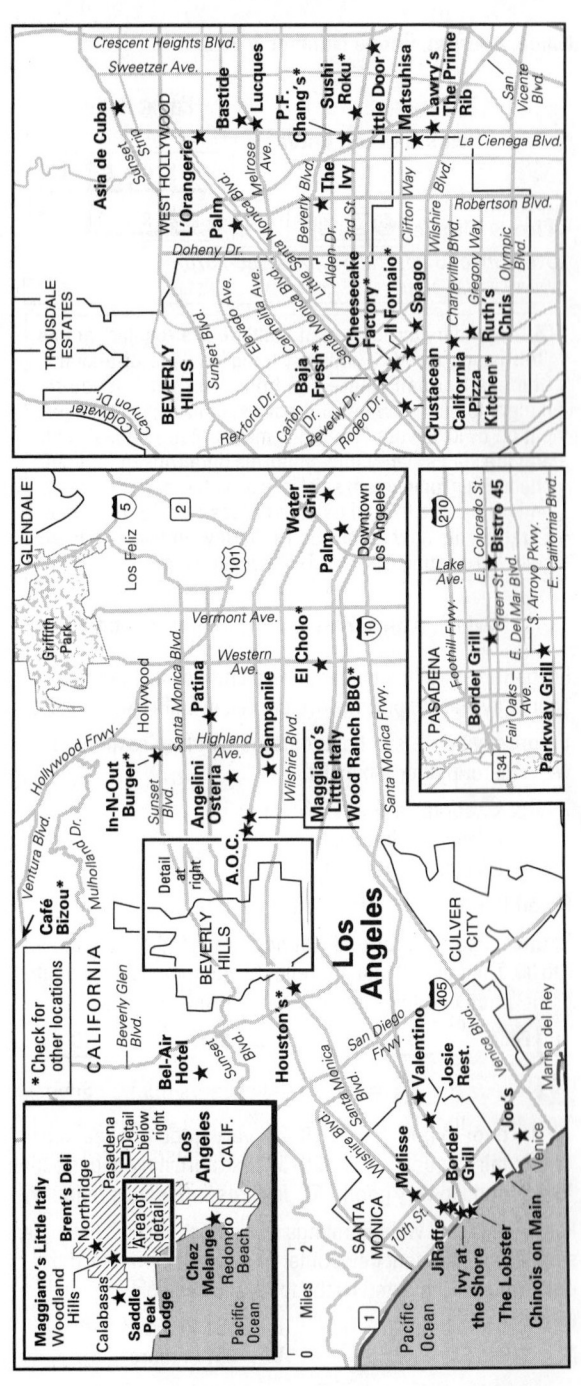

GREATER LOS ANGELES

Top Food

- **28** Matsuhisa
  Katsu-ya
- **27** Nobu Malibu
  Mélisse
  Sushi Sasabune
  Sushi Nozawa
  Bastide
  Derek's
  Sona
  Water Grill
  Christine
  Josie Rest.
  Chinois on Main
  Patina
  Saddle Peak Lodge
  Mori Sushi
  Bistro 45
  Joe's
  Campanile
  Valentino
  Gina Lee's Bistro
- **26** Spago
  Bel-Air Hotel
  Angelini Osteria
  JiRaffe
  L'Orangerie
  Brent's Deli
  Belvedere, The
  Diaghilev
  Shiro
  Brandywine
  Chameau
  Cafe Blanc
  Iroha
  Frenchy's Bistro
  Mako*
  La Cachette
  Alex
  Yujean Kang's
  Grace

By Cuisine

American (New)
- **27** Mélisse
  Josie Rest.
  Saddle Peak Lodge
- **26** Grace
- **25** Leila's

American (Traditional)
- **25** Grill, The
  Clementine
- **24** 555 East
  Uncle Bill's Pancake
  Shenandoah Cafe

Asian/Pan-Asian
- **27** Chinois on Main
- **23** Asia de Cuba
- **21** Typhoon
  Zen Grill
- **19** Buddha's Belly

Barbecue
- **22** Johnny Rebs'
  Dr. Hogly Wogly's
  Lucille's Smokehse.
- **20** Mr. Cecil's
  Wood Ranch BBQ

Cal-Asian
- **27** Gina Lee's Bistro
- **26** Shiro
- **25** Cinnabar
- **24** Max Rest.
- **23** 2117

Californian
- **27** Derek's
  Christine
  Joe's
- **26** Spago
  JiRaffe

Caribbean/Latin
- **24** Xiomara
- **23** Asia de Cuba
  Prado
- **22** Versailles
- **21** Bamboo

Chinese
- **26** Yujean Kang's
- **24** Mon Kee's
  Yang Chow
- **23** Ocean Star
  NBC Seafood

10   subscribe to zagat.com

Top Ratings*

Excluding places in Orange County, and those with low voting.

Greater Los Angeles' Most Popular

1. Café Bizou
2. Cheesecake Factory
3. Spago
4. Campanile
5. Matsuhisa
6. Chinois on Main
7. Water Grill
8. Valentino
9. JiRaffe
10. Joe's
11. P.F. Chang's
12. Lucques
13. Patina
14. Mélisse
15. Bel-Air Hotel
16. Crustacean
17. Ivy, The
18. Lawry's Prime Rib
19. California Pizza Kit.
20. Houston's
21. Asia de Cuba
22. Baja Fresh
23. Bistro 45
24. Border Grill
25. Sushi Roku*
26. Angelini Osteria
27. Ruth's Chris
28. Il Fornaio
29. El Cholo
30. Josie Rest.
31. A.O.C.
32. In-N-Out Burger
33. Palm*
34. Parkway Grill
35. Saddle Peak Lodge
36. L'Orangerie
37. Ivy at the Shore
38. Maggiano's Little Italy
39. Bastide
40. Little Door
41. Lobster, The*
42. Chez Melange
43. Wood Ranch BBQ*
44. Brent's Deli
45. Michael's
46. Chaya Brasserie
47. Ciudad
48. Versailles
49. Arroyo Chop Hse.
50. Claim Jumper

It's obvious that many of the restaurants on the above list are among the Los Angeles area's most expensive, but if popularity were calibrated to price, we suspect that a number of other restaurants would join the above ranks. Given the fact that both our surveyors and readers love to discover dining bargains, we have added a list of 80 Best Buys on page 17. These are restaurants that give real quality at extremely reasonable prices.

---

* Indicates a tie with the restaurant directly above

get updates at zagat.com

Top Food

Coffee Shops/Diners
- 26 Sweet Lady Jane
- 22 Apple Pan
- 21 Cora's Coffee
  - Johnnie's Pastrami
  - Blueberry

Continental
- 26 Brandywine
- 25 Röckenwagner
- 24 Raymond, The
  - Dal Rae
  - Checkers

Delis
- 26 Brent's Deli
- 24 Langer's Deli
- 21 Nate 'n Al's
  - Barney Greengrass
- 20 Greenblatt's Deli

Dim Sum
- 23 Ocean Star
  - NBC Seafood
  - Empress Pavilion
- 22 Ocean Seafood
- 21 Sea Empress

Eclectic
- 26 Chez Melange
- 25 5 Dudley
- 24 Depot
- 21 Literati Café
- 19 Authentic Cafe

Fast Food
- 24 In-N-Out Burger
- 23 Zankou Chicken
- 22 Philippe the Original
  - Gumbo Pot
- 21 Poquito Mas

French (Bistro)
- 26 Frenchy's Bistro
  - Julienne
- 25 Pinot Bistro
- 24 Pastis
  - Mistral

French/Cal-French
- 27 Bastide
  - Patina
  - Bistro 45
- 26 Bel-Air Hotel
  - L'Orangerie

Greek
- 24 Papa Cristo's
- 23 Taverna Tony
- 22 Papadakis Tav.
- 21 Great Greek
  - Delphi Greek

Hamburgers
- 24 In-N-Out Burger
- 23 Father's Office
- 22 Tommy's
  - Apple Pan
- 20 26 Beach Café

Indian
- 24 Bombay Cafe
- 22 Tantra
  - Akbar
  - Surya India
  - Nawab of India

Italian
- 27 Valentino
- 26 Angelini Osteria
  - Posto
  - Giorgio Baldi
- 25 Madeo

Japanese
- 28 Matsuhisa
  - Katsu-ya
- 27 Nobu Malibu
  - Sushi Sasabune
  - Sushi Nozawa

Mediterranean
- 27 Christine
  - Campanile
- 26 A.O.C.
- 25 Reg. Bev. Wilshire
- 24 Gardens

Mexican
- 24 Tlapazola Grill
- 23 El Tepeyac
  - La Serenata/Garibaldi
- 22 La Serenata Gourmet
  - Guelaguetza

Middle Eastern
- 24 Sunnin
- 23 Zankou Chicken
- 22 Carousel
- 21 Javan
  - Carnival

Top Food

Pizza (Californian)
- 26 Spago
- 25 Parkway Grill
- 23 Granita
- 20 Caioti Pizza
- 18 California Pizza Kit.

Pizza (Italian)
- 25 Village Pizzeria
- 24 Casa Bianca
- 23 Farfalla Trattoria
- Abbot's Pizza
- 22 Mulberry St. Pizz.

Seafood
- 27 Water Grill
- 24 Mon Kee's
- 23 Seashell
- Ocean Ave.
- NBC Seafood

South American
- 25 Mario's Peruvian
- 24 Carlito's Gardel
- 22 Picanha Churr.
- 20 Galletto
- 19 Inka Grill

Southern/Cajun/Creole
- 24 Shenandoah Cafe
- 22 Johnny Rebs'
- Ragin' Cajun Cafe
- Roscoe's Hse. of Ckn.
- Gumbo Pot

Steakhouses
- 26 Fleming's Prime
- Ruth's Chris
- Mastro's Steak.
- 25 Lawry's Prime Rib
- Arroyo Chop Hse.

Thai
- 24 Saladang
- 23 Palms Thai
- Talesai
- 21 Tuk Tuk Thai
- 20 Chan Dara

Vegetarian/Health Food
- 21 Urth Caffé
- 20 Inn/Seventh Ray
- 19 Real Food Daily
- 18 Mäni's Bakery
- Newsroom Café

By Special Feature

Bakeries/Desserts
- 27 Campanile
- 26 Sweet Lady Jane
- 25 Clementine
- 21 Le Pain Quotidien
- 20 Il Fornaio

Breakfast
- 24 Uncle Bill's Pancake
- 23 Marston's
- 22 Roscoe's Hse. of Ckn.
- 21 Doughboys
- John O'Groats

Brunch
- 27 Saddle Peak Lodge
- Joe's
- Campanile
- 26 Bel-Air Hotel
- Brent's Deli

Business Dining
- 27 Mélisse
- Derek's
- Water Grill
- Josie Rest.
- Patina

Hotel Dining
- 26 Bel-Air Hotel
- Bel-Air Hotel
- Belvedere, The
- Penin. Bev. Hills
- Diaghilev
- Wyndham Bel Age
- Chez Melange
- Palos Verdes Inn
- 25 Reg. Bev. Wilshire
- Reg. Bev. Wilshire

"In" Places
- 28 Matsuhisa
- Katsu-ya
- 27 Nobu Malibu
- Mélisse
- Sushi Nozawa

Late Dining
- 26 Iroha
- 24 In-N-Out Burger
- 23 Zankou Ckn.
- Ivy, The
- Dan Tana's

Top Food

Lunch
- *28* Matsuhisa
  Katsu-ya
- *27* Mélisse
  Sushi Sasabune
  Sushi Nozawa

Newcomers/Rated
- *27* Bastide
  Sona
- *26* Grace
  A.O.C.
- *21* Opaline

Newcomers/Unrated
- Amuse Café
- Chloe
- Dolce Enoteca
- Noé
- Señor Fred

People-Watching
- *27* Chinois on Main
  Patina
  Gina Lee's Bistro
- *26* Spago
  Grace

Power Scenes
- *28* Matsuhisa
- *27* Bastide
  Sona
  Water Grill
  Patina

Prepared Food
- *26* Julienne
- *25* Clementine
- *23* Zankou Chicken
- *18* Marmalade Café
- *17* Sandbag's Sand.

Worth a Trip
- *27* Nobu Malibu
    Malibu
  Christine
    Torrance
  Saddle Peak Lodge
    Calabasas
  Gina Lee's Bistro
    Redondo Beach
- *26* Frenchy's Bistro
    Long Beach

By Location

Beverly Hills
- *28* Matsuhisa
- *26* Spago
  Belvedere
  Cafe Blanc
  Mako

Brentwood
- *25* Takao
  Peppone
- *24* Zax
  Vincenti
  Toscana

Chinatown
- *24* Mon Kee's
  Yang Chow
- *23* Empress Pavilion
- *22* Philippe the Original
  Ocean Seafood

Downtown
- *27* Water Grill
- *25* R-23
  Arnie Morton's
- *24* Langer's Deli
  Palm

Hollywood/East Hollywood
- *27* Patina
- *25* Mario's Peruvian
- *24* In-N-Out Burger
- *23* Zankou Chicken
  Vert

Malibu
- *27* Nobu Malibu
- *23* Granita
  Malibu Seafood
  Taverna Tony
- *22* Geoffrey's

get updates at zagat.com   13

Top Food

Pasadena/South Pasadena
- *27* Derek's
- Bistro 45
- *26* Shiro
- Yujean Kang's
- *25* Maison Akira

San Fernando Valley/East
- *28* Katsu-ya
- *27* Sushi Nozawa
- *26* Iroha
- *25* Pinot Bistro
- Emmanuel

San Fernando Valley/West
- *27* Saddle Peak Lodge
- *26* Brent's Deli
- Brandywine
- *25* Hirosuke
- *24* Yang Chow

San Gabriel Valley
- *24* Rest. Devon
- Dal Rae
- *23* Ocean Star
- El Tepeyac
- NBC Seafood

Santa Monica/Venice
- *27* Mélisse
- Josie Rest.
- Chinois on Main
- Joe's
- Valentino

South Bay
- *27* Christine
- Gina Lee's Bistro
- *26* Chez Melange
- *24* Reed's
- Depot, The

Third Street - LA
- *26* A.O.C.
- *25* Locanda Veneta
- G. Garvin's
- *24* Michelia
- *23* Sushi Roku

West Hollywood
- *27* Bastide
- Sona
- *26* L'Orangerie
- Diaghilev
- Lucques

West LA
- *27* Sushi Sasabune
- Mori Sushi
- *25* Hamasaku
- Hide Sushi
- *24* Bombay Cafe

Westwood
- *24* Sunnin
- *22* Tengu
- Lamonica's Pizza
- Tanino
- *21* Sprazzo Cuc. Ital.

Top Decor

- **29** Cicada
  Bel-Air Hotel
- **28** L'Orangerie
  Inn/Seventh Ray
  Madison, The
- **27** Grace
  Saddle Peak Lodge
  Reg. Bev. Wilshire
  La Boheme
  Geoffrey's
  Little Door
  Oceanfront
  Crustacean
  Ritz-Carlton Hunt.
  Diaghilev
- **26** Belvedere, The
  Yamashiro
  Bastide
  Gardens
  One Pico

Koi
Dar Maghreb
Il Cielo
Polo Lounge
Tantra
Checkers
Eurochow
- **25** Spago
  Michael's
  Asia de Cuba
  Firefly*
  Katana
  Thousand Cranes
  Mélisse
  Campanile
  Patina
  Alex
  Monsoon Cafe
  Bistro Gdn./Coldwater
  Chez Mimi

Outdoors

Asia de Cuba
Bastide
Bel-Air Hotel
Cafe des Artistes
Il Cielo
Inn/Seventh Ray

Ivy, The
Lobster, The
Michael's
Nobu Malibu
Saddle Peak Lodge
Spago

Romance

Bel-Air Hotel
Brentwood Rest.
Cafe Del Rey
Chez Mimi
Four Oaks
Il Cielo

Inn/Seventh Ray
Josie Rest.
Michael's
Patina
Saddle Peak Lodge
Valentino

Stargazing

Brentwood Rest.
Buffalo Club
Campanile
Crustacean
Dan Tana's
Grill on Hollywood

Ivy, The
Maple Drive
Mastro's Steak.
Mr. Chow
Nate 'n Al's
Spago

Views

Asia de Cuba
Cafe Del Rey
Fenix/Argyle
Geoffrey's
Getty Center
Gladstone's Malibu

Hump, The
Lobster, The
One Pico
Sky Room
Windows
Yamashiro

get updates at zagat.com

LA/Hollywood/W. Hollywood   F | D | S | C

ABC Seafood   20 | 10 | 14 | $20
205 Ord St. (New High St.), Chinatown, 213-680-2887
◪ Expect a "virtual zoo" at lunchtime at this cavernous Chinese seafood house in Chinatown that's long been renowned for its "fabulous dim sum"; despite a "dingy setting" and "machinelike waiters", regulars insist that the food is "as good as it gets without going to Monterey Park" – and the "free parking is a plus."

Ago   21 | 20 | 19 | $46
8478 Melrose Ave. (La Cienega Blvd.), West Hollywood, 323-655-6333
◪ "Good-looking people in black" make this "semi-glitzy" Northern Italian "hangout" a "hip" favorite among West Hollywood's 'in' crowd; it's a "great stop" for "amazing gnocchi" and "celebrity sightings", but if you aren't on the A-list, expect "no attention at all."

Alessi Ristorante & Bar ⓢ   ∇ 22 | 18 | 19 | $38
6602 Melrose Ave. (Highland Ave.), Los Angeles, 323-935-1197
■ This "high-end" Melrose Northern Italian ristorante makes a fine "meeting place" for residents of Hancock Park and Hollywood; credit its "genuinely good" fare (notably the "outstanding pastas"), the "attractive" decor anchored by an impressive oil painting done by artist Maya Garcia and the "live music" featured on most nights.

ALEX ⓢ   26 | 25 | 24 | $70
6703 Melrose Ave. (Citrus St.), Los Angeles, 323-933-5233; www.alexrestaurant.com
■ A "great talent" who's "quickly heading for the top echelon", Alex Scrimgeour pleases with "inventive yet comforting" Cal-French fare (don't miss the goat cheese soufflé salad) at his "warm, wood-paneled" "special-occasion" "favorite" on Melrose that's convenient to the Hollywood studios; groupies gush it's definitely "worth the splurge", for this is "as good as it gets."

Alto Palato   22 | 22 | 21 | $38
755 N. La Cienega Blvd. (bet. Santa Monica Blvd. & Sherwood Dr.), West Hollywood, 310-657-9271
■ "Always underrated", this "affordable" West Hollywood Italian earns props for "perfect" thin-crust pizzas from a wood-burning oven and other "fabulous" fare served in a "high-ceilinged" room by a staff that's "always there to help, but otherwise invisible"; the "superb" Wednesday night regional special is "one of the best deals in town."

Ammo   23 | 16 | 18 | $30
1155 N. Highland Ave. (bet. Fountain Ave. & Santa Monica Blvd.), Hollywood, 323-871-2666; www.ammocafe.com
■ In the industrial heart of Hollywood, "young and so hip" diners lock and load on "fabulous", "invitingly quirky"

LA/Hollywood/W. Hollywood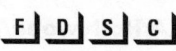

Californian comfort food such as "miraculous" turkey meatloaf at this "chic" "hole-in-the-wall" cafe; "helpful", "competent" service helps mute grumbles over the "echo-chamber" acoustics in the "stark", "tiny box of a space."

Anarkali ▽ 18 | 16 | 18 | $20
7013 Melrose Ave. (La Brea Ave.), Los Angeles, 323-934-6488

■ Pros promise you'll "love the shrimp vindaloo" at this "reliable", "reasonably priced" Indian stalwart in Melrose, but "every dish is a winner"; the "mysterious" decor raises a few eyebrows, but there's nothing suspect about the "warm, friendly" service.

Angeli Caffe 22 | 14 | 19 | $30
7274 Melrose Ave. (Poinsettia Pl.), Los Angeles, 323-936-9086; www.angelicaffe.com

■ At her "casual", "friendly" Melrose Italian sporting an industrial look, cookbook author and radio-show host Evan Kleiman (an "invaluable LA treasure") offers an "amazing, cerebral foodie experience", starting with "fabulous" breads that would "make a perfect meal with just a drizzle of olive oil"; the Thursday night family-style theme dinners are a "definite must."

ANGELINI OSTERIA Ⓜ 26 | 16 | 21 | $42
7313 Beverly Blvd. (Poinsettia Pl.), Los Angeles, 323-297-0070; www.angeliniosteria.com

■ "Gino Angelini delivers what others just promise" at his "bustling", "authentic" Italian in La Brea, offering "wonderful country" cuisine on a "cleverly designed menu that allows you to graze or gorge" and a "knowledgeable" staff that "times your courses perfectly"; the "noisy", "cramped" space leaves many "underwhelmed" ("alta cucina in a coffee shop"), but for most the biggest "difficulty is getting reservations."

Angelique Cafe Ⓢ 21 | 13 | 18 | $16
840 S. Spring St. (bet. 8th & 9th Sts.), Downtown, 213-623-8698

■ An "incredible find" in "desolate" Downtown, this "unpretentious" French cafe "in the center of the Fashion District" is a "joy for lunch" to "garment-industry" types, dishing out "tasty" "real bistro" fare ("great pâté, even for a liver hater") "sans attitude", in a "cute", "charming" setting; the main drawback is that it "closes super early."

Antonio's Ⓜ ▽ 21 | 17 | 21 | $23
7470 Melrose Ave. (bet. Fairfax & La Brea Aves.), Los Angeles, 323-655-0480

■ Local hero Antonio Gutierrez "greets you at the door" of his "family-operated" Melrose Mexican serving "*que bueno*" "authentic Mexico City cuisine", including moles that are some of the "best in the city"; "if you're lucky" the "extremely personable host" will regale you with "stories of

LA/Hollywood/W. Hollywood | F | D | S | C |

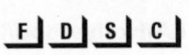

the movie stars that grace the walls" of the "atmospheric" room where mariachi bands perform on weekends.

A.O.C. | 26 | 23 | 24 | $46 |
8022 W. Third St. (Laurel Ave.), Los Angeles, 323-653-6359
■ "Bacchus wouldn't know where to begin" at the Lucques team's instant new hit on Third Street – the "wonderful" wine bar offering 50 vintages by the glass, "sublime" cheese and charcuterie bar or "inventive" French/Med–accented "Californian tapas" menu offering "drama in every bite"; the staff "knows its stuff" and offers "great recommendations", and the "chic, modern" rooms allow the "panorama of great tastes" to "shine forth"; one caveat: those "little plates at not-so-little prices" can add up fast.

Arnie Morton's of Chicago | 25 | 21 | 23 | $53 |
435 S. La Cienega Blvd. (San Vicente Blvd.), Beverly Center, 310-246-1501
735 S. Figueroa St. (bet. 7th & 8th Sts.), Downtown, 213-553-4566
www.mortons.com
■ "Heaven for carnivores" or a "vegetarian's worst nightmare", this "classic" steakhouse trio in Beverly Center, Downtown and Burbank offers "huge portions of prime cow" that are "presented as raw slabs" and live lobsters on rolling carts for you to choose from, in a throwback setting where you half-expect to "see Sinatra in the corner puffin' on a cigar"; "bring your appetite" and "your credit card" for the "big fat steaks at a big fat price."

ASIA DE CUBA | 23 | 25 | 20 | $50 |
Mondrian Hotel, 8440 Sunset Blvd. (bet. La Cienega Blvd. & Olive Dr.), West Hollywood, 323-848-6000
■ The hottest spot on the Sunset Strip, adjacent to the trendy Sky Bar in the hip Mondrian Hotel, this "chichi" affair is a "definite must for out-of-towners", offering a "fabulous fusion" of Asian and Caribbean cuisines in "big family-style portions" and an "enchanting" setting with a "gorgeous patio" overlooking Hollywood and other "first-rate views, both architectural and human"; the staff can be "knowledgeable" and "helpful" or just plain "arrogant."

Asian Noodles | – | – | – | I |
643 N. Spring St. (Cesar Chavez Blvd.), Chinatown, 213-617-1083
Another hint that LA's Chinatown isn't moving to the suburbs, this stylish, high-tech Chinese has roots in Manila, where the Ma Mon Luk family owns seven restaurants; despite the name, they offer more than noodle dishes, including an adobo chicken pizza.

Astro Burger ●🥡 | 19 | 9 | 15 | $9 |
7475 Santa Monica Blvd. (bet. Fairfax & La Brea Aves.), West Hollywood, 323-874-8041
☑ This pair of "no-frills" patty purveyors in West Hollywood and Montebello sends "carnivores" into "burger orbit" with

LA/Hollywood/W. Hollywood

F	D	S	C

"humongous" hamburgers and "rocks the world" of vegetarians as well with a "good selection" of "veggie-friendly" choices; it stays "open long after the bars are closed", attracting an "amusing" post-"clubbing" crowd.

Authentic Cafe
| 19 | 15 | 15 | $24 |

7605 Beverly Blvd. (bet. Curson & Stanley Aves.), Los Angeles, 323-939-4626; www.authenticcafe.com

☑ A "cool crowd" descends on this "cramped" Fairfax bistro serving a "varied, eclectic" American Southwestern menu covering a "diverse territory", from a "skirt steak that rocks" to Szechuan dumplings; many agree the "recent face-lift was needed" – now if only something could be done about the "slow", "erratic" service.

BAJA FRESH MEXICAN GRILL ⊄🅼🅂
| 20 | 11 | 15 | $9 |

8495 W. Third St. (La Cienega Blvd.), Los Angeles, 310-659-9500; www.bajafresh.com

■ The "favorite fast-food option of the health-conscious and foodies alike", this bourgeoning, "remarkably consistent" chain dishes out "fresh", "quick", "cheap" Mexican fare ("monstrous" burritos, "addictive" salsa, "incredible" fish tacos) in "clean, bright" rooms; amigos boast that it "kicks the frijoles" of its rivals.

Balboa
| 25 | 24 | 21 | $54 |

The Grafton Hotel, 8462 W. Sunset Blvd. (La Cienega Blvd.), West Hollywood, 323-650-8383; www.balboaprime.com

■ For "excellent" NY strip on the Sunset Strip, this "hot", "clubbing" crowd flocks to this "sexy", "sophisticated" West Hollywood steakhouse run by the Sushi Roku folks; while the menu of "mouthwatering" beef, "great seafood" and "amazing sides" is the main draw, the "people-watching is half the treat" in the "beautiful", "mazelike" dining room; the service is "friendly", if not always "polished."

Barbara's at the Brewery ⓈⒷ
| △ | 18 | 13 | 15 | $20 |

Brewery Art Complex, 620 Moulton Ave. (Main St.), Downtown, 323-221-9204

■ A "hidden gem" in the "middle of nowhere", this "very chill", "boho hang" located Downtown near the Golden State Freeway is the "only place to eat" for the "eclectic, arty" crowd at the Brewery artists' colony, so expect to see plenty of piercings and tats in the "industrial" room; "excellent" burgers stand out on the "limited" Cal-Eclectic menu that complements an "extensive" bar list.

Barefoot Bar & Grill
| 18 | 20 | 18 | $30 |

8722 W. Third St. (bet. George Burns Rd. & S. Robertson Blvd.), Los Angeles, 310-276-6223; www.barefootrestaurant.com

■ A "shoe-in" for "drinks after work", this "winner" across the street from Cedars offers a "great happy hour" and a "serviceable", "moderately priced" Californian menu with

get updates at zagat.com 25

LA/Hollywood/W. Hollywood   F D S D C

"something for everyone", from "especially good" sushi to "fresh" pastas; there's nothing shoddy about the "comfy" quarters graced with "artwork by locals" (with a private room upstairs) or "friendly" staff that's "nice to look at."

Barfly ◐ ☒   15 19 13 $37
8730 W. Sunset Blvd. (bet. Holloway Rd. & La Cienega Blvd.), West Hollywood, 310-360-9490

☑ Even the "doorman is too cool for school" at this West Hollywood 'in' spot where "posing" and "people-watching" take precedence over the Cal-French cuisine and the room's "so dark you can't see what you're eating" anyway; the staff is so "rude," some find it "entertaining."

Bar Marmont ◐   16 23 15 $30
8171 Sunset Blvd. (Havenhurst Dr.), West Hollywood, 323-650-0575; www.committedinc.com

☑ The focus is on "drinks, decor and celebrities" at this "gorgeous" West Hollywood watering hole next to the historic Chateau Marmont on the Sunset Strip, where "stars" can be seen in the "beautiful", "private" setting and the French fare is "surprisingly good"; the drinks "ain't cheap" and the service can be "snooty", but fans feel it's "worth it" for a taste of the "fabulousness that is LA."

Basix Café   17 15 17 $20
8333 Santa Monica Blvd. (N. Flores St.), West Hollywood, 323-848-2460; www.basixcafe.com

"Consistency is the hallmark" of this "cheap", "reliable" Cal-Italian in West Hollywood that appeals to a largely gay crowd with a "crowd-pleasing menu" of "simple dishes done well" and a "nice mellow" setting, with a dog-friendly patio that's "great in summer"; though the service can be "spotty", the "guy-candy" waiters are usually "kind."

BASTIDE   27 26 27 $96
8475 Melrose Pl. (La Cienega Blvd.), West Hollywood, 323-651-5950

Years (and millions of dollars) in the making and "well worth the wait", this "tiny jewel" in West Hollywood is the "hottest ticket in town", "setting a new standard" for French dining in LA with chef/co-owner Alain Giraud's "divine" Provençal cuisine, served in five "fantastic" tasting menus, a "fabulous" 900-label all-Gallic wine list (with 40 choices by the glass), Andrée Putman's "gloriously understated" design and "impeccable" service.

BCD Tofu House ◐   21 14 12 $13
1021 S. Los Angeles St. (12th St.), Downtown, 213-746-2525
868 S. Vermont Ave. (W. 7th St.), Koreatown, 213-386-8558
3575 Wilshire Blvd. (Kingsley Ave.), Koreatown, 213-382-6677
869 S. Western Ave. (bet. 8th & 9th Sts.), Koreatown, 213-380-3807

■ "Cheap" and "dependable", this "no-frills" 24/7 Korean chain is the place to go for "way awesome" "bubbling tofu

26   subscribe to zagat.com

LA/Hollywood/W. Hollywood F | D | S | C |

hot pot", made "as spicy as you want it to be", that's "perfect on cold, rainy days" or after "a night out and too much to drink"; novices "never knew" bean curd "could taste this good."

Belly ◐ ▽ 17 | 18 | 14 | $21 |
7929 Santa Monica Blvd. (Fairfax Ave.), West Hollywood, 323-822-9264; www.bellylounge.com
◪ Though it's named after the gut, the scene is strictly "hip" at this West Hollywood "hole-in-the-wall" where "twentysomethings" and "reality-show rejects" "go to socialize and drink"; it serves a "surprisingly tasty" "LA spin on tapas" that's complemented by "delicious" sangria and "fun martinis", but most agree "it's not about the food."

Berri's Pizza Cafe ◐ – | – | – | I |
8412 W. Third St. (Orlando St.), Los Angeles, 323-852-0642
With three branches all over town, this inexpensive Italian-Med chain provides a laid-back space where omelets are available in the morning, and the rest of the day is filled with exotic salads, sandwiches, pastas and pizzas – including Moroccan, French and Greek versions.

Bice 19 | 19 | 19 | $37 |
Hollywood & Highland, 6801 Hollywood Blvd. (Highland Ave.), Hollywood, 323-962-3474; www.biceristorante.com
◪ A "great transplant from NY", this paesano pair in Pasadena and Hollywood offers "well-prepared, flavorful" Italian fare, including "exceptional pastas", and "friendly", "polished" service in a "fun" atmosphere; while the former is "good for an expense account", its "unflashy" sibling is "reasonably priced."

Bistro 21 ⓈⓂ ▽ 25 | 16 | 25 | $43 |
Cienega Ctr., 846 N. La Cienega Blvd. (bet. Waring & Willoughby Aves.), West Hollywood, 310-967-0021
■ "Haute cuisine in a mini-mall" is not an oxymoron at this West Hollywood "sleeper" offering "excellent, imaginative" French-Japanese cuisine ("I couldn't believe the wasabi sorbet") by a "genius" of a chef and "professional" service in an "intimate, personal" atmosphere that excuses the storefront digs; many a crony confesses that a visit to this "mom-and-pop winner" "boosts my spirits."

Bliss Ⓜ ▽ 23 | 27 | 20 | $49 |
650 N. La Cienega Blvd. (Melrose Ave.), West Hollywood, 310-659-0999
■ There's scarcely a sign in front of this bunkerlike New American neophyte in West Hollywood, and behind the windowless exterior hides a "drop-dead gorgeous interior" where "the cool meet the chic" to create a "total Hollywood scene"; nearly as "exciting" are chef Gabriel Morales' (ex Balboa) "outstanding preparations" and "hottie" waiters who help make this one of the "sexiest rooms" in town.

get updates at zagat.com

LA/Hollywood/W. Hollywood | F | D | S | C |

Bourbon Street Shrimp & Grill | 17 | 17 | 17 | $20 |
8454 Melrose Ave. (La Cienega Blvd.), West Hollywood, 323-653-2640

■ There's "nothing fancy" about this "feel-good" duo in West Hollywood and West LA dishing out "delish peel-and-eat shrimp" and other "basic" Cajun/Creole eats in an "informal" setting that's "like being in the Quarter in New Orleans"; purists pooh-pooh it as a "poor imitation" that "wouldn't last long in the Big Easy"; P.S. Fat Tuesday specials ("half-priced entrees") are a "big-time bargain."

Buddha's Belly | 19 | 17 | 20 | $25 |
7475 Beverly Blvd. (Gardner St.), Los Angeles, 323-931-8588; www.bbfood.com

■ "Be sure to rub the Buddha's big belly as you enter" this "hip, fresh" but "serious" newcomer on Beverly Boulevard where "inspired" Pan-Asian fare prepared in an "open kitchen" will "open your taste buds"; the "young, energetic" staff is "attentive", and the "gleaming", "airy" setting illuminated by "oversized lamps hanging overhead" is "gloriously clean"; another blessing: it's "priced right."

Ca'Brea | 22 | 20 | 20 | $37 |
346-348 S. La Brea Ave. (bet. 3rd & 4th Sts.), Los Angeles, 323-938-2863

■ The La Brea cousin of Ca' del Sole and Locanda Veneta makes up for a "so-so location" in a traffic-heavy area with "fine" Northern Italian "comfort food" that's "simple" and "well-prepared", and a "wonderful space" brightened with "fun" artwork by local artists and a "warm" ambiance; it works equally well as a "quick power-lunch" spot or a "place to fall in love – with your date or the risotto."

Cadillac Cafe | 19 | 16 | 18 | $21 |
359 N. La Cienega Blvd. (Beverly Blvd.), West Hollywood, 310-657-6591

■ For "real food at real prices", fans are down with this "funkadelic" "hangout" in West Hollywood serving a "Dada-inspired" New American menu, served by an, er, "interesting-looking" staff in a room filled with "ever-changing art"; you can also "sit outside and watch people come and go from the strip club down the block."

Cafe des Artistes | 19 | 22 | 17 | $38 |
1534 N. McCadden Pl. (Sunset Blvd.), Hollywood, 323-469-7300; www.cafedesartistes.info

■ "Hidden" "in the heart of Hollywood", Jean-Pierre Bosc's (of Mimosa) "well-run" French bistro is a "nice cozy hideaway for celebrities" and others looking for a "chill night out" in a "romantic" "French country" setting; "you feel like you've left the city" on the "charming, romantic" back patio, and the "garden atmosphere" makes the "dependable" Gallic fare "taste even better."

LA/Hollywood/W. Hollywood F | D | S | C |

Café Med   17 | 16 | 16 | $25 |
8615 Sunset Blvd. (Sunset Plaza Dr.), West Hollywood, 310-652-0445

■ Bice's "cool", "cheaper" spin-offs both serve "reasonably priced" "basic" Italian fare that "pleases everyone" and alfresco dining that make up for the "hit-or-miss" service; it's "see-and-be-seen" at the West Hollywood location, where you can "watch the pretty people on Sunset Boulevard" from the outdoor tables, while its Pasadena sibling boasts a "pleasant patio" of its own.

Cafe Pinot   22 | 23 | 21 | $41 |
700 W. Fifth St. (Flower St.), Downtown, 213-239-6500; www.patinagroup.com

■ "Another of the Patina Group wonders", this Downtown Cal-French is a "civilized oasis" next to the "lovely garden" of the Main Library, with a "well-shaded" outdoor patio that's "beautiful in summer" and bright, "airy" interior as well as a menu of "delicious, inventive" dishes; it's a "can't-miss for business or romance", as well as pre- or "after-theater pleasure."

Cafe Stella ⓈⓂ   21 | 18 | 16 | $32 |
3932 Sunset Blvd. (bet. Hyperion & Sanborn Aves.), Los Feliz, 323-666-0265

■ You'll "feel like you're sitting in a Paris cafe" at this "small, tasteful" Silver Lake French, a "charming" "super-Euro" "hideaway" where "everyone has a fabulous accent", even as it projects a "good neighborhood vibe"; "solid steaks and seafood" anchor the "short" menu of "simple yet delicious" "classics."

Cafe Sushi ●   – | – | – | M |
8459 Beverly Blvd. (N. La Cienega Blvd.), Los Angeles, 323-651-4020

Though it may be overshadowed by nearby standouts such as Matsuhisa, Sushi Roku and Koi, this solid, midpriced Fairfax Japanese near the Beverly Center still attracts a loyal following of local finatics who crave sushi and sashimi at reasonable prices without a scene, in a setting where a black wardrobe isn't required.

Cafe Tartine   – | – | – | I |
7385 Beverly Blvd. (Martel Ave.), Los Angeles, 323-938-1300

With cooks formerly from Les Deux Cafés in the kitchen, it's no surprise that this casual-looking French entry offers the sort of menu you might find on the Left Bank, built around bread FedExed from Paris' Poilâne bakery, and used in open-face 'tartines' of roast beef and aïoli, country pâté with apples, curried chicken and more; this being LA, you can wash your sandwich down with either cappuccino or soy milk.

get updates at zagat.com

LA/Hollywood/W. Hollywood F | D | S | C

Caffe Latte 18 | 9 | 16 | $16
6254 Wilshire Blvd. (Crescent Heights Blvd.), Los Angeles, 323-936-5213
■ Early-birds extol this "bustling" New American on the Wilshire Miracle Mile as the "perfect neighborhood breakfast spot", serving the "best" "fresh-roasted" java to the "best-looking people", as well as "dreamy poppy-seed muffins", "good" omelets and other "yummy carbo-laden" dishes that are "reason enough to get out of bed"; the space is nondescript but the ambiance is "laid-back", and the air "smells wonderfully of coffee."

California Chicken Cafe ⊠ 21 | 9 | 15 | $10
6805 Melrose Ave. (bet. Mansfield Ave. & Orange Dr.), Los Angeles, 323-935-5877; www.californiachickencafe.com
■ The bird is the word at this "inexpensive" chicken chain that "blows away pretenders" with "fresh, healthy" poultry dishes, from "perfect rotisserie chicken" to some of the "biggest wraps" around, and a "nice range of sides"; "long lines" and "noisy, crowded" rooms contribute to make it a "great take-out" choice of many.

CALIFORNIA PIZZA KITCHEN 18 | 14 | 17 | $18
Beverly Ctr., 121 N. La Cienega Blvd. (bet. Beverly Blvd. & 3rd St.), Beverly Center, 310-854-6555
Wells Fargo Ctr., 330 S. Hope St. (bet. 3rd & 4th Sts.), Downtown, 213-626-2616
Hollywood & Highland, 6801 Hollywood Blvd. (Highland Blvd.), Hollywood, 323-460-2080
www.cpk.com
■ A "chain that never misses", this California pizza "institution" (with locations nationwide) offers a "great variety" of gourmet pies (including the "excellent" BBQ chicken version) that are "consistently" "fresh"; "noisy" rooms with "sterile" decor, "bright" lights and lots of "kids" are to be expected, but you always "know you're getting something good for not much money."

California Wok 18 | 9 | 15 | $15
Cienega Plaza, 8520 W. Third St. (La Cienega Blvd.), Los Angeles, 310-360-9218
◪ An "appealing" choice for "cheap", "fresh" Chinese that "tastes healthy", this Sino trio (with branches in Encino and West LA) comes "highly recommended for takeout" (a "half-order is enough for one") or "fast, fast, fast delivery", if only because the digs are so "depressing"; skeptics find the fare "acceptable but not exceptional."

CAMPANILE 27 | 25 | 24 | $50
624 S. La Brea Ave. (bet. 6th St. & Wilshire Blvd.), Los Angeles, 323-938-1447; www.campanilerestaurant.com
■ "Believe every good thing you've heard" about this "unique gem" in La Brea that's "always a winner" for its

LA/Hollywood/W. Hollywood F | D | S | C

"amazing" Cal-Med cuisine, "legendary" Thursday grilled-cheese nights, "incredible weekend brunches" and "divine" breads from the adjacent La Brea Bakery; the high-ceilinged structure, commissioned by Charlie Chaplin, boasts an "Italian" courtyard and "glorious" dining room to create a setting "at once sophisticated and charming."

Canter's ● | 15 | 8 | 13 | $16

419 N. Fairfax Ave. (bet. Beverly Blvd. & Melrose Ave.), Los Angeles, 323-651-2030

◪ This 24/7 Fairfax "landmark" (circa 1931) is "what a deli should be", dishing out sandwiches that'll "fill you up" and chicken soup that'll "cure anything", as well as "wonderful" baked goods; the "smells of pickles, corned beef and smoked fish" fill the "kitschy" space sporting an "acid-trip" of a ceiling, where a "crusty" staff slings "insults and matzos" at a "varied" crowd that's a "microcosm of LA"; live musical acts play in the Kibitz Room next door.

CARLITO'S GARDEL | 24 | 22 | 23 | $34

7963 Melrose Ave. (Fairfax Ave.), Los Angeles, 323-655-0891; www.carlitosgardel.com

■ "Authentically Argentinian" fare with an Italian flair and a "wonderfully Latin ambiance" make for a "magical escape" at this "seductively charming" family-run chophouse in Melrose; "one-of-a-kind steaks" and other "sumptuous" dishes are "loving prepared" and served by a "helpful", "knowledgeable" staff in a room that's "dark, but not so romantic you can't go with friends."

Carousel Ⓜ | 22 | 16 | 20 | $23

High Plaza, 5112 Hollywood Blvd. (Normandie Ave.), Hollywood, 323-660-8060; www.carouselrestaurant.com

■ "Funky" (Hollywood) and "fancy" (Glendale), these Armenian/Middle Eastern twins couldn't be more different – the former is a Thai Town mini-mall "hole-in-the-wall" where you can "sit down" or get your "food to go"; the latter boasts "gracious" service and an "attractive dining room", plus live music and belly dancers on weekends, "but no takeout"; what they share is "wonderfully authentic" fare.

Casbah Cafe | ▽ 18 | 21 | 16 | $13

3900 W. Sunset Blvd. (Hyperion Blvd.), Silver Lake, 323-664-7000

■ A Los Feliz/Silver Lake "hipster" clientele rocks this casbah for "delicious" French-Moroccan breakfasts, pastries and baked goods, "good coffee" and "great mint teas" in an "elegant" setting; it's a "nice neighborhood hangout" where you can "relax and watch the street scene", but "a little too pricey" for some.

Cassell's Ⓢ⇄ | ▽ 19 | 6 | 13 | $10

3266 W. Sixth St. (Vermont Ave.), Koreatown, 213-480-8668

◪ Patty pundits are split over the signature sandwich at this Koreatown hamburger stalwart – pros insist it's "still

get updates at zagat.com

LA/Hollywood/W. Hollywood F | D | S | C |

the best in town" while foes declare it a "shadow of its former self"; the space may be "faded", too, but it's still "busy during lunch", thanks to an "excellent" buffet where you can "fix your burger your way" and dress it with the "outstanding" homemade mayonnaise.

Celestino Italian Steak House 23 | 19 | 22 | $51 |
8908 Beverly Blvd. (bet. Doheny Dr. & Robertson Blvd.), West Hollywood, 310-858-5777; www.celestinodrago.com
■ "*Molto bene*" say meateaters to "melt-in-your-mouth" steaks of all-natural, low-fat Piedmontese beef, like the "incredible" porterhouse for two at Celestino Drago's West Hollywood Italian steakhouse; nearly as "impressive" is the "friendly", "professional" staff that waits on you in the "cozy", "old-school" room.

Cha Cha Cha 19 | 17 | 16 | $25 |
656 N. Virgil Ave. (Melrose Ave.), Los Feliz, 323-664-7723
☑ "Always fun, always crowded", this "brassy, bold" duo offers a "colorful jolt of the Caribbean" with "flavorful jerk chicken" and other "vivid" fare and a "cutely kitschy" decor; the Silver Lake sibling is located on an "edgy street" while the Long Beach location is more sedate.

CHAMEAU ⌧ Ⓜ 26 | 15 | 21 | $33 |
2520 Hyperion Ave. (bet. Griffith Park Blvd. & Tracy St.), Silver Lake, 323-953-1973
■ A "hidden treasure" in Silver Lake, this BYO French-Moroccan "charmer" offers a "menu that changes with the seasons, yet is consistently delightful", showcasing a "fusion of unexpected styles" that's "lick-your-fingers fabulous"; the storefront setting can be "noisy", but the atmosphere is "comfortable" and the service is "friendly", and "no corkage fee" "keeps the costs down"; N.B. open for dinner Thursdays–Saturdays only.

Chan Dara 20 | 17 | 18 | $25 |
310 N. Larchmont Blvd. (Beverly Blvd.), Hancock Park, 323-467-1052
1511 N. Cahuenga Blvd. (Sunset Blvd.), Hollywood, 323-464-8585
www.chandara.com
☑ While this popular Thai chain is for employing some of the "most beautiful waitresses in LA", cynics observe they "seem to be better at standing around than serving you"; nearly lost amid all the "eye candy" are "nicely prepared" dishes such as the "sublime" crying tiger beef salad and "excellent" crab fried rice; N.B. Chan Darette in Marina del Rey is a more casual sibling specializing in noodle dishes.

Chao Krung – | – | – | I |
111 N. Fairfax Ave. (W. 3rd St.), Los Angeles, 323-932-9482; www.chaokrung.com
Since 1976, this elegant Thai across from the Farmer's Market has been a destination for solid Siamese cooking

LA/Hollywood/W. Hollywood   F | D | S | C

Chaya Brasserie   24 | 23 | 22 | $45
8741 Alden Dr. (bet. Beverly Blvd. & 3rd St.), West Hollywood, 310-859-8833; www.thechaya.com

■ A "tried-and-true favorite" "after 20 years", this Asian-Eclectic attracts a "beautiful Hollywood crowd without the attitude" with "never boring" creations, "beautiful" Gallic-looking decor and "attentive", "eager-to-please" service; "divine vodka infusions" and the "best martinis in town" ensure "lots of bar action every night."

Checkers Downtown   24 | 26 | 23 | $48
Hilton Checkers Hotel, 535 S. Grand Ave. (bet. 5th & 6th Sts.), Downtown, 213-624-0000; www.checkershotel.com

■ Even after major renovations, this Cal-Continental housed in the Hilton Checkers Hotel remains a "soothing" "oasis of quiet elegance in Downtown"; "exceptional", "delicious" fare contributes to an experience that's "never short of enchanting" (as long as "you have four hours to spare"), be it for an "expense-account lunch", "wonderful afternoon tea" or "pre-theater dining"; N.B. there's free shuttle service to the Music Center.

Cheebo ☻   – | – | – | I
7533 W. Sunset Blvd. (Sierra Bonita Ave.), Hollywood, 323-850-7070; www.cheebo.com

This Hollywood pizzeria in a Mondrian-esque setting (it's hard to miss a building painted bright orange), with tables covered with white butcher paper, takes an alternative approach to the genre, selling it by 'slab' – either foot-long or yard-long ones, potentially topped with ingredients both classic and out there; in case you're curious, the name is phonetic for the Italian word *cibo*, meaning 'food.'

Chianti   22 | 20 | 21 | $41
7383 Melrose Ave. (bet. Fairfax & La Brea Aves.), Los Angeles, 323-653-8333

■ The Northern Italian fare's "so good you don't mind not being able to see it" at this Melrose "throwback" to 1938 (the site of the wrap party for *Gone With the Wind*) with a "dark", "romantic" room where "you might see a famous duo"; the atmosphere is "calming", and the waiters are "old enough to be your grandfather" and "just as caring."

Chianti Cucina   22 | 16 | 20 | $33
7383 Melrose Ave. (bet. Fairfax & La Brea Aves.), Los Angeles, 323-653-8333

■ "No fancy garb required" at Chianti's "cheaper", "low-key" "little sibling" next door serving the "same" "solid"

get updates at zagat.com   33

LA/Hollywood/W. Hollywood F | D | S | C

Italian fare as its elder; the atmosphere is "casual" and it gets a bit "noisy" in the comparatively "well-lit" room where "you can actually see your food" as well as the drying pastas hanging from racks over the counter.

Chi Dynasty   20 | 16 | 19 | $21

2112 Hillhurst Ave. (bet. Ambrose Ave. & Los Feliz Blvd.), Los Feliz, 323-667-3388; www.chidynasty.com

■ "Some of the best Chinese outside of Monterey Park" ("wonderful whole fish", "amazing chicken salad", "the best Szechuan string beans") can be found at this "good ol' Mandarin" in Los Feliz; the "upscale" room is "understated" and the atmosphere is "pleasant", if "non-hip" ("saw Tommy Lee here"), making it a fine place to "take mom and dad."

Chin Chin   17 | 13 | 16 | $20

Sunset Plaza, 8618 Sunset Blvd. (bet. La Cienega Blvd. & Palm Ave.), West Hollywood, 310-652-1818; www.chinchin.com

◪ Fans of this "always reliable" "Cal-Chinese" chain attest the chicken salad is "the best anywhere", the potstickers are "excellent" and the 'dim sum and then some' is a "great value", excusing "barely adequate" service and "take-out" decor; purists pan the "Americanized" eats as a "pallid imitation of the real thing", but defenders praise it as a "tasty modern twist on traditional" Middle Kingdom fare.

Chow Fun   – | – | – | I

686 N. Spring St. (Ord St.), Chinatown, 213-626-1678

With its high ceilings and oversized picture windows, this newly opened Chinese is the antithesis of the traditional Chinatown eatery; its tapas-style menu is fairly revisionist as well, moving away from egg rolls into a world of 'sushi' made with noodles, salads of fruits and vegetables and udon with Creole chicken sausage.

Ciao Trattoria   22 | 21 | 21 | $33

815 W. Seventh St. (bet. Figueroa & Flower Sts.), Downtown, 213-624-2244; www.ciaotrattoria.com

■ Though this Northern Italian is housed in a "fabulous" "historic" Downtown building in a "convenient location" and boasts a "beautiful interior", cronies crack it's all about the "chow, baby", that's "tastefully prepared", "fresh and flavorful"; it's a "good alternative" "before the theater or opera", and the staff does its best "to get your party out in time" for the show.

CICADA ⊠   23 | 29 | 23 | $46

617 S. Olive St. (bet. 6th & 7th Sts.), Downtown, 213-488-9488

■ LA's No. 1 for Decor in this *Survey*, this "beautiful art deco" venue is housed in a former Downtown haberdashery (note the many drawers) in the restored Oviatt Building, with "lots of dark wood" and "Lalique crystal everywhere"; "crowds are not a problem" in the "huge" space, and the

34   subscribe to zagat.com

LA/Hollywood/W. Hollywood F | D | S | C

"outstanding" Northern Italian cuisine and "professional" service make it a "place to savor" where you can "put on the Ritz" and "feel as if you're in a glamorous '40s movie"; N.B. the apartment upstairs is available for private parties.

Cinespace ▽ 18 | 21 | 18 | $34
6356 Hollywood Blvd. (bet. Cosmo St. & Ivar Ave.), Hollywood, 323-817-3456; www.cine-space.com

How "typically Hollywood" – a restaurant/movie theater, showing revivals and independents and serving New American fare in a "cool, dark, modern" space; while some feel it has "more of a club" feel with "lots of celebrities" that's "better for the scene than the food", others enthuse it's a "great concept" that's "a lot of fun" for a "date."

Ciudad 22 | 20 | 19 | $35
Union Bank Plaza, 445 S. Figueroa St. (5th St.), Downtown, 213-486-5171; www.ciudad-la.com

■ The Too Hot Tamales (Mary Sue Milliken and Susan Feniger) go Nuevo Latino at this "boisterous" Downtown "oasis" serving "inventive" dishes and a "cornucopia of rum varieties"; "Diego Rivera would love" the "bright, modernist" decor that evokes a "fantasy '50s Latin America – Mexico City, Havana and Buenos Aires all rolled into one."

Clafoutis ● 18 | 18 | 17 | $27
Sunset Plaza, 8630 W. Sunset Blvd. (Pine Tree Pl.), West Hollywood, 310-659-5233; www.clafoutisrestaurant.com

"If you can pronounce the name of the place, that's half the battle" at this French Bistro "smack in the middle of the Sunset Strip" with a sidewalk patio from which to observe "streams of actress wanna-bes, foreign businessmen, club kids and bewildered tourists" over "scrumptious desserts and awesome coffee" while surrounded by an "industry crowd" and "poseurs galore."

Cobras & Matadors 21 | 17 | 18 | $29
7615 W. Beverly Blvd. (bet. Fairfax & La Brea Aves.), Los Angeles, 323-932-6178

■ Expect to stand in a "line out the door" for a "*buenos noche*" at Steve Arroyo's Fairfax Spanish where you can "nibble to your heart's content" on "tantalizing" tapas in a "cool, dark" space or at one of the outdoor tables and BYO wine with no corkage if it's purchased from the shop next door; it's "noisy" and "crowded", but the atmosphere is "low-key" with "no attitude."

Cole's P.E. Buffet ⊠ ▽ 17 | 12 | 15 | $13
Pacific Electric Bldg., 118 E. Sixth St. (bet. Los Angeles & Main Sts.), Downtown, 213-622-4090

A "classic LA experience" and a "must" for "tourists", this "scenic", "old-world" Downtown Traditional American (circa 1908) has appeared in more than 400 films and TV shows and offers a "taste of history – and the dust to prove

get updates at zagat.com 35

it"; cognoscenti counsel "stay with the French dip" that "can't be beat" and "you'll be glad you did."

Cravings ◐ 17 | 17 | 15 | $29

Sunset Plaza, 8653 W. Sunset Blvd. (La Cienega Blvd.), West Hollywood, 310-652-6103

◪ Many "love" this West Hollywood Cal-Med "just for its location" that's "perfect for watching the parade of shoppers and poseurs strolling down Sunset" from sidewalk tables where you can "brunch with the stars", making the "mediocre" eats almost an afterthought; defenders, though, point out there's some "fine" fare to be found, such as "excellent" salads and "ahi tuna with fresh avocado."

Cynthia's 22 | 15 | 17 | $36

8370 W. Third St. (La Cienega Blvd.), Los Angeles, 323-658-7851; www.cynthias-restaurant.com

◪ While all agree the "awesome home-cooked" eats at this Third Street Traditional American, from "sensational" fried chicken to "must-have" blackberry cobbler, make a visit to the cramped storefront "worthwhile", surveyors are split over "infamous" chef-owner Cynthia Hirsch: fans say "meeting her is a trip" (and she "sure knows how to pick a pack of glam-guy servers"), while foes feel she's "crossed the line" with her "tirades."

Daily Grill 17 | 16 | 17 | $25

Beverly Connection Shopping Ctr., 100 N. La Cienega Blvd. (bet. Beverly Blvd. & 3rd St.), Los Angeles, 310-659-3100; www.dailygrill.com

◪ This chain knockoff of The Grill in Beverly Hills offers "solid, generous" portions of "all-American" "classics" such as "monstrous chicken pot pies" and Cobb salad you can "count on" in a "casual", "family-friendly" setting; though it's "lost its appeal" for some, pros give it props for doing a "solid job within a narrow range."

Dan Tana's ◐ 23 | 18 | 22 | $44

9071 Santa Monica Blvd. (Doheny Dr.), West Hollywood, 310-275-9444

■ The "steaks are tender and the waiters are tough" at this dinner-only West Hollywood Italian and "industry watering hole" where it "helps to be in show biz"; while you "can order your favorite dish named after a mogul or star", for carnivores, the "fantastic" NY cut is an "offer you can't refuse"; there's "always a buzz" in the "old-school" setting, with a "real kind" of "bar scene" and the "best bartenders in the world."

Dar Maghreb 22 | 26 | 22 | $45

7651 Sunset Blvd. (bet. Fairfax & La Brea Aves.), Hollywood, 323-876-7651; www.darmaghrebrestaurant.com

■ Take a "trip to Morocco for under 50 bucks" at this Hollywood "hideaway" for "an evening of Middle Eastern

LA/Hollywood/W. Hollywood F | D | S | C |

hospitality" in a "dazzling", "palatial interior" where you can "relax on big fluffy couches" and watch a "belly dancer" gyrate to "deafening music" as you "eat with your hands" through a "family-style" "feast" of "meat-intensive" fare; the "charming", "accommodating" staff contributes to the "unique experience" that's "always fun for a big party."

Delmonico's Seafood Grille ◐   20 | 17 | 19 | $35 |
9320 W. Pico Blvd. (bet. Beverly & Doheny Drs.), Los Angeles, 310-550-7737; www.delmonicosseafoodgrille.com

■ "Dependable fresh seafood", "excellent steaks" and "fantastic martinis" await at this deep-sea duo in Pico-Robertson near Century City and Pasadena's Paseo Colorado, the former a "great industry hangout" where you can see "lots of studio execs", the latter notable for its "Craftsman-inspired bar"; the "nice tall booths" are a "must for enjoyment" in the "loud" rooms, and though the service can be "shoddy" at times, it's also "sometimes stellar."

DIAGHILEV ⊠Ⓜ   26 | 27 | 28 | $69 |
Wyndham Bel Age Hotel, 1020 N. San Vicente Blvd. (Sunset Blvd.), West Hollywood, 310-854-1111; www.wyndham.com

■ At this "lavish" West Hollywood Franco-Russian in the Wyndham Bel Age Hotel (voted this *Survey*'s No. 1 for Service in LA), "you don't have to be a celebrity to be treated like one" by fabled maitre d' Dmitri Dmitrov and an "incredible" staff that does its "absolute best" to make you "feel special"; it's "spectacular in every way", from a "sumptuous", "formal" space to "delicious chilled vodkas" and a "selection of caviars difficult to match", and though you'll have to brace yourself for "mild apoplexy when you get the bill", pros promise it's "worth the splurge."

Dolce Enoteca e Ristorante ◐   – | – | – | E |
8284 Melrose Ave. (Sweetzer Ave.), Hollywood, 323-852-7174; www.dolceenoteca.com

The space that was the home to Le Chardonnay has been redesigned as a dark, hyper-modern Italian with a bar that has a blazing gas fire against its back wall; the place is attracting a stylish crowd hungry for small dishes like fried olives and prosciutto with dried figs, as well as larger dishes like swordfish carpaccio and risotto with Gorgonzola.

Doughboys ◐   21 | 12 | 14 | $16 |
8136 W. Third St. (Crescent Heights Blvd.), Los Angeles, 323-651-4202

◪ Everyone from "LA's most happening" to "would-be somebodies" endure "lines down the block" for the "best breakfasts in town" and "perfect" brunches at this "casually quaint" Third Street American; neither "obnoxious waits" nor a "too-cool-for-school staff" can diminish the joy of landing an outdoor table in this "priceless" scene and

LA/Hollywood/W. Hollywood F | D | S | C

tucking into "lovingly prepared" sandwiches or "red velvet cake" that "rocks."

Duke's Coffee Shop　　　15 | 11 | 14 | $17
8909 Sunset Blvd. (San Vicente Blvd.), West Hollywood, 310-652-3100

☑ "Wait on line, sit, order, eat, leave" – the ritual's simple at this "rock 'n' roll hash house" in West Hollywood, the "hippest breakfast spot on the Strip", where "rockers wearing sunglasses stumble in" for "great corned beef hash", "greasy fries" and other "hearty" "hangover" fare; it's a scene "straight out of a Quentin Tarantino movie."

Du-par's ◐　　　13 | 9 | 13 | $14
Farmers Mkt., 6333 W. Third St. (Fairfax Ave.), Los Angeles, 323-933-8446
Ramada Inn, 8571 Santa Monica Blvd. (La Cienega Blvd.), West Hollywood, 310-659-7009
www.dupars.com

☑ Although surveyors rate the fare at this "old-school" American coffee shop chain only "a notch higher than Denny's", many "keep coming back" for pancakes that are the "best this side of anywhere", "pies, pies, pies" and a hearty helping of "nostalgia"; skeptics insist its "legendary" status is "all in the mind", while defenders call it a "fun throwback to the diners of yesteryear."

Edendale Grill Ⓜ　　　13 | 24 | 15 | $34
2838 Rowena Ave. (bet. Auburn & Rokeby Sts.), Silver Lake, 323-666-2000; www.edendalegrill.com

☑ While the owners of this "ultrahip" Traditional American newcomer to Silver Lake earn applause for the "beautiful redo" of the circa-1920s firehouse where it's housed, critics feel it's still "getting its legs" in the kitchen and dining room, with "erratic" cooking and "sketchy" service; P.S. a drink at the "gorgeous" bar, a "throwback to days gone by", "is a must."

EL CHOLO　　　18 | 18 | 17 | $21
1121 S. Western Ave. (bet. Olympic & Pico Blvds.), Koreatown, 323-734-2773; www.elcholo.com

■ For many, this "classic" Mexican chain dating back to 1923 is the "first place to go" for "true blue" south-of-the-border fare, including "amazing" green corn tamales "worth waiting six months for" (they're served May–October only), "guac that rocks" and margaritas that'll "knock your socks off"; P.S. regulars especially recommend the original on Western for its atmospheric "courtyard."

El Coyote Cafe　　　11 | 14 | 17 | $17
7312 Beverly Blvd. (bet. Fairfax & La Brea Aves.), Los Angeles, 323-939-2255

☑ The numbers don't reflect the "persistent popularity" of this Fairfax "icon" that's been "around as long as the La Brea

LA/Hollywood/W. Hollywood　　F | D | S | C

tar pits" (since 1931), serving "cheap", "messy" "Mexican for the masses" and "lethal" margaritas ("leave the car at home") in a space that's a "cross between '70s Tijuana and a '50s trailer park"; for those who still "don't get it", amigos add: "you can spend $10 here and walk out stuffed."

Electric Lotus ●　　19 | 21 | 17 | $22
4656 Franklin Ave. (Vermont Ave.), Los Feliz, 323-953-0040; www.electriclotus.com
■ An "insane library of curries" will "wake up your taste buds" at this "way-cool funky Indian for the hipster crowd" in Los Feliz serving "gigantic platters" of "healthier" fare; a space with a "sensuous, colorful" "Bombay chic" decor and "killer DJs" spinning tunes (at "ear-splitting levels") on weekends make it a "place to go for loud fun times with a group of friends."

EL TEPEYAC ⌘　　23 | 9 | 17 | $12
812 N. Evergreen Ave. (bet. Cesar E. Chavez & Wabash Aves.), East LA, 323-267-8668
■ "Dress down and eat up" at this "bare-bones" Mexican "mecca" in East LA (known as Manuel's to locals) where "USC medical students", "Westside and Valley folks" and "tourists" alike queue for the "biggest burritos you've ever seen" (the "gigantic Hollenbeck" is a "meal for two") and other "excellent" fare; expect "long lines", though the "wait is usually minimal" at the Monterey Park branch.

EM Bistro ☒　　∇ 23 | 23 | 23 | $44
8256 Beverly Blvd. (Sweetzer Ave.), Los Angeles, 323-658-6004
■ One of the players on Fairfax's "new Beverly Boulevard restaurant row", this American bistro is making a mark with "fantastic" comfort food notable for its "beautiful presentation and balance of flavors"; the "A+ desserts" are an "outrageous way to finish an evening", though the "plush banquettes" and "soothing lighting" make the room "so comfortable you may not want to leave."

Empress Pavilion　　23 | 14 | 15 | $20
Bamboo Plaza, 988 N. Hill St. (Bernard St.), Chinatown, 213-617-9898
■ The "dowager of dim sum", this sprawling hall in old Chinatown "replicates the dim summeries of Hong Kong" with the "best Chinese chefs" preparing "tempting morsels" that are wheeled out on carts by "sourpuss" servers in a "noisy", "cavernous" space where "lines snake out the door" at lunch and on weekends; finatics advise "don't miss dinner", when "solid" seafood dishes are served.

Engine Co. No. 28　　20 | 22 | 20 | $33
644 S. Figueroa St. (bet. 7th St. & Wilshire Blvd.), Downtown, 213-624-6996; www.engineco.com
■ A "Downtown landmark", this homage to "old-fashioned American cuisine" housed in a "beautiful", "historic"

LA/Hollywood/W. Hollywood   F | D | S | C

restored firehouse dishes out "straightforward" "comfort food for grown-ups" in a "classy", "boys' club" setting (lots of wood, brass, glass); it works equally well for a "not-so-formal business lunch", before a "show" or a "game at the Staples Center."

Fabiolus Café   20 | 15 | 19 | $21

5255 Melrose Ave. (Van Ness Ave.), Los Angeles, 323-464-5857
6270 Sunset Blvd. (bet. Gower & Vine Sts.), Hollywood, 323-467-2882
www.fabiolus.com

■ "Old-style Italian" is the theme of this duo popular for its "reliable pastas and risotto" – the Melrose branch is a mainstay for "industry types" from nearby Paramount who come to "eye each other" over a "fast", "filling", "tasty" lunch, while the Sunset location is "walking distance to the Pantages" and a "fine choice for pre-Arclight meals" as well; "huge portions at low prices" and "friendly service" – "what's not to like?"

Factor's Famous Deli   16 | 10 | 15 | $18

9420 W. Pico Blvd. (Rexford Dr.), Los Angeles, 310-278-9175

■ A West LA "fixture" that's "still going strong" after 55 years, this "classic" Jewish deli serves "all the standards", including "mile-high sandwiches" and "huge salads", that are "worth every penny when you're woozy on a Sunday morning"; "waitresses who are all clones of my mother, with attitude", help create the requisite "back-in-NYC feeling"; P.S. go for the "nice patio in back few people know about."

Farfalla Trattoria   23 | 17 | 18 | $27

1978 Hillhurst Ave. (Finley Ave.), Los Feliz, 323-661-7365

■ *Amici* insist "they never miss" at this small storefront Italian in Los Feliz, where you "may have to wait outside" for a table some nights, but your patience is rewarded with "outstanding, authentic", "reasonably priced" dishes, including "perfectly prepared" pastas and "exquisite" veal, "intelligent", "accommodating" service and a "homey", "welcoming" setting; it's so "very busy" that it perhaps "could use a bigger space."

Farm of Beverly Hills   18 | 17 | 16 | $26

The Grove at Farmer's Mkt., 189 The Grove Dr. (Beverly Blvd. & 3rd St.), Los Angeles, 323-525-1699;
www.farmofbeverlyhills.com
See review in Westside Directory.

Fat Fish ●   ∇ 28 | 25 | 27 | $27

616 N. Robertson Blvd. (bet. Melrose Ave. & Santa Monica Blvd.), West Hollywood, 310-659-3882; www.fatfishla.com

■ A "fabulous" sushi selection and other "excellent, innovative" Asian-accented Fusion dishes, plus a "great sake list" and "adventurous drinks" get this "ambitious"

40   subscribe to zagat.com

LA/Hollywood/W. Hollywood   F | D | S | C

West Hollywood newcomer "rocking and rolling", but "without the high prices"; "friendly", "fantastic" service and a "cool, Zen-like" space also earn it a "thumbs up."

Feinstein's at the Cinegrill   – | – | – | M
7000 Hollywood Blvd. (Orange Dr.), Hollywood, 323-769-7269
In the grandly historic Hollywood Roosevelt Hotel (where the very first Academy Awards were presented in 1928), in a room filled with art deco elegance, is this stage for both singer Michael Feinstein, who performs here when he's in town (he splits his time between NYC and LA), and Makoto Tanaka (Mako), who's moved on from his trademark Cal-Asian into a world of Cal-French cuisine; in sum – elegant food for an elegant space.

Fenix at the Argyle   21 | 24 | 21 | $51
Argyle Hotel, 8358 Sunset Blvd. (La Cienega Blvd.), West Hollywood, 323-848-6677; www.argylehotel.com
The "terrace under the shade of the concrete palms" with a "cityscape view of LA" and a "Hollywood Golden Age decor" that "transports diners back to the '30s" are the stars of this Cal-Asian housed in the landmark Argyle Hotel in the heart of the Sunset Strip; the cuisine earns mixed reviews ("fantastic" vs. "mediocre"), and though it comes in "large portions", many feel it's still "overpriced."

Figaro Brasserie   ▽ 17 | 24 | 14 | $29
1802 N. Vermont Ave. (bet. Franklin Ave. & Hollywood Blvd.), Los Feliz, 323-662-1587; www.figarorestaurants.com
"Authentic in food, atmosphere" and "spotty" service that "can go either way", this Los Feliz brasserie offers "classic French dishes" in a "beautiful" venue with "curbside tables" that resembles a "Parisian cafe"; phobes fume you can "fly to Paris and eat in less time than it takes to get served", but for Francophiles the Gaul-ing treatment "makes the adventure even better."

Flavor of India   ▽ 21 | 16 | 18 | $23
9045 Santa Monica Blvd. (Doheny Dr.), West Hollywood, 310-274-1715; www.theflavorofindia.com
It's "like being on Brick Lane in London" at this "charming" West Hollywood located between The Palm and the Troubadour on busy Santa Monica Boulevard, where "gracious waiters" serve "solid", "tasty" dishes in a "kitschy" space with a covered patio; it's "reasonably priced" and the "buffet on weekends is pleasant."

Flora Kitchen   15 | 15 | 12 | $19
460 S. La Brea Ave. (6th St.), Los Angeles, 323-931-9900
A "super place for a fun lunch" that's even "better for breakfast", this La Brea Cal-Med is situated "in a flower shop", so diners have "something beautiful to look at" while they tuck into a "menu of light favorites", from "yummy pancakes and scones" to "healthy sandwiches and soups";

get updates at zagat.com

LA/Hollywood/W. Hollywood   F | D | S | C

the "floral scents make it a nice place to linger" too, in spite of "slow, distracted" service from an "attitudey" staff.

Formosa Cafe ●   11 | 19 | 14 | $22
7156 Santa Monica Blvd. (La Brea Ave.), West Hollywood, 323-850-9050

☑ Cineastes sigh if only the "walls could talk" at this "kitschy" Chinese-American, a "classic Hollywood haunt" (circa 1929) "seething with history", while cynics sniff it's "basically a bar" that works "better as a movie set than a place to eat"; mai tais and other "strong drinks", plus a "heavy noir atmosphere", also make it a "good place to go after your significant other dumps you."

410 Boyd ⌧   19 | 15 | 16 | $24
410 Boyd St. (San Pedro St.), Downtown, 213-617-2491

■ "Power brokers" venture to this "cool, arty hangout" in an "edgy place" between Little Tokyo and Skid Row for a "refreshing break from the standard expense-account" scene, to dine alongside "Downtown artists" on "upscale" Cal fare with "bold flavors", "beautifully served" in a setting that's "as casual as it gets."

Frankie & Johnnie's ●   18 | 10 | 15 | $19
8947 W. Sunset Blvd. (Hilldale Ave.), West Hollywood, 310-275-7770

☑ "You feel like you're in Greenwich Village" boast boosters of this pizzeria pair in West Hollywood and Beverly Hills dishing out "serious" Big Apple–style "big pies with thin crusts" and a "variety of pasta dishes" in a space that looks like "my dining room"; skeptics scoff "I'd rather pop in a Mama Leone's", but at least it's "better than Shakey's."

Fred 62 ●   16 | 16 | 12 | $16
1850 N. Vermont Ave. (Franklin Ave.), Los Feliz, 323-667-0062

☑ Dig into a Belly Bomb omelet, Bearded Mr. Frenchy (French toast) or other "whimsically named" dishes at this "eccentric" Eclectic 24/7 diner in Los Feliz while you "hang with Eastside hipsters", and you just may spot "Drew Barrymore canoodling at the counter"; detractors deride it as a "distilled swingers'" scene for the "tragically hip" and "trust-fund existentialists", with "sub-par" eats and "atrocious" service, but none of that seems to matter when "it's 3 AM, you've been drinking all night and it's open."

Gaucho Grill   18 | 15 | 16 | $21
7980 Sunset Blvd. (Laurel Ave.), West Hollywood, 323-656-4152; www.gauchogrillusa.com

☑ "Not exactly Buenos Aires", but if you're a "trendy carnivore" and "garlic-lover" "in the mood for beef or chicken", this Argentinean chain is a "solid performer", offering "generous servings" and "so many meat choices" in a "warm", "cozy" setting; wags may wonder whether

LA/Hollywood/W. Hollywood F | D | S | C

"*gaucho* means bland", but for many it's an "easy" "alternative to eating at home" and a "very good bargain."

Genghis Cohen   19 | 15 | 18 | $23
740 N. Fairfax Ave. (Melrose Ave.), Los Angeles, 323-653-0640
■ They "understand what a real egg roll is" at this Fairfax spot serving Sino fare that's "as close to NY Chinese as it gets", but definitely not kosher ("salt-and-pepper shrimp", anyone?); occasional "celebrity" sightings ("I sat next to Halle Berry – yes!") can lighten up the "dark" room, and "live entertainment" in the adjacent club is "always fun."

G. Garvin's ☒   25 | 18 | 21 | $44
8420 W. Third St. (bet. Croft & Orlando Aves.), Los Angeles, 323-655-3888
■ "Ask Gerry Garvin what to order" at his Third Street production that "consistently delivers" "fantastic, creative" and "well-presented" Southern-accented New American fare, from a "must-have" ribs appetizer to some of the "best fried chicken around"; though the room's "a little cramped", the atmosphere is "intimate" and "charming", and the staff is not only "well-informed", but "gorgeous" to boot.

Girasole ☒ Ⓜ   23 | 16 | 21 | $28
225½ N. Larchmont Blvd. (bet. Beverly Blvd. & 3rd St.), Hancock Park, 323-464-6978
■ "Big taste in a tiny location" awaits at this "charming, family-run" BYO Northern Italian on Larchmont (with "no corkage" and a "wine store next door") near Paramount Studios, where "amazing homestyle" dishes such as "heavenly" osso buco are "simple but elegant" and "beautifully prepared"; the "cozy" space "only seats a small family", so "you must reserve."

GRACE Ⓜ   26 | 27 | 26 | $52
7360 Beverly Blvd. (Fuller Ave.), Los Angeles, 323-934-4400; www.gracerestaurant.net
■ An "unpretentious, yet chic" crowd "as eclectic and exciting as the menu" flocks to Richard Drapkin and Amy Knoll's "high-class newcomer" in Fairfax, where Michael Berman's "beautiful" decor "exudes elegant warmth", chef Neal Fraser's "Nouveau American dream" embodies his "gift for nuance and playful juxtapositions", an "impressive wine selection enhances the cuisine" and a "professional, personable" staff "always makes you feel embraced"; foodies rejoice "for once, the place where you want to be seen is a place where you want to dine."

Grand Lux Café   19 | 20 | 19 | $25
Beverly Ctr., 121 N. La Cienega Blvd. (Beverly Blvd.), Beverly Center, 310-855-1122
■ The Cheesecake Factory "ups the ante" with this "higher-end" Beverly Center spin-off serving a "broader" New American menu "with more winners than losers" in a

LA/Hollywood/W. Hollywood F | D | S | C

"glitzy", "cavernous" room "straight out of Vegas" ("where's the choreographed fountain?"), though regulars of the parent may recognize the "huge portions" and "long waits"; "be sure to save room for dessert", for "the beignets are as good as you'll get west of New Orleans", and yes, it does serve cheesecake.

Greenblatt's Deli & Fine Wines ● 20 | 11 | 16 | $19
8017 Sunset Blvd. (Laurel Ave.), Hollywood, 323-656-0606
☑ A Hollywood "staple" since 1926, this "true Jewish deli" "ain't just chopped liver", but a "world-class" wine shop as well ("where else can you have a '61 Lafite with your corned beef?"); "big nosh" sandwiches, a "great selection by the glass" and "incredible" chocolate cake excuse the "blah surroundings", while the "chicken matzo soup" is the "only remedy for a broken heart."

Griddle Cafe, The – | – | – | I
7916 Sunset Blvd. (Fairfax Ave.), Hollywood, 323-874-0377; www.thegriddlecafe.com
Leonardo DiCaprio and a fair-sized crew of Hollywood's young turks have been sighted at this Sunset Boulevard breakfast joint, a destination for low-octane Hollywood power meals, communing with a plate of ham and eggs or mom's French toast slathered in organic maple syrup, which can be found on every table.

GRILL ON HOLLYWOOD, THE 21 | 19 | 19 | $39
6801 Hollywood Blvd. (Highland Ave.), Hollywood, 323-856-5530; www.thegrill.com
☑ The "friendliest, most comfortable restaurant" in the Hollywood & Highland complex say fans, this spin-off of The Grill offers "huge portions of hearty American" fare in a "classy bistro setting"; while cynics sniff it "can't compete" with its illustrious elder (except in "price"), the upside is that it "isn't nearly as busy", either.

Gumbo Pot 22 | 8 | 15 | $11
Farmer's Mkt., 6333 W. Third St. (Fairfax Ave.), Los Angeles, 323-933-0358; www.thegumbopotla.com
■ Cronies crow it's "worth battling the crowds" at the Farmer's Market for Cajun/Creole fare that's "as close as you can get to the Big Easy in LA"; while some grumble over the "food-court" setting, for fans the "alfresco dining is icing on the cake" ("why pay more for fancy tablecloths?").

Hamburger Hamlet 15 | 13 | 15 | $18
6914 Hollywood Blvd. (N. Highland Ave.), East Hollywood, 323-467-6106
9201 Sunset Blvd. (N. Doheny Dr.), West Hollywood, 310-278-4924
www.hamburgerhamlet.com
☑ An "LA institution" for 54 years, this ubiquitous American chain is a "reliable standby" for a "sit-down burger" and other "consistent" comfort food "classics" served in "oddly

LA/Hollywood/W. Hollywood F | D | S | C

relaxing", "dark wood" settings; cynics shrug "nothing special, nothing horrible" and "kind of dated", but still many regulars concede this "neighborhood favorite" will "always have a place in my heart."

Hard Rock Cafe   12 | 20 | 14 | $20
Beverly Ctr., 8600 Beverly Blvd. (San Vicente Blvd.), Beverly Center, 310-276-7605; www.hardrock.com

☑ This worldwide American chain is "still rock 'n' roll" to fans who "just want some escapist fun" gawking at the "great memorabilia" and rubbing elbows with hordes of "teens and tourists" in a "clamorous", "kitschy cool" setting; the "completely average" fare is "more like easy listening than hard rock", but the "people-watching and ambiance are what draw 'em in."

Harold & Belle's   – | – | – | M
2920 W. Jefferson Blvd. (bet. Arlington Ave. & Crenshaw Blvd.), Los Angeles, 323-735-3376

Always jammed, this upscale Southerner in Mid-City garners a loyal local clientele with giant portions of Cajun-Creole fare, including a much-revered gumbo; expect a wait on weekends in the comfortable (if crowded) bar, and go as hungry as you can, because you can bring home bags that'll fill you for days.

Hillmont ⓢⓜ   21 | 17 | 15 | $32
4655 Hollywood Blvd. (Vermont Ave.), Hollywood, 323-669-3922

☑ An "unconventional steakhouse", to say the least ("Sizzler meets *Blade Runner*"), this trendy Hollywood "dining hall for hipsters" is an "excellent place for a fun group", offering "ample servings" of "thick, juicy" steaks and "deliciously heavy" sides at "better than average prices"; wags, though, wish the staff would "spend less time looking in the mirror."

Hirozen ⓢ   24 | 9 | 19 | $32
8385 Beverly Blvd. (Orlando Ave.), Beverly Center, 323-653-0470; www.hirozen.com

■ "Don't come here, it's mine" growl groupies of this "tiny" "treasure" hidden in the Beverly Center mall, a "real sushi bar without the famous, overpriced name" serving a "diverse menu" of "fresh, succulent" fin fare in a "cramped" "hole-in-the-wall"; the service can feel "rushed" when it's "super-crowded", but "everyone is treated like family", whether you're a "Hollywood type or not."

Hollywood Canteen ●ⓢ   ▽ 16 | 19 | 15 | $26
1006 N. Seward St. (Romaine St.), Hollywood, 323-465-0961

☑ An "industry" "favorite for lunch", "off the beaten track near the post-production houses" in Hollywood, this "hipster canteen" is more about "people-watching" than its "hit-or-miss" Italian-accented New American fare; the "ever-changing decor can't make up its mind", while the patio keeps its "cool."

get updates at zagat.com 45

LA/Hollywood/W. Hollywood F | D | S | C

Hollywood Hills ◐ 14 | 14 | 15 | $19
1745 N. Vermont Ave. (Prospect Ave.), Hollywood, 323-661-3319
◪ You "can be as healthy or sinful as you wish" with the "big breakfast menu" at this "hipster coffee shop" in Los Feliz that's also "perfect" for Sunday "brunch with a Bloody Mary"; otherwise the fare is merely "passable" and the service is "iffy", but the space is "what all Hollywood diners should look like – dark, plush and slightly haunted", with a "myriad of celebrity pix on the wall."

Hop Li 19 | 11 | 15 | $18
526 Alpine St. (Yale St.), Chinatown, 213-680-3939
◪ "If you can't find it here, maybe it doesn't exist" boast boosters of this Chinese duo in Chinatown and West LA with an "extensive menu" of "traditional" dishes that "taste true"; opinions of the decor range from "dull" to "blah", and the "surly" staff's "rudeness" is almost legendary, but the "allure" is in the "generous portions" of "tasty", "well-prepared" fare that make it such a "great value."

House, The Ⓜ 22 | 20 | 20 | $40
5750 Melrose Ave. (Arden Blvd.), East Hollywood, 323-462-4687
■ At this East Hollywood New American housed in an "authentic California bungalow", chef Scooter Kanfer "aims to please" by creating "the kind of comfort food you only wish you'd grown up with", including "magically prepared Farmer's Market vegetables"; "personal" service and an "intimate" ambiance add allure; P.S. "don't miss the prix fixe Sunday dinner."

House of Blues 15 | 20 | 14 | $32
8430 Sunset Blvd. (Olive Dr.), West Hollywood, 323-848-5100; www.hob.com
◪ The Sunday "gospel brunch is memorable" and the "fantastic" music and "spirited energy" make the "Cajun specialties even spicier" and "everything taste better" at this Sunset Strip Southerner offering up "good-for-the-soul" food and some of the "best blues" around; the fare "should come free with the concert" contend critics, who also carp over "cattle-call" service and a "cafeteria" scene.

Hugo's 19 | 12 | 17 | $20
8401 Santa Monica Blvd. (bet. King's Rd. & Orlando Ave.), West Hollywood, 323-654-3993
■ Celebs in West Hollywood and families in Studio City come to this casual New American duo for "innovative breakfasts", "creative brunch selections" and "more varieties of tea than you can ever imagine"; the atmosphere is "warm" and the "friendly" staff "handles crowds better than most other places", which is fortunate since there's often a line "spilling out onto the sidewalk."

LA/Hollywood/W. Hollywood   F | D | S | C

Il Capriccio on Vermont   23 | 16 | 23 | $23
1757 N. Vermont Ave. (bet. Kingswell & Melbourne Aves.), Los Feliz, 323-662-5900

■ The "owner seems to know everyone and makes you feel at home" at this "family-run Italian bistro" in Los Feliz where "better-than-usual renditions" of "authentic homestyle" cooking are "served attentively and with personal care" by "twin waiters" in a "small, busy space that makes you feel like you're on Mulberry Street"; N.B. it's still BYO, but since obtaining a liquor license it now charges a $3 corkage fee.

Impresario M   ∇ 17 | 21 | 19 | $44
LA Music Ctr., 135 N. Grand Ave. (bet. 1st & Temple Sts.), Downtown, 213-972-7333; www.patinagroup.com

◪ Joachim Splichal's Cal-Italian located atop the Music Center Downtown is not only "wonderfully convenient" but offers "beautiful views" as well; it combines an "elegant" buffet and table service in order to "move the pre-theater crowds" along, but many still object to the idea of a "self-service cafeteria line" "at these prices."

India's Oven   19 | 11 | 16 | $19
7231 Beverly Blvd. (bet. Alta Vista Blvd. & Formosa Ave.), Los Angeles, 323-936-1000

◪ "Always reliable" for "straightforward" "traditional Indian at a decent price", this pair in Fairfax and West LA "doesn't try to be anything it isn't"; the plain rooms could use an "update", but the booths are "comfy" and the service is "friendly", and the "bountiful portions" of "stick-to-the-ribs" fare make it a "very good value."

India's Tandoori   19 | 11 | 18 | $18
5947 W. Pico Blvd. (S. Point View St.), Los Angeles, 323-936-2050

◪ The "friendly staff always gets it right" at this "better-than-average" Indian chain where the "tandoori chicken's a must-try" and the curries are "flavorful and satisfying"; the digs are "not much to look at", but it's "too much of a bargain" for many to notice.

IN-N-OUT BURGER ●   24 | 10 | 18 | $7
3640 Cahuenga Blvd. (Lankershim Blvd.), Hollywood, 800-786-1000
7009 Sunset Blvd. (Orange Dr.), Hollywood, 800-786-1000
www.in-n-out.com

■ The "epitome of the American burger 'n' fries", this chain's "double-double, animal-style" and "freshly cut" fries are a "rebuff to every criticism of SoCal"; the service is "better than most fast-food places", and while "long lines at the drive-through" are to be expected, "it's worth the wait" for this "gift from heaven" that surveyors voted this *Survey*'s best Bang for the Buck.

---

get updates at zagat.com   47

LA/Hollywood/W. Hollywood F D S C

Ita-Cho 🈂️Ⓜ️ 22 | 13 | 19 | $32
7311 Beverly Blvd. (bet. Fuller Ave. & Poinsettia Pl.), Los Angeles, 323-938-9009
■ The "wonderful", "authentic" *izakaya*-style small plates ("miso eggplant to die for", "lotus root with kick") at this Fairfax Japanese "make you realize sushi is not the only dish from Japan" – in fact, it's not even on the menu, though "luscious slabs" of sashimi are; "lingering is no-go" here, where the service is "faster than McDonald's."

IVY, THE ☾ 23 | 24 | 21 | $51
113 N. Robertson Blvd. (bet. Beverly Blvd. & 3rd St.), Beverly Center, 310-274-8303
■ A "classic that's still classy", this New American is a "true Hollywood experience" with "paparazzi parked out front" and "guaranteed celebrity sightings" in the "froufrou" "Laura Ashley–country house" setting, with predictably "snotty" service "if you're not an A-lister"; still, many fans "would go even if it were just me and the walls" (and "on the company's dime") for its "simple food prepared perfectly" and served in "large" (but "damn expensive") portions.

Jacopo's ☾ 17 | 8 | 14 | $16
8166 Sunset Blvd. (Crescent Heights Blvd.), West Hollywood, 323-650-8128; www.jacopos.com
See review in Westside Directory.

Jan's ☾ 11 | 6 | 15 | $14
8424 Beverly Blvd. (Croft Ave.), Beverly Center, 323-651-2866
◪ "Exactly what it purports to be", this "no-frills" "late-night" Beverly Center coffee shop is an "old-school" eatery where "you can sit by yourself and relax with a paper" over "big portions" of "standard" fare like "turkey burgers"; but cynics sniff about the "unremarkable" food that will suit you "if you're over 80, a cop" or a "stoned biker."

JAR 23 | 18 | 22 | $48
8225 Beverly Blvd. (Harper Ave.), Beverly Center, 323-655-6566; www.thejar.com
■ Über-chef Mark Peel (Campanile) and hyper-talented Suzanne Tracht (Jozu) have "one great restaurant here" is what surveyors say about this "trendy" Beverly Center Cal-accented American serving "hearty, conscientiously prepared" fare like "pot roast like mom never made" as well as "excellent" braised and broiled meats and fish with assorted sauces; sure, this "minimalist everything" spot is "loud" and "pricey", but "star sightings are guaranteed."

Jitlada Ⓜ️ ▽ 22 | 11 | 17 | $22
5233½ W. Sunset Blvd. (bet. Harvard Blvd. & Kingsley Dr.), East Hollywood, 323-667-9809
■ "They definitely pack heat" at this "spicy", "tasty Thai", albeit in a "nondescript" East Hollywood strip-mall setting;

subscribe to zagat.com

LA/Hollywood/W. Hollywood | F | D | S | C |

it's best to "ignore the decor and enjoy the food", and with that fiery breath you've acquired, "don't expect to go out afterwards, unless it's to chase vampires."

Johnnie's New York Pizzeria & Caffe | 18 | 11 | 15 | $15 |
350 S. Grand Ave. (W. 4th St.), Downtown, 213-617-3992
Museum Park Sq., 5757 Wilshire Blvd. (bet. Curson & Masselin Aves.), Los Angeles, 323-904-4880
■ This Italian group's "traditional East Coast pizza" turns out to be "surprisingly good for a chain" and makes NYers "not miss New York so much"; counter "service is slow", so the "reliable delivery" may be the way to go.

Johnny Rockets ● | 16 | 15 | 16 | $12 |
6801 Hollywood Blvd. (Highland Ave.), Hollywood, 323-465-4456
Beverly Connection, 100 N. La Cienega Blvd. (Oakwood Ave.), Los Angeles, 310-657-6073
Farmer's Mkt., 6333 W. Third St. (Fairfax Ave.), Los Angeles, 323-937-2093
7507 Melrose Ave. (Gardner St.), Los Angeles, 323-651-3361
www.johnnyrockets.com
■ "Fun, funky", "'50s-style retro diner" chain that dishes up "reliable" burgers and fries that would make "Homer Simpson happy", along with "old-fashioned milkshakes" and the "BLTs of your childhood"; most maintain that "it's a step above fast food" and its "back-to-the-future" vibe makes it a "good choice for families."

Jones Hollywood ● | 18 | 20 | 15 | $27 |
7205 Santa Monica Blvd. (2 blocks west of La Brea Ave.), West Hollywood, 323-850-1727; www.committedinc.com
■ It's "so dark you can't see the food" at this "cool, cool, cool spot for Hollywood hipsters" with "lots of eye candy" and "loud music" that "leaves little room for conversation"; despite a "neglectful" staff, the retro Italian-American fare is "surprisingly good", "reasonably priced" and served in a "great atmosphere"; "if James Dean were still around, this is the place where he'd be."

Kabob & Chinese | ∇ 19 | 10 | 14 | $20 |
9180 W. Pico Blvd. (bet. Beverly & Doheny Drs.), Los Angeles, 310-274-4007
☑ When the need for kosher Chinese-Persian strikes (as long as it's not on Friday night or Saturday before sundown), fans head for this glatt duo in Beverlywood and West LA; but while the "juicy beef or lemony chicken kebabs" are certifiably kosher, the service is certifiably "nonexistent."

Katana ● | 21 | 25 | 19 | $49 |
8439 W. Sunset Blvd. (bet. La Cienega Blvd. & Sweetzer Ave.), West Hollywood, 323-650-8585; www.sushiroku.com
■ "The beautiful people" have made this Sushi Roku spin-off, just across from Roku's Balboa steakhouse on the Sunset

LA/Hollywood/W. Hollywood F | D | S | C |

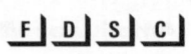

Strip, in the historic building that's home to Miramax, a "Hollywood hot spot with incredible food"; "sit outside on the patio" at this "real hipster scene" that features "three bars" – one for sushi, another for *robatayaki* and a third for exotic cocktails; "amazing" "interior design by Dodd Mitchell" makes it the sort of place where you "might see the entire cast of *Charlie's Angels* – I did!"

Kinara Cafe M   – | – | – | M |
656 N. Robertson Blvd. (bet. Melrose Ave. & Santa Monica Blvd.), West Hollywood, 310-657-9188; www.kinaraspa.com
The latest concept from Joachim and Christine Splichal (of Patina and Pinot), this high-end spa run by Christine serves a menu created by Joachim of upscale spa chow – chilled pea soup, open-faced tartines, Scottish salmon on couscous – and a three-course fixed-price menu; until recently, it was open only to those who were there to be fluffed, buffed and puffed – now it's open to everyone.

King's Road Cafe   18 | 14 | 16 | $15 |
8361 Beverly Blvd. (King's Rd.), Beverly Center, 323-655-9044
■ Caffeine freaks find "coffee that's stronger than Arnold Schwarzenegger" at this "bustling" American, just a few blocks from the Beverly Center, which features a menu that runs from pancakes to sandwiches and salads; it's a "laid-back" setting where "directors read their scripts" and "disheveled actors start their days late"; P.S. there are "dog-friendly tables outside."

Kitchen, The ●   22 | 13 | 16 | $19 |
4348 Fountain Ave. (W. Sunset Blvd.), Silver Lake, 323-664-3663
■ A "funky local diner with an ambitious menu", this "tiny" Traditional American in hyper-hip Silver Lake is "often crowded" with "late-night" denizens hungry for "large portions of home cooking", including an "incredible pistachio-crusted salmon"; "you have to bring your own wine", which keeps the tab tolerable.

Koi   23 | 26 | 18 | $49 |
730 N. La Cienega Blvd. (bet. Melrose Pl. & Waring Ave.), West Hollywood, 310-659-9449; www.koirestaurant.com
■ "Is this a restaurant or a photo shoot? – everything looks just so at this trendy Asian" West Hollywood "hot spot" where "celebrity sightings are a given"; "amazing food" – "creative, new-wave sushi" like "wonderful spicy seared tuna with fried onion" and the "best Kobe beef" – is also served in the "fab", feng-shuied "Zen space", so most maintain it's "well worth the money, the wait and the trip."

Kokomo Cafe   18 | 9 | 12 | $15 |
Farmer's Mkt., 6333 W. Third St. (Fairfax Ave.), Los Angeles, 323-933-0773
◪ There are "good breakfasts and lunches" at this Farmer's Market Southern-Californian, an "ultrahip" outdoor spot

LA/Hollywood/W. Hollywood F | D | S | C

that "only true LA insiders know of", "but brace yourself for deplorable service" – "come with the patience to wait"; N.B. there's a jazz brunch on Saturday and Sunday.

Koo Koo Roo 16 | 8 | 13 | $11
445 S. Figueroa St. (bet. 4th & 5th Sts.), Downtown, 213-629-1246
255 S. Grand Ave. (3rd St.), Downtown, 213-620-1800
301 N. Larchmont Blvd. (Beverly Blvd.), Hancock Park, 323-962-1500
5779 Wilshire Blvd. (bet. Courtyard Pl. & Curson Ave.), Los Angeles, 323-954-7200
8520 Santa Monica Blvd. (La Cienega Blvd.), West Hollywood, 310-657-3300
www.kookooroo.com
■ This "tasty, healthy fast-food" chicken chain earns a loyal following with its "original skinless" version that fans "can't live without"; it's a "real time and money saver", just be warned about the "inept" service.

Kung Pao Chinese Bistro 17 | 13 | 17 | $17
Fan Fair Mall, 7853 Santa Monica Blvd. (Fairfax Ave.), West Hollywood, 323-848-9888
■ A "good neighborhood Chinese" option, this chainlet offers "tasty" entrees at "reasonable prices", plus a "separate veggie menu" featuring "healthy" faux-meat dishes; the "decor is nothing to write home about", which may make it better for "quick delivery."

La Boca del Conga Room ▽ 17 | 21 | 16 | $33
5364 Wilshire Blvd. (La Brea Ave.), Los Angeles, 323-938-1696; www.congaroom.com
◪ Mid-Wilshire Nuevo Latino co-owned by Jennifer Lopez and Jimmy Smits (among others), with "colorful dishes" that are a prelude to "thigh-thinning, butt-firming Latin dancing" "in the club upstairs"; the food may "need work", but the "beautiful people and mojitos" help make up for it.

LA BOHEME 24 | 27 | 24 | $43
8400 Santa Monica Blvd. (N. Orlando Ave.), West Hollywood, 323-848-2360
■ The decor is somewhere between "*Phantom of the Opera*" and a "gothic *Alice in Wonderland*" at this West Hollywood Cal-French where "velvet curtains, grand chandeliers" and a "roaring fireplace" are the "theatrical" backdrop for "outstanding food" served by an "excellent" staff; it's "romantic", but even the mismatched maintain "I've never had a bad meal here even when on a bad date."

La Bottega Marino ▽ 22 | 14 | 19 | $20
Larchmont Village, 203 N. Larchmont Blvd. (bet. Beverly Blvd. & W. 1st St.), Hancock Park, 323-962-1325
■ With locations in old-money Hancock Park and the new-money Westside, this "consistently good" spot is a "small

LA/Hollywood/W. Hollywood   F | D | S | C

Italian market and deli" featuring "high-end" imported groceries and "substantial sandwiches" by day and a cafe serving "delicious" and "affordable" dishes by night; the BYO Hancock Park branch also offers a traditional country breakfast on weekends.

La Korea Korean BBQ ⑤Ⓜ — | — | — | I
6333 W. Third St. (Fairfax Ave.), Los Angeles, 323-936-3930
Korean restaurants are expanding beyond Koreatown and Gardena, with this one debuting at the ethnically diverse Farmer's Market, where it sits across the way from the Gumbo Pot; look for a casual, neat-as-a-pin stand offering a good cross section of Korean cooking for beginners: mung-bean pancakes and battered tofu (with maple syrup) for breakfast and barbecue and bibimbop for lunch and dinner, with several kimchi options to crank the heat level up a notch.

La Luna 20 | 18 | 19 | $32
113 N. Larchmont Blvd. (bet. Beverly Blvd. & 1st St.), Hancock Park, 323-962-2130; www.ristorantelaluna.com
■ "Consistent" Northern Italian in Larchmont Village, where "good pastas, pizzas and seafood" are served by a "friendly" staff in a "warm", rustic open-kitchen space; there are "enjoyable" outdoor tables to tempt people-watchers.

LANGER'S DELI ⑤ 24 | 8 | 17 | $15
704 S. Alvarado St. (7th St.), Downtown, 213-483-8050
■ Fans say this Downtown deli "institution" serves the "best pastrami in America" – "hand-cut", "mouthwatering" meat "piled high" on "rye to die for"; the only drawback is it's in a "scary area" ("if you need a fake ID, you're in the right neighborhood"), so those who are "freaked by the location" "call in their order and pull up for curbside delivery", and other brave souls take the "subway, which stops here"; N.B. closes at 4 PM Monday–Saturday.

La Paella ⑤ 23 | 19 | 22 | $31
476 S. San Vicente Blvd. (bet. Ashcroft & Dorrington Aves.), West Hollywood, 323-951-0745
■ One of SoCal's few Spaniards, this "intimate" Iberian south of the Beverly Center is the place to go for the namesake creation of "succulent clams, mussels, perfectly seasoned rice and saffron" served by an "excellent" staff; it's also a "cute, quiet and romantic" spot where you can indulge in "tasty sangria" and "authentic tapas."

La Parrilla 21 | 15 | 18 | $19
1300 Wilshire Blvd. (Witmer St.), Downtown, 213-353-4980
2126 E. Cesar Chavez Ave. (Chicago St.), East LA, 323-262-3434
3129 W. Sunset Blvd. (Silver Lake Blvd.), Los Feliz, 323-661-8055
▣ There's "no question the guacamole and tortillas are fresh – they're made right in front of you" at this Mexican trio; "yes, the decor is kitschy", the service "can be sketchy"

LA/Hollywood/W. Hollywood　　F | D | S | C

and the mariachi bands can be "extra loud", but "generous portions" of "savory" fare make up for most glitches.

La Salsa　　16 | 9 | 13 | $10
601 W. Fifth St. (Grand Ave.), Downtown, 213-623-6390; www.lasalsa.com

◪ "Convenient" Mexican chain where you get "lots of" "fresh, tasty" "inexpensive" eats "for the price" including "good fish tacos and burritos"; while critics complain about the "faux" "Americanized" fare and the fact that the competition has stolen much of its fire, the consensus is "it is what it is" – "not the best, not the worst."

La Serenata de Garibaldi　　23 | 18 | 19 | $28
1842 E. First St. (bet. Boyle Ave. & State St.), Boyle Heights, 323-265-2887; www.laserenataonline.com

■ "Fantastico" "gourmet Mexican" duo in East LA and Santa Monica whose "exquisite, imaginative soups", "innovative fish dishes" and "wondrous sauces" make them "islands of great food in a sea of Tex-Mex"; service "can leave something to be desired", but devotees declare "everyone I've taken there loves it."

Le Pain Quotidien　　21 | 18 | 15 | $17
8607 Melrose Ave. (Westbourne Dr.), West Hollywood, 310-854-3700; www.painquotidien.com

■ With branches in the more food-obsessed parts of town, this bakery/cafe chain has hit the ground running with "fragrant, fresh bread", "the best baguettes", a "host of terrific pastries" like chocolate mousse cake and "soups, salads and open-faced sandwiches that are perfect for lunch" whether you sit on the "great patio" or at "communal tables"; sure, it's "pricey" and an "Atkins nightmare", but that doesn't stop the starch-starved from storming the place.

Le Petit Bistro　　20 | 19 | 18 | $32
631 N. La Cienega Blvd. (Melrose Ave.), West Hollywood, 310-289-9797; www.lepetitbistro.net

■ "You'll feel like you're in Paris" at this trio of French bistros with "reliable" dishes like the "best baby lamb chops" and "can't-go-wrong steak frites" served in "pretty" settings; while service is "sometimes good, sometimes Gallic" and the atmosphere can be "noisy", no one's complaining about an "authentic" experience at a "reasonable price."

Le Petit Four　　20 | 17 | 18 | $29
Sunset Plaza, 8654 W. Sunset Blvd. (Sunset Plaza Dr.), West Hollywood, 310-652-3863; www.lepetitfour.com

■ "Opt for patio seating" at this industry-heavy watering hole, a "high-stylin' place to eat" in the heart of Sunset Plaza, where you can "rub elbows with out-of-work actresses and wanna-be Hollywood agents" and watch "scantily clad women and 50-year-old cheeseballs in Ferraris"; the French bistro fare is "surprisingly good", the

get updates at zagat.com

LA/Hollywood/W. Hollywood — F | D | S | C

"wine list is reasonable" and you can "unwind with an espresso after your meal."

Le Petit Greek — 20 | 15 | 19 | $27
127 N. Larchmont Blvd. (bet. Beverly Blvd. & 1st St.), Hancock Park, 323-464-5160

■ Hancock Park Hellenic (near Paramount) with "reliably good food", a "friendly" staff and appealing "outdoor seating on a summer evening"; it's a "little pricey for what it is", but it's "convenient" and one wit wagers he "goes there so often the staffers think I'm stalking them."

Les Deux Cafés — 19 | 24 | 13 | $49
1638 N. Las Palmas Ave. (bet. Hollywood Blvd. & Selma Ave.), Hollywood, 323-465-0509; www.lesdeux.info

◪ This "happening" Hollywood "celeb hangout" and "magical" "oasis" "hidden" in a "cozy" Craftsman house with a "beautiful garden patio" features "excellent" organic French food that's billed as being hormone and steroid free; but foes fume over "overpriced" fare" and "god-awful service" from a staff with "more attitude than Madonna."

Linq ❂ — 22 | 24 | 20 | $44
8338 W. Third St. (bet. Orlando & Sweetzer Aves.), Los Angeles, 323-655-4555; www.linqlounge.com

■ An "urban hipster bistro" where the "management takes the time to kiss cheeks", this Third Street Californian inspires *amour* from admirers who gush "how do I love thee? let me count the ways" – among them, the "fabulously understated decor" with its "fountain wall" and fireplace, "surprisingly good food" and "apple martinis to die for"; natch, it's best to "dress to impress" at this trendy spot.

LITTLE DOOR, THE — 22 | 27 | 19 | $47
8164 W. Third St. (bet. Crescent Heights Blvd. & La Jolla Ave.), Los Angeles, 323-951-1210

■ The entrance isn't so small that it doesn't admit an "eclectic mix of hipsters, continentals" and celebs to this "Third Street hideaway", an "incredibly romantic" room with "candles everywhere" and an "enchanting indoor garden patio"; "excellent, imaginative" French fare with "Moroccan flair" and a "worldly wine selection" make it a "culinary heaven" that's far removed from the outside "hustle and bustle" and lead its lovers to say "*j'adore* The Door."

Locanda Veneta — 25 | 17 | 21 | $43
8638 W. Third St. (bet. Robertson & San Vicente Blvds.), Los Angeles, 310-274-1893; www.locandaveneta.com

■ "Beautiful food for beautiful people" awaits at this "tiny", celeb-heavy Venetian near Cedars-Sinai, a "landmark that lives up to the hype", where "everything is excellent", including the "exquisite grilled shrimp" and "best gnocchi in LA"; service is "hospitable", and "even though they pack 'em in, you can have a romantic dinner here."

LA/Hollywood/W. Hollywood F | D | S | C

Lola's ●   17 | 19 | 17 | $28
945 N. Fairfax Ave. (bet. Romaine St. & Willoughby Ave.), West Hollywood, 213-736-5652; www.lolasla.com

■ A "must for martini lovers", with over 50 versions and bars front and back, this West Hollywood New American also offers "excellent mac 'n' cheese", "meatloaf and delicious mashed potatoes"; but mainly it's a "swanky" watering hole for "hip/cool Hollywood types" ("are there any 'real' people" here?), which makes it a "great place to take out-of-towners to show them what LA is all about."

L'ORANGERIE Ⓜ   26 | 28 | 26 | $84
903 N. La Cienega Blvd. (Romaine St.), West Hollywood, 310-652-9770; www.orangerie.com

■ New chef Christophe Eme has helped this "fabulous, old-world" West Hollywood Classic French regain its "exquisite, sumptuous" edge, making it the "standard bearer" for "elegant dining"; with its "beautiful indoor-garden setting", "gracious service" and "attention to detail", this "big-night-out", "special-occasion", "romantic" "paradise" is "ridiculously expensive but worth twice as much"; N.B. "don't forget a coat and tie."

Lotería! Grill   ▽ 25 | 11 | 18 | $10
Farmer's Mkt., 6333 W. Third St. (S. Fairfax Ave.), Los Angeles, 323-930-2211

■ The brainchild of Wharton School of Business graduate Jimmy Shaw, this Farmer's Market stand is earning raves for "fantastic" and "authentic Mexican street chow", from "the best tacos in town bar none" with "juicy, flavorful fillings" to "mole to die for"; "reasonable prices" and "helpful" service add to the *olés*.

Louise's Trattoria   15 | 14 | 16 | $21
232 N. Larchmont Blvd. (Beverly Blvd.), Hancock Park, 323-962-9510
7505 Melrose Ave. (Gardner St.), Los Angeles, 323-651-3880
10645 W. Pico Blvd. (bet. Manning & Overland Aves.), Los Angeles, 310-475-6084
4500 Los Feliz Blvd. (Hillhurst Ave.), Los Feliz, 323-667-0777
www.louises.com

◪ After a management change, this longtime Cal-Italian chain has returned to its original ownership and its tradition of "handmade" food from an open-kitchen at "reasonable prices"; but the less enthused assert the "great locations in all the hot spots around town are the draw", adding that while the bill is "fair, so is the food quality."

LUCQUES   26 | 23 | 24 | $53
8474 Melrose Ave. (La Cienega Blvd.), West Hollywood, 323-655-6277; www.lucques.com

■ Best known these days as the parent of A.O.C., Suzanne Goin's "laid-back but upscale" West Hollywood Cal-French

LA/Hollywood/W. Hollywood   F | D | S | C |

is a "sublime experience" that begins with plates of the "namesake olives" brought to your table, along with "almonds dipped in salt", and continues through the various "outstanding" courses served by a "top-notch" staff; you'll feel you're in "your own private ski lodge", where "no matter what you choose, it'll be great" (even if "you'll need a dictionary to figure out the menu"); P.S. the $30 "prix fixe Sunday dinner is the deal of a lifetime."

Madame Wu's Asian Bistro   12 | 18 | 13 | $27 |
The Grove at Farmer's Mkt., 189 The Grove Dr. (bet. Beverly Blvd. & W. 3rd St.), Los Angeles, 323-965-8150
◪ "Perfect for a quick dinner" "on the way to or from a movie" thanks to its "convenient Grove location", this Sino-Japanese remake of the fabled Madame's Santa Monica spot offers "great" weekend dim sum and a "lovely" sushi bar; though the "marginal" fare and "unprofessional service" "bear little resemblance to the original", the "bordello" decor and balcony overlooking the theater lobby make it a "fun stop."

MADEO   25 | 19 | 25 | $47 |
8897 Beverly Blvd. (bet. Doheny Dr. & Robertson Blvd.), West Hollywood, 310-859-4903
■ While it draws its share of "stars and wanna-bes", "few people seem to know" about this "elegant, grown-up" West Hollywood Northern Italian, resulting in a "quiet" ambiance and "lots of space for diners"; "consistently" "fabulous" "old-fashioned" cooking and "proper service" from a staff of "professional waiters, not actors" in a "comfortable" (if "dated") setting represent "what fine dining should be" and make this spot "one of the classiest in town."

MAGGIANO'S LITTLE ITALY   19 | 20 | 19 | $26 |
The Grove at Farmer's Mkt., 189 The Grove Dr. (Fairfax Ave.), Los Angeles, 323-965-9665; www.maggianos.com
■ "Italian in work boots" is how some describe the "hearty" "soul food" at this Southern Italian chain where "everything is huge" – the "humongous" "family-style platters" big enough to "feed a small farming community", "large", "'50s-style" dining rooms, "crowds" and "ridiculously long lines"; for parents it's the "perfect 'let-the-kids-make-noise' crowd-pleaser."

Magic Carpet   ▽ 20 | 11 | 14 | $18 |
8566 W. Pico Blvd. (La Cienega Blvd.), Los Angeles, 310-652-8507
■ Neophytes can discover the "unknown delight of melawach" and the rest of the "rainbow of tastes" at this "authentic", "unpretentious" kosher Yemenite specialist in Pico-Robertson; devotees declare there's "no better hummus anywhere" and the "excellent" fare is "so worth the wait" for service from the "slow" staff; N.B. closed Friday night through Saturday for the Sabbath.

LA/Hollywood/W. Hollywood F | D | S | C

Mandarette   19 | 15 | 16 | $26
8386 Beverly Blvd. (bet. N. King's Rd. & N. Orlando Ave.), West Hollywood, 323-655-6115; www.mandarette.com
■ "If it's good enough for Barry Diller, it's good enough for me" declare dazzled devotees of this West Hollywood Chinese serving "amazing Nouveau Chinese offerings" in a "sparse", "minimalist" space where "stars" like "Warren Beatty and Annette Bening" are "treated like real folks for a change" by an "alternately pleasant and gruff" staff that "doesn't seem to recognize them."

Mandarin Deli   21 | 9 | 13 | $13
727 N. Broadway (bet. Alpine & Ord Sts.), Chinatown, 213-623-6054
356 E. Second St. (bet. Central Ave. & San Pedro St.), Little Tokyo, 213-617-0231
◪ What it "lacks in grace and style" (and service and decor), this Chinese chain makes up for with "large portions" of "amazing" Mandarin fare "like you've never tasted", such as "excellent" handmade noodles, "delicious" scallion pancakes and "unique" dumplings, at prices that are a "steal"; it's the "perfect dive."

Mäni's Bakery   18 | 11 | 13 | $12
519 S. Fairfax Ave. (bet. 3rd St. & Wilshire Blvd.), Los Angeles, 323-938-8800; www.manisbakery.com
■ "Health food so delicious you'll think it's bad for you" is the hallmark of these "hipster bakery"/cafe twins in Pico-Robertson and Santa Monica that are "neighborhood staples" for "wonderful desserts" with "no guilt", a "cuppa Joe" or "great" turkey chili that "even Garfield would approve"; "what's the point of fat-free sweets if they're taste-free?" wags wonder, arguing that "sometimes we need a little fat."

Manna ⌧   – | – | – | M
3377 W. Olympic Blvd. (bet. Gramercy Ave. & St. Andrews Pl.), Koreatown, 323-733-8516
The "smoky" aroma of BBQ "permeates your senses and not your clothes" at this Koreatown outpost of a South Korean chain, where the dining area is all "protected outdoor seating"; the "curt, hyper-efficient" staff comes running when you use the "calling bell on the table."

Marino ⌧   ∇ 22 | 17 | 24 | $34
6001 Melrose Ave. (Wilcox Ave.), East Hollywood, 323-466-8812
■ Chef-owner Ciro Marino "meets you at the door and makes you feel welcome" at his "little bit of NY-ish heaven" in East Hollywood that serves as the "unofficial Paramount commissary", dishing out "solid" "Italian comfort food"; the "wonderfully personal" service and "old-world" atmosphere almost make you feel as if you're in "a *Saturday Night Live* skit" about a "comfortably untrendy", "friendly old joint."

get updates at zagat.com

LA/Hollywood/W. Hollywood F | D | S | C

MARIO'S PERUVIAN 25 | 5 | 15 | $15
5786 Melrose Ave. (Vine St.), East Hollywood, 323-466-4181
■ "Substance without style" "sounds odd, but it works in a big way" at this East Hollywood "hole-in-the-wall" serving "huge portions" of the "best Peruvian" fare around at "very low prices" in a "bare-bones" space that'll tempt you to "close your eyes while you eat"; items such as "lomo saltado prepared to perfection" and "camarones de saltado to die for", and a "magical green sauce" "make the 45-minute wait seem totally reasonable."

Marix Tex Mex Café 17 | 15 | 16 | $21
1108 N. Flores St. (Santa Monica Blvd.), West Hollywood, 323-656-8800; www.marixtexmex.com
■ Though they both serve the same "fierce" margaritas and "hearty, natural" Tex-Mex fare, these "loud and louder" twins are "totally different" in atmosphere – the slightly "more upscale" Santa Monica branch is "perfect for after the beach", while the Boys Town location is one of the "cruisiest spots in WeHo", where the "sizzling fajitas" are nearly as hot as the "local talent."

Marouch M ▽ 24 | 12 | 16 | $20
4905 Santa Monica Blvd. (N. Edgemont St.), East Hollywood, 323-662-9325; www.marouchrestaurant.com
◪ The neighborhood's "scary", but "the food makes up for it" at this East Hollywood Armenian-Lebanese offering "some of the finest grilled meats you can find" in a rec-room setting; it's "chronically understaffed", so "you may want to ask for your check when they deliver" your order.

McCormick & Schmick's 19 | 19 | 19 | $33
Library Tower, 633 W. Fifth St. (Grand Ave.), Downtown, 213-629-1929; www.mccormickandschmicks.com
■ A "taste of home" for "Pacific Northwesterners", this chain of "corporate" "brasserie-style" seafooders "excels at what it aims for", an "unbelievable variety" of "fresh fruits of the sea", including "yummy oyster platters", "reliably delivered" (if somewhat "by the book") in "dark, smoky, men's club" settings; "it's not the Water Grill, but they try."

Mel's Drive-In ☽ 15 | 17 | 16 | $14
1650 N. Highland Ave. (Hollywood Blvd.), Hollywood, 323-465-2111
8585 Sunset Blvd. (La Cienega Blvd.), West Hollywood, 310-854-7200
www.melsdrive-in.com
■ For many who believe that "a little grease never hurt anyone", "there's no better place for a burger and a malt" or a "black-and-white shake" than this "fun retro" diner trio, though "health nuts can also find enough" to choose from on the menu; the Sunset Strip location, open 24/7, is a popular "post–bar hopping" "detox spot" for the "semi-famous"; N.B. the third branch is in Sherman Oaks.

LA/Hollywood/W. Hollywood   F | D | S | C

Menjin ⌧   _ | _ | _ | I
8393 Beverly Blvd. (N. La Cienega Blvd.), Los Angeles, 323-653-9915
Located in the same Fairfax shopping mall as the popular Hirozen, this inexpensive Siamese newcomer offers a daily menu of tapas-style Thai dishes (à la Rambutan in Silver Lake), served up at large tables in a small space; deep-fried ice cream seals the deal.

Mexico City   18 | 15 | 16 | $22
2121 Hillhurst Ave. (Avocado St.), Los Feliz, 323-661-7227
◪ "Potent margaritas", "the best beef fajitas burrito west of El Paso" and "what do they put in the guacamole?" – this Los Feliz cantina is "not your ordinary Mexican", serving south-of-the-border fare that's "authentic and full of flavor"; amigos aver the "food's worth having to shout" above the "noise" in the "kitschy" room, or at servers who could use a bit of "remedial training."

Miceli's   15 | 19 | 19 | $23
1646 N. Las Palmas St. (Hollywood Blvd.), Hollywood, 323-466-3438
◪ "Singing waiters", "red-and-white checkerboard tablecloths" and "Chianti bottle decorations" make for a "campy, over-the-top evening" at this Italian duo in Hollywood and Universal City that's "fun, fun, fun for families"; "affordable menu choices" of "basic" red-sauce fare may be fine for "hungry actors stretching a buck", but many come for "the atmosphere" rather than the cooking, which can be "hit-or-miss."

Michelia ⌧   24 | 20 | 23 | $34
8738 W. Third St. (S. George Burns Rd.), Los Angeles, 310-276-8288
■ "Every dish is a pure delight" at this French-Vietnamese "oasis of quiet" on busy Third Street across from Cedars-Sinai, where "truly talented" "chef Kimmy Tang dishes up tantalizingly tasty" dishes that are served with a "tableside charm unmatched at pricier restaurants" in a "serene" room where you "can even hold a conversation"; "don't miss the lobster stir-fried with scallions and black peppercorns."

Milky Way   ▽ 18 | 16 | 21 | $24
9108 W. Pico Blvd. (Doheny Dr.), Los Angeles, 310-859-0004
■ "For a hug and some comfort soup" regulars recommend this "tidy", "spacious" kosher dairy Pico-Robertson owned by "Steven Spielberg's mom", Leah Adler, who's "there every night to greet you", "and will tell all"; besides "blintzes that re-establish your center of gravity", it also offers "healthy", "unusual choices" on a menu that's "great for vegetarians and non-vegetarians alike."

get updates at zagat.com   59

LA/Hollywood/W. Hollywood F | D | S | C

Mimi's Cafe 18 | 17 | 18 | $18
2925 Los Feliz Blvd. (bet. Revere & Seneca Aves.), Silver Lake, 323-668-1715; www.mimiscafe.com

■ A "wonderful stop off the freeway" and a "place to go for a no-frills bite with friends", this fast-growing, "higher-end", "French-themed" American chain earns points for "delicious breakfast entrees", including "tasty muffins" and "pain perdu to die for", and other "steady, consistent" fare at "coffee-shop prices"; not surprisingly, it "caters to families."

Mimosa ⊠ Ⓜ 22 | 17 | 20 | $41
8009 Beverly Blvd. (bet. N. Edinburgh & N. Laurel Aves.), Los Angeles, 323-655-8895; www.mimosarestaurant.com

■ The "most authentic bistro in LA", Jean-Pierre Bosc's Fairfax District French has just the right "je ne sais quoi" to go along with the "best côte de boeuf", "mac 'n' cheese to die for" and other "flavorful" "old favorites", as well as "friendly" service and an "intimate", "country-inn" setting.

Mirabelle ● ▽ 20 | 20 | 21 | $32
8768 Sunset Blvd. (bet. Horn Ave. & N. Sherbourne Dr.), West Hollywood, 310-659-6022

■ Though it's located in an area that's "way too impressed with itself", this family-owned Californian stalwart is "not as trendy, obnoxious or pricey as some" others on the Sunset Strip, and therein lies one of its "charms"; add to that "well-prepared and -presented" fare, "friendly, accommodating" service and "great star-spotting."

Mishima 20 | 14 | 18 | $16
8474 W. Third St. (La Cienega Blvd.), Los Angeles, 323-782-0181; www.mishima.com

■ A "mainstay for low-budget, casual dining", this Japanese noodle shop chain "never leaves you hungry", dishing out "great bowls" of "slurpy" soba and udon, and a "good mix of sushi", at "rock-bottom prices"; "long lines" can be a bit soba-ring, but the "quick" staff will "get you in and out fast."

Miyagi's ● 14 | 16 | 14 | $30
8225 Sunset Blvd. (Crescent Heights Blvd.), West Hollywood, 323-650-3524

☒ It's like a "sushi-themed frat party" at this West Hollywood Japanese better known for its "hip" scene and "all-you-can-eat" Mondays than the "decent" fin fare, "uninspired" decor or "nonexistent" service; "late at night" "the place goes off", and while "it may not be the best sushi you've ever had, it might be the best time you've ever had eating it."

Moishe's ⊄ ▽ 21 | 8 | 15 | $11
Farmer's Mkt., 6333 W. Third St. (Fairfax Ave.), Los Angeles, 323-936-4998

■ "Who knew" you could find some of the "best falafel this side of Israel" at a "Farmer's Market stand"? – many, it

60 subscribe to zagat.com

LA/Hollywood/W. Hollywood F | D | S | C

seems, since this Middle Easterner is "always crowded", thanks to "fabulous" hummus and tabbouleh that's "worth getting on line for", and a chicken kebab plate "you don't want to miss"; do watch out for "lots of garlic."

MON KEE'S 24 | 10 | 17 | $22
679 N. Spring St. (Ord St.), Chinatown, 213-628-6717
■ After "more than 25 years" this "frenetic" Cantonese seafooder is still a "dependable" "Chinatown standby" that "delivers every time" with "justly famous" fin fare, including "delicious" crabs, "super tasty scallops" and "killer" shrimp; the decor's "a little run down" at this "hole-in-the-wall", but the service is "fast" and the atmosphere is "cordial."

Monsieur Marcel – | – | – | I
Farmer's Mkt., 6333 W. Third St. (Fairfax Ave.), Los Angeles, 323-939-7792
Bistro meets sidewalk stand at this surprising, affordable French wine and cheese bar/charcuterie on the eastern edge of the Farmer's Market in Fairfax, offering a solid vin list of some 500 labels and more than 200 varieties of fromage, as well as popular steak specials, in an open-air setting; jazz on weekends adds allure.

Morels First Floor Bistro 17 | 20 | 18 | $31
The Grove at Farmer's Mkt., 189 The Grove Dr. (bet. Fairfax Ave. & 3rd St.), Los Angeles, 323-965-9595
■ In the very center of the Grove at Farmer's Market, this "wonderfully French" bistro serves a "fantastic" number of "divine" cheeses and Gallic fare that "doesn't disappoint" in an "authentic" setting with "reproductions of French painters" gracing the walls; there's "great people-watching" on the outdoor patio.

Morels French Steakhouse M 19 | 22 | 19 | $48
The Grove at Farmer's Mkt., 189 The Grove Dr. (bet. Fairfax Ave. & 3rd St.), Los Angeles, 323-965-9595
■ Perhaps "not as well known as its neighbor downstairs", this "spacious" upstairs, upscale Gallic steakhouse over the First Floor Bistro "keeps you above the hustle and bustle below" and boasts an "outdoor patio overlooking the Grove"; "outstanding" steaks and "fantastic cheese fondue" are among the "many choices" on the menu, and "all are done well."

Morton's S 25 | 22 | 24 | $53
8764 Melrose Ave. (bet. N. Robertson & N. San Vicente Blvds.), West Hollywood, 310-276-5205
■ When it's "beef" you "crave", "treat yourself like Hollywood royalty" at this West Hollywood Cal-American that's "still a scene after all these years" (site of the annual *Vanity Fair* Oscar party), serving "fabulous" "Chicago-style" steaks and "veal that's worth the guilt" in a "clubby" setting with plenty of "celeb sightings"; the service is "impeccable",

LA/Hollywood/W. Hollywood F | D | S | C |

but it doesn't hurt to "have some in."

Moun of Tunis ▽ 21 | 22 | 23 | $32 |
7445½ Sunset Blvd. (bet. N. Gardner & N. Vista Sts.), Hollywood, 323-874-3333; www.mounoftunisrestaurant.com

■ Hollywood's "rock 'n' roll Tunisian" is a "great introduction to the culinary world of North Africa", offering an "amazing" "mélange of flavors" and "obscene" portions in a "festive" setting, where the "belly dancing is spectacular" and the service is "friendly and helpful"; it's "loads of fun for kicking it with pals", though you may find it hard to "eat with your hands and cheer the dancers at the same time."

Moustache Café 18 | 15 | 17 | $28 |
8155 Melrose Ave. (N. Kilkea Dr.), Los Angeles, 323-651-2111

■ "So sue me, I love the old-fashioned French cuisine" at this Gallic Bistro duo in Melrose and Westwood defiant devotees declare, and while the decor may be "a bit tired" the "consistently good" fare "doesn't disappoint"; the "heaven-sent" "chocolate soufflé" is a "special splurge."

Musso & Frank Grill ⓈⓂ 18 | 19 | 19 | $36 |
6667 Hollywood Blvd. (Highland Ave.), Hollywood, 323-467-7788

■ A "Hollywood classic" (circa 1919) that's "never gone out of style", this Traditional American "brings back the Golden Age of Hollywood", with "grumpy old" waiters who may have "been there since it opened" serving "great grilled meats and chops" and "stiff drinks" "good enough for Faulkner or Fitzgerald" in a "mahogany womb" that looks like a "movie set" where "you expect Bogart to walk in at any moment"; it's "history à la carte", and it "can get pricey."

Nak Won Korean ⓈⓂ – | – | – | I |
3879 Wilshire Blvd. (Western Ave.), Koreatown, 213-389-3800

In the midst of block after block of Korean barbecue houses with no decor worth mentioning comes this newly opened one that stands out because of its bright colors and highly modern, neon-lit look; it's an eatery out of *Blade Runner*, with a stylish snack-focused menu, including spicy rice cakes with ramen noodles.

Newsroom Café 18 | 14 | 16 | $18 |
120 N. Robertson Blvd. (bet. Alden Dr. & W. Beverly Blvd.), Beverly Center, 310-652-4444

■ "Picky eaters" and "carnivores" alike praise the "healthy and tasty", "veggie-friendly" fare at this "chic, hipster" West Hollywood Eclectic with a large, cavernous room where "you always see stars", and "where else can you get wheatgrass and vodka shots?"; the "smaller" Santa Monica satellite may be somewhat "less inspired", but partisans find the atmosphere there "friendlier."

LA/Hollywood/W. Hollywood   F | D | S | C

Nick & Stef's Steakhouse   24 | 21 | 22 | $51
Wells Fargo Ctr., 330 S. Hope St. (bet. 3rd & 4th Sts.), Downtown, 213-680-0330; www.patinagroup.com
■ Named after his twin sons, Joachim Splichal's Downtown steakhouse offers 12 of everything on its menu, from "phat" steaks of "prime cuts aged in-house" to "awesome sides"; "excellent" service, a "beautiful" decor and one of the "best happy-hour deals in town" add allure.

Nishimura Ⓢ   ▽ 28 | 24 | 26 | $60
8684 Melrose Ave. (N. San Vicente Blvd.), West Hollywood, 310-659-4770
■ Chef Hiro Nishimura "dazzles" at his West Hollywood Japanese, a "wonderful find" (if you can, as there's "no sign in front") for "fabulous" raw fin fare "seasoned to perfection", served in a "pristine" setting that "gives new meaning to the word minimalist"; insiders fret "if people knew how great this place was, it'd be impossible to get in."

Noah's New York Bagels   16 | 11 | 13 | $7
250 N. Larchmont Blvd. (Beverly Blvd.), Hancock Park, 323-466-2924; www.noahs.com
◪ While "California natives" "travel for miles" for this popular chain's "flavorful" bagels and "great schmears", transplanted Gothamites give a Bronx cheer to the "bloated rolls with holes" that have "nothing NY about them except the price"; surveyors from both coasts agree that the service is like watching "chaos theory in action."

Noé Ⓢ Ⓜ   – | – | – | E
Omni Los Angeles Hotel, 251 S. Olive St. (2nd St.), Downtown, 213-356-4100; www.omnilosangeles.com
Gaddabout chef Robert Gadsby has surfaced at this opulent Downtown newcomer in the Omni; the stylish room of cobalt blue and tan has terra-cotta cement floors, and the 'progressive' American cuisine takes culinary sojourns to Italy, France, Japan and Thailand.

Noura Cafe   19 | 20 | 15 | $17
8479 Melrose Ave. (La Cienega Blvd.), West Hollywood, 323-651-4581
■ A "reliable" option for "tasty" Middle Eastern fare at a "great price", this "funky" spot located directly across from Ago in West Hollywood boasts a "relaxed" setting with "cozy" "couches set around low tables" inside and an outdoor patio "with a Moroccan garden feel"; it's "good, delicious fun", especially if you're "dining on a budget."

Nyala Ethiopian   20 | 15 | 17 | $18
1076 S. Fairfax Ave. (bet. W. Olympic Blvd. & Whitworth Dr.), Los Angeles, 323-936-5918; www.nyala-la.com
■ "One of Little Ethiopia's best", this West Hollywood venue is a "hands-on experience" whereby you "scoop

get updates at zagat.com   63

LA/Hollywood/W. Hollywood F | D | S | C |

up" the "aromatic" stews with "pancakelike" injera bread and follow your meal with coffee "so strong it makes you high"; "it's hard to run up a big bill, so explore to your heart's content", but as the food "sends you to exotic lands", the service may "take some time to catch up to you."

Ocean Seafood   22 | 14 | 16 | $21 |
750 N. Hill St. (bet. Alpine & Ord Sts.), Chinatown, 213-687-3088
■ For a "lunch under 30 minutes", the daytime dim sum at this Sino seafooder in Chinatown is "truly excellent", but the service "will scare the hell out of you"; in the evening, you "choose your fish, clams, prawns and lobsters at the entrance" and then await a more leisurely "royal feast."

Off Vine   22 | 22 | 22 | $35 |
6263 Leland Way (Vine St.), Hollywood, 323-962-1900; www.offvine.com
■ A "charming Craftsman house with a roaring fireplace" is the "very romantic", "rustic" setting for this Californian located in the heart of Hollywood, "close to the theaters", where "nicely presented, comforting" dishes, "lovely wines" and a "heavenly choice of dessert soufflés" are served; tell the "wonderful staff" that "you're going to a show and the service improves" noticeably.

Opaline ⊠   21 | 22 | 23 | $46 |
7450 Beverly Blvd. (Vista St.), Los Angeles, 323-857-6725; www.opaline.org
■ David Rosoff, former sommelier at Michael's, brings his "refreshing approach to wine" to Fairfax's super busy Beverly Boulevard with an "intelligently constructed" list to go along with an "attractive, well-designed menu" of "inventive" Cal-Med dishes that are "not for the faint of palate"; "gracious hosts" and a "knowledgeable staff" provide "wonderful" service in a "sexy, modern" room with a "classy, calm" decor.

Original Pantry Bakery ⊄   14 | 8 | 15 | $13 |
875 S. Figueroa St. (9th St.), Downtown, 213-627-6879
◪ "You get what you pay for" at this Downtown "dive that never disappoints", the "classic diner" offspring of the adjacent Original Pantry Cafe, which dishes out "huge portions" of "greasy" American fare including what some call the "best breakfast in LA" – it "ain't healthy, but it sure is tasty"; N.B. the kitchen closes at 3 PM.

Original Pantry Cafe ●⊄   15 | 9 | 16 | $15 |
877 S. Figueroa St. (9th St.), Downtown, 213-972-9279
◪ "Killing me loudly with cholesterol", this Downtown 24/7 "landmark" is the "Holy Grail of greasy spoons", a "slice of LA history with character" that "delights at all hours", serving "comfort food with a capital C", including "steaks as good as Morton's" and "must-have" coleslaw, with the "ambiance other places dream about."

LA/Hollywood/W. Hollywood F | D | S | C

Orso 21 | 22 | 21 | $39
8706 W. Third St. (east of Robertson Blvd.), Los Angeles, 310-274-7144

■ The West Coast cousin of an NYC Italian, this "celebrity hangout" on Third Street combines "NY savvy in cuisine and service with a glorious California patio" with "stars above and at every table" and a "total Hollywood scene at lunch"; its "excellent" thin-crust pizzas and "authentic", "perfectly prepared" Northern dishes make it a "reliable" option "when you don't know where to eat."

Osteria Nonni ▽ 19 | 12 | 15 | $23
3219 Glendale Blvd. (Glenfeliz Blvd.), Atwater Village, 323-666-7133

■ A "boutique restaurant in an unexpected area", this "reliable" "neighborhood" red-sauce Italian in obscure Atwater prepares "homestyle" "Roman dishes you hardly find anyplace else", like "fantasy"-inducing lemon chicken, as well as "homemade rounds of bread" that "come to your table steaming"; it's "noisy" and "fun", like "eating at your Italian grandma's house."

Otto's 15 | 15 | 16 | $37
LA County Music Ctr., 135 N. Grand Ave. (1st St.), Downtown, 213-972-7322; www.patinagroup.com

◪ Although there have been "huge improvements since the Patina Group took over" this Downtown Californian, with a "redesigned menu" and a "cheese platter that's just the thing before a performance", it's still mostly "location, location, location" that attracts a "captive audience" of "legal types from the nearby courthouse" and Music Center patrons who "mingle with the maestros" after a show.

Pace ⌀Ⓜ – | – | – | M
2100 Laurel Canyon Blvd. (Kirkwood Dr.), West Hollywood, 323-654-8583

No one seems to be in a rush at this Laurel Canyon Cal-Italian cafe, housed in the cottage that was once home to Caioti, where 'casual' is the operative word and the prices are exceedingly reasonable for the earthy, healthy fare; the good vibe comes at no additional cost.

Pacific Dining Car ◐ 22 | 20 | 22 | $49
1310 W. Sixth St. (bet. Alvarado & Figueroa Sts.), Downtown, 213-483-6000; www.pacificdiningcar.com

■ The "food is heavy, the wine is choice and the mood is business" at this venerable steakhouse duo, a "throwback to the glory days of eating out", serving "succulent meats" in a "refined atmosphere"; at the Downtown branch you can "dine with political movers and shakers" in "comfy red booths" or "get a prime rib-eye at 3:30 AM" (it's open 24/7); the Santa Monica location is "peaceful and unhurried", and its kitchen closes at 2 AM.

get updates at zagat.com   65

LA/Hollywood/W. Hollywood   F | D | S | C

Paladar ▽ 19 | 24 | 19 | $33
1651 Wilcox Ave. (bet. Hollywood Blvd. & Selma Ave.), Hollywood, 323-465-7500

■ A "sleek, modern", "wonderfully low-lit" setting and "awesome" mojitos that could "make Hemingway rise from the dead" highlight this new Cuban production in Hollywood by the folks behind Tengu, where a "well-priced", "contemporary" menu that includes "outstanding" pork chops and "fantastically flavored frites" is served by an "attentive" staff.

Palermo 16 | 15 | 19 | $18
1858 N. Vermont Ave. (bet. Franklin Ave. & Hollywood Blvd.), Los Feliz, 323-663-1178

■ "You always get more than you paid for" at this "friendly" family-owned pizzeria/Southern Italian duo in Los Feliz and Montrose serving the "best pizzas for miles around", "hearty", "down-home" red-sauce fare and "75-cent glasses of wine" in a "cheesy", "energetic" room "packed with locals" and the "LAPD (they always get a table)"; N.B. the Los Feliz branch is an excellent stop before a show at the nearby Greek Theatre.

PALM 24 | 20 | 22 | $54
9001 Santa Monica Blvd. (bet. Doheny Dr. & Robertson Blvd.), West Hollywood, 310-550-8811
1100 S. Flower St. (11th St.), Downtown, 213-763-4600
www.thepalm.com

■ This "great, no-nonsense steakhouse" duo "holds its own in a tough market" with "beautiful, thick, juicy" steaks, "lobsters cooked to perfection" and the "yummy Gigi Salad" (named after the late, beloved maitre d'), served by "professionals" in an "old-world classy" setting of "deep booths and cocktail lounge lighting"; "celebrities and suits" dominate the scene at the West Hollywood original, while the Downtown branch is the "pre-Staples place to be."

PALMS THAI ☻ 23 | 14 | 18 | $18
5273 Hollywood Blvd. (Hobart Blvd.), East Hollywood, 323-462-5073; www.palmsthai.com

■ Home of the "legendary" "singing Thai Elvis", this sprawling East Hollywood Siamese is "always a blast", and "wise men say eat here for authentic Thai" dishes and a "'wild things' menu that offers unique meat dishes for the brave of heart"; the service is "attentive and prompt", the "entertainment is unparalleled" and, "oh yeah, it's cheap too"; N.B. open until 3 AM.

Pane e Vino 20 | 21 | 17 | $32
8265 Beverly Blvd. (Sweetzer Ave.), Los Angeles, 323-651-4600; www.panevinola.com

■ "Forget the celebrities" and "dressed-in-black industry people", "the food and atmosphere are the real stars" at

LA/Hollywood/W. Hollywood   F | D | S | C

this Fairfax Northern Italian, with a "lovely", "oh-so-chic" patio that's a "great setting for a romantic date" (if you don't mind the "trendy smokers" lighting up); though the service "can be slow", it's still a "great way to spend an evening or afternoon" "catching up with old friends over tasty pizza."

PAPA CRISTO'S M   24 | 10 | 19 | $15
2771 W. Pico Blvd. (Normandie Ave.), Koreatown, 323-737-2970; www.papacristo.com

■ "You'll laugh, you'll cry, you'll go away stuffed to the seams" at this "big fat Greek bistro" in Koreatown "with amazing food and amazing personality", offering "enormous portions" of "lusty", "authentic" "Aegean fare" and "super-friendly service" that make up for the "cafeteria" setting and a location that's "not the best"; the reservation-only Thursday night family meals are a "culinary and cultural treat" and a chance to "belly-dance with a large group of friends and strangers."

Pastis   24 | 21 | 20 | $40
8114 Beverly Blvd. (Crescent Heights Blvd.), Los Angeles, 323-655-8822

■ There's "always something interesting on the menu" at this "authentic" Fairfax bistro "where French expats go" for "earthy", "inspired" Gallic "home cooking" and a "perfect wine list", served in a "lovely" space that'll "remind you of your childhood . . . if you spent your summers in Provence"; "delightful" service rounds out a "memorable" experience that's "perfect for a first date."

PATINA ⓢ   27 | 25 | 26 | $69
5955 Melrose Ave. (bet. Highland Ave. & Vine St.), East Hollywood, 323-467-1108; www.patinagroup.com

■ Joachim Splichal's flagship Cal-French on the edge of Hollywood provides a "benchmark of what fine dining should be" – namely, "divine, beautifully executed" cuisine, an "impressive" wine list, an "extremely professional" staff and a "lovely", elegantly understated space that's "conducive to a quiet meal"; though the "food's as expensive as a hotel room", this "classic" "embodies the phrase 'you get what you pay for'", so "break the bank open and enjoy" a "mind-blowing" experience.

Patinette Cafe at MOCA M   16 | 13 | 13 | $19
Museum of Contemporary Art, 250 S. Grand Ave. (bet. 2nd & 3rd Sts.), Downtown, 213-626-1178; www.patinagroup.com

◪ For a "quick lunch" at the Museum of Contemporary Art, this Splichal-owned Continental-French offers "imaginative" salads and sandwiches in a "tiny", modern space that's "urbane and slick – yet comfy", with a "pleasant" outdoor patio that's "delightful on a nice day"; while the staff is "nice", their numbers are "not sufficient" and consequently it's often "hard to get waited on."

get updates at zagat.com   67

LA/Hollywood/W. Hollywood | F | D | S | C |

Pat's ▽ 20 | 16 | 20 | $32 |
9233 W. Pico Blvd. (Glenville Dr.), Beverlywood, 310-205-8705
■ Pros praise this "upscale" Beverlywood spot as the "best non-dairy kosher in LA", dishing out "generous portions" of "fabulous", "creative" Cal-Italian fare by a "broad-minded" kitchen that's willing to "cook steaks rare"; the staff is "friendly" and the ambiance is "nice", and though "you're paying more, it's worth it."

Pentimento Cafe ▽ 18 | 15 | 16 | $22 |
LA County Museum of Art, 5905 Wilshire Blvd. (Fairfax Ave.), Los Angeles, 323-857-4761; www.patinagroup.com
☑ "Surprisingly elegant for a museum cafe", this Patina Group scion at LACMA is an "attractive alternative to the cafeteria", with a "small, eclectic" menu of "light" Continental fare and desserts that are "works of art"; just "don't expect Patina standards."

Pete's Cafe & Bar ▽ 22 | 22 | 23 | $21 |
400 S. Main St. (W. 4th St.), Downtown, 213-617-1000
■ A "welcome addition to the thriving loft community", this Downtown New American in a restored vintage building is a "noisy, fun" "hangout" with "old-style charm", offering a "thoughtful" menu ("superb" tomato bisque, a burger that's a "carnivore's dream"), "well-selected" wine list and "friendly" service; if it had a "shuttle to the Theater District", it would be many a surveyor's "top choice."

P.F. CHANG'S CHINA BISTRO 20 | 20 | 18 | $24 |
Beverly Ctr., 121 N. La Cienega Blvd. (bet. Beverly Blvd. & 3rd St.), Beverly Center, 310-854-6467; www.pfchangs.com
■ "Mass-market" "Ameri-Chinese at its finest" that's "tasty despite its chaininess" is how fans describe the fare (including "awesome" lettuce wraps that "everyone loves") at this "hip-hop-happening" chain; "expect to wait an hour" for a table in the "tastefully decorated" room where an "energetic" staff is "in tune with the vibe of the crowd."

Philippe the Original ⊄ 22 | 14 | 15 | $11 |
1001 N. Alameda St. (Ord St.), Chinatown, 213-628-3781; www.philippes.com
■ An "amazing cross section of Angelenos" come to "dine at a shrine" to the French dip (purportedly its birthplace), this "self-serve LA landmark" (circa 1908) near Dodger Stadium, where the "awesome" signature sandwich is served in a "period" room with "sawdust on the floors" and a "black-and-white movie vibe"; insiders warn the house mustard can "hurt your insides from your nose to your toes."

Pho Café ◐⊄ – | – | – | I |
2841 W. Sunset Blvd. (Silver Lake Blvd.), Silver Lake, 213-413-0888
One of the most successful of the new wave of Vietnamese spots to appear, this brightly lit entry sits adjacent to

LA/Hollywood/W. Hollywood F | D | S | C

Rambutan Thai in a Silver Lake mini-mall with difficult parking; items like pho (rice noodle soup), bun (rice noodles without soup), fine cha gio (egg rolls) and goi cuon (spring rolls) come at prices that are about the same as dining at a fast-food chain; club-kid bonus: open daily until midnight.

Pho 79   20 | 7 | 12 | $10
727 N. Broadway (bet. Alpine & Ord Sts.), Chinatown, 213-625-7026
■ Pho-natics flock to this Vietnamese chain that stretches from the Eastside to Orange County to "get rejuvenated" by bowls of "masterful" pho, as well as "great spring rolls" and other "authentic" dishes; the digs are "clean and cheap" and the staff is "friendly" but it's clear "they want you to eat and run", so "forget about asking for water."

Pig, The   19 | 11 | 14 | $17
612 N. La Brea Ave. (south of Melrose Ave.), Los Angeles, 323-935-1116; www.thepigcatering.com
■ "This little piggy goes wee wee wee all the way into your stomach" gush groupies of this "cute" "Memphis-style BBQ" in La Brea run by chef Daly Thompson and wife/pastry chef Liz, a "perfect simulacra of a rib joint" serving "fabulous brisket and chicken wings", "down-home style ribs" and "desserts as huge as the entrees" (including the "fantastic apple crumble") on "checkered tablecloths."

Pig 'n' Whistle   16 | 20 | 15 | $25
6714 Hollywood Blvd. (Highland Ave. & Vine St.), Hollywood, 323-463-0000
◪ "You feel like a star in the '40s" at this "refurbished Hollywood hangout of years gone by" (circa 1927), though purists object to the "big screen TV" that "uglifies" the otherwise "beautiful old space", which is "romantic even without the beds in the back"; while the Continental cooking is "decent", most agree this watering hole is still "better for drinks than dinner."

Pink's Famous Chili Dogs ●⇍   21 | 7 | 13 | $8
709 N. La Brea Ave. (Melrose Ave.), Los Angeles, 323-931-4223; www.pinksholllywood.com
■ Frankly speaking, you'll need "comfortable shoes to wait on line" at this La Brea "legend" serving "lick-your-fingers" "messy" chili-cheese dogs that are "heaven on a bun"; skeptics can't "understand its religious following", but dogged devotees can't resist stopping here "after not getting enough to eat at a fancy restaurant."

Pinot Hollywood ●☒   22 | 21 | 21 | $42
1448 N. Gower St. (Sunset Blvd.), Hollywood, 323-461-8800; www.patinagroup.com
■ A "class act" that's "worth the investment", this Pinot production "brings in the young and hip of Hollywood" from the surrounding studios and production houses for

LA/Hollywood/W. Hollywood | F | D | S | C |

"must-have mustard chicken" and other "solid" Cal-French bistro fare, as well as an "excellent martini bar"; "comfy" banquettes and a fireplace grace the "sophisticated" dining room, while on the outdoor patio you can dine "both under and among the stars."

Poquito Mas ◐ | 21 | 9 | 15 | $10 |
8555 Sunset Blvd. (Londonderry Pl.), West Hollywood, 310-652-7008; www.poquitomas.com

■ "*Mucho mas, por favor*" exclaim amigos of this "fresh-Mex" chain that "blows the others out of the water" with "fantastic" fare that's "healthfully cooked" ("carnitas from heaven", "incredible steak burritos", "to-die-for fish tacos"); it's "speedy" and "inexpensive" and the "decor isn't much", but fans find it "hard to call it 'fast food.'"

Prado | 23 | 18 | 21 | $31 |
244 N. Larchmont Blvd. (bet. Beverly Blvd. & 3rd St.), Hancock Park, 323-467-3871

■ A "great place to eat after a yoga class down the street" on Larchmont Boulevard, Cha Cha Cha's upscale Caribbean sibling offers "adventurous Pan-American" dishes that are a "quirky change from the usual" fare (just "order anything in black pepper sauce") in a "quiet", "totally cool" setting; fans marvel at the staff that seems able to anticipate "your every thought before you decide."

Prego | 19 | 19 | 19 | $34 |
Howard Hughes Ctr., 6081 Center Dr. (Sepulveda Blvd.), Downtown, 310-670-7285

■ Spread out from the Valley to just north of LAX (along with an outpost in OC), this "reliable" Northern Italian quartet offers a "quiet", "high-end" dining experience, with "freshly made pastas" and the "best breadsticks" in "pleasant", "airy" rooms; a few mavericks find them "overly formulaic", and service sometimes comes with "attitude", but most agree it's a "safe bet" and "considerably better than the average chain."

Prizzi's Piazza | ▽ 23 | 20 | 20 | $29 |
5923 Franklin Ave. (bet. Bronson & Tamarind Aves.), Hollywood, 323-467-0168

■ "At these prices, you don't expect homemade pasta", "excellent gourmet pizzas" or "garlic breadsticks without peer", but that's what you'll find (along with a "few Fox-TV starlets") at this "neighborhood" Italian in Beachwood Canyon; the "cozy" room has just a "hint of hip" and the service is "commendable", but *amici* advise "get there early", for it's "tiny" and "doesn't accept reservations."

Rambutan Thai | – | – | – | I |
2835 W. Sunset Blvd. (Silver Lake Blvd.), Silver Lake, 213-273-8424

"Don't be intimidated by the outward appearance" of this unexpectedly "swank" newcomer in Silver Lake (Tuk Tuk

LA/Hollywood/W. Hollywood   F | D | S | C

Thai's sibling) sporting gentle lights and rich red walls that belie its mini-mall surroundings; the "Thai tapas" menu, which consists of small dishes with monikers such as Beef Waterfall and Drunken Noodles, puts a contemporary "spin on many classics."

Real Food Daily   19 | 15 | 17 | $20
414 N. La Cienega Blvd. (bet. Beverly Blvd. & Melrose Ave.), Beverly Center, 310-289-9910; www.realfood.com

■ With branches in West Hollywood, Santa Monica and now in Beverly Hills, this "all organic, no meat, no dairy" Vegetarian offers a menu that "isn't protein deficient" and includes "decadent desserts that won't leave you groaning in your yoga class the next morning"; "good luck finding a smiling face" among the staff, though.

Roscoe's House of Chicken 'n Waffles ●   22 | 8 | 16 | $14
1514 N. Gower St. (bet. Hollywood & Sunset Blvds.), Hollywood, 323-466-7453
106 W. Manchester Ave. (Main St.), Los Angeles, 323-752-6211
5006 W. Pico Blvd. (La Brea Ave.), Los Angeles, 323-934-4405

■ A "Hollywood legend" that's grown into a chain of five, this affordable soul food specialist serves a "timeless pairing" of fried "chicken that falls from the bone" and "soft, fluffy" waffles that aficionados "don't eat separately, but both in the same bite"; throw in some "grits submerged in butter" and mac 'n' cheese "like grandma used to make" and you may "never make it at home again."

R-23   25 | 22 | 21 | $48
923 E. Second St. (bet. Alameda St. & Santa Fe Ave.), Downtown, 213-687-7178; www.r23.com

■ The name refers to the railroad tracks between Second and Third Streets, the location of this "diamond in the rough" offering "fresh", "exotic" Japanese cuisine in a "unique loft district, film-noir setting" with a high-ceilinged room and "cool cardboard chairs" (by Frank Gehry); it's "hard to find", but "stellar sushi" and "creative appetizers" are "worth the detective work."

Saddle Ranch Chop House ●   16 | 18 | 18 | $25
8371 Sunset Blvd. (bet. Crescent Heights & La Cienega Blvds.), West Hollywood, 323-656-2007

■ "Texan-sized servings" big "enough to fill two cowboys" aren't the only reason you feel like you're "eating at a barn" at this "rustic", "western-style" Sunset Strip steakhouse across from the House of Blues with an "all-you-can-eat rib night" and "rockin' riding" on a mechanical bull (hint: try it before you eat); most agree this "college bar" is "not about food", but more about "strong drinks" and "the bull."

get updates at zagat.com

LA/Hollywood/W. Hollywood F | D | S | C

Seoul Jung ▽ 22 | 24 | 21 | $35
Wilshire Grand Hotel & Ctr., 930 Wilshire Blvd. (Figueroa St.), Downtown, 213-688-7880; www.thewilshiregrand.com

■ "Dine like Korean royalty" at this "refined", "serene" "jewel inside the Wilshire Grand Hotel", where you can cook the "delicious BBQ meat" "yourself" or "let them do it for you right at your table" and "you won't come out smelling like bulgoki", thanks to a "spotless, well-ventilated" space; for a true "a feast for the eyes and palate", regulars recommend the "10-course Emperor's Banquet", which you have to "order 24 hours in advance."

Shabu Shabu House Ⓜ 23 | 10 | 17 | $20
127 Japanese Village Plaza Mall (bet. Central Ave. & San Pedro St.), Little Tokyo, 213-680-3890

■ "Satisfy your shabu-shabu craving" at this "assembly-line" Japanese in Little Tokyo where diners "roll up their sleeves and dip lean bits of meat and vegetables into boiling water" that come with "steamed white rice and a trio of delicious sauces"; it's "not for a leisurely dinner with friends" since "most seats are at the counter", and it's best to "go early" since the lines are often "out the door."

Sharky's Mexican Grill 19 | 12 | 15 | $11
1716 N. Cahuenga Blvd. (Hollywood Blvd.), Hollywood, 323-461-7881; www.sharkys.com

■ "Healthy", organic, seafood-centric "Nu-Mex" fare ("excellent shrimp burritos", the "best tempura mahi mahi" and free-range chicken) makes this affordable Mexican chain "different" from most fast-food joints, as well as nice touches such as tortilla chips "seasoned with a hint of lime"; you still "fetch your own tray when they call your number", though.

Sofi 20 | 21 | 19 | $30
8030¾ W. Third St. (bet. Crescent Heights Blvd. & Fairfax Ave.), Los Angeles, 323-651-0346

■ "You're far from LA" when you "walk down a narrow alley to a terrace garden" at this Greek located a short walk from the Farmer's Market with a "romantic, hidden" patio "tented in beautiful bougainvillea" and waiters who "treat you like Apollo" as they bring out "authentic mezedes" as well as "standards like gyros and souvlaki"; it's a "wonderful hideaway" that can do without the theatrical "dancing and smashing plates."

SONA 27 | 24 | 24 | $73
401 N. La Cienega Blvd. (bet. Beverly Blvd. & Melrose Ave.), West Hollywood, 310-659-7708; www.sonarestaurant.com

■ One of this *Survey*'s top newcomers, this West Hollywood New French is owned and operated by two "rising stars on the LA dining scene", David and Michelle Myers (chef and pastry chef, respectively); "divine" tasting menus of

LA/Hollywood/W. Hollywood   F | D | S | C |

"amazing savory creations" with Asian and New American influences and "out-of-this-world" desserts are served by "people who really care" in a "minimalist Zen" room.

Sonora Cafe   22 | 22 | 21 | $36 |
180 S. La Brea Ave. (bet. Beverly Blvd. & 3rd St.), Los Angeles, 323-857-1800; www.elcholo.com

■ "From the wonderful folks who brought us El Cholo", this "fabuloso" La Brea Southwesterner "mixes Mexican and Spanish flavors" with the tastes of Arizona and New Mexico in an "imaginative" way; the "cozy" room with a "huge fireplace" is "elegant enough to impress a date, but not stuffy", and there's a private room above the bar.

Soot Bull Jeep   22 | 6 | 14 | $22 |
3136 Eighth St. (Catalina St.), Koreatown, 213-387-3865

■ Bulgoki buffs flock to this Koreatown Korean for "authentic", "first-rate" BBQ that you "cook yourself" over "real coals" (versus the more common gas grills) that make "real smoke" that'll "ooze from your pores for hours"; it's "not for the faint of heart" or "dry-clean-only attire", and the "surly" staff speaks "iffy English", but "what does that matter when you're eating so well and so affordably?"; N.B. it has a Newport Beach sibling, Yi Dynasty, that serves the same menu.

Souplantation   15 | 10 | 12 | $11 |
Beverly Connection Mall, 8491 W. Third St. (La Cienega Blvd.), Los Angeles, 323-655-0381; www.souplantation.com

■ Fans call this "up-to-date" chain of "all-you-can-eat" buffets an "American dream" where you can "feast on ten pounds of food for just $8" and still "feel like you've eaten healthy"; besides offering a "fresh feast" for "salad lovers", there's "something for every taste", including "soup, potato, pasta and pizza"; it's "everything a family of five could want."

Spanish Kitchen ●   15 | 20 | 15 | $39 |
826 N. La Cienega Blvd. (bet. Melrose Pl. & Santa Monica Blvd.), West Hollywood, 310-659-4794

◢ You'll feel like you're in a "hacienda" at this "trendy" location on La Cienega, a "reinvented Hollywood landmark" where longtime Eastsider Hugo Molina creates "gourmet Mexican" dishes; but foes find it "overpriced", and not even the "beautiful" decor is "worth the attitude."

Standard, The ●   16 | 21 | 15 | $28 |
The Standard Hotel, 550 S. Flower St. (6th St.), Downtown, 213-892-8080
The Standard Hotel, 8300 Sunset Blvd. (Sweetzer Ave.), West Hollywood, 323-650-9090
www.standardhotel.com

■ "Everything from Thai shrimp rolls to banana splits" can be found on the "eclectic", "comfort-chic" menu at Andre Balazs' "funky" pair of 24/7 hyper-trendy, retro "upscale"

get updates at zagat.com

LA/Hollywood/W. Hollywood F | D | S | C

hotel coffee shops located in the middle of the Sunset Strip and Downtown; the decor is a "feast for the eyes" and the "sweet" staff does its best to meet the "bizarre requests" of the "beautiful hangers-on" and "club kids" who frequent these "diners gone Hollywood."

Sunset Room 🚫Ⓜ️   17 | 21 | 15 | $43
1430 N. Cahuenga Blvd. (bet. DeLongpre Ave. & Sunset Blvd.), Hollywood, 323-463-0004; www.thesunsetroom.com

◪ It's a "power scene" at this "cool and trendy", "upscale" Hollywood Cal-Med supper club "best known for its star-studded industry clientele", where "dinner turns into a be-seen nightclub" for "industry types" who come to "eat, drink and be very merry"; be sure to bring names with you because "the bouncer won't let you in until you drop some", and "don't valet-park your car unless you want to wait until your warranty expires to get it back."

Surya India   22 | 17 | 21 | $25
8048 W. Third St. (Crescent Heights Blvd.), Los Angeles, 323-653-5151

■ "Contemporary" Cal-Indian dishes that "dazzle with flavor" and "gracious" service raise this "plain and simple" spot near the Farmer's Market "above the curry-in-a-hurry crowd"; the "chicken mandalorian saves the day", while "wonderful curries" and "great breads" are also "worth returning to" this "neighborhood find."

Sushi Mon   20 | 13 | 16 | $25
Japanese Restaurant 🚫Ⓜ️
8562 W. Third St. (San Vicente Blvd.), Beverly Center, 310-246-9230

■ Pros promise you'll get "more bang for the buck" at this Japanese "culinary artist" across from Cedars-Sinai serving "cost-effective" portions of "creative rolls" that'll "turn even a non-sushi eater into a believer"; service can be "ultra attentive or completely indifferent", and regulars worry "if it gets too crowded, I'm going to regret telling you about it."

SUSHI ROKU   23 | 22 | 18 | $44
8445 W. Third St. (La Cienega Blvd.), Los Angeles, 323-655-6767; www.sushiroku.com

■ "Hip sushi" and a "crowd that matches" can be found at this stylish, "high-energy", "Cal-influenced" Japanese trio (Third Street, Santa Monica and Pasadena) where "low-key fashionistas rub elbows with industry types" in a "modern" room; "they know what they're doing" in the kitchen, creating "maki that's inventive, but not ridiculous" and other dishes that "ain't cheap."

SWEET LADY JANE   26 | 12 | 15 | $14
8360 Melrose Ave. (La Cienega Blvd.), West Hollywood, 323-653-7145; www.sweetladyjane.com

■ "How sweet the taste" at this "sardine-size" coffee shop on Melrose Avenue serving "great coffee" paired with

subscribe to zagat.com

LA/Hollywood/W. Hollywood F | D | S | C

"decadent", "exquisite", "heavenly" cakes and desserts that are nearly "too pretty to eat", and "worth every pound you have to work off at the gym" – that is, if "you're lucky enough to get one of the small tables" in the "cramped" room where you'll have to make your way "through throngs of eager brides-to-be lined up for wedding-cake tastings."

Swingers ◐   16 | 17 | 15 | $15
Beverly Laurel Motor Hotel, 8020 Beverly Blvd. (Laurel Ave.), Los Angeles, 323-653-5858; www.swingersrestaurant.com
■ "You get homestyle potatoes from a waitress in fishnet stockings" at this late-night diner duo in Fairfax and Santa Monica, the "ultimate hangout after a night of club-hopping" or for a "hangover brunch", offering a "novel-sized menu" of American "standbys" served by an "über-hip" staff "that's as much fun to watch as the patrons."

Taix French Restaurant   16 | 14 | 19 | $26
1911 Sunset Blvd. (Alvarado St.), Echo Park, 213-484-1265; www.taixfrench.com
■ A "longtime favorite run by the same family" since 1927, this "LA institution" in Echo Park, "convenient to the Music Center and Dodger Stadium", offers "reasonably priced" "French" "staples" that were "classic before I was born", along with a "large" wine list, in a setting "so old-fashioned it's funky"; some find the fare a "major downer", but for most it's an "excellent value."

Talesai   23 | 18 | 19 | $27
9043 Sunset Blvd. (Doheny Dr.), West Hollywood, 310-275-9724
■ This "upscale" Thai trio stays a "step above most of the competition" thanks to "healthy portions" of "fabulous" fare, "contemporary" rooms and a "welcoming" ambiance; the West Hollywood original is surrounded by hard-rock clubs, while the Beverly Hills location is a more casual cafe; the Studio City spin-off, near the studios, is separately owned, but serves the same menu.

Tam O'Shanter Inn   21 | 22 | 21 | $31
2980 Los Feliz Blvd. (Boyce Ave.), Atwater Village, 323-664-0228; www.lawrysonline.com
■ "Once considered the Disney commissary", this Scottish-themed American run by Lawry's is one of the "old dames of the LA restaurant scene" that's "aged as well as the beef" served by "brisk", "smiling lassies" in a "Tudor-inspired" setting; "you feel you're going back in time" at Christmas when the carolers come out, or on Robert Burns' birthday, which is celebrated with haggis and bagpipes.

TANTRA Ⓜ   22 | 26 | 17 | $30
3705 Sunset Blvd. (bet. Edgecliffe Dr. & Lucile Ave.), Silver Lake, 323-663-8268
■ The father-and-son team of Navraj and R.J. Singh (India's Oven) have gone far "beyond the typical" to create this

LA/Hollywood/W. Hollywood | F | D | S | C |

"hip and trendy", "upscale" Indian in the avant-garde wilds of Silver Lake, where the "tantalizing" cuisine of a world-class chef from London, Vineet Bhatia (Zaika), and cocktails with names like "Comfortably Numb" are served in a "spectacular", "ultra-swanky" setting with Bollywood movies playing on plasma screens.

Taylor's Prime Steaks | 21 | 16 | 19 | $32 |
3361 W. Eighth St. (bet. Normandie & Western Aves.), Koreatown, 213-382-8449; www.taylorssteakhouse.com
■ "You feel like you should pay more" at this chophouse duo that's "all about steaks" "with no frills", served in a "wonderfully smoky" "men's club" setting complete with "big red booths" and waiters who've "been around the block"; while a few give a "slight edge" to the newer La Cañada-Flintridge outpost, purists insist "you can't beat the old-school" ambiance of the Koreatown original.

Tesoro Trattoria ⑤ | 20 | 19 | 20 | $32 |
California Plaza, 300 S. Grand Ave. (3rd St.), Downtown, 213-680-0000; www.tesorotrattoria.com
■ A "convenient" "good bet before the Music Center" (with "free shuttle and free parking"), this "small" but "classy" Downtown Northern Italian sibling of Ciao Trattoria is also "perfect for an intimate" meal or "business luncheon"; "excellent lobster ravioli", "tasty pastas" and other dishes are "well worth the wait" "when it's busy."

Thousand Cranes, A | 23 | 25 | 23 | $44 |
New Otani Hotel, 120 S. Los Angeles St. (bet. 1st & 2nd Sts.), Little Tokyo, 213-253-9255
■ "Actually, several restaurants in one", this Little Tokyo hotel Japanese offers a tempura station where the "grumpy" chef is a "master" of fried fare, "fabulous" shabu-shabu tables where you can cook your own, a small sushi bar serving "amazing" seafood and a Sunday brunch buffet with a "good variety" of dishes; the "elegant" room is adjacent to a "beautiful" rooftop garden with a "great night view."

Toast Bakery & Cafe | ▽ 21 | 16 | 16 | $16 |
8223 W. Third St. (Harper Ave.), Los Angeles, 323-655-5018
■ Breakfasters and brunchers "can't go wrong" at this "new, competitive" Miracle Mile cafe, an "egg-white eater's heaven" offering a "vast menu" of "tasty, inexpensive delights" and "good people-watching on Third Street"; "delicious muffins", "awesome banana pudding" and an "exceptional" veggie burger are "worth the wait" on weekends, when you can expect "huge lines."

Todai | 14 | 11 | 12 | $24 |
Beverly Ctr., 8612 Beverly Blvd. (bet. La Cienega & San Vicente Blvds.), Beverly Center, 310-659-1375; www.todai.com
☒ "Nothing fancy" at this "cafeteria-style" "all-you-can-eat sushi" chain that's "well suited for beginners" and

LA/Hollywood/W. Hollywood F | D | S | C

"chowhounds" "looking for quantity over quality", with "plenty of eats for the non–raw food lover"; if the "fun of gorging outweighs the mediocrity" of the fare, you'll "get your money's worth" here.

Tom Bergin's 13 | 16 | 18 | $17
840 S. Fairfax Ave. (bet. Olympic & Wilshire Blvds.), Los Angeles, 323-936-7151

■ Paper shamrocks on the wall emblazoned with the names of regulars like "Ronald Reagan" are a "badge of pride" at this "traditional Irish bar" near Fairfax and Wilshire where the "fish 'n' chips are the real deal" and the "kitchen turns out great steak and lamb" as well; still, most come here mainly for the "warm, publike atmosphere" and the "coldest Guinness in town."

Tommy's ●⌀ 22 | 5 | 15 | $7
2575 W. Beverly Blvd. (Rampart Blvd.), Echo Park, 213-389-9060; www.originaltommys.com

■ "God's own chili-burger" can be found at this "must-see LA landmark", a sprawling 24/7 stand near Dodger Stadium where you must stand on line for "awesome, greasy, calorie-filled chili-cheeseburgers"; for fans, there's "nothing better than a triple and chili fries at midnight", so "load up on the jalapeños and indigestion be damned."

Tommy Tang's Ⓜ 19 | 13 | 16 | $28
7313 Melrose Ave. (bet. Fairfax & La Brea Aves.), Los Angeles, 323-937-5733; www.tommytangs.com

☑ Telegenic toque Tommy Tang's Melrose production is the showcase for "Cal-meets-Thai at its best", with an "eclectic", "somewhat Americanized" menu suitable for neophytes "who wouldn't be comfortable in more authentic restaurants"; the interior is "spartan" and the service can be "goofy", but the "awesome drag show on Tuesdays" makes up for them; P.S. "try anything with shredded duck."

Trastevere 18 | 18 | 17 | $26
Hollywood & Highland, 6801 Hollywood Blvd. (Highland Ave.), Hollywood, 323-962-3261; www.trastevereristorante.com

■ A slightly "upscale" option that "won't break the budget", this Southern Italian pair in the Hollywood & Highland complex and on the Third Street Promenade serves "satisfying", "more than serviceable" red-sauce fare paired with a "decent", "reasonable" wine list; the outdoor patios and "touristy" locations are a "perfect" combination for "people-watching."

Traxx Ⓢ 21 | 23 | 19 | $37
Union Station, 800 N. Alameda St. (bet. Cesar Chavez Ave. & Frwy. 101), Downtown, 213-625-1999; www.traxxrestaurant.com

■ The "most delicious Metro transfer you'll find" awaits at this "attractive" New American bistro located in "historic"

LA/Hollywood/W. Hollywood   F | D | S | C

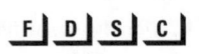

Union Station where the "art deco" room takes you "back into the '20s" and you can "watch the world walk by" from a "table on the concourse"; many are "wowed" by the "inventive" fare, and feel it's "underappreciated" because the "classic" setting is so "special".

Tuk Tuk Thai   21 | 18 | 19 | $18
8875 W. Pico Blvd. (bet. Doheny Dr. & Robertson Blvd.), Los Angeles, 310-860-1872
■ A "shiny pearl in the unlikely oyster of Beverlywood", this "tantalizingly affordable" Siamese (with a tuk tuk jitney hanging over the entrance) is a casual cafe destination for "authentic home cooking", including "curries made fresh daily", and "crisp, fresh Thai beer", brought to you by "beautiful, friendly servers" in a "small, noisy" room.

Ubon   23 | 18 | 19 | $28
Beverly Ctr., 8530 Beverly Blvd. (La Cienega Blvd.), Beverly Center, 310-854-1115
■ "Matsuhisa Lite" is what fans call this "affordable" Nobu outpost "tucked away in the Beverly Center" offering a "good blend of dishes that have trickled down from its more expensive", "hard-to-get-into" siblings, "at a fraction of the cost"; "beautifully prepared noodles", "heavenly sashimi" and "inventive bento boxes" served in a "mellow" setting by a "friendly" staff make this "little place a big bargain."

Ulysses Voyage   – | – | – | M
6333 W. Third St. (Fairfax), Los Angeles, 323-939-9728; www.ulyssesvoyage.com
A rarity in the Old Farmer's Market – a sit-down restaurant that's actually fancy enough for a special occasion – this traditional-looking Greek begins the day with a selection of breakfast dishes (eggs scrambled with feta, many forms of filo filled with everything from manouri cheese to wild greens) and moves from there through a selection of dishes both familiar (moussaka, pastitsio) and not so familiar, such as *soutzoukakia* (long, narrow lamb meatballs) and *stifado* (beef stew).

URTH CAFFÉ   21 | 14 | 14 | $14
8565 Melrose Ave. (bet. La Cienega & San Vicente Blvds.), West Hollywood, 310-659-0628; www.urthcaffe.com
■ "Get your New Age on" at this West Hollywood cafe serving "fresh, simple" New American dishes and "amazing organic coffee" in a surprisingly "cramped, stressful" space that's "always packed" with "scenesters and their miniature dogs"; the staff is "cool" and the fare is "excellent for the money", but the "long waits" can be "unbearable."

Uzbekistan ◐   ▽ 20 | 13 | 16 | $22
7077 Sunset Blvd. (La Brea Ave.), Hollywood, 323-464-3663
■ "When you think you've tried everything", head over to this Hollywood Uzbekistani specialist for "tasty", "unusual"

LA/Hollywood/W. Hollywood | F | D | S | C |

dishes "you might not find anywhere else on this continent", including "lots of lamb" and dumplings that "rival the best of North China", served by an "earnest" staff with "a lot of spirit"; it's a "fantastic value", and ideal for a "large group."

vermont | 22 | 22 | 20 | $39 |
1714 N. Vermont Ave. (Prospect Ave.), Los Feliz, 323-661-6163; www.vermontrestaurantonline.com

■ "Celebrating what's good about life – people, food and wine" – this "friendly" Los Feliz Californian is a "soothing" spot where the "tragically hip" come for "delicious", "exceptional" fare at lunch or dinner or "cocktails before the Greek" in an "elegant", yet "laid-back" room; "your bill will be high", but insiders insist it's "worth it."

Versailles | 22 | 9 | 17 | $16 |
1415 S. La Cienega Blvd. (Pico Blvd.), Los Angeles, 310-289-0392

■ "Don't forget mega-breath mints" when you head for this "cheap, cheap, cheap", "cafeteria"-like Cuban chain famous for its "legendary", "amazing" garlic chicken and "melt-in-your-mouth" pork, which you can wash down with "pitchers of sangria that will give you visions of the tropics"; don't be daunted by "lines hanging out the door", for the service is "lightning fast."

Vert | 23 | 20 | 20 | $36 |
6801 Hollywood Blvd., 4th fl. (Highland Ave.), Hollywood, 323-491-1300; www.wolfgangpuck.com

■ "Puck does the South of France" at this "moderately priced" modern French bistro, conceived by Wolfgang and run by brother Klaus (a "real gentleman"), a "refreshing oasis" that may be "the best reason to go to Hollywood & Highland"; a "diverse" menu of "impressive" Gallic fare with Italian accents is served by a "patient, helpful" staff in a "colorful" space that includes a "well-appointed" bar.

VILLAGE PIZZERIA | 25 | 12 | 18 | $12 |
131 N. Larchmont Blvd. (bet. Beverly Blvd. & 3rd St.), Hancock Park, 323-465-5566; www.villagepizzeria.net

■ Even "a kid from the Bronx can find a slice" to love in Hancock Park at this "Brooklyn" import serving what many call the "best NY-style pizza in LA"; the "cramped" storefront space is full of Big Apple "shtick" and boasts a "comfy" outdoor patio where you can take in the "Larchmont Boulevard hustle and bustle"; hey, "if it's good enough for Kathy Bates, it's good enough for me."

WATER GRILL | 27 | 24 | 25 | $55 |
544 S. Grand Ave. (bet. 5th & 6th Sts.), Downtown, 213-891-0900; www.kingsseafood.com

■ "Poseidon would be proud" of this upscale "seafood lovers' paradise" next to the Downtown Biltmore, "a star by any definition" thanks to veteran chef Michael Cimarusti's

LA/Hollywood/W. Hollywood F | D | S | C

"transcendent" nautical cuisine that devotees deem the "best in LA, period"; "fish so fresh they almost bite back", "impeccable" service "without the attitude" and a "lovely", "urban" setting all go into this "expensive", "serious homage to seafood in all its glory."

White Lotus M ▽ 17 | 26 | 15 | $45
1743 N. Cahuenga Blvd. (Hollywood Blvd.), Hollywood, 323-463-0060; www.whitelotushollywood.com
■ A "beautiful place filled with beautiful people", this "fabulously lush, expensively decorated" Cal-Asian/sushi bar (the Sunset Room's sibling) just north of Hollywood Boulevard is the "hot bodies'" destination of the moment for a "complete night of dinner, drinks and dancing"; the "interesting array of eye candy" and the "gorgeous" decor make the "admirable" fare seem almost "irrelevant."

Windows S ▽ 19 | 24 | 19 | $49
Transamerica Ctr., 1150 S. Olive St. (bet. 11th & 12th Sts.), Downtown, 213-746-1554
☒ Boasting one of the "best views of the Downtown skyline" (that "glows even brighter by the light of a jumbo martini"), this high-end Californian atop the Transamerica Center is "hard to beat if you're trying to impress out-of-towners"; while fans approve of the menu that's "expanded beyond its steak-eater core", critics grouse that the vistas can't make up for the "lackluster food" or "disappointing" service.

Wokcano ● – | – | – | M
913 S. Figueroa St. (bet. 9th St. & Olympic Blvd.), Downtown, 213-892-8999
8408 W. Third St. (S. Orlando Ave.), Los Angeles, 323-653-1998
Located Downtown near Staples and in Fairfax close to the Beverly Center, this moderately priced Pan-Asian duo offers Chinese and sushi, by a chef from a grand hotel in Shanghai and a Japanese chef from a grand hotel in Las Vegas, respectively; the latter branch is open until 2 AM on weekdays, 4 AM on weekends.

Wolfgang Puck Cafe 17 | 15 | 16 | $22
Virgin Megastore Complex, 8000 N. Sunset Blvd. (N. Crescent Heights Blvd.), West Hollywood, 323-650-7300; www.wolfgangpuck.com
■ Call them "Spago Lite", these "quick", "dependable" Cal cafes offer "unique twists on traditional favorites", including WP classics such as "smoked salmon pizza" and "Chinois chicken salad" in a "jazzy" setting; it's a "less expensive way to enjoy the delights of a Wolfgang Puck experience."

WOOD RANCH BBQ & GRILL 20 | 16 | 18 | $23
The Grove at Farmer's Mkt., 189 The Grove Dr. (bet. Fairfax Ave. & 3rd St.), Los Angeles, 323-937-6800; www.woodranch.com
■ Expect "super-long waits" at this ultra-popular modern barbecue chain where a "basket of brisket comes with

LA/Hollywood/W. Hollywood | F | D | S | C |

real wood flavor" and the dish of choice is the "delicious tri-tip" that's "so tender it beats the best filet"; add beef ribs that "melt in your mouth", "garlicky rolls" and more, all at "reasonable prices", and you have "satisfaction all around."

Woo Lae Oak | 21 | 20 | 18 | $32 |
623 S. Western Ave. (bet. 6th St. & Wilshire Blvd.), Koreatown, 213-384-2244; www.woolaeoak.org

■ A "good introduction" to Korean cuisine, this BBQ duo offers "delicious", "refined", "traditional" fare you "cook yourself" on "tabletop grills", and "you'll have so much fun you won't even realize you cooked your own dinner"; the La Cienega branch is "elegant" and "hip", while the Koreatown location is "more authentic."

Yabu | 23 | 15 | 19 | $26 |
521 N. La Cienega Blvd. (south of Melrose Ave.), West Hollywood, 310-854-0400

■ "Shhh, don't tell" whisper fans of this Japanese noodle duo that's "not known for sushi – but should be", serving "excellent" raw fin fare as well as "big bowls" of udon and soba that "hit the spot"; there's "always a wait" at the West LA location, while the West Hollywood branch boasts a "lovely outdoor garden with lots of smokers" that makes you feel like you're in "suburban Tokyo."

YAMASHIRO | 19 | 26 | 20 | $37 |
1999 N. Sycamore Ave. (Franklin Ave.), Hollywood, 323-466-5125; www.yamashirorestaurant.com

■ "The view is spectacular" from this Cal-Asian "hideaway" high on a hill above the Hollywood lights, set in a former residence designed like an imperial palace with a "large, impressive dining area" and "romantic Japanese gardens" where you can "take a stroll and kiss your love under the moonlit sky"; cronies put in a good word for the "improved" cuisine and "wonderful" service.

Yang Chow | 24 | 11 | 18 | $21 |
819 N. Broadway (bet. Alpine & College Sts.), Chinatown, 213-625-0811

■ The "absolutely superb slippery shrimp" are a "must" at this "extremely popular" Chinese trio, but "everything on the menu is worth trying", such as "awesome hot-and-sour soup", "excellent steamed fish" and other "fabulous" dishes at "bargain prices", which make up for the "noisy", nondescript setting; P.S. "make sure you ask for William" the waiter at the Chinatown branch.

ZANKOU CHICKEN ●⌀ | 23 | 5 | 12 | $10 |
5065 W. Sunset Blvd. (Normandie Ave.), East Hollywood, 323-665-7845

■ Fowl fans flock to this "cheap, cheap, cheap" Armenian poultry chain "made famous in a Beck song", where the "rotisserie roasted bird is succulent and the garlic sauce

LA/Hollywood/W. Hollywood F | D | S | C |

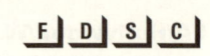

sublime"; it's "obvious the profits aren't spent on the decor", and "if you're looking for 'please' and 'thank you', look elsewhere", but who cares when you're eating the "best chicken on the planet."

Zen Grill 21 | 15 | 17 | $22 |
8432 W. Third St. (bet. La Cienega Blvd. & Orlando Ave.), Los Angeles, 323-655-9991

■ The contemplative name notwithstanding, this Pan-Asian duo is always "noisy" and "crowded" with pilgrims who come for "cheap, fresh" dishes, such as the "absolutely delicious" calamari salad, that are "worth the wait", though some may yearn for non-being while sitting in a "cramped" room where "you can't hear your own conversation."

Zita Trattoria ⓢ ▽ 19 | 17 | 19 | $30 |
825 W. Ninth St. (Figueroa St.), Downtown, 213-488-0400; www.zitala.com

■ It's "bucatini and biker shorts" at this "slightly less formal Italian" where "lawyers" go for a "casual business lunch" or "before heading to the Staples Center" across the street; "straightforward" fare at "decent prices", a "modern decor" and a "lively happy hour" make it "worth recommending" fans attest.

Zucca 21 | 24 | 21 | $43 |
801 Tower, 801 S. Figueroa St. (8th St.), Downtown, 213-614-7800; www.patinagroup.com

■ The "chandeliers alone are worth a visit" to Joachim Splichal's "drop-dead gorgeous" "oasis" near the Staples Center that's "hard to beat" for "business entertaining" or "before a Lakers game"; "creative" Italian dishes and selections from an "adventurous wine list" are "pricey but worth every penny", and "you'll be amazed what they can do with the lowly pumpkin" (*zucca*) for which it's named.

The Westside

Top Food

- **28** Matsuhisa
- **27** Nobu Malibu
  - Mélisse
  - Sushi Sasabune
  - Josie Rest.
  - Chinois on Main
  - Mori Sushi
  - Joe's
  - Valentino
- **26** Spago

Top Decor

- **29** Bel-Air Hotel
- **28** Inn/Seventh Ray
- **27** Reg. Bev. Wilshire
  - Geoffrey's
  - Oceanfront
  - Crustacean
- **26** Belvedere, The
  - Gardens
  - One Pico
  - Il Cielo

Top Service

- **27** Bel-Air Hotel
  - Belvedere, The
- **26** Reg. Bev. Wilshire
  - Mélisse
  - Mori Sushi
  - Valentino
- **25** Michael's
  - Lawry's Prime Rib
  - Gardens
  - Josie Rest.

Top Value

1. In-N-Out Burger
2. Noah's NY Bagels
3. Lamonica's Pizza
4. Literati Café
5. Baja Fresh
6. Apple Pan
7. Poquito Mas
8. Abbot's Pizza
9. Jody Maroni's Sausage
10. Asahi Ramen

By Location

Beverly Hills
- **28** Matsuhisa
- **26** Spago
  - Belvedere, The
  - Cafe Blanc
  - Mako

Brentwood
- **25** Takao
  - Peppone
- **24** Zax
  - Vincenti
  - Toscana

Malibu
- **27** Nobu Malibu
- **23** Granita
  - Malibu Seafood
  - Taverna Tony
- **22** Geoffrey's

Santa Monica/Venice
- **27** Mélisse
  - Josie Rest.
  - Chinois on Main
  - Joe's
  - Valentino

West LA
- **27** Sushi Sasabune
  - Mori Sushi
- **25** Hamasaku
  - Hide Sushi
- **24** Bombay Cafe

Westwood
- **24** Sunnin
- **22** Tengu
  - Lamonica's Pizza
  - Tanino
- **21** Sprazzo Cuc. Ital.

The Westside Restaurant Directory

The Westside F | D | S | C

Abbot's Pizza 23 | 7 | 15 | $10
1811 Pico Blvd. (18th St.), Santa Monica, 310-314-2777
1407 Abbot Kinney Blvd. (California Ave.), Venice, 310-396-7334
■ At this pair of "creative" pizzerias in Santa Monica and Venice, the "zany chefs ring a bell whenever someone puts a tip in the jar", which happens often, given that it cooks up some of the "best" pies around (made with a revisionist "bagel crust" that gives them a special crunch); the seating is "limited" and the decor is of the "hole-in-the-wall" variety, but that's just "part of its charm."

Airstream Diner ☉ 15 | 18 | 13 | $18
9601 Little Santa Monica Blvd. (Camden Dr.), Beverly Hills, 310-550-8883
◪ Chef-owner Fred Eric of Fred 62 in Los Feliz has motored into Beverly Hills, setting up shop in a retro-modern space that captures the smooth look of an Airstream trailer; the "gigantic" American menu is filled with familiar diner staples and more "interesting items" (like deep-fried mac 'n' cheese balls), and it's open 24/7, but brace yourself for his trademark "nonexistent" service.

Akbar Cuisine of India 22 | 14 | 20 | $24
3115 Washington Blvd. (Lincoln Blvd.), Marina del Rey, 310-574-0666
2627 Wilshire Blvd. (bet. Princeton & 26th Sts.), Santa Monica, 310-586-7469
www.akbarcuisineofindia.com
■ Run by a wine-obsessed owner, this Indian trio with "subdued" decor regularly wanders off the chutney path but rewards adventurous appetites with "lip-smacking good" specialties (a caveat: "order the vindaloo hot and be prepared to drink the raita to quench the fire"); while the menu is fairly extensive, those in-the-know advise the only "three words" you need to say here are "tandoori sea bass."

A La Tarte Bistrot Ⓜ ∇ 16 | 16 | 14 | $25
1037 Swarthmore Ave. (bet. Monument St. & Sunset Blvd.), Pacific Palisades, 310-459-6635
◪ In the restaurant-deprived Pacific Palisades, devotees laud this "cutesy" "slice of France" where you can partake of an alfresco weekend brunch out on the terrace along "SoCal's Riviera"; the "authentic" French bistro fare is "reasonably priced", though less enthusiastic sorts mutter that what's really "authentic" here is the staff's "attitude" ("very snotty"), and quip that the quarters have "less room than my wife's shoe closet."

Alejo's 21 | 8 | 16 | $17
4002 Lincoln Blvd. (bet. Maxella Ave. & Washington Blvd.), Marina del Rey, 310-822-0095
■ "If you love garlic", this pair of stinking roses is a "must"; whether you visit the "hole-in-the-wall" flagship in Marina

The Westside | F | D | S | C |

del Rey or the spacious Westchester offshoot with a "nicer neighborhood vibe", you may need to enroll in a "garlic detox program" after feasting on a "bargain" meal that kicks off with "addictive" bread and "infused oil"; "don't be fooled by the decor – just believe in the line of people waiting at the door."

Allegria | 21 | 16 | 19 | $30 |
22821 PCH (south of Malibu Pier), Malibu, 310-456-3132
■ Feted by its celebrity Malibu fans, this "genuine trattoria" is a "perfect neighborhood Italian" hangout, one of the "best places to see the stars in a casual setting" while tucking into "exquisite" pizzas, "reliable" risottos and "full-flavored" seafood at moderate prices; it's a "great spot when driving up the coast", especially if you "request a table out on the patio."

All India Café | 21 | 13 | 17 | $19 |
Santa Monica Plaza, 12113 Santa Monica Blvd. (Bundy Dr.), West LA, 310-442-5250; www.allindiacafe.com
■ This "inexpensive" duo in West LA and Pasadena goes "beyond the standard-issue" curry joints with a "many-layered" menu featuring many "uncommon items" "more likely to be found in an Indian home"; the service is "uneven" and the decor "unremarkable", but the "outstanding" fare makes the "blah" setting "tolerable."

Amuse Café | – | – | – | M |
796 Main St. (Brooks Ave.), Venice, 310-450-1956; www.amusecafe.com
Youthful Brooke Williamson, along with her former Zax sous-chef, Nick Roberts, has headed west to a quirky, beach-adjacent space near avant-garde Abbot Kinney where she's given a new coat of paint (and a new outdoor patio) to an old wooden house; the New American menu consists of 'Little Plates' (e.g. caramelized onion and Gruyère tart) and 'Bigger Plates' (e.g. roasted halibut with soba noodles).

Anna's | 15 | 13 | 17 | $22 |
10929 W. Pico Blvd. (bet. Veteran Ave. & Westwood Blvd.), West LA, 310-474-0102; www.annaitalian.com
☑ "Gloriously heavy food from the bottom half of the Boot"-shaped country awaits at this "kid-friendly" Westside Southern Italian that's an "old-fashioned red-booth delight" straight out of "the '50s"; though hecklers hiss that the fare is heading in the direction of "Chef Boyardee", diehards declare "like Old Man River, it just keeps rolling along."

Antica Pizzeria | 17 | 16 | 16 | $21 |
Villa Marina Mktpl., 13455 Maxella Ave. (Lincoln Blvd.), Marina del Rey, 310-577-8182; www.latrattoria.com
☑ "Don't come if you want the same old pepperoni" warn devotees who declare this "underrated" Marina del Rey Italian's "fabulous thin-crust" pies the "most authentic

get updates at zagat.com

The Westside | F | D | S | C |

Neapolitan pizzas" in town; "terrific specials" like penne alla vodka also earn praise, and the outdoor patio is a "nice" touch, but overall the setting is "not much", while the service is "uneven" at best.

APPLE PAN ⓂⒻ 22 | 11 | 19 | $11
10801 W. Pico Blvd. (Glendon Ave.), West LA, 310-475-3585
■ Even "agents and lawyers [stand] in line for french fries" at this "Smithsonian display of a real burger joint" in West LA, where "nothing has changed in many years" and everything's "absolutely perfect – except for the wait"; standards like the "terrific" hickory burgers and "addictive apple pie à la mode" make it a "great tradition to pass on to your kids."

Asahi Ramen Ⓕ 21 | 8 | 17 | $11
2027 Sawtelle Blvd. (bet. La Grange & Mississippi Aves.), West LA, 310-479-2231
☑ "Lots of bang for the buck" at this "friendly" Sawtelle Boulevard Japanese dishing out "killer ramen" in "bowls bigger than your head" and "generous portions" of some of the "best gyoza and fried rice on the Westside"; the storefront looks like it was decorated on a "shoestring budget", but no one seems to mind – there's "always a line."

Asakuma 22 | 16 | 19 | $31
11701 Wilshire Blvd. (Barrington Ave.), West LA, 310-826-0013
141 S. Robertson Blvd. (bet. Charleville & Wilshire Blvds.), Beverly Hills, 310-659-1092
Hoyt Plaza, 2805 Abbot Kinney Blvd. (Washington Blvd.), Marina del Rey, 310-577-7999
11769 Santa Monica Blvd. (bet. Granville & Stoner Aves.), West LA, 310-473-8990
www.asakumarestaurant.com
☑ "Incredibly fresh sushi" and fin fare such as "deep-fried catfish" and "blackened cod to die for" at this Westside Japanese (with take-out outlets throughout town) make up for the "difficult parking"; the "eh" decor is definitely "not trendy", but there are "celebrities everywhere."

Asuka 19 | 13 | 18 | $30
1266 Westwood Blvd. (Wilshire Blvd.), Westwood, 310-474-7412
☑ "Old Faithful" to its fans, this "casual" Westwood Japanese has earned a "loyal following" among students, offering "something for everyone – sushi on the left, teppanyaki on the right"; detractors dismiss the "generic-looking" fare as "consistently so-so" and are equally indifferent to the "minimal decor."

Aunt Kizzy's Back Porch 20 | 14 | 17 | $20
Villa Marina Mktpl., 4325 Glencoe Ave. (Mindanao Way), Marina del Rey, 310-578-1005; www.auntkizzys.com
■ "Bring your appetite" and "wear loose pants" to this Marina BYO Southerner dishing out "scrumptious" fried

The Westside   F | D | S | C

chicken, some of the "best pork chops in the city" and other "mighty fine eats" served in a "down-home atmosphere" that's "like sitting on the back porch, but without the bugs", where you'll "forget you're in a mini-mall"; N.B. all-you-can-eat Sunday brunch.

Avenue   19 | 24 | 18 | $51
301 N. Cañon Dr. (Dayton Way), Beverly Hills, 310-275-2900
☑ At this "exquisitely stylish" Beverly Hills New American, the "lush, intimate", "very Manhattan" decor designed by local lion Dodd Mitchell is one of the "sexiest in LA", with the added attraction of "celebrities at almost every table"; the cuisine is "innovative without pretensions" and "visually stunning" in its own right, and though the service can resemble "amateur hour" and the tabs can be a "little hard to take", many are confident this newcomer's "going to last."

A Votre Sante   17 | 11 | 15 | $19
13016 San Vicente Blvd. (26th St.), Brentwood, 310-451-1813
☑ "Everything's good for you" on the "reasonably priced" menu at this Brentwood American that's a "good choice for the yoga set", serving "creative" "natural" fare "without sacrificing taste"; "bland, bland, bland" is the chief beef of bashers who find the "healthy food" and "spartan digs" "too hip for anyone other than starving vegetarians."

Axe ⓜ   21 | 18 | 16 | $31
1009 Abbot Kinney Blvd. (B'way), Venice, 310-664-9787; www.axerestaurant.com
☑ The name's pronounced ah-shay at this "chic", "local hang for the Venetian Zen set" where "fresh", "well-thought-out" Californian fare is served in a "stark" space that inspires mixed reactions ("serene", "beautiful" vs. "like a jail"), with a "superb" outdoor garden for drinks; the biggest axe foes have to grind: "you could cut through the attitude with an 'ah-shay.'"

Babalu   19 | 15 | 16 | $23
1002 Montana Ave. (10th St.), Santa Monica, 310-395-2500
■ "Everything Caribbean" can be found at this "eclectic" Santa Monica "hole-in-the-wall" that's a "great break from shopping" on tony Montana Avenue; "creative Cal-tropical" fare makes up the menu, but leave room for the "truly special" desserts, including pies "to die for", or just "have them for dinner"; frequent "celebrity sightings" may help take your mind off the "cramped" seating.

Back on the Beach   13 | 18 | 13 | $17
445 PCH (California Blvd.), Santa Monica, 310-393-8282
☑ Though it's "perfectly fine", the Cal fare is "secondary" to the "fantastic" setting of this Santa Monica "beach cafe" where you can "burrow your toes in the sand", "watching the waves rush in" and the "occasional hot

get updates at zagat.com   89

The Westside   F D S C

rollerbladers" roll by; needless to say, it's "great for kids" – just remember to "bring sunglasses and sunscreen."

BAJA FRESH MEXICAN GRILL   20 | 11 | 15 | $9
475 N. Beverly Dr. (Little Santa Monica Blvd.), Beverly Hills, 310-858-6690
11690 San Vicente Blvd. (Barrington Ave.), Brentwood, 310-826-9166
Villa Marina Mktpl., 13424 Maxella Ave. (Del Rey Ave.), Marina del Rey, 310-578-2252
Westwood Village, 10916 Lindbrook Ave. (Westwood Blvd.), Westwood, 310-208-3317
www.bajafresh.com
See review in LA/Hollywood/W. Hollywood Directory.

Ballona Fish Market   20 | 19 | 20 | $33
Villa Marina Ctr., 13455 Maxella Ave. (Lincoln Ave.), Marina del Rey, 310-822-8979

■ If the fish "were any fresher, it'd swim to your table" at Hans Röckenwagner's Marina del Rey seafooder swear fans who are hooked by a "dazzling selection" of "unusual" offerings like skate served on "artistic plates" in a setting that recalls a "back porch of a summer cottage by the lake"; critics "unimpressed" by the fare are still hopeful it "may get better", so "keep trying, Mr. Röck."

Bamboo   21 | 16 | 16 | $24
10835 Venice Blvd. (bet. Overland Ave. & Sepulveda Blvd.), Palms, 310-287-0668; www.bamboorestaurant.net

■ Not to be confused with the Bamboo Inn in Sherman Oaks, this Palms Caribbean is a "find", offering "hearty, tasty", "reasonably priced" fare, "down-to-earth" service and a "swank postcolonial" setting that makes you "feel worlds away from the neighborhood"; the lush tropical greenery surrounding the outdoor patio can make the place a "bit hard to find."

Bandera   21 | 20 | 20 | $29
11700 Wilshire Blvd. (Barrington Ave.), West LA, 310-477-3524; www.banderarestaurants.com

■ A slightly more upscale spin-off of Houston's, this West LA spot attracts a "youngish", "beautiful" crowd with "great" live jazz nightly and a "super bar scene" that's "always entertaining", but it's also "mastered American cuisine" ("amazing spit-roasted chicken and steaks", "great skillet cornbread"); the "log-cabin-meets-the-big-city" interior is a "little dark", but the "food lightens things up"; N.B. there's also a branch in Corona del Mar.

Barney Greengrass   21 | 19 | 17 | $28
Barneys New York, 9570 Wilshire Blvd., 5th fl. (Camden Dr.), Beverly Hills, 310-777-5877

■ For a "taste of NY", deli devotees come to this Beverly Hills outpost sitting atop Barney's with a "lovely patio" that

The Westside   F D S C

offers "awesome views" and "prices to match" its "rooftop" setting, where "agents", industry "young turks" and sundry "glitterati" graze on smoked fish that's "heaven on earth", "amazing" salmon and "H&H bagels from NY" while observing that the "dude waiting on Ben Affleck is as good-looking as Ben Affleck."

Barney's Gourmet Hamburger ⓢ ≠   — — — I

Brentwood Country Mart, 225 26th St. (San Vicente Blvd.), Brentwood, 310-899-0133; www.barneyshamburgers.com

A popular SF patty chain heads south to open this basic stand offering a choice of four-dozen burgers (beef, chicken, turkey and tofu) to affluent Brentwood locals who usually come to the Country Mart to read the paper and drink latte in the open air; options range from a basic flame-broiled model to the Maui Waui, topped with pineapple and teriyaki.

Beach House Ⓜ   18 19 19 $41

100 W. Channel Rd. (PCH), Santa Monica, 310-454-8299

◪ Across the road from the beach, this Santa Monica New American has "recovered from being hip" to become a "dark, romantic" spot where you "won't be pushed aside by wanna-bes in black"; the "creative" menu can be "hit or miss", but the lemon-drop martinis are the "best around", and the waiters, who "look like they just finished a photo shoot", "take extra care to make you feel at home."

Beau Rivage   20 23 20 $43

26025 PCH (Malibu Canyon Rd.), Malibu, 310-456-5733; www.beaurivagerestaurant.com

◪ A "pioneer" in Malibu, this "grown-up" Mediterranean across from the ocean is "as romantic as a restaurant can be without being in Paris", with a "gorgeous, unexpected" decor, "fireplaces in winter and outdoor dining in summer"; contrarians carp that it's a "paradise with flaws", namely a "tired", "overpriced" menu, but it still remains a popular choice "up the coast" for a "special, leisurely dinner."

Bel-Air Bar & Grill   21 21 21 $38

662 N. Sepulveda Blvd. (Church Ln.), Bel Air, 310-440-5544; www.belairbarandgrill.com

■ The owners of this "classy" Bel Air "hangout" close to the Getty Museum "make sure your visit is a wonderful experience", a task made easier by "consistently good" Cal fare, a "room with grand style", "cozy bar" and "romantic outdoor patio"; a "safe bet for the area", it's a "great location for meeting between the Valley and the city."

BEL-AIR HOTEL   26 29 27 $63

Bel-Air Hotel, 701 Stone Canyon Rd. (Sunset Blvd.), Bel Air, 310-472-1211; www.hotelbelair.com

■ Bon mots abound for this "supreme" Cal-French in Bel-Air where you feel like you've "crossed the bridge to paradise"

get updates at zagat.com   91

The Westside | F | D | S | C |

as you dine in the "absolutely stunning" room or on the patio surrounded by a "spacious, verdant garden", and for a "special, special" event, Table One, a private room in the kitchen, is well worth making a "reservation months in advance"; the cuisine is "exquisite", and the "excellent" staff "makes anyone feel like the President"; N.B. the bar was voted Most Popular in our *LA Nightlife Survey*.

BELVEDERE, THE | 26 | 26 | 27 | $63 |

Peninsula Beverly Hills Hotel, 9882 Little Santa Monica Blvd. (Wilshire Blvd.), Beverly Hills, 310-788-2306; www.peninsula.com

■ This Californian housed in the Peninsula Beverly Hills is "one of the top destinations" in town thanks to chef Bill Bracken's "superb" cuisine and an "incredibly elegant" dining room with an "old-world", "grand hotel" feel, where "there's always a celebrity sighting" (CAA is right next door); many feel that "service is the real star", thanks to a "professional" staff that can "handle a party of 10 with absolute aplomb" and "makes every guest feel welcome."

Benihana | 19 | 18 | 21 | $32 |

38 N. La Cienega Blvd. (Wilshire Blvd.), Beverly Hills, 323-655-7311
1447 Fourth St. (B'way), Santa Monica, 310-260-1423
www.benihana.com

◪ The "witty" chefs' "juggling and chopping" show at this Japanese grill chain would "do Circus Maximus proud", which is why it's such a "great place to take the kids", but adults anoint it the "king of teppanyaki" for its "consistently" "tasty" fare; those who find "volcanoes made from onion slices" "passé" and "boring" may be heartened to know that some branches now offer sushi bars.

Benny's BBQ | ∇ 16 | 4 | 14 | $14 |

4077 Lincoln Blvd. (bet. Maxella Ave. & Washington Blvd.), Marina del Rey, 310-821-6939

◪ "It ain't Texas", but this "no-frills" Marina del Rey BBQ is the "only flame in town" for some, but surveyors are divided over the fare ("best ribs on the Westside" vs. "it smells better than it tastes"); all agree that "takeout" is the way to go, for while the "little shack" is "cute", "there's no room or decor."

Berri's Pizza Cafe ◐ | - | - | - | I |

9360 Wilshire Blvd. (Crescent Dr.), Beverly Hills, 310-276-0164
8415 Pershing Dr. (Manchester Ave.), Playa del Rey, 310-823-6658
See review in LA/Hollywood/W. Hollywood Directory.

Billingsley's | - | - | - | I |

11326 W. Pico Blvd. (Sawtelle Blvd.), West LA, 310-477-1426

A SoCal landmark for more than 50 years, this American duo in West LA and Van Nuys offers big orders of steak, chicken, barbecue and seafood at prices that are at least

The Westside   F | D | S | C

a decade behind the times in equally retro rooms; they're also among the increasingly rare places in LA where you can enjoy a proper drink at a proper bar.

Bistro 31 ⓢ   ▽ 23 | 14 | 18 | $28
Art Institute of Los Angeles, 2900 31st St. (Ocean Park Blvd.), Santa Monica, 310-314-6057

■ "Soon-to-be-chefs" prepare "attractive, high-quality" fare for "half the price it would cost in a real restaurant" at this student-run Santa Monica Californian, while "nervous" waiters-in-training "are so cute" and "eager-to-please", though some "fumbling" is to be expected; still, the "excitement of discovering a new toque makes this place worth a try"; N.B. open Mondays–Wednesdays only.

BJ's ☽   17 | 15 | 16 | $18
939 Broxton Ave. (bet. Leconte & Weyburn Aves.), Westwood, 310-209-7475; www.bjsbrewhouse.com

☑ The "epitome of college-life restaurants", this "pizza-and-beer" chain also functions as a "great sports bar" ("just don't go during a Lakers playoff game, unless you like crowds"), serving deep-dish pies that "hit the spot" and an "impressive array of beers on tap"; needless to say, it's "not good for conversation."

Blueberry   21 | 15 | 15 | $15
510 Santa Monica Blvd. (5th St.), Santa Monica, 310-394-7766

☑ "Watch the street scene while enjoying an omelet" at this "trendy" Santa Monica "breakfast place" where nearly "everything is blue" in the "funky" decor and on the menu ("awesome pancakes", "tasty" mini-muffins, "excellent" lemonade all made with the eponymous berry); "free coffee" while you stand on line goes a long way toward curing those "long-waits-on-weekends" blues.

Blue on Blue   ▽ 18 | 23 | 17 | $43
Avalon Hotel, 9400 W. Olympic Blvd. (Cañon Dr.), Beverly Hills, 310-277-5221; www.avalon-hotel.com

■ Housed in Beverly Hills' Avalon Hotel, a retro-modern boutique inn that appeared on "*I Love Lucy* episodes", this "hip hangout" offers "poolside dining" in "romantically secluded" cabanas that make it one of the "best places for a party", and American fare that's "outta sight", though the place is "so cool" it almost "doesn't matter"; "well-made" drinks are another plus, but be careful, for "after two martinis, the pool beckons."

Bob Morris' Paradise   13 | 17 | 15 | $26
Cove Beach Cafe
28128 PCH (Paradise Cove Rd.), Malibu, 310-457-2503

☑ "You can't get closer to the beach" than this north Malibu American, a "fun, casual destination" for "a drink with an ocean view" of "unbelievable West Coast sunsets", though as the numbers indicate, not much else; the service is

get updates at zagat.com   93

The Westside | F | D | S | C |

"sporadic" and the food "mediocre", but of course if the menu were better, "the wait would be even longer."

Bombay Bite | – | – | – | I |
1051 Gayley Ave. (Le Conte Ave.), Westwood, 310-824-1046; www.bombaybite.com
This modern-looking Indian newcomer in the heart of Westwood Village specializes in the cooking of Bombay, which means a selection of street snacks like frankies, along with *pav bhaji* (assorted vegetables flavored with cilantro) and paneer chili (a type of cottage cheese stir-fried with diced onions and bell peppers).

BOMBAY CAFE | 24 | 17 | 20 | $26 |
12021 W. Pico Blvd. (Bundy Dr.), West LA, 310-473-3388
■ Consistently the top-rated Indian for its "fabulous", "out-of-the-ordinary", "nouvelle" fare that "wakes up your taste buds and has them crying for more", this West LA spot is "worth going out of your way"; though it's "often very crowded", the "helpful", "knowledgeable" staff "does a good job" and the atmosphere is "warm and inviting", albeit "noisy."

Bombay Palace | 21 | 21 | 20 | $30 |
8690 Wilshire Blvd. (bet. Hamel & Willaman Drs.), Beverly Hills, 310-659-9944; www.bombaypalace.com
■ It's "like eating in a museum or gallery" at this "elegant" Beverly Hills Indian where "delectable" dishes from the subcontinent are "well prepared and presented" and served by a "gracious" staff in an "upscale, sophisticated" setting; there's "something for every taste, from spicy to mild", and while the "portions seem small, they fill you up."

BORDER GRILL | 21 | 19 | 19 | $30 |
1445 Fourth St. (bet. B'way & Santa Monica Blvd.), Santa Monica, 310-451-1655; www.bordergrill.com
■ A "different kind of south-of-the-border" experience awaits at the Too Hot Tamales' (Mary Sue Milliken and Susan Feniger) Mexican duo in the form of "adventurous", "inventive" fare served in "bold", "hip" settings; "too noisy" is how some describe the scene at the Santa Monica branch, but while the Pasadena location is "not nearly as raucous", its "mall atmosphere" raises a few eyebrows.

Bourbon Street Shrimp & Grill | 17 | 17 | 17 | $20 |
10928 W. Pico Blvd. (Kelton Ave.), West LA, 310-474-0007
See review in LA/Hollywood/W. Hollywood Directory.

Brasserie des Artistes | 17 | 13 | 17 | $34 |
8300 Wilshire Blvd. (San Vicente Blvd.), Beverly Hills, 323-655-6196; www.brasseriedesartistes.com
◪ While some may pause at a place offering "hearty French food and karaoke" (on Fridays and Saturdays), *amis* insist this Beverly Hills brasserie is as "authentic" as they come,

The Westside　　　　　F | D | S | C

serving "fun fare for Francophiles", including the "best steak tartare"; a few feel the cooking's prone to "mood swings", but many more "want to become regulars."

Bravo Cucina　　　　　18 | 14 | 18 | $23
1319 Third St. Promenade (bet. Arizona Ave. & Santa Monica Blvd.), Santa Monica, 310-394-0374; www.bravocucina.com
2400D Main St. (Hollister Ave.), Santa Monica, 310-392-7466
■ A "cozy neighborhood find" on Santa Monica's bustling Third Street Promenade (with a pizza outpost on Main Street, Bravo Pizzeria), this Italian offers "satisfying", "delicious", "healthy" choices and "great people-watching" from an outdoor patio; cynics, though, find it "convenient but nothing more."

Breeze　　　　　21 | 22 | 20 | $41
Century Plaza Hotel & Spa, 2025 Ave. of the Stars (Constellation Ave.), Century City, 310-277-2000
■ "Perfect for lawyerly lunches" or "drinks after work", this "upscale" hotel Californian in the Century Plaza offers a "diverse menu" that ranges from "sushi to steak" and a "great raw bar"; the "light, airy" space is "calming" even when filled with "every attorney in Century City", but at times the staff can be "hard to find"; P.S. the "awesome" weekend brunch offers "so much to choose from."

Brentwood Restaurant & Lounge　23 | 21 | 22 | $44
148 S. Barrington Ave. (Sunset Blvd.), Brentwood, 310-476-3511; www.brentwoodrestaurant.com
■ As "dark and comfy as a good Bordeaux", this "upscale" New American is "Brentwood's most public private club" attracting "lots of star power" in a "quiet" setting "safe from paparazzi"; the "diverse" menu of "great comfort food" is "solid all around", but most agree the "face of the place" is "exceptional" host David Rozansky, with his "warm, friendly" mien and "amazing knowledge of wine."

Brighton Coffee Shop　　　17 | 9 | 16 | $15
9600 Brighton Way (Camden Dr.), Beverly Hills, 310-276-7732
■ A "part of local history" since 1930, this "classic" coffee shop gives you a "feel of what Beverly Hills was like in the old days" as you tuck into "heavenly" pancakes or the "best chicken salad sandwich on earth"; "convenient" for breakfast and a "real treat" for lunch, it's also a "great place to stop while you shop till you drop."

Broadway Deli ☾　　　　16 | 14 | 14 | $20
1457 Third St. Promenade (B'way), Santa Monica, 310-451-0616; www.broadwaydeli.com
■ A "perfect place to chill after a long day of shopping", this "international" deli on Santa Monica's Third Street

get updates at zagat.com　　　　　　　　　95

The Westside | F | D | S | C |

Promenade serves up a "huge", "eclectic" menu that's a mix of "traditional and nontraditional" along with a "hot" wine list in a "modern" room with an "SF" look; purists pooh-pooh it as a "pseudo-deli" that "doesn't live up to the real thing", though the "NY-style service" is an authentic touch.

Buca di Beppo | 14 | 17 | 17 | $22 |
1442 Second St. (Santa Monica Blvd.), Santa Monica, 310-587-2782; www.bucadibeppo.com

☑ For quintessential "family-style dining", "come with a group" to this "kitschy" Southern Italian chain dishing out "crazy" portions of "hearty" fare in "wacky"-looking rooms that are closer to "Disneyland" than Rome, where the staff "suffers large parties with a smile" and "everybody leaves full and happy"; P.S. "reserve well in advance" for the "kitchen table" where you can "watch the chefs work."

Buffalo Club ⓈⓂ | 21 | 21 | 18 | $48 |
1520 Olympic Blvd. (15th St.), Santa Monica, 310-450-8600

■ Go "back into the world of NY speakeasies" at this "hidden", "swanky" "gem" in a "transitional neighborhood" of Santa Monica with a "handsome" "old-school" interior and a "breathtaking" outdoor patio where "celebrities" gather; the "classic" American fare ("steaks like buttah", "heaven"-sent mac 'n' cheese) has a "creative spark", which might be useful to light up the "too dark" room.

CAFÉ BIZOU | 23 | 19 | 21 | $29 |
Water Garden, 2450 Colorado Blvd. (bet. Cloverfield Blvd. & 26th St.), Santa Monica, 310-582-8203; www.cafebizou.com

■ Voted Most Popular in this *Survey* going away, this Cal-French trio is "always reliable", "always superb" and "always interesting", thanks to a "formula that doesn't feel like a formula", with "exceptional" appetizers and "delicious entrees and desserts" at "bargain" prices ("$2 corkage... enough said"), plus a "friendly" staff that "tries to please"; the only drawback is that it's "always packed", so wear your "standing shoes."

CAFE BLANC ⓈⓂ | 26 | 16 | 23 | $46 |
9777 Little Santa Monica Blvd. (N. Linden Dr.), Beverly Hills, 310-888-0108

■ "Stark blanc" in aspect and "microscopic" in scale, this Beverly Hills "hole-in-the-wall" is the showcase for chef-owner Tomi Harase's "sophisticated fusion" of French and Pacific Rim cuisines memorable for "flavors that are delicate but always surprising and oh-so-fresh" on a menu that "changes daily"; the "wonderful gourmet lunch specials" are a "bargain" that'll "suit even the collegiate budget."

Cafe Brasil | 19 | 12 | 13 | $16 |
10831 Venice Blvd. (Westwood Blvd.), Palms, 310-837-8957

■ A "variety" of "tasty", "authentic" Brazilian dishes, from "delicious" BBQ to "excellent" feijoada, is served at this

The Westside   F | D | S | C

"down-to-earth" Palms BYO that's not far from Sony Studios; the "bare-bones" decor and "self-service" may be "one step up from a cafeteria", but the atmosphere is "refreshing."

Cafe Del Rey   24 | 23 | 21 | $42
4451 Admiralty Way (bet. Lincoln Blvd. & Via Marina), Marina del Rey, 310-823-6395; www.cafedelrey.com

■ Fans aver "when it's on its game", this Marina del Rey Pacific New Waver "can rival the biggest names" on the strength of its "inventive, brilliant" cuisine, "perfect" setting with a "romantic" "view of the Marina" and "gracious" service; though the "top-drawer ambiance" is marred somewhat by the "noise level", this spot remains a "favorite for special occasions."

Cafe '50s ●   14 | 17 | 16 | $13
838 Lincoln Blvd. (Lake St.), Venice, 310-399-1955
11623 Santa Monica Blvd. (bet. Barry & Federal Aves.), West LA, 310-479-1955
www.cafe50s.com

◪ The "shakes alone are worth the trip" to this "'50s-style" diner trio on the Westside and in Sherman Oaks sporting "bright red booths and coin-op jukeboxes" and a "fun", "kid-friendly" atmosphere (including "pajama nights"), but the "Americana" fare is "average" and "predictable"; still, it offers one of the "best breakfasts in LA"; N.B. all three locations are independently owned.

Cafe Misto   19 | 15 | 18 | $24
Highlands Plaza, 538 Palisades Dr. (Sunset Blvd.), Pacific Palisades, 310-573-1411

■ You "won't go away hungry" from this "perennial" "locals' favorite" in Pacific Palisades offering "large servings" of "solid, if unspectacular" Italian fare at "reasonable prices" and "friendly" service in "simple" quarters; while some sniff there's "not much to write home about", defenders tout it as a "good choice" for "relaxing dining" in the area.

Cafe Montana   20 | 16 | 18 | $28
1534 Montana Ave. (16th St.), Santa Monica, 310-829-3990

◪ "Fantastic" for brunch but perhaps "best for breakfast", Babalu's sibling on Santa Monica's boutiquish Montana Avenue is a popular stop with "ladies who lunch", "stroller moms" and "celebrities" alike for "light", "flavorful" Californian fare and "sensational" desserts; though it's "always busy", the staff is "accommodating" and a "casual no-socks" ambiance fills the "chic" glass-box setting.

Caffe Delfini   23 | 18 | 21 | $35
147 W. Channel Rd. (PCH), Santa Monica, 310-459-8823
Fred Segal, 500 Broadway (5th St.), Santa Monica, 310-395-5699

■ "You could be on the Riviera" rather than a "cozy little corner of Santa Monica Canyon" at this "adorable" "hidden

The Westside   F | D | S | C

gem" half a block from the beach offering "wonderfully straightforward", "authentic" Italian cuisine and "vibrant, welcoming" service in a "small" space; though the "close quarters" are a bit too "intimate" for some, the "super-romantic setting" makes it "one of the best date spots in town"; N.B. the mall outlet serves breakfast and lunch only.

Caffe Pinguini M   ▽ 19 | 19 | 18 | $33
6935 Pacific Ave. (Culver Blvd.), Playa del Rey, 310-306-0117; www.caffepinguini.com

◼ The "flip-flops" crowd comes to this Northern Italian "sleeper" in "laid-back" Playa del Rey for alfresco dining in a "beautiful, romantic" setting; oenophiles whine about the "overpriced" wines, while others mutter about a service "overhaul", but most deem the fare "with a Continental flair" "worth a return visit."

California Chicken Cafe ⑤   21 | 9 | 15 | $10
2401 Wilshire Blvd. (24th St.), Santa Monica, 310-453-0477
2005 Westwood Blvd. (bet. Olympic & Santa Monica Blvds.), West LA, 310-446-1933
www.californiachickencafe.com
See review in LA/Hollywood/W. Hollywood Directory.

CALIFORNIA PIZZA KITCHEN   18 | 14 | 17 | $18
207 S. Beverly Dr. (bet. Olympic & Wilshire Blvds.), Beverly Hills, 310-275-1101
210 Wilshire Blvd. (bet. 2nd & 3rd Sts.), Santa Monica, 310-393-9335
Westwood Village, 1001 Broxton Ave. (Weyburn Ave.), Westwood, 310-209-9197
www.cpk.com
See review in LA/Hollywood/W. Hollywood Directory.

California Wok   18 | 9 | 15 | $15
12004 Wilshire Blvd. (Bundy Dr.), West LA, 310-479-0552
See review in LA/Hollywood/W. Hollywood Directory.

Canal Club   18 | 19 | 17 | $30
2025 Pacific Ave. (Venice Blvd.), Venice, 310-823-3878

◼ The "decor is an experience by itself" at this "cool" "SoHo at the beach" in Venice, a "party spot" offering an Eclectic menu with "something for everyone", "fabulous" "bargain" sushi bar happy hour and "DJs on weekends"; it's a "wonderful local hangout" where you can "start your evening or finish it with variety."

C & O Trattoria   19 | 16 | 18 | $19
31 Washington Blvd. (Pacific Ave.), Marina del Rey, 310-823-9491; www.cotrattoria.com

■ "Cheap wine" self-served on an "honor system" and "sing-alongs of 'That's Amore!'" in a "crowded" room make this Marina del Rey Southern Italian a "rambunctious" scene that "won't cost a lot"; "huge" "family-style" portions of

98   subscribe to zagat.com

The Westside   F | D | S | C

red-sauce fare will fill you up, if the "endless servings" of "addictive", "hot, buttery" garlic knots don't.

Capo ☒ Ⓜ   25 | 24 | 23 | $68

1810 Ocean Ave. (Pico Blvd.), Santa Monica, 310-394-5550; www.foodcowest.com

■ "Everything exceeds expectations . . . including the price" at Bruce Marder's "special-occasion" Italian in Santa Monica serving "amazing dishes you'll be hard-pressed to find anywhere else" made with produce from his "organic home garden", meats and seafood cooked on an open grill and wines that'll "rock your world"; "you might see a celebrity or two" in the "beautiful", "rustic" space, where a "smart, friendly" staff provides "attentive" service; fans wax philosophical – "quality doesn't come cheap."

Casa Antigua Cantina   18 | 22 | 19 | $30

12217 Wilshire Blvd. (Bundy Dr.), West LA, 310-820-2540; www.casaantigua.com

■ "High-end Mexican with a French twist" by a chef who cooked at Maxim's in Mexico City and a "fantastic" space with "museum-quality" decor await at this "exotic, original" West LA cantina that's "very different from your run-of-the-mill" south-of-the-border spot; all agree it shows "promise", though a few feel it needs to be more "consistent" in order to "be a great restaurant."

Casablanca   21 | 19 | 21 | $22

220 Lincoln Blvd. (Rose Ave.), Venice, 310-392-5751

■ Cineastes are shocked, shocked to discover "authentic Mexican" fin fare and the "best homemade tortillas in town" at this "campy" Venice tribute to the eponymous classic sporting a "Moroccan setting" with "Claude, Bogey and Ingrid all over the walls" and a "piano in the corner"; it's perfect for "movie buffs who like seafood Veracruz style."

Cézanne   ▽ 22 | 23 | 22 | $48

Le Merigot Hotel, 1740 Ocean Ave. (bet. Colorado Ave. & Pico Blvd.), Santa Monica, 310-395-9700; www.lemerigothotel.com

■ "Tastefully cooked, well seasoned" Cal-French cuisine, an "elegant room" and "flawless" service make this Santa Monica Cal-French housed in the Marriott-owned Le Merigot "better than your standard hotel restaurant"; there's "no view of the ocean" from its location "near the beach" "but not on it", but that doesn't take away its "romantic" appeal "for a special evening out"; P.S. it's also a "wonderful place for brunch on the patio."

Cha Cha Chicken   20 | 12 | 13 | $12

1906 Ocean Ave. (Pico Blvd.), Santa Monica, 310-581-1684

■ A "beachside" "picnic stand" with a "colorful outdoor patio", Cha Cha Cha's Santa Monica spin-off "isn't upscale or even fast", but it's "worth the drive" for "awesome",

get updates at zagat.com

The Westside | F | D | S | C |

"mouthwatering jerk chicken enchiladas"; "if you're jonesing for that Caribbean island you went to last vacation, this is the spot to get your fix" cheaply.

Chan Dara | 20 | 17 | 18 | $25 |
11940 W. Pico Blvd. (Bundy Dr.), West LA, 310-479-4461
Villa Marina Mktpl., 13490 Maxella Ave. (Lincoln Blvd.), Marina del Rey, 310-301-1004
www.chandara.com
See review in LA/Hollywood/W. Hollywood Directory.

Chart House | 19 | 21 | 18 | $34 |
18412 PCH (Topanga Canyon Rd.), Malibu, 310-454-9321
13950 Panay Way (Via Marina St.), Marina del Rey, 310-822-4144
www.chart-house.com
◪ While opinions are split about the fare at this stalwart surf 'n' turf chain ("wonderful steaks", "fabulous", "fresh" seafood vs. "nothing special", "overpriced"), there's no quibbling over the "great views of the harbor and the ocean" common to all branches; lettuce lovers lament that some locations no longer offer the "remarkable" salad bar.

Chaya Venice | 22 | 21 | 19 | $41 |
110 Navy St. (Main St.), Venice, 310-396-1179;
www.thechaya.com
■ This "beachy" Venice "version of Chaya" is "always a happening scene" with a high "star-spotting factor", where "power lunch combines with chic casualness"; "delectable" Cal-Asian dishes such as "miso codfish that melts in your mouth" "look as good" as the "hip crowd with wandering eyes", and "for a taste of the place without the price tag", try the "wonderful sushi happy hour."

CHEESECAKE FACTORY | 20 | 18 | 18 | $23 |
364 N. Beverly Dr. (Brighton Way), Beverly Hills, 310-278-7270
11647 San Vicente Blvd. (bet. Barrington Ave. & Wilshire Blvd.), Brentwood, 310-826-7111
4142 Via Marina St. (Admiralty Way), Marina del Rey, 310-306-3344
www.thecheesecakefactory.com
◪ At this popular, "reliable" American-Eclectic chain the "mind-boggling" menu has "something for everyone", and "everybody knows it as you can tell from the lines"; a "dizzying array of choices" and "humongous portions", topped off by "giant slices of heavenly cheesecake", make you feel "like you're eating in a dream."

Chez Jay | 18 | 15 | 17 | $30 |
1657 Ocean Ave. (Colorado Ave.), Santa Monica, 310-395-1741;
www.chezjays.com
■ *Tout le* Santa Monica, from "salty old beach bums" to "high-powered Hollywood producers", frequents this "funky" surf 'n' turf "dive" for "juicy" steaks, "fresh" fin fare (including "superior" sand dabs) and "great breakfasts" in

The Westside | F | D | S | C |

a "dark" space that looks "like a small-town bowling alley", albeit one with "sawdust and peanut shells underfoot."

Chez Mimi ⓜ | 21 | 25 | 20 | $41 |
246 26th St. (San Vicente Blvd.), Santa Monica, 310-393-0558

■ "Step through the gates into a serene evening of delicious dining" at this "bit of France" in Santa Monica near the Brentwood border that's as "charming and cozy" as a "French country inn", with an "excellent courtyard patio" and "quaint", "fireplace"-equipped interior; "mussels to die for", "divine onion soup" and other "standards" also win praise, smoothing over complaints about the staff's "surly" attitude and "phony French accents."

Chin Chin | 17 | 13 | 16 | $20 |
206 S. Beverly Dr. (Gregory Way), Beverly Hills, 310-248-5252
11740 San Vicente Blvd. (bet. Barrington & Montana Aves.), Brentwood, 310-826-2525
Villa Marina Mktpl., 13455 Maxella Ave. (Lincoln Blvd.), Marina del Rey, 310-823-9999
www.chinchin.com
See review in LA/Hollywood/W. Hollywood Directory.

CHINOIS ON MAIN | 27 | 20 | 23 | $54 |
2709 Main St. (bet. Ashland Ave. & Ocean Park Blvd.), Santa Monica, 310-392-9025; www.wolfgangpuck.com

■ "So-o-o many excellent dishes to choose from" at this Santa Monica "destination" that's once again Wolfgang Puck's highest-rated for Food in the *Survey*, thanks to "creative, inspiring" and "beautifully presented" French-influenced Asian cuisine, brought to table by a staff that's usually "accommodating" but sometimes "aloof"; a few feel the "'80s" decor is due for a "face-lift" in the "tight squeeze" of a space, but wags note it's a "great place to people-watch, 'cause you can't hear them" in the "din."

Chloe Ⓢ | – | – | – | M |
333 Culver Blvd. (Vista del Mar), Playa del Rey, 310-305-4505; www.chloerestaurant.com

The most stylish eatery to open in hyper-casual Playa, and located just three blocks from the beach, this tiny, spare-looking Californian is the creation of veterans of Patina, Cicada, Pinot Bistro and Joe's, who have taken over a simple storefront in which they serve items like a soup of petite peas and vanilla and braised pork shoulder with golden potato puree.

Cholada | ▽ 25 | 12 | 22 | $18 |
18763 PCH (Topanga Beach Dr.), Malibu, 310-317-0025

■ A "terrific find for a Thai fix" that's "inexpensive and filling", this Malibu cult favorite is a "jewel on PCH", "right across from the ocean", offering "creative", "authentic"

The Westside	F	D	S	C

Siamese "home cooking" in a "casual" "beach shack" where you'll "feel like you're dining in Thailand."

Chung King 18 | 11 | 17 | $16
11538 W. Pico Blvd. (bet. Federal Ave. & Gateway Blvd.), West LA, 310-477-4917

◼ "Tasty", "no-frills" Chinese and "amazing lunch specials" are the draw at this West LA Mandarin that enjoys a large following among the "parking patrol" and "police"; still, while you may "feel safe" surrounded by LA's finest in the "plain" room, with such "fast" service and "atrocious parking" – "did someone say takeout?"

Clay Pit 22 | 16 | 19 | $26
145 S. Barrington Ave. (Sunset Blvd.), Brentwood, 310-476-4700; www.theclaypitinc.com

◼ An "excellent variety" of "impressive" Indian dishes with the "right amount of spices" attracts savvy "Brentwood locals" to this "stylish", "affordable" spot where you're "treated like family" and may catch a glimpse of "a star or two" in the "bright, airy" and "relaxing" space with floor-to-ceiling windows.

CLEMENTINE ⊠ 25 | 14 | 15 | $15
1751 Ensley Ave. (Santa Monica Blvd.), Century City, 310-552-1080

◼ One of the "best lunch spots anywhere near Century City", this "quintessential" Cal cafe has earned a "cult following" with "awesome" sandwiches, "delicious, creative" soups, "sensational salads" and "irresistible desserts"; but some feel "parking's impossible", the room's often "jam-packed" and sometimes there's "not enough help" to handle the crush.

Cobra Lily ◐⊠ ▽ 20 | 19 | 17 | $31
8442 Wilshire Blvd. (Hamilton Dr.), Beverly Hills, 323-651-5051

◼ At this "fashiony" Beverly Hills spin-off of Cobras & Matadors housed in the former space of C Bar, "every bite is delectable" from the "inspired" Spanish tapas menu ("outstanding octopus, appealing asparagus and charming churros y chocolate"), and the "fun bar scene is always packed", with wines poured from bottles that sit in a "big zinc tub on the bar"; the red interior is "sexy" and "elegant."

Coral Tree Café – | – | – | I
11645 San Vicente Blvd. (Barrington Ave.), Brentwood, 310-979-8733; www.coraltreecafe.net

This handsomely redone Brentwood cafe with a sizable outdoor patio offers an eclectic menu of organic-leaning Cal-Italian items, which translates into the likes of curried chicken salad, a sandwich caprese, vegan soups and sundry panini (with the option of real cheese or the soy version); the coffee served is also 'certified organic, shade grown and fair traded.'

The Westside F D S C

Cora's Coffee Shoppe 21 | 14 | 15 | $17
1802 Ocean Ave. (Pico Blvd.), Santa Monica, 310-451-9562
■ Über-chef Bruce Marder bought this "old Santa Monica dive" adjacent to his upscale Capo and "reimagined it" as a "coffee shop with an edge" serving "high quality" fare "at a fraction of the price" of its sibling; while a few feel it "lost some of its original charm" in the redo, it still has a "dive" look with a "cute little counter right out of Edward Hopper"; there's also an outdoor patio for "alfresco dining near the beach."

Crazy Fish 19 | 7 | 13 | $24
9105 W. Olympic Blvd. (Doheny Dr.), Beverly Hills, 310-550-8547
◪ The line at the door of this Beverly Hills Japanese is "the eighth wonder of the world", but "young, hip" fans swear the "yummy, creative" sushi is "worth [not only] the wait", but the "dingy" digs, "fluorescent" lighting and "famously rude" service as well; critics find the "Americanized" fare a "little too crazy" for comfort, but the "large portions at reasonable prices" make it "perfect for college kids."

Crocodile Café 16 | 15 | 17 | $21
101 Santa Monica Blvd. (Ocean Ave.), Santa Monica, 310-394-4783; www.crocodilecafe.com
■ "They know what they do, and they do it well" at this "poor man's Spago" (it's actually a spin-off of Parkway Grill), a "dependable" Cal chain that's "super in its niche", serving a "wide selection" of "solid", "well-prepared" fare, including grilled dishes from a "wood-burning oven", and "reliable" service; the "roomy interiors" are augmented by outdoor patios that are "great for the kids."

CRUSTACEAN ⊠ 24 | 27 | 21 | $54
9646 Little Santa Monica Blvd. (Bedford Dr.), Beverly Hills, 310-205-8990; www.secretkitchen.com
■ "You feel like you're walking on water" at this "see-and-be-seen" Beverly Hills Vietnamese, and not only from the "heavenly seafood" and other "out-of-this-world" fare, but also the below-floor koi pond leading into a "fantastique" "version of colonial Vietnam"; "there must be gods" in the touted "secret kitchen" where house specials such as the "great spicy Dungeness crab" and "garlic noodles to die for" are discreetly prepared.

Daily Grill 17 | 16 | 17 | $25
Brentwood Gardens, 11677 San Vicente Blvd. (Barrington Ave.), Brentwood, 310-442-0044; www.dailygrill.com
See review in LA/Hollywood/W. Hollywood Directory.

D'Amore's Pizza Connection 20 | 7 | 15 | $14
22601 PCH (Cross Creek Rd.), Malibu, 310-317-4500
■ "Bostonians would be proud" of the "great East Coast pizzas" at this popular pie chain, while "amazing thin crusts"

The Westside   F | D | S | C

will make "NYers take note" and the "native Chicagoans will drool over the Sicilian version"; like many "good takeout" places, it has "minimal decor", but the staff "goes out of its way to help."

Da Pasquale   21 | 13 | 18 | $27
9749 Little Santa Monica Blvd. (bet. Linden & Roxbury Drs.), Beverly Hills, 310-859-3884

■ "CAA agents" deal over lunches of "delicious" Northern Italian fare ("terrific" pastas, bread you "could make a meal of") at this "chic but still intimate" Beverly Hills "retreat"; there's "nothing fancy" about the decor and the "tables are a bit close" to one another, but the "friendly" staff "always makes you feel at home."

Delphi Greek Cuisine ⌀   21 | 13 | 20 | $23
1383 Westwood Blvd. (Wilshire Blvd.), Westwood, 310-478-2900

■ "No dancing or plate-throwing, just delicious" Greek fare at this "cozy", "mom-and-pop" Westwood Hellenic south of UCLA popular with students and visiting dignitaries like "Michael Dukakis" and "Walter Mondale"; the space is "cramped" and the decor is "cheesy" and a bit "dreary", but the "service couldn't be friendlier."

De Mori   20 | 20 | 18 | $42
421 N. Rodeo Dr. (Santa Monica Blvd.), Beverly Hills, 310-274-1500

■ Co-owner and namesake Silvio De Mori is "as gracious and accommodating as ever" at this "charming" Italian on Rodeo Drive serving "scrumptious pastas" and other "homestyle" fare; the "beautiful outdoor patio" is a "quiet oasis in the midst of Beverly Hills", except on weekends, when live jazz really "makes this place worth checking out."

Di Stefano   16 | 15 | 20 | $21
1076 Gayley Ave. (bet. Kinross & Weyburn Aves.), Westwood, 310-208-5117

☒ "One of the last grown-up restaurants in Westwood", this "local hangout" serves "big portions" of "old-world Italian at old-world prices" with bread that's "always warm and fresh" in an "intimate, relaxing" atmosphere that's "perfect for a date or the family"; it's also a good "choice before a movie" – the "friendly" staff will "get you in and out" in time for the show.

Divino   22 | 17 | 21 | $33
11714 Barrington Ct. (Sunset Blvd.), Brentwood, 310-472-0886

■ "Exemplary host" Goran Milic "treats everyone like a personal guest" at his "high-end" Brentwood Northern Italian where dishes like the "must-try" rigatoni al ragu and "excellent" gnocchi are "worth the challenge" of parking at its mini-mall location; "conscientious" service from a

The Westside   F | D | S | C

"friendly" staff and a "quaint", "inviting" room add to its "character and charm."

Drago   25 | 21 | 23 | $45
2628 Wilshire Blvd. (26th St.), Santa Monica, 310-828-1585; www.celestinodrago.com

■ The Santa Monica "flagship" of Celestino Drago's "growing family of restaurants", this "sophisticated" Italian "keeps rolling" with the "ambitious, highly skilled" chef's "upscale", "authentic" Northern and Southern dishes that "delight", such as pumpkin tortellini and the "best black risotto this side of Italy", at "affordable prices"; the room is "beautiful" and the "polished" service exudes "confidence and panache" instead of the usual "attitude."

Duke's Malibu/Huntington Beach   16 | 20 | 18 | $28
21150 PCH (Las Flores Canyon Rd.), Malibu, 310-317-0777; www.hulapie.com

◪ All you need for a "sunny weekend" – "cocktails, coeds", plus a "beer and a burger at the barefoot bar" – awaits at this Hawaiian duo in Malibu and Huntington Beach, where some of the "hottest" "people-watching" vies with "million-dollar views" of the ocean in a "casual" setting with a "surfer" decor and "fun island vibe"; the "so-so" fare is almost an afterthought to "sipping a cool tall one" and watching the "waves crashing against the windows and dolphins swimming by."

EL CHOLO   18 | 18 | 17 | $21
1025 Wilshire Blvd. (10th St.), Santa Monica, 310-899-1106; www.elcholo.com
See review in LA/Hollywood/W. Hollywood Directory.

El Dorado Cantina   13 | 16 | 13 | $27
11777 San Vicente Blvd. (bet. Barrington & Montana Aves.), Brentwood, 310-207-0150; www.eldoradocantina.com

◪ A bit of "Hollywood in Brentwood" for a "younger crowd", this "night club trying to be a [Mexican] restaurant" "turns from fiesta to party" "after 10 PM" when "junior agents" and "twentysomething" "eye candy" mingle at the bar or "in the velvet room"; the "mediocre" fare is an "afterthought" and the service can be "dreadful", but pros point out you're "going for the scene."

El Pollo Inka   18 | 11 | 15 | $15
11701 Wilshire Blvd. (Barrington Ave.), West LA, 310-571-3334; www.elpolloinka.com

■ "Savory, comforting chicken" and a "magic green sauce" that "makes everything taste good" highlight the "large menu" of "yummy" Peruvian cooking at this "affordable" chain that's a "treat when you want something different"; the decor may be "kitschy" but the service is "super-quick", and several of the branches offer live music and salsa dancing on weekends.

get updates at zagat.com

The Westside

| F | D | S | C |

El Texate
| – | – | – | I |

316 Pico Blvd (4th St.), Santa Monica, 310-399-1115
One of a growing number of Westside Oaxacans, this Santa Monica Mexican attracts a sizable late-night crowd of clubbers as well as keglers from the bowling alley next door with mole of many colors and big portions at low prices, and real margaritas from a real bar.

El Torito
| 14 | 14 | 15 | $18 |

13715 Fiji Way (Lincoln Blvd.), Marina del Rey, 310-823-8941; www.eltorito.com

◪ A "good standby" for "competent" Mexican fare, this group is "different from most chains", offering "guacamole made at your table" and "chef's special regional menus" in addition to "all the familiar staples"; while the "plastic" decor fails to impress, several locations are on the water, offering "great views" of "sailboats and sunsets."

El Torito Grill
| 17 | 16 | 16 | $22 |

9595 Wilshire Blvd. (Camden Dr.), Beverly Hills, 310-550-1599; www.eltorito.com

■ At El Torito's "slightly upscale" sibling chain, modern, "healthy" takes on classic Mexican cuisine are a "little pricier, but *muy bien* for the money", and amigos take special note of the "fresh tortillas made on the premises"; a "fun happy hour" and "awesome" Sunday brunches add allure, while private party spaces make it a good choice for "group events."

Encore
| ▽ 21 | 24 | 21 | $50 |

St. Regis Hotel, 2055 Ave. of the Stars (bet. Galaxy Way & Olympic Blvd.), Century City, 310-277-6111; www.stregis.com

■ After several false starts, this French establishment housed in the St. Regis Hotel in Century City has a new chef and management who have turned it into a "fine dining experience" in a "beautiful" room where "you can carry on a conversation"; there's a "magical touch in every dish" and the "staff caters to every whim", all of which makes it a "perfect place for a romantic evening" as well as a "power breakfast or business lunch."

Enterprise Fish Co.
| 18 | 17 | 16 | $29 |

174 Kinney St. (Main St.), Santa Monica, 310-392-8366; www.enterprisefishco.com

■ "So many choices" but "nothing complicated" at this "solid" Santa Monica seafooder a block from the Pacific serving "succulent crab legs" and fin fare "properly cooked" over a mesquite grill; a few feel the kitchen could be "more enterprising", but the "bar scene is fun", and the "inviting" outdoor patio with fire pit is recommended for "romantic" dining or "cocktails with friends"; P.S. "can't beat" the "lobster specials on Mondays and Tuesdays."

The Westside   F | D | S | C

Eurochow   18 | 26 | 17 | $43
1099 Westwood Blvd. (Kinross Ave.), Westwood, 310-209-0066; www.eurochow.com

◪ At Mr. Chow's Sino-Italian sibling in Westwood Village, "every table feels as if it's its own set" "in a Stanley Kubrick film" in the "stunning" all-white space with a clear "glass floor over the wine cellar"; while the menu "concept sounds promising", foes find the "execution disappointing"; still, the "extensive" martini list is "something to write home about", though the "snobbish" staff may "seat you in Siberia" "unless you're someone."

Falafel King ☻   18 | 6 | 13 | $9
1315 Third St. Promenade (bet. Arizona Ave. & Santa Monica Blvd.), Santa Monica, 310-587-2551
1059 Broxton Ave. (bet. Kinross & Weyburn Aves.), Westwood, 310-208-4444

■ For an "honest introduction to Middle Eastern" cuisine or just a "tasty" "quick fix", this no-look pair in Westwood Village and Santa Monica offers "great bang for the buck" with its "salty, yummy falafel" and other staples; the interior encourages "sitting outside and watching people stroll by", but the service is "solid."

Farm of Beverly Hills   18 | 17 | 16 | $26
439 N. Beverly Dr. (bet. Brighton Way & Santa Monica Blvd.), Beverly Hills, 310-273-5578; www.thefarmofbeverlyhills.com

■ Like a "breath of fresh air in Beverly Hills", this 90210 pastoral is where the "healthy, wealthy" set flocks for "upscale" Cal comfort dishes, served by a "sitcom-pretty" staff in a "glassy, classy" setting with a "natural outdoors feel" and "celebrity spotting" aplenty; the branch in the Grove at the Farmer's Market is a "great place for dinner before a movie" next door, and both are popular sites for "business or casual lunches", albeit a bit "overpriced."

FATHER'S OFFICE   23 | 14 | 11 | $19
1018 Montana Ave. (bet. 10th & 11th Sts.), Santa Monica, 310-393-2337

■ A "religious experience" awaits at this Santa Monica brewpub in the form of its renowned hamburger, a "juicy slab of beef" "covered in blue cheese and caramelized onions", served with "sweet potato fries that take your breath away" but "no ketchup" (or substitutions); you can wash it down with one of "more than 30 microbrews", but first you have to wade through a "three-deep" crowd to order at the "bowling lane–sized bar" (no table service).

Feast from the East ☒   21 | 6 | 14 | $10
1949 Westwood Blvd. (bet. Olympic & Santa Monica Blvds.), West LA, 310-475-0400; www.feasteast.com

■ "Has anyone ever ordered anything but Chinese chicken salad?" at this unassuming West LA Asian where the

get updates at zagat.com

The Westside F D S C

signature dish is so "amazing" and "unique" it "needs to be patented"; the digs are "functional" and not much else, so it's "best for takeout", even though "parking's a joke"; still, if you get "what they're famous for", it "makes circling the block worth it."

5 DUDLEY ⓜ 25 | 14 | 22 | $45
5 Dudley Ave. (bet. Oceanfront Walk & Speedway), Venice, 310-399-6678
■ "Quirky and absolutely brilliant", this "sweet", "tiny" Venice "beach hole-in-the-wall" is a "must for those looking for something different", where a "little kitchen that could" creates a "shape-shifting" menu of "delectable" Eclectic dishes, recited by a "hyper-informed" staff that deserves an "Oscar for best presentation"; you feel like you're at "a talented chef's house for a dinner party" in the "hip", "intimate" setting that's full of "character (or characters?)."

Four Oaks ⓜ 23 | 24 | 23 | $53
2181 N. Beverly Glen Blvd. (Beverly Glen Pl.), Bel Air, 310-470-2265; www.fouroaksrestaurant.com
■ "Get lost in Bel Air" at this "beautiful", "woodsy retreat" in a canyon between Sunset and Mulholland, where chef-owner Peter Roelant "keeps surprising you" with his "impressive", "exquisite" French-accented New American cuisine; whether in the "warm, inviting" "room with a fireplace", on the "lovey-dovey" outdoor patio or in the "gorgeous" garden, the "romantic" setting is a "sure way to win your date's heart", and the "wonderful" service won't hurt your cause.

Frankie & Johnnie's ◐ 18 | 10 | 15 | $19
9533 Santa Monica Blvd. (N. Beverly Dr.), Beverly Hills, 310-860-1155
See review in LA/Hollywood/W. Hollywood Directory.

French Country Cafe ⓢ ▽ 18 | 12 | 14 | $22
231 N. Beverly Dr. (Wilshire Blvd.), Beverly Hills, 310-273-4332
■ Where ladies who lunch go for a "quick, delicious" bite and a "little piece of France" "without the pretense", this Beverly Hills bistro is "perfect for a salad and a glass of wine" during a "shopping breather"; the "specials are just that", and the decor is "warm and charming."

Fritto Misto 21 | 11 | 19 | $19
601 Colorado Ave. (6th St.), Santa Monica, 310-458-2829
■ "Your imagination is the only limit" to what you can order at this "unpretentious", "great-value" Cal-Italian pair in Santa Monica and Hermosa Beach where you can "build your own pasta", or stick to your "low-carb" regimen with "veggie options" and "salads to die for"; the "garage"-like room may be "loud and cramped", but the service is "friendly and welcoming"; P.S. the "BYO policy in Hermosa [a $1.50 corkage fee] knocks down your tab."

The Westside   F | D | S | C |

Fromin's Restaurant & Deli   15 | 9 | 16 | $16 |
1832 Wilshire Blvd. (19th St.), Santa Monica, 310-829-5443
◪ "For a cozy dinner with the family", this deli duo in Santa Monica and Encino is the "real deal at a bargain price", where the "honest" fare is "as dependable as" the "friendly" service; together the two excuse the "cafeteria" seating and "'70s" decor that's way "overdue for a makeover."

Galley, The   20 | 18 | 19 | $33 |
2442 Main St. (bet. Ocean Park & Pico Blvds.), Santa Monica, 310-452-1934
■ Purportedly the oldest spot in Santa Monica (circa 1934), Captain Ron Schur's "rollicking", "unpretentious" surf 'n' turf "old-timer" is where you get "incredible" littleneck clams and "marvelous" steaks with a helping of "kitsch" in the "nautical-theme" setting; there's "so much history" here (at "modern-day prices").

GARDENS   24 | 26 | 25 | $53 |
Four Seasons Hotel, 300 S. Doheny Dr. (Burton Way), Beverly Hills, 310-273-2222; www.fourseasons.com
■ It's "like being in another country" at this "powerhouse" in the Beverly Hills Four Seasons, where the "excellent" Cal-Med cuisine, especially the "fabulous" Sunday brunch, an "ocean of sushi, waffles and everything in between", is "as impressive as the celebs" who light up the "beautiful room"; the staff is "knowledgeable" and "sexy, sexy, sexy."

Gardens on Glendon   19 | 21 | 18 | $33 |
1139 Glendon Ave. (Lindbrook Dr.), West LA, 310-824-1818; www.gardensonglendon.com
■ An "oasis in Westwood" with "nary a student in sight", this "lovely, if a little dated", upscale Californian housed in a "beautiful old building" is "excellent for a business lunch or dinner with your parents"; the "solid" menu offers a "nice choice of user-friendly dishes", but it's the "guacamole made at your table" that "keeps [many] coming back."

Gate of India   ∇ 21 | 15 | 16 | $25 |
115 Santa Monica Blvd. (Ocean Ave.), Santa Monica, 310-656-1664
◪ Putting its "own spin" on Indian cuisine, this "cute" Santa Monica storefront offers "exquisite", "nontraditional" dishes such as the "rich, decadent" coconut malai curry that are "superb" enough to "convert naysayers"; even true believers, however, are put off by the "spotty" service.

Gaucho Grill   18 | 15 | 16 | $21 |
11754 San Vicente Blvd. (bet. Montana & S. Barrington Aves.), Brentwood, 310-447-7898
1251 Third St. Promenade (3rd St.), Santa Monica, 310-394-4966
www.gauchogrillusa.com
See review in LA/Hollywood/W. Hollywood Directory.

get updates at zagat.com

The Westside | **F** | **D** | **S** | **C** |

GEOFFREY'S
| 22 | 27 | 22 | $47 |

27400 PCH (Malibu Canyon Rd.), Malibu, 310-457-1519; www.geoffreysmalibu.com

■ While fans find the fare "fabulous" and the service "outstanding", they're "almost besides the point" compared to the "incomparable", "postcard-perfect" view at this Malibu Californian situated on a cliff high above the Pacific; the "breathtakingly romantic" open-air setting will make "you feel like a movie star" "vacationing on the Riviera", but it's "not a place to go if you're in a hurry or on a budget."

Getty Center, Restaurant at the Ⓜ
| 21 | 24 | 21 | $38 |

The Getty Ctr., 1200 Getty Center Dr. (Frwy. 405), Brentwood, 310-440-6810; www.getty.edu

■ While the views from its "stunning location" are "drop dead" "spectacular" and the "spacious" room is "world-class" at the Getty's "spacious", upscale seasonal Cal spot, foodies insist the "art is in the kitchen", where "inventive", "beautifully presented" dishes are prepared; "attentive" service contributes to a "tranquil" dining experience "after walking through the museum."

Giorgio Baldi
| 26 | 18 | 20 | $53 |

114 W. Channel Rd. (PCH), Santa Monica, 310-573-1660

■ "Giorgio cooks like an angel" at his "sublime" Santa Monica Northern Italian half a block from the beach, creating "heavenly", "authentic" dishes for a "devoted clientele" that includes a "who's who in the industry"; the room is "small" and often "crowded", the staff can be "haughty if you're not a celebrity" and the "bill can creep up on you", but for a "star-studded" "night in Italy", *amici* insist, "it doesn't get any better than this."

Gladstone's Malibu
| 16 | 19 | 16 | $31 |

17300 PCH (Sunset Blvd.), Pacific Palisades, 310-573-0212; www.gladstones.com

☒ Fans and foes agree this Pacific Palisades seafooder is a "classic LA experience" – to the former this means "huge portions" of fin fare, an "unbeatable" ocean vista, "great margaritas" and "chipper, perky service"; to the latter, it's nothing more than an "overpriced" "tourist trap" where "you pay for the view", and a "wait, even with a reservation", is to be expected.

Globe Venice Beach
| ▽ 20 | 18 | 17 | $38 |

72 Market St. (Pacific Ave.), Venice, 310-392-8720

■ "Just steps from the beach", this "sophisticated" SF import has found a following in Venice Beach with "simple, well-prepared" New American fare, a "hopping bar" scene and an ambiance that's "just the right amount of funky without crossing the line to pretentiousness"; "exposed brick walls" give an "urban" feel to the "adorable" space.

The Westside   F | D | S | C

Granita Ⓜ   23 | 23 | 21 | $48
Malibu Colony Plaza, 23725 W. Malibu Rd. (PCH), Malibu, 310-456-0488; www.wolfgangpuck.com

■ Though it's "just off the beach", there's "no ocean view" at this Wolfgang Puck production located in a Malibu shopping mall, though there's plenty of sea in the room's "distinctive" "underwater motif"; "great stargazing" and "imaginative, perfectly prepared" Cal-Med cuisine are "surprising for its strip-mall location"; P.S. the "bread basket is a meal in itself", so "remember to leave room."

Gray Whale   ▽ 22 | 19 | 23 | $41
6800 Westward Beach Rd. (PCH), Malibu, 310-457-5521; www.graywhale.com

◪ At this surfside Continental nestled in a hidden cove in Malibu, you can "view dolphins frolicking in the waves", the "best sunsets in the world" and "even whales" as you tuck into "exceptional" cuisine such as the "excellent" steak Diane prepared tableside; the "formal service" makes it something of an "odd duck at the beach."

GRILL, THE   25 | 21 | 25 | $47
9560 Dayton Way (Wilshire Blvd.), Beverly Hills, 310-276-0615; www.thegrill.com

■ The "people-watching is incomparable" at this "NY steak joint in the heart of Beverly Hills", an "industry hot spot" where "heavy hitters" "power lunch" over "awesome veal chops and filet mignon" and other "sturdy" American comfort fare in a "clubby", "old-school" setting; still, the "professional" staff in "white jackets" provides "excellent service" to "everyone who steps through the door, even if you aren't from CAA."

Guelaguetza   22 | 8 | 17 | $16
11127 Palms Blvd. (Sepulveda Blvd.), Palms, 310-837-1153

■ For a taste of "what Mexican food should be", this Palms Oaxacan specialist is "worth visiting again and again" for "exquisite" cooking from the south of Mexico, especially "anything with black mole", the "deep, rich and savory" "Rolls Royce" of sauces that fanatics "could eat like soup"; if you "close your eyes, you're in Oaxaca", which is preferable to the "nondescript" room.

Guido's   20 | 18 | 23 | $35
11980 Santa Monica Blvd. (Bundy Dr.), West LA, 310-820-6649
3874 Cross Creek Rd. (PCH), Malibu, 310-456-1979; www.guidosmalibu.com

◪ "Superb", "old-world" service from an "unobtrusive" staff that "knows how to treat guests", "dependable", "quality" Northern Italian fare and a "comfortable" setting where you "can actually have a conversation" are what "attract an older crowd" to this veteran duo in West LA and Malibu.

get updates at zagat.com

The Westside

| | F | D | S | C |

Gulfstream
| | - | - | - | M |

Century City Shopping & Mktpl., 10250 Santa Monica Blvd. (Century Park W.), Century City, 310-553-3636; www.houstons.com

This latest concept from the people who gave us Houston's (and Bandera) is located in the space that was once home to Steven Spielberg's thematic hero sandwich shop Dive!; the previous incarnation's submarine theme has been replaced with what might be called 'Houston's: The Next Generation', with ceilings curved like ocean waves and a seafood-heavy menu of cherrywood smoked trout dip, cedar plank salmon and red snapper with rock shrimp sauce.

Gyu-kaku
| | 22 | 16 | 18 | $27 |

10925 W. Pico Blvd. (bet. Kelton & Midvale Aves.), West LA, 310-234-8641; www.gyu-kaku.com

■ "Korean-style Japanese BBQ – or is it Japanese-style Korean BBQ?" . . . whatever, the meat's "fantastic" and the bibimbop's "the best" at this West LA outpost of a Japan-based yakiniku chain where you "cook your own food" in a "friendly", "casual", but "crowded" setting that's a "fun" "group experience"; two caveats from cognoscenti: the "portions are small" and "pricey", and "hope you don't mind long waits."

Hal's Bar & Grill ◐
| | 20 | 20 | 18 | $35 |

1349 Abbot Kinney Blvd. (bet. Main St. & Venice Blvd.), Venice, 310-396-3105; www.halsbarandgrill.com

■ A "bit of SoHo on Abbott Kinney", this veteran Venice New American is a "big hangout for the art crowd", where "beautiful people" "troll the bar" or tuck into "creative variations" of old standards, served in a space resembling a "NY loft"; "always wear black and maybe bring earplugs", for the scene is "hip" and the "noise level's unreal."

Hamasaku ⓢ
| | 25 | 18 | 21 | $47 |

11043 Santa Monica Blvd. (Sepulveda Blvd.), West LA, 310-479-7636

■ Groupies gush they must "catch their fish in heaven" at this high-end Westside Cal-Japanese, where "master" chefs create "luscious", "incredible variations on sushi and sashimi" in addition to "superb, beautifully presented cooked dishes"; chef-owner Toshi Kihara is a "fantastic host" who "makes everyone feel like a celebrity" in this "star hangout" "tucked away in the corner of a strip mall."

Hama Sushi
| | 24 | 12 | 17 | $38 |

213 Windward Ave. (Main St.), Venice, 310-396-8783

■ Located next to the California Sushi Academy, this "funky dive" is the Venice hipoisie's "favorite" for "fresh" sushi in a "rowdy", "beachy" setting where "everyone sings and toasts", and the "entertaining chefs" cap off the evening with a rendition of "'Hotel California' at the top of their

The Westside F | D | S | C

lungs"; afishionados advise neophytes not to "play it safe", but rather "order the specials, no matter what they are."

Hamburger Hamlet   15 | 13 | 15 | $18
122 S. Beverly Dr. (Wilshire Blvd.), Beverly Hills, 310-274-0191
11648 San Vicente Blvd. (bet. Montana Ave. & Wilshire Blvd.), Brentwood, 310-826-3558
2927 Sepulveda Blvd. (National Blvd.), West LA, 310-478-1546
www.hamburgerhamlet.com
See review in LA/Hollywood/W. Hollywood Directory.

Hide Sushi M⌿   25 | 10 | 16 | $26
2040 Sawtelle Blvd. (bet. La Grange & Mississippi Aves.), West LA, 310-477-7242
■ Arrive "early to put your name on the chalkboard" at this cash-only cult favorite Japanese on Sawtelle where the "line extends out the door" for "fresh, fresh, fresh" sushi "so cheap they're practically giving it away"; the "decor rivals a discount clothing store dressing room" and the "staff can be downright ornery", but with "prices like this", afishionados have "no reason to go anywhere else."

Hop Li   19 | 11 | 15 | $18
10974 W. Pico Blvd. (Westwood Blvd.), West LA, 310-441-3708
See review in LA/Hollywood/W. Hollywood Directory.

Hop Woo   – | – | – | M
11110 W. Olympic Blvd. (S. Sepulveda Blvd.), West LA, 310-575-3668
Serious Sinophiles should not be put off by the mini-mall location or lack of parking of this midpriced storefront Cantonese seafooder in West LA, a hotbed of serious lobster (almost always selling at discount) and live prawns pulled fresh from the tanks that line one wall; it's also known for its Peking duck.

HOUSTON'S   21 | 19 | 20 | $29
Westfield Shoppingtown, 10250 Santa Monica Blvd. (Century Park W.), Century City, 310-557-1285
202 Wilshire Blvd. (2nd St.), Santa Monica, 310-576-7558
www.houstons.com
■ Fans attest "you can't go wrong" at these outposts of a national chain that are "always on the mark" with "reliable" "all-American" comfort food "done right", served in "dimly lit", "high-end surroundings" with "cozy booths"; "long waits for a table for lunch and dinner" that rival those at the "DMV" are proof that "they must be doing something right."

Hump, The   25 | 23 | 22 | $52
Santa Monica Airport, 3221 Donald Douglas Loop S. (Centinela Ave.), Santa Monica, 310-313-0977;
www.thehump-sushi.com
■ Named after a World War II supply route, this Santa Monica Japanese takes off with "first-rate" sushi and a

The Westside	F	D	S	C

"heavenly setting at the airport", where you can "watch planes take off 50 feet away" while tucking into "pricey", "hard-core" fare, including "live sweet shrimp" and seafood "so fresh it's still moving on your plate", that's "not for the squeamish" or the "bargain-hunting"; the "cool, romantic" glass-box space, surrounded by the airport lights, is a "great place to bring a date."

Hu's Szechwan
22 | 6 | 17 | $16

10450 National Blvd. (bet. Motor & Overland Aves.), Palms, 310-837-0252

■ "Everything's tasty – if it's delivered" from this Palms Chinese "hole-in-the-wall" serving "excellent" Szechuan cuisine in a "charmless" location with "almost no parking"; if you "don't care about atmosphere", you can "BYO and feast for little money" on "huge portions" of "addictive dumplings and shrimp" and other "authentic" dishes that are "among the best on the Westside."

i Cugini
21 | 21 | 20 | $36

1501 Ocean Ave. (B'way), Santa Monica, 310-451-4595; www.icugini.com

■ A "family favorite" that also works for "impressive dates or business meetings", this scion of King's Seafood Co. (King's Crab Lounge, King's Fish House, Ocean Ave, Seafood, Water Grill) "just off the Santa Monica beach" offers "consistently strong" Italian fare and seafood "prepared perfectly" in an open kitchen, "beautiful" decor and a "totally enjoyable" patio "with an ocean view"; the service is "friendly" and the Sunday brunch, featuring jazz music and a "scrumptious buffet", "makes all others seem insipid."

Il Buco
22 | 16 | 20 | $31

107 N. Robertson Blvd. (Wilshire Blvd.), Beverly Hills, 310-657-1345

■ A "neighborhood pleasure", this "cozy" spot on the edge of Beverly Hills offers a "great Italian experience", thanks to "simple", "delicious" dishes, such as the popular "favorite" pumpkin ravioli and "wonderful breads", and "flawless" service "without a trace of BH attitude"; the ambiance is "welcoming" but some regulars are not when they insist: "don't tell anyone about this place."

Il Cielo
20 | 26 | 21 | $45

9018 Burton Way (bet. Almont & Wetherly Drs.), Beverly Hills, 310-276-9990; www.ilcielo.com

■ "Go with someone special" to what many call the "most romantic restaurant in LA", a "charming" Tuscan cottage in Beverly Hills with "dreamy" gardens and "date-pleasing" old-world decor; the "mature, friendly" staff is "attentive without being overbearing" and the "lovely" Italian fare is "surprisingly good", all of which make it the "perfect place for a special occasion" or to "pop the question."

The Westside   F | D | S | C |

IL FORNAIO   20 | 19 | 19 | $29 |
301 N. Beverly Dr. (Dayton Way), Beverly Hills, 310-550-8330
1551 Ocean Ave. (Colorado Ave.), Santa Monica, 310-451-7800
www.ilfornaio.com

■ The "bread takes the cake" at this chain of bakery/Italians that offers a "delicious alternative" to the norm with an "authentic" menu of "solid standbys and interesting specials" as well as "irresistible" baked goods and "sumptuous" desserts; though the service can "vary by location", the decor is consistently "classy and hip."

Il Forno   21 | 13 | 20 | $28 |
2901 Ocean Park Blvd. (bet. 29th & 30th Sts.), Santa Monica, 310-450-1241
2450 Colorado Ave. (26th St.), Santa Monica, 310-449-9244 ⊠
www.ilfornocaffe.com

■ The "food, owners and servers are all so very Italian" at this "neighborhood favorite" next to Santa Monica Airport (and its branch on Colorado Avenue) where locals go for "delicious, unpretentious", "reasonably priced" fare and "friendly", "attentive" service in a "low-key" setting that's "perfect" when "you want a tablecloth but don't want to get dressed up."

Il Grano ⊠   24 | 18 | 23 | $39 |
11359 Santa Monica Blvd. (bet. Corinth & Purdue Aves.), West LA, 310-477-7886

■ "For the meal of a lifetime" cognoscenti counsel, "let Sal Marino make what he wants" at his West LA Italian, where his "passion" and "dedication to superlative ingredients" are evident in the "freshest produce and fish" that go into his "fabulous" seafood and "flavorful pastas"; "amicable" service and a "quiet", "unpretentious" setting create an "inviting atmosphere" for a "truly unique dining experience."

Il Moro   22 | 20 | 21 | $35 |
11400 W. Olympic Blvd. (Purdue Ave.), West LA, 310-575-3530;
www.ilmoro.com

■ An "oasis in a concrete desert", with a "romantic, serene" patio that "feels far from the rush of Olympic Boulevard", this West LA Northern Italian is a "good place to impress a guest", "client" or "business associate"; "fabulous pastas", "fantastic" risotto and other "outstanding" dishes are prepared in an open kitchen and "beautifully served in a gorgeous setting" with a "wonderful" private room.

Il Pastaio   24 | 16 | 20 | $33 |
400 N. Cañon Dr. (Brighton Way), Beverly Hills, 310-205-5444;
www.celestinodrago.com

■ "Nobody makes pasta and risotto like Giacomino Drago", who presides over this "terrific, not-so-secret" haunt in Beverly Hills offering "big taste in a tiny space"; while the "tables are so close you have no choice but join in your

get updates at zagat.com   **115**

The Westside   F D S C

neighbor's conversation", the "classy" staff makes up for the "claustrophobic" setting and may even "serve you a little something on the house while you peruse the menu."

India's Oven   19 | 11 | 16 | $19
11645 Wilshire Blvd. (bet. Barrington & Barry Aves.), West LA, 310-207-5522
See review in LA/Hollywood/W. Hollywood Directory.

India's Tandoori   19 | 11 | 18 | $18
11819 Wilshire Blvd. (bet. Granville & S. Westgate Aves.), West LA, 310-268-9100
See review in LA/Hollywood/W. Hollywood Directory.

Indo Cafe M   ▽ 22 | 11 | 19 | $19
10428½ National Blvd. (Motor Ave.), Palms, 310-815-1290
■ This "tiny hole-in-the-wall" BYO in working-class Palms is "definitely worth hitting" for "cheap", "incredibly tasty, authentic" Indonesian cuisine served in a "friendly", "welcoming" atmosphere; while the "bare-bones" quarters now "have a little flesh" after a recent redo, for most it's still the "food that pleases the eye" rather than the decor.

INN OF THE SEVENTH RAY   20 | 28 | 20 | $35
128 Old Topanga Canyon Rd. (4 mi. north of PCH), Topanga, 310-455-1311; www.innoftheseventhray.com
■ Like a "little piece of heaven", the "idyllic", "creekside" setting of this Topanga Canyon Californian, nestled amid "towering pine trees" where "coyotes watch you eat", is an "otherworldly experience"; while it's not strictly vegetarian, the "healthy, socially conscious" menu includes many vegan options ("truly superb faux duck") among its "delicious, nutritious" offerings; "beautiful place, beautiful food" – "who cares if the service is slow?"

IN-N-OUT BURGER ●   24 | 10 | 18 | $7
13425 Washington Blvd. (Centinela Ave.), Culver City, 800-786-1000
9245 W. Venice Blvd. (Robertson Blvd.), Culver City, 800-786-1000
922 Gayley Ave. (Wilshire Blvd.), Westwood, 800-786-1000
www.in-n-out.com
See review in LA/Hollywood/W. Hollywood Directory.

Islands   16 | 16 | 17 | $14
350 S. Beverly Dr. (Olympic Blvd.), Beverly Hills, 310-556-1624
404 Washington Blvd. (Via Marina), Marina del Rey, 310-822-3939
10948 W. Pico Blvd. (Veteran Ave.), West LA, 310-474-1144
www.islandsrestaurants.com
■ This "family-oriented Hawaiian-style hamburger" chain "has it all" – a "diverse menu selection" to "please hungry kids or adults", service "with a smile from friendly folks wearing aloha gear" and a "boffo tropical setting"; "bring

The Westside

| F | D | S | C |

your appetite and your earplugs" to these "dens of din", and "don't wear your Sunday best."

IVY AT THE SHORE ◐   23 | 21 | 20 | $50
1541 Ocean Ave. (bet. B'way & Colorado Ave.), Santa Monica, 310-393-3113

■ While "not as star-studded" as the Robertson Boulevard original, this "fun", "comfortable" outpost offers "fabulous" New American classics and "world-class" Ivy gimlets in a "resort casual" space across from the Santa Monica pier; as a "receptacle of disposable income", it concedes nothing to its elder sibling ("the only thing missing from the dessert tray are the smelling salts").

Jaan   ▽ 18 | 25 | 23 | $59
Raffles L'Ermitage Hotel, 9291 Burton Way (bet. Foothill Rd. & Maple Dr.), Beverly Hills, 310-278-3344; www.jaanrestaurant.com

◪ Since the departure of longtime chef David Myers from this "quiet dining room of an upscale Beverly Hills hotel", new chef Bruno Lopez has introduced a modern French/New American menu that's served in a "pretty", polished space; surveyors note that it's not unusual to experience "mediocrity and excellence in the same evening."

Jack Sprat's Grille   18 | 11 | 16 | $20
10668 W. Pico Blvd. (Overland Ave.), West LA, 310-837-6662; www.jackspratsgrille.com

■ "Tasty food for the always-on-a-diet crowd" is the draw at this West LA "health-conscious" Californian dishing up complimentary "delish soft pretzels instead of bread", "killer air-baked fries" and "salads that are too big to finish"; it's "small" and "noisy", but "reliable" "for times when you're feeling virtuous but still want to eat well."

Jacopo's ◐   17 | 8 | 14 | $16
490 N. Beverly Dr. (Little Santa Monica Blvd.), Beverly Hills, 310-858-6446
15415 Sunset Blvd. (Via de la Paz), Pacific Palisades, 310-454-8494
11676 W. Olympic Blvd. (Barrington Ave.), West LA, 310-477-2111
www.jacopos.com

◪ Surveyors are split on this long-standing Westside trio (with a location in West Hollywood) of "basic", "everyday" Italian "joints": proponents say it "delivers on the simple things", so it's "good for a quick pizza or bowl of pasta", particularly if you have "young children"; but opponents pan it as "pricey" for "mediocre" pies in a "bare-bones" setting.

James' Beach   18 | 18 | 18 | $34
60 N. Venice Blvd. (Pacific Ave.), Venice, 310-823-5396

■ The "patio brunch is what California is all about", along with "lots of beautiful people on hot nights" hanging at the "great outdoor bar" at this Venice Traditional American;

The Westside

| F | D | S | C |

there's "enjoyable" "comfort" food like fried chicken, but this is basically a "happening scene" "where the beach dudes and dudettes go to pretend they're in West Hollywood."

Javan 21 | 14 | 18 | $22
11500 Santa Monica Blvd. (Butler Ave.), West LA, 310-207-5555
■ There are "mounds of rice" and "anything with lamb is great", but it's mostly "meat on a stick that appeals to every man's inner Neanderthal" at this "pleasant Persian" on the Westside; it's a "cheerful, big-scale" place when it comes to "portions, families and noise" but not when it comes to price.

Jimmy's Tavern ⊠ – | – | – | M
10543 W. Pico Blvd. (Patricia Ave.), West LA, 310-446-8808; www.jimmystavern.us
The fabled Jimmy Murphy – boulevardier, raconteur and man-about-town – returns with a mini-version of Jimmy's (his former Century City place) at this newcomer across from the Rancho Park Golf Course; look for the pianist situated next to the fireplace, a menu of the eponymous owner's longtime classics – French onion soup, Dublin Bay prawn salad – and sundry new Continental dishes from chef David Fouts (Beach House, Josie's, Granita).

Jinky's 21 | 10 | 16 | $13
1447 Second St. (B'way), Santa Monica, 310-917-3311
See review in San Fernando Valley/Burbank Directory.

JIRAFFE 26 | 22 | 24 | $49
502 Santa Monica Blvd. (5th St.), Santa Monica, 310-917-6671; www.jirafferestaurant.com
■ "Have the blood orange martini" when you arrive at chef-owner Raphael Lunetta's "perfect", "always a pleasure" Californian on the edge of the Third Street Promenade, where "fabulous" "four-star food without the four-star price and stuffiness" is served by an "excellent, unobtrusive" staff in a "beautiful" bi-level setting ("upstairs is quieter"); in short, it "lives up to its tall name."

Jody Maroni's Sausage Kingdom 19 | 6 | 13 | $9
2011 Ocean Front Walk (20th Ave.), Venice, 310-822-5639
Westfield Shoppingtown, 10250 Santa Monica Blvd. (Century Park W.), Century City, 310-556-0899
Howard Hughes Ctr., 6081 Center Dr. (bet. Culver & Washington Blvds.), Culver City, 310-348-0007
www.jodymaroni.com
■ "You won't need a computer to access these hyperlinks" found all over town (though the original is on the Venice Boardwalk), whose fans know that "eating a Jody's sausage is a life-altering experience"; "one of LA's great food inventions", this "California icon astounds the taste buds" and come in almost "any flavor", from the "great chicken-apple" to the "andouille with onions and peppers."

The Westside | F | D | S | C |

JOE'S Ⓜ | 27 | 21 | 23 | $46 |
1023 Abbot Kinney Blvd. (bet. Main St. & Westminster Ave.), Venice, 310-399-5811; www.joesrestaurant.com
■ "Joe Miller delivers creative, vibrant food" at his Venice production, a "consistently outstanding" Californian where "you can sit by the kitchen and watch him work his magic" in a space that began as a single storefront and has expanded into a "charming" warren of rooms; "excellent value for what you get" means that "it's a great place to go", and you might even see "Hillary Swank at brunch."

Johnnie's New York Pizzeria & Caffe | 18 | 11 | 15 | $15 |
10251 Santa Monica Blvd. (bet. Ave. of the Stars & Beverly Glen Blvd.), Century City, 310-553-1188
342 N. Beverly Dr. (bet. Brighton & Dayton Ways), Beverly Hills, 310-246-0099
22333 PCH (1 mi. south of Malibu Pier), Malibu, 310-456-1717
Hoyt Plaza, 2805 Abbot Kinney Blvd. (Washington Blvd.), Marina del Rey, 310-821-1224
1456 Third St. Promenade (Colorado Ave.), Santa Monica, 310-395-9062
11870 Santa Monica Blvd. (bet. Amacost & Westgate Aves.), West LA, 310-820-7420
See review in LA/Hollywood/W. Hollywood Directory.

Johnnie's Pastrami ●≠ | 21 | 9 | 15 | $12 |
4017 S. Sepulveda Blvd. (bet. Washington Blvd. & Washington Pl.), Culver City, 310-397-6654
■ "Sit outdoors next to the fire pits" or "pick songs from the jukeboxes on the indoor tables" at this Culver City "classic" deli/coffee shop where "the pastrami is excellent" and the "pickles are wonderful"; it's a "local institution" that's "open late" and attracts all kinds of Angelinos who drive everything "from pickups to Bentleys."

Johnny Rockets ● | 16 | 15 | 16 | $12 |
Westfield Shoppingtown, 10250 Santa Monica Blvd. (Century Park W.), Century City, 310-788-9020
474 N. Beverly Dr. (Little Santa Monica Blvd.), Beverly Hills, 310-271-2222
Howard Hughes Ctr., 6081 Center Dr. (Sepulveda Blvd.), Culver City, 310-670-7555
1322 Third St. Promenade (Wilshire Blvd.), Santa Monica, 310-394-6362
www.johnnyrockets.com
See review in LA/Hollywood/W. Hollywood Directory.

John O'Groats | 21 | 12 | 18 | $15 |
10516 W. Pico Blvd. (Beverly Glen Blvd.), Rancho Park, 310-204-0692
■ Named for the northernmost town in Scotland, this non-Scottish (except for the oatmeal) New American, across

get updates at zagat.com 119

The Westside   F | D | S | C

from the Rancho Park Golf Course serves up "ecstasy-inducing buttermilk biscuits", "perfectly cooked farm-fresh eggs" and the occasional "lobster eggs Benedict"; it can be "crowded" and the "tables and chairs don't match, but who cares when the food tastes this good?"

JOSIE RESTAURANT   27 | 24 | 25 | $55
2424 Pico Blvd. (25th St.), Santa Monica, 310-581-9888; www.josierestaurant.com

■ Supporters say Josie Le Balch is the "most creative chef to hit Santa Monica in years" – she's a "master at cooking game" and turning it into "heaven on a plate", and her "truffle fries give new meaning to the phrase 'oh my God!'"; a "polished" staff presides over this "understated but exquisite" New American "where everything tastes and feels like the best", "so if you're game this is the place."

JR's BBQ   ▽ 24 | 8 | 20 | $17
3055 S. La Cienega Blvd. (Blackwelder St.), Culver City, 310-837-6838

■ This "little hole-in-the-wall" in the industrial zone where Fairfax and La Cienega meet is a "trip down to Tennessee without the headache of LAX"; ribs "so good they'll have you speaking with a drawl" are served with "three kinds of sauce" and the "best-ever baked beans" by a "friendly" staff, which adds to its "addictive" appeal.

JR Seafood   20 | 11 | 15 | $21
11901 Santa Monica Blvd. (Amacost Ave.), West LA, 310-268-2463

■ Going to this Santa Monica Boulevard seafooder is "like having Chinatown on the Westside" and has saved many the long trip Downtown for "fine hot-and-sour soup", "great shrimp in black bean sauce" and dim sum at lunchtime; service can be "surly", but the food is a "bargain both in quantity and quality."

Juliano's Raw   - | - | - | I
609 Broadway (6th St.), Santa Monica, 310-587-1552; www.julianosraw.com

Juliano made his mark in San Francisco with a belief in the virtue of eating it raw; now, he's set up shop in an industrial-looking space in Santa Monica, where he offers 'Gourmet Living Cuisine', meaning meatless and resolutely uncooked items like unheated soups, mock salmon sushi and a 'cheezeburger', with smoothies to wash it all down.

Junior's   16 | 9 | 14 | $17
2379 Westwood Blvd. (W. Pico Blvd.), West LA, 310-475-5771

◪ Since 1959, this sprawling Westside deli "institution" has been dishing out Jewish "comfort food" like corned beef sandwiches, chicken soup and cheesecake to "crowds" of "regulars"; but bashers who bemoan the "run-down" setting and only "so-so" fare say "it will do in a pinch, but isn't worth seeking out."

The Westside   F | D | S | C

Kabob & Chinese   ▽ 19 | 10 | 14 | $20
11330 Santa Monica Blvd. (Corinth Ave.), West LA, 310-914-3040
See review in LA/Hollywood/W. Hollywood Directory.

Kate Mantilini ●   17 | 17 | 17 | $30
9101 Wilshire Blvd. (Doheny Dr.), Beverly Hills, 310-278-3699
◪ Open until at least midnight, this "timeless" Traditional American is the "hip", "late-night" "place to go in Beverly Hills" for "consistent" "upscale coffee shop comfort food" like rotisserie chicken and white chili; wallet-watchers dub it "too expensive", but as people-watchers patiently explain "it's good for star sightings – that's why you have to pay so much for macaroni 'n' cheese."

Kay 'n Dave's   18 | 13 | 19 | $17
262 26th St. (San Vicente Blvd.), Santa Monica, 310-260-1355
15246 Sunset Blvd. (bet. Monument St. & Swarthmore Ave.), Pacific Palisades, 310-459-8118
■ These "cheap, healthy" Mexicans in Santa Monica and the Palisades may be "Americanized", but they're also "kid-friendly" and have their walls decorated with "young customers' drawings"; "no weekend is complete without a trip here" for "salsa I can drink by the bowl" in this lard-free, can-free, microwave-free zone that makes them "something-for-everyone" spots.

Killer Shrimp   20 | 10 | 15 | $20
523 Washington Blvd. (Via Marina), Marina del Rey, 310-578-2293
■ "Like the name states", these shellfish shacks in the Marina and Studio City focus on "delectably spicy peel-and-eat shrimp" in a "hot sauce eaten with bread (for dipping), pasta or rice"; "they may have only one thing on the menu" and it's served up by "punk rockers with attitude", but it's seafood the "way sex should be – hot, messy and satisfying."

Knoll's Black Forest Inn ⑤Ⓜ   23 | 20 | 23 | $40
2454 Wilshire Blvd. (bet. Chelsea Ave. & 25th St.), Santa Monica, 310-395-2212
■ "Warm", "old-world" family-run establishment with the "best German food in LA", including "excellent Wiener schnitzel" and a seasonal "white asparagus menu that shouldn't be missed"; "it's decorated beautifully, especially during the Christmas holidays", and in summer the "patio area is the place to be."

Koo Koo Roo   16 | 8 | 13 | $11
435 N. Beverly Dr. (Little Santa Monica Blvd.), Beverly Hills, 310-859-3434
262 S. Beverly Dr. (bet. Charleville Blvd. & Gregory Way), Beverly Hills, 310-274-3121

(continued)

get updates at zagat.com

The Westside | F | D | S | C |

(continued)
Koo Koo Roo
11650 San Vicente Blvd. (Darlington Ave.), Brentwood, 310-207-3232
2002 Wilshire Blvd. (20th St.), Santa Monica, 310-453-8767
255 Main St. (Rose Ave.), Venice, 310-452-3722
11066 Santa Monica Blvd. (Sepulveda Blvd.), West LA, 310-473-5858
12081 Wilshire Blvd. (S. Bundy Dr.), West LA, 310-477-4321
www.kookooroo.com
See review in LA/Hollywood/W. Hollywood Directory.

Koutoubia ▫ ∇ 23 | 23 | 21 | $37 |
2116 Westwood Blvd. (bet. Mississippi Ave. & W. Olympic Blvd.), West LA, 310-475-0729; www.koutoubiarestaurant.com
■ "Round up your friends for a feast" at this "hidden gem on Westwood Boulevard", a "wonderful Moroccan in a caravansary setting" where you "sit on low couches, eat" "delicious food" "with your fingers" and feel like "you've left LA"; while some "could do without the belly dancer" (weekend nights only), most say the "helpful", "personable" owner adds to the place's appeal.

La Bottega Marino ∇ 22 | 14 | 19 | $20 |
11363 Santa Monica Blvd. (Purdue Ave.), West LA, 310-477-7777
See review in LA/Hollywood/W. Hollywood Directory.

La Bruschetta Ristorante ▫ 21 | 17 | 22 | $34 |
1621 Westwood Blvd. (bet. Massachusetts & Ohio Aves.), Westwood, 310-477-1052; www.labruschettaristorante.com
■ "Angelo is the consummate host" who's "always there to ensure his customers are happy" at this "neighborhood Italian that's a step above" in Westwood; everyone gets a "complimentary bruschetta appetizer" at this "old-world" establishment with "excellent pasta and tender veal."

LA CACHETTE 26 | 24 | 24 | $55 |
10506 Santa Monica Blvd. (bet. Beverly Glen Blvd. & Overland Ave.), Century City, 310-470-4992; www.lacachetterestaurant.com
■ "Light French isn't an oxymoron" at this Century City star with a Californian accent where chef-owner Jean François is "fantastic in the kitchen", preparing "well-presented, innovative dishes" complemented by an "extensive wine list"; a "stellar staff" presides over an "elegant", "softly lit" setting that's "perfect for special occasions or a romantic date"; it's "pricey" and attracts an "older crowd."

La Dijonaise Cafe 20 | 16 | 18 | $19 |
Helms Bldg., 8703 Washington Blvd. (Helms Ave.), Culver City, 310-287-2770
■ "Delicious food for breakfast, lunch and dinner" is what fans find at this "authentic" French "bistro in the heart of

The Westside F | D | S | C

Culver City", where "they make croissants the way they're supposed to be made", "wonderful crêpes" and "delicious coq au vin"; "everything is Farmer's Market fresh" and prices are "reasonable."

L.A. Farm 20 | 22 | 20 | $38
3000 W. Olympic Blvd. (bet. Centinela Ave. & Stewart St.), Santa Monica, 310-449-4000; www.lafarm.com

■ A "sparkling island of good taste in an otherwise dreary neighborhood" of Santa Monica studios and production houses (it sits in the George Lucas–owned Skywalker Studios near Sony Records and MGM), this Cal-French is also an industry hang for "power lunches" when "lawyers, agents and actors galore" gather in the "sunlit atrium" "for good eavesdropping" and "Zone-friendly meals."

Lamonica's NY Pizza 22 | 11 | 15 | $9
1066 Gayley Ave. (Kinross St.), Westwood, 310-208-8671

■ "Wicked good pizza, thin and crispy", makes this Westwood storefront "decorated to look like a NY subway station" "heaven for transplanted" Manhattanites who particularly praise the mushroom and "spicy sausage" pies; it's an "open-late", "no-frills (get in, get out)" "bang-for-the-buck" spot that "students can afford."

La Salsa 16 | 9 | 13 | $10
9631 Santa Monica Blvd. (bet. Bedford & Camden Drs.), Beverly Hills, 310-276-2373
11740 San Vicente Blvd. (Gorham Ave.), Brentwood, 310-826-7337
1401 Third St. Promenade (Santa Monica Blvd.), Santa Monica, 310-587-0755
11901 Santa Monica Blvd. (Amacost Ave.), West LA, 310-473-7880
1154 Westwood Blvd. (Lindbrook Dr.), Westwood, 310-208-7083
www.lasalsa.com
See review in LA/Hollywood/W. Hollywood Directory.

La Scala 22 | 17 | 21 | $31
434 N. Cañon Dr. (bet. Brighton Way & Little Santa Monica Blvd.), Beverly Hills, 310-275-0579

■ After moving up the street to a "lovely", "roomier" new location, this "old-school Beverly Hills" Northern Italian still serves the "best chopped salad anywhere" and other "classics" to a crowd full of "familiar old Hollywood faces" in a "comfortable neighborhood" setting; the "friendly" service "hasn't changed" either, and regulars say "just keep it that way, thank you."

La Scala Presto 17 | 13 | 17 | $23
11740 San Vicente Blvd. (Barrington Ave.), Brentwood, 310-826-6100

■ The "chopped salad is what lures" many fans to this "less expensive version" of La Scala in Brentwood, though

get updates at zagat.com

The Westside | F | D | S | C |

the Bolognese is "worth the trip" and the "pizza's a winner", too; the atmosphere is "terrific", and "warm summer evenings on the patio" are "always enjoyable."

La Serenata de Garibaldi | 23 | 18 | 19 | $28 |
1416 Fourth St. (bet. B'way & Santa Monica Blvd.), Santa Monica, 310-656-7017
See review in LA/Hollywood/W. Hollywood Directory.

La Serenata Gourmet | 22 | 14 | 17 | $23 |
10924 W. Pico Blvd. (Westwood Blvd.), West LA, 310-441-9667
■ The menu leans more toward *antojitos* (small dishes) at this "super-casual", "delicious" West LA offspring of La Serenata de Garibaldi that "elevates simple tacos to an art form", serves "unbeatable mole and fish" and "reminds you Mexico has a cuisine, and a fine one"; since "you can't beat it for the price", no wonder it's "popular."

Lavande | ▽ 20 | 25 | 21 | $51 |
Loews Santa Monica Beach Hotel, 1700 Ocean Ave. (bet. Pacific & Seaview Terraces), Santa Monica, 310-576-3180
◪ The "gorgeous formal room" and the "ocean views" are like a "dream" at this Med housed in the Loews Santa Monica Beach Hotel; the "attentive" service "can't be beat" and the "romantic" setting is "great for a quiet dinner" of "fine" cuisine, but many still say "they miss Alain Giraud."

La Vecchia Cucina | 21 | 17 | 20 | $31 |
2654 Main St. (bet. Hill St. & Ocean Park Blvd.), Santa Monica, 310-399-7979; www.lavecchiacucina.com
■ "NY-style" Northern Italian that's a "solid neighborhood" Santa Monica "favorite" in a "great location" where the "pizzas and pastas are always tasty", and the "olive oil and garlic dipping sauce with bread keeps us returning for more"; claustrophobics complain that the "only downside" is that "tightly packed tables" mean "it can get noisy and crowded", but loyalists like that "lively vibe."

LAWRY'S THE PRIME RIB | 25 | 22 | 25 | $43 |
100 N. La Cienega Blvd. (Wilshire Blvd.), Beverly Hills, 310-652-2827; www.lawrysonline.com
■ "Save the lo-cal fish dinner for another night", for this Beverly Hills dowager is a "landmark" meat mecca that also offers side dishes that "are nothing to scoff at either"; a "uniformed staff" pushes "retro serving carts" through a sprawling series of paneled spaces that resemble a "grand ballroom"; N.B. Lawry's Cavery, the cheaper, more casual Costa Mesa offshoot, features hand-carved sandwiches.

Le Marmiton | 18 | 13 | 15 | $26 |
1327 Montana Ave. (14th St.), Santa Monica, 310-393-7716
■ Take a "sidewalk seat and watch the rich and famous" pass by on Santa Monica's trendy Montana Avenue at this "modest" French bistro featuring classics like coq au vin,

The Westside | F | D | S | C |

"great crêpes and omelets" for breakfast and "take-out goodies" to put together a "perfect feast"; the food "could be more cutting edge" considering the neighborhood and "*beaucoup d'attitude*" from the staff, but "reasonable prices" appeal to most.

Le Pain Quotidien | 21 | 18 | 15 | $17 |
9630 Little Santa Monica Blvd. (bet. Bedford & Camden Drs.), Beverly Hills, 310-859-1100
11702 Barrington Ct. (bet. Barrington Ave. & Sunset Blvd.), Brentwood, 310-476-0969
www.painquotidien.com
See review in LA/Hollywood/W. Hollywood Directory.

Le Petit Bistro | 20 | 19 | 18 | $32 |
11829 Wilshire Blvd. (Westgate Ave.), West LA, 310-575-3777; www.lepetitzinc.net
See review in LA/Hollywood/W. Hollywood Directory.

Le Petit Café ⌂ | 22 | 15 | 21 | $28 |
2842 Colorado Ave. (bet. Stewart & Yale Sts.), Santa Monica, 310-829-6792; www.lepetitcafe.info
■ A "pleasing, little" price-is-right place, this "slice of France" in a "funky" corner of Santa Monica features the chef-owner's "utterly consistent" and "delicious" cooking, from "fabulous lobster bisque" to bouillabaisse and cassoulet; "it's not much to look at", but it's "homey" and has "plenty of loyalists" who pronounce it "delightful."

Le Saigon ⓂØ | ▽ 23 | 7 | 19 | $11 |
11611 Santa Monica Blvd. (bet. Barry & Federal Aves.), West LA, 310-312-2929
■ "Crowded little hole-in-the-wall" in West LA offering "reliable", "absolutely mouthwatering" Vietnamese food – "each dish is better than the next", from the "fresh vegetables to the shrimp and pork spring rolls"; throw in "low prices" and "what more could you ask for?"

Lilly's French Cafe & Wine Bar | 21 | 20 | 17 | $35 |
1031 Abbot Kinney Blvd. (bet. B'way & Westminster Ave.), Venice, 310-314-0004
■ "Proof that the French are our friends", this "bit of Paris in Venice" is best appreciated from the "outdoor patio in a beautiful garden" where the "friendly staff" will "guide you through" an "authentic" French bistro menu that's backed up by a "good wine list" (55 by the glass); there are "great lunch specials," and it's also "cheerful" for Sunday brunch.

Literati Café | 21 | 22 | 20 | $13 |
12081 Wilshire Blvd. (S. Bundy Dr.), West LA, 310-231-7484; www.literaticafe.com
■ This Brentwood "neighborhood" Eclectic is "packed" with literate locals like screenwriters and "students with laptops" who like the "relaxing", "cozy" atmosphere, which

The Westside F | D | S | C

includes a fireplace, mellow music and "whimsical photos of celebrities", along with "delicious" soups, salads and desserts with a health-food emphasis and "excellent organic coffee" and teas; "service is quick and friendly, and the price can't be beat."

LOBSTER, THE 23 | 24 | 21 | $47
1602 Ocean Ave. (Santa Monica Pier), Santa Monica, 310-458-9294; www.thelobster.com

■ Even the "spunky" "staff stops to watch the sunset" at this Santa Monica Pier American seafooder that boasts a "beautiful ocean" vista, along with the "fabulous" cooking of Allyson Thurber, who "just keeps getting better" as dishes like "great lobster" ("prepared all sorts of ways") and "sublime scallops" attest; "amazing", albeit "noisy" on a summer night, this is "the best place in LA to leave work early for."

Locanda del Lago 20 | 19 | 20 | $34
231 Arizona Ave. (3rd St. Promenade), Santa Monica, 310-451-3525; www.lagosantamonica.com

■ "Perfect after a movie on the Promenade" or "for lunch on Farmer's Market Wednesday", this "always pleasant" Northern Italian that specializes in the cooking of the Lake District features "excellent" dishes like "perfect classic osso buco with saffron risotto" served by a "polite staff"; the rustic interior is "comfortable", but the "outside tables are the best place for people-watching."

Louise's Trattoria 15 | 14 | 16 | $21
264 26th St. (Minerva St.), Brentwood, 310-451-5001
1008 Montana Ave. (10th St.), Santa Monica, 310-394-8888
www.louises.com

See review in LA/Hollywood/W. Hollywood Directory.

Lunaria ⊠ 19 | 19 | 18 | $38
10351 Santa Monica Blvd. (Beverly Glen Blvd.), Century City, 310-282-8870; www.lunariajazzscene.com

◪ Part restaurant, part "cool" jazz club with a wall that slides open during the evening, turning both spaces into one, this Century City French-Italian is a "reliable" spot for "food, music and conversation" according to fans, but the less-swayed are "unimpressed" because the riffs are "better than" the fare.

MAKO ⊠ 26 | 20 | 23 | $45
225 S. Beverly Dr. (Charleville Blvd.), Beverly Hills, 310-288-8338; www.makorestaurant.com

■ Chef Makoto Tanaka's "talent for Asian cuisine is unparalleled" and on display at the Beverly Hills spot he runs with his wife Lisa Brady, where the "flavor combos are nothing short of amazing" on the "tapanese" menu of "fabulous" small plates; "sampling's a blast" and "sharing is fun" in the "Zen minimalist" room with a "warm, friendly"

The Westside F | D | S | C |

ambiance that serves as an "industry hangout at lunch and foodie scene at night."

Malibu Seafood 23 | 11 | 13 | $16 |
25653 PCH (1½ mi. north of Malibu Canyon Rd.), Malibu, 310-456-3430; www.malibufishandseafood.com
◪ At this "super-casual" seafood shack across from the beach in Malibu, the "view of the Pacific can't be beat", nor can the "fresh fish" that "might have been swimming in it this morning", "cooked any way you want"; the "decor's spectacular" "if you count the ocean", otherwise it's just outdoor "picnic tables", so "don't wear anything fancier than beach clothes."

Mandarin, The 20 | 18 | 17 | $32 |
430 N. Camden Dr. (bet. Brighton Way & Santa Monica Blvd.), Beverly Hills, 323-272-0267
■ "Old Hollywood still comes" to this "reliable" Chinese "standby" in Beverly Hills for "plucky duck", "great cold noodles with peanut sauce", "amazing lettuce wraps" and other "solid" Sino "classics", served by a "friendly" staff, while aficionados lunch in the "noodle shop in the back"; devotees declare "after all these years, it still rocks."

Manhattan Wonton Company 16 | 17 | 15 | $30 |
151 S. Doheny Dr. (bet. Charleville & Wilshire Blvds.), Beverly Hills, 310-888-2804
◪ The look of this sprawling Sino spot next to Beverly Hills' WGA Theater is "hip and new" but the menu is "retro" "NY-style Chinese" all the way, from the "egg rolls" and "duck sauce" to "succulent dumplings" that evoke memories of "Sunday nights"; it's "expensive" and the service can be "clueless", but fans "end up here quite often" anyway.

Mäni's Bakery 18 | 11 | 13 | $12 |
2507 Main St. (Ocean Park Blvd.), Santa Monica, 310-396-7700; www.manisbakery.com
See review in LA/Hollywood/W. Hollywood Directory.

Maple Drive ☒ 23 | 22 | 21 | $45 |
345 N. Maple Dr. (Alden Dr.), Beverly Hills, 310-274-9800; www.mapledriverestaurant.com
■ "You'd be hard-pressed to get a bad meal" at this "high-end" "show business hangout" "hidden away" in an entertainment complex on a "quiet" Beverly Hills backstreet, where "power brokers" and assorted "pretty people" tuck into "inspired" takes on American "old favorites", such as the "best meatloaf around", to the strains of "lovely" live jazz that fill the "ultrahip, modern" room most nights.

Marguerite ▽ 20 | 16 | 16 | $20 |
123 Washington Blvd. (Pacific Ave.), Marina del Rey, 310-822-5379
■ It's "like sitting in Paris" at this "perfect little French cafe" just "blocks from Venice Beach" that's a "delight for

get updates at zagat.com

The Westside

| F | D | S | C |

breakfast" or a "relaxed Sunday brunch", with "baguettes and coffee" that are "pure bliss" and "pastries that leave you saying ooh-la-la"; the service can be "slow" (hint: "hire more waiters"), however, so remember the "sunscreen if you want to eat outside."

Marix Tex Mex Café ⊠ — 17 | 15 | 16 | $21
118 Entrada Dr. (PCH), Santa Monica, 310-459-8596; www.marixtexmex.com
See review in LA/Hollywood/W. Hollywood Directory.

Marmalade Café — 18 | 17 | 17 | $23
3894 Cross Creek Rd. (PCH), Malibu, 310-317-4242
710 Montana Ave. (7th St.), Santa Monica, 310-395-9196
■ For "breakfast, brunch, lunch and dinner", this growing chain of "elegant, casual" Cal-American shops impresses with an "endless menu" of "sensational" soups, "generous" sandwiches, "outstanding" baked goods, "amazing" desserts and more; the "charming" setting is "nice for families and friends"; P.S. "if you don't want to eat out", try the "prepared foods counter."

Mastro's Steakhouse — 26 | 24 | 23 | $57
246 N. Cañon Dr. (bet. Clifton & Dayton Ways), Beverly Hills, 310-888-8782; www.mastrossteakhouse.com
■ A "hip place for the young and old" alike, this "classic steakhouse" in Beverly Hills is an "adult carnivore's dream", offering "perfectly prepared" steaks and "interesting" sides, "oversized" martinis and "fabulous" Cosmos in a "warm, inviting" downstairs dining room, while upstairs, there's a "party every night" in the "fun but loud", "Vegas"-like piano lounge; P.S. for private dining, the "all-white" Gallery Room is an "intimate, elegant cocoon of calm."

MATSUHISA — 28 | 17 | 23 | $68
129 N. La Cienega Blvd. (bet. Clifton Way & Wilshire Blvd.), Beverly Hills, 310-659-9639; www.nobumatsuhisa.com
■ Voted LA's No. 1 for Food for the fifth consecutive year, Nobu Matsuhisa's Beverly Hills flagship is "one place where you'll ignore the Hollywood celebrities" and focus on the "magnificent" Japanese cuisine, from "super-fresh" sushi to "melt-in-your-mouth" Kobe beef ("for the full experience", the omakase menu "shines"); the "cramped" space is "ho-hum" by comparison, and hoi polloi hiss at the "velvet rope system", but it's "still the best", so "brush up on your cheek kisses, wear black" and "bring a fat wallet."

Matteo's Ⓜ — 20 | 18 | 19 | $38
2321 Westwood Blvd. (bet. Pico Blvd. & Tennessee Ave.), West LA, 310-475-4521
■ For a "step back in time, when restaurants were clubby, service was professional and no one had ever heard of cholesterol", this "old-school Italian" in West LA is a place you can "relax and enjoy" "Jersey-style" red-sauce fare

The Westside   F | D | S | C |

in a "classic" room full of "history", where a "piano player plays fun standards" and the "ghosts of Milton Berle", "Frank and Sammy" are probably "holding court."

Matteo's Hoboken   19 | 10 | 18 | $21

2323 Westwood Blvd. (bet. Pico Blvd. & Tennessee Ave.), West LA, 310-474-1109

■ Matteo's "little brother stands on its own" next door to its elder sibling, dishing out "cheap, hearty" Southern Italian "homestyle favorites", and those in the know "love the daily specials"; it's "perfect for lunch", an "early dinner before a movie" or when you're "on the run."

Maxwell's Cafe   19 | 12 | 16 | $14

13329 Washington Blvd. (Walgrove Ave.), Venice, 310-306-7829

■ A "Sunday morning tradition in Marina del Rey", this "mainstay for locals" dishes out "heaping portions" of "honest American" fare for breakfast and lunch that'll "last you the entire day"; the "cool beach cottage" setting is "always crowded" and "noisy", and unless you "get there early", you can expect to "wait in line."

McCormick & Schmick's   19 | 19 | 19 | $33

Two Rodeo, 206 N. Rodeo Dr. (Wilshire Blvd.), Beverly Hills, 310-859-0434; www.mccormickandschmicks.com
See review in LA/Hollywood/W. Hollywood Directory.

MÉLISSE   27 | 25 | 26 | $71

1104 Wilshire Blvd. (11th St.), Santa Monica, 310-395-0881; www.melisse.com

■ This *Survey*'s No. 1 American has a French accent and a "refined", "curiously Continental feel" that gives some pause – "wait, is this LA?"; chef-owner Josiah Citrin "gets it all right" with his "incredible" creations, especially the "spectacular" tasting menus that "change as often as the silverware", paired with an "obscene" wine list; add to that the "best cheese trolley in town", "warm, discreet" service and a "romantic" room and you have a "true culinary experience" that's "pricey" but "worth every dollar."

Menemsha   18 | 18 | 17 | $41

822 Washington Blvd. (Abbott Kinney Blvd.), Venice, 310-822-2550

▲ Bringing a "little East Coast flair" to Venice, this "New England"–style nautical newcomer is "worth the trip for the lobster roll" that's "better than those on Martha's Vineyard" and other "fresh", "basic" seafood, served in a "large", "funky" room that's a "mix of trendy and cozy"; the service can be "mixed", as the staff is "still finding its sea legs."

MICHAEL'S   25 | 25 | 25 | $59

1147 Third St. (bet. California Ave. & Wilshire Blvd.), Santa Monica, 310-451-0843; www.michaelssantamonica.com

■ "Still going strong after 25 years", this "expense-account" "classic" in Santa Monica gets its "staying power" from

The Westside   F | D | S | C

"delicious, innovative" New American cuisine, a "beautiful setting" with a "romantic", "luscious garden patio" and a "professional" staff; while a few feel the cooking's "no longer cutting edge" and the service can be "difficult", things tend to pick up when chef "Michael McCarty is on the premises", and for the "famous and not-so-famous" alike, it remains a "perennial favorite for special occasions."

Mi Ranchito Family Mexican   ▽ 18 | 13 | 16 | $15

12223 Washington Blvd. (Centinela Ave.), Culver City, 310-398-8611

■ You may "never see more stuff on walls in your life" as you will at this "cheesy" Culver City Mexican, but "don't let the wacky decorations fool you" advise amigos, for it's "serious" about its "delicious", "authentic", "affordable" fare; the staff "makes you feel at home", and the "margaritas will make you forget your worries."

Mishima   20 | 14 | 18 | $16

11819 Wilshire Blvd. (Barrington Ave.), West LA, 310-966-1062; www.mishima.com

See review in LA/Hollywood/W. Hollywood Directory.

Mojo   ▽ 18 | 25 | 17 | $43

W Hotel, 930 Hilgard Ave. (Le Conte Ave.), Westwood, 310-443-7820

☑ Housed in Westwood's W Hotel with an "amazing, modern decor" that's "oh-so-LA", this Nuevo Latino manages to be "hot, spicy and cool, all at the same time", with a "clever, tempting" menu and a poolside annex that's a stylish way to "spend a warm summer afternoon"; cynics sniff it's "high on style but lacking in substance", while others, distracted by the "sexy", "smiling" staff and "beautiful blondes and guys draped around the room", shrug "food? – can't remember."

Monsoon Cafe   18 | 25 | 18 | $27

1212 Third St. Promenade (bet. Arizona Ave. & Wilshire Blvd.), Santa Monica, 310-576-9996; www.global-dining.com

■ You feel like you're in "Bangkok" (or "the Tiki Room at Disneyland") once you step into the "huge", "exotic" space of this Pan-Asian on Santa Monica's Third Street Promenade; while many feel "you really go for the decor", insiders insist "everything is executed well" on the "interesting", "eclectic" menu (the "pupu appetizers are the way to go").

Monte Alban   ▽ 21 | 8 | 19 | $16

11927 Santa Monica Blvd. (bet. Amacost & Brockton Aves.), West LA, 310-444-7736

■ The "delicate, complex" moles are "divine" at this "authentic" West LA Mexican that's a "must for those wanting to experiment with Oaxacan cuisine"; the setting's "nothing to speak of", but the atmosphere's "cheerful" and the staff is "pleasant" and "always there without being too

The Westside | F | D | S | C |

clingy", and the "yummy regional dishes" at "bargain prices" give you "lots of bang for the buck."

Moonshadows | 16 | 18 | 15 | $35 |
20356 PCH (Big Rock Dr.), Malibu, 310-456-3010; www.moonshadowsmalibu.com
■ The "owners of Allegria" have "done wonders" in "rehabbing" this "Malibu legend" into a "chic" spot where you can "unwind and watch the sunset" and the "waves crashing in" from the patio over "fresh, flavorful" New American fare; while some feel the kitchen and staff are "still working out the kinks", many agree it's "taken a turn for the better", and the ocean view is as "glorious" as ever.

MORI SUSHI ⊠ | 27 | 21 | 26 | $54 |
11500 W. Pico Blvd. (Gateway Blvd.), West LA, 310-479-3939
■ Morihiro Onodera is "a true original" who "outdoes himself every time" at his "upscale", "understated" ("the name isn't even on the sign") West LA Japanese, with "magical presentations" of "exquisite" sushi; it's a "highly personal" "purist's delight", where the toque "hulls his own rice", grates wasabi "before your eyes" and even "makes his own serving dishes", and the tasting menu is truly an "unforgettable experience" that leaves groupies gushing "omakase, omigod!"

Mort's Deli | 15 | 10 | 14 | $15 |
1035 Swarthmore Ave. (W. Sunset Blvd.), Pacific Palisades, 310-454-5511
◪ "Mort may be gone" but his "spirit lives on" at this "old reliable" deli, a Pacific Palisades "landmark" where "local politicos and resident stars" drop in for "simple, heavy" "comfort food at all hours"; "don't expect anything fancy", just "a lot of heart."

Moustache Café | 18 | 15 | 17 | $28 |
1071 Glendon Ave. (bet. Kinrose & Weyburn Aves.), Westwood, 310-208-6633
See review in LA/Hollywood/W. Hollywood Directory.

Mr. Cecil's California Ribs | 20 | 11 | 16 | $21 |
12244 W. Pico Blvd. (Bundy Blvd.), West LA, 310-442-1550
■ At this "itsy, bitsy" BBQ shack in West LA and its new full-size Sherman Oaks sibling, the "succulent" ribs that "need no sauces" are so "addictive" you'll "wake up the next morning wanting more"; the decor's a bit "cheesy", but it's a "fun, funky" spot that's "nice for families" ("just hose the kids off after dinner"), even if it is a bit "on the spendy side."

Mr. Chow | 22 | 20 | 20 | $55 |
344 N. Camden Dr. (bet. Brighton Way & Wilshire Blvd.), Beverly Hills, 310-278-9911; www.mrchow.com
■ Showcasing "more stars than the sky", this Beverly Hills "celebrity 'it' spot" is where the "hip crowd" goes for

The Westside F | D | S | C |

Chinese that's "edgy" and "unique", but comes in second to all the "eye candy"; it "helps a lot to be a regular" if you want to "be treated with decency", but the "unbelievably expensive" menu makes that difficult unless you're on an "expense account."

Mulberry Street Pizzeria   22 | 10 | 15 | $13 |
347 N. Cañon Dr. (bet. Brighton & Dayton Ways), Beverly Hills, 310-247-8998
240 S. Beverly Dr. (bet. Charleville Blvd. & Gregory Way), Beverly Hills, 310-247-8100

■ Proving to Angelenos that "NY is good for something", this pizzeria chain offers "excellent", "crispy" "thin-crust" pies (the "white pizza is heavenly") in a "no-frills" Big Apple setting "without the attitude"; on good days you can "have a slice with the stars" while you get the dish on them in the *NY Post*, which is provided at the counter.

Musha   ▽ 25 | 20 | 22 | $25 |
424 Wilshire Blvd. (bet. 4th & 5th Sts.), Santa Monica, 310-576-6330

■ It's "really like a pub in Tokyo" at this *izakaya* duo in Santa Monica and Torrance that's "not your run-of-the-mill sushi joint", instead offering "tapas"-like Japanese pub grub from "three different menus"; the "great selection" of "creative, original" dishes that are "priced well" and a "fun", "friendly" atmosphere make it "great for a group."

Napa Valley Grille   20 | 23 | 19 | $39 |
1100 Glendon Ave. (Lindbrook Dr.), Westwood, 310-824-3322;
www.constellationconcepts.com

■ You "feel like you're in the wine country" at Cafe del Rey's cousin that offers a "taste of NoCal" in Westwood with a "spacious", "comfortable", "rustic" room highlighted by a large open kitchen and sprawling bar, "creative" Californian cuisine "that works" and a "tremendous" Cal-only wine selection; despite "uneven" service, it's a "nice place to take out-of-town friends or clients."

Natalee Thai   20 | 17 | 18 | $19 |
998 S. Robertson Blvd. (Olympic Blvd.), Beverly Hills, 310-855-9380
10101 Venice Blvd. (Clarington Ave.), Palms, 310-202-7003
www.nataleethai.com

■ "Tasty", "trendy" Thai cuisine and "cool", "modern" decor are the draw at these "reliable" Siamese twins in Beverly Hills and Palms, and the sushi bar is a "great addition"; "big portions" at "bargain prices" and "quick", "friendly" service help make up for the "deafening" "din."

Nate 'n Al's   21 | 10 | 18 | $20 |
414 N. Beverly Dr. (bet. Brighton Way & Little Santa Monica Blvd.), Beverly Hills, 310-274-0101

■ This Beverly Hills "landmark" is an "old-style NY Jewish deli with a Hollywood twist" where the "people-watching's

The Westside

F | D | S | C

great", the corned beef's "to die for" and the rye bread is "manna from heaven"; you're as likely to "catch Larry King" in "the next booth" as "find your waitress", but when you do she'll "know everything you like and what you should eat", just "like your mother"; P.S. "you can't get a table between noon and two."

Nawab of India 22 | 15 | 20 | $26
1621 Wilshire Blvd. (bet. 16th & 17th Sts.), Santa Monica, 310-829-1106

■ "Sublime" shrimp curry, "tempting tandoori, divine dal" and other "authentic" dishes with "more flavors than an entire spice rack" fill out the "extensive menu" at this Santa Monica Indian where the "fabulous lunch buffet" is a "great bargain"; the "quiet room with "white tablecloths" and "comfy booths" is "elegant and romantic", and the service is "friendly and helpful."

Neptune's Net 16 | 9 | 9 | $17
42505 PCH (2 mi. north of Leo Carillo Beach), Malibu, 310-457-3095

■ An "LA rite of passage", this Malibu "roadside joint" on PCH near the Ventura County line is the "ultimate beach seafood dive" where "bikers and surfer dudes" mingle over "chowder, lobsters and fried everything", "cold beer" and "a view of the ocean"; "no need to brush off the sand before entering", as the decor and service are "nonexistent."

Newsroom Café 18 | 14 | 16 | $18
530 Wilshire Blvd. (bet. 5th & 6th Sts.), Santa Monica, 310-319-9100

See review in LA/Hollywood/W. Hollywood Directory.

Nic's ⊠ 22 | 23 | 21 | $41
453 N. Cañon Dr. (Little Santa Monica Blvd.), Beverly Hills, 310-550-5707; www.nicsbeverlyhills.com

■ A "bohemian outpost in Beverly Hills", "Larry Nicola's up-to-date old-fashioned supper club" attracts "an interesting mix of blue hairs and hipsters" with "incredible", "first-rate" New American fare, a "fabulous", "ultrahip" martini bar and "dynamite live jazz" on weekends; while some wonder where "all the gorgeous waiters" have gone, Larry is always a "gracious host" who "makes you feel like the most important person in town."

Nizam 20 | 16 | 21 | $24
10871 W. Pico Blvd. (Westwood Blvd.), West LA, 310-470-1441

■ "Easy to miss, but impossible to forget", this storefront Indian across from the Westside Pavilion is many surveyors' "first choice" for "wonderful, delicious" dishes ("killer eggplant", "excellent samosas") "served with care" by an "attentive, personable" owner and staff; cronies counsel midday is the "time to go", when it serves one of the "best lunch buffets in LA."

get updates at zagat.com 133

The Westside   F | D | S | C |

Noah's New York Bagels   16 | 11 | 13 | $7 |
11911 San Vicente Blvd. (Montana Ave.), Brentwood, 310-472-5651
Marina del Rey Shopping Ctr., 546 Washington Blvd. (Via Marina), Marina del Rey, 310-574-1155
1426 Montana Ave. (14th St.), Santa Monica, 310-587-9103
10910 Lindbrook Dr. (bet. Gayley Ave. & Westwood Blvd.), Westwood, 310-209-8177
www.noahs.com
See review in LA/Hollywood/W. Hollywood Directory.

NOBU MALIBU   27 | 21 | 23 | $59 |
3835 Crosscreek Rd. (PCH), Malibu, 310-317-9140; www.nobumatsuhisa.com

■ The "star clientele" will "blow you away" at this Malibu outpost of the Nobu Matsuhisa empire where the "celebrity-watching is only outmatched by the insanely fresh cuts of fish" and other "fabulous, creative Japanese dishes"; the sushi will "hook you like a drug" (and, at "$5 a bite", cost nearly the same), while the omakase menu is even "better than sex", and the "terrific staff treats everyone like a regular" in the "casual", "relaxed" setting where "you can get decked out or wear sweatpants" with equal ease.

Ocean Ave. Seafood   23 | 20 | 21 | $40 |
1401 Ocean Ave. (Santa Monica Blvd.), Santa Monica, 310-394-5669; www.oceanave.com

■ "A table by the window at sunset, a bowl of Manila clams and a bottle of wine" make for a definitive "Southern Californian" experience at this "first-class fish fantasia" above the beach in Santa Monica; with the "freshest possible" fin fare served by "hot waiters" in a "handsome, comfortable" room, one of the "best oyster bars in LA" and a "killer view" of the Pacific "right across the street", it "hits all the marks, all the time."

OCEANFRONT   22 | 27 | 23 | $49 |
Casa Del Mar, 1910 Ocean Way (Pico Blvd.), Santa Monica, 310-581-7714; www.hotelcasadelmar.com

■ "Elegant", yet "relaxing", this Californian lodged in Santa Monica's Hotel Casa Del Mar is the "most fabulous place on the beach" with one of the "best ocean sunsets in SoCal"; Quinn Hatfield is a "hot young chef to watch", creating "wonderful", "high-end" dishes almost "too good to be true"; "drinks by the fireplace" and "early evening jazz" "perfectly complement the mood."

Olive Garden   11 | 12 | 14 | $18 |
936 Westwood Blvd. (Weyburn Ave.), West LA, 310-824-7588; www.olivegarden.com

☑ "Enough with the jokes" storm loyalists of this national chain who "aren't ashamed to admit" their affinity for its "decent" "Americanized" Italian at "low" prices, but wags

The Westside　　　　　　　　　F ▮ D ▮ S ▮ C ▮

can't resist – "it's the pits", "if mama cooked like this I would've left her in Italy"; still, it's "kid-friendly" and a "good value" for "families on a budget."

ONE PICO　　　　　　　　　　　24 ▮ 26 ▮ 23 ▮ $51 ▮
Shutters on the Beach, 1 Pico Blvd. (Ocean Ave.), Santa Monica, 310-587-1717; www.shuttersonthebeach.com
■ At the crux of some of the best beach dining in Santa Monica, this New American housed in Shutters on the Beach is "class all the way", offering "beautiful ocean views" from a "striking", "elegant" room and a "pleasant" outdoor patio, a "decadent cuisine that makes you decide when you're coming back before you even leave" and "gracious", "attentive" service; in sum, it's a "wonderful experience for special occasions."

Outlaws Bar & Grill　　　　　▽ 18 ▮ 13 ▮ 18 ▮ $19 ▮
230 Culver Blvd. (Vista del Mar), Playa del Rey, 310-822-4040
■ You "must be very hungry when you arrive" at this "noisy" Playa del Rey pub serving "man-sized burgers" and "more ribs than you can eat" to "local cowfolk"; the setting is "fun and informal", with "waitresses who talk back" and an outdoor deck that's "nice for dining" and "drinking beer" in the summer.

Pacific Dining Car ◐　　　　　22 ▮ 20 ▮ 22 ▮ $49 ▮
2700 Wilshire Blvd. (Princeton St.), Santa Monica, 310-453-4000; www.pacificdiningcar.com
See review in LA/Hollywood/W. Hollywood Directory.

Pacifico's　　　　　　　　　　19 ▮ 15 ▮ 19 ▮ $20 ▮
9341 Culver Blvd. (south of Venice Blvd.), Culver City, 310-559-3474; www.pacificos.net
■ Howdy Kabrins (founder of La Salsa) rides again at this Culver City production that's a "big step up from typical Mexican seafood", dishing out "generous servings" of "tasty fish for any palate" in a "spartan" "fast-food" setting with a "nice" outdoor patio.

Paco's Tacos　　　　　　　　　19 ▮ 14 ▮ 17 ▮ $16 ▮
4141 S. Centinela Ave. (bet. Culver & Washington Blvds.), Mar Vista, 310-391-9616; www.pacoscantina.com
■ "Handmade tortillas from heaven" are "worth the wait" at this "family-friendly" Mexican duo in Mar Vista and Westchester that's a "favorite date place" on weekends; it's an "easy choice" for many, thanks to "cheap" eats and "attentive service", though opinions are divided on the decor that "constantly changes to fit holidays."

Palomino　　　　　　　　　　　18 ▮ 20 ▮ 19 ▮ $34 ▮
10877 Wilshire Blvd. (Glendon Ave.), Westwood, 310-208-1960; www.palomino.com
■ A horse of a different color, this "handsome" Westwood Village Cal-Med is "one of the few places where people of

The Westside

| F | D | S | C |

all ages feel comfortable", from families with kids to "bar aficionados"; the "handsome", "minimalist" decor "makes one feel happy to be there" tucking into "earthy and almost sensual, Italian-inspired" dishes or meeting friends over "great-looking drinks and martinis"; the staff may be a bit "under-trained", but the service is "generally warm."

Pammolli ⊘   24 | 23 | 24 | $41
9513 Little Santa Monica Blvd. (Rodeo Dr.), Beverly Hills, 310-273-7588; www.pammolli.com

■ Dramatically improved scores indicate this "lovely, quiet" Northern Italian "charmer in the heart of Beverly Hills" has "overcome a slow beginning" to become an "exceptional" performer, thanks to chef Massimo Ormani's (ex Locanda Veneta) "delicious, hearty" but "never heavy" cuisine, "friendly, witty" service and "enchanting" setting; it's a "classy" act that's "not intimidating" – but "not for those on a budget", either.

Pastina ⊘   20 | 16 | 20 | $30
2260 Westwood Blvd. (bet. Olympic & Pico Blvds.), West LA, 310-441-4655

■ A "real sleeper", this "inexpensive" Westside Italian is a "neighborhood secret" where "the pastas are always al dente", the "specials are usually good" and the "bread alone is worth a visit"; the atmosphere is "warm" and "friendly", and the "hospitality makes you feel at home", which is why so many regulars bring their "visiting relatives and friends."

Patrick's Roadhouse ⊄   ▽ 17 | 18 | 16 | $18
106 Entrada Dr. (PCH), Santa Monica, 310-459-4544

■ "Get down and dirty with the stars" at this "dusty roadside gem" in Santa Monica that "welcomes bathing suits and flip-flops" (which is good, for the beach is across the street) as it keeps true to its "greasy-spoon roots" with "great breakfasts" and "fine cheap beach brunches" (fans "dream about" the banana pancakes), and a "mishmash of living room castaways" filling the "funky" room.

Pearl Dragon   ▽ 16 | 17 | 17 | $37
15229 Sunset Blvd. (bet. Monument St. & Swarthmore Ave.), Pacific Palisades, 310-459-9790

◪ The "hippest spot in the Palisades" may also be the "only place to get sushi" with the "only full bar" in town, and perhaps because there's "not much else to compete with", it's "expensive for what it is" and you can expect to "spend a while waiting for service"; still, the "light" Asian fusion dishes are "tasty" and the decor is "trendy."

Pedals   21 | 23 | 19 | $28
Shutters on the Beach, 1 Pico Blvd. (Ocean Ave.), Santa Monica, 310-587-1707; www.shuttersonthebeach.com

■ A "true gem in the sand", this Cal-Italian at Santa Monica's Shutters on the Beach shares the same "magnificent ocean

The Westside   F | D | S | C

view" with One Pico upstairs; it's a "favorite for breakfast, brunch or lunch" "by the beach", where you can watch "the world walk by" over "reliable, fresh" fare served by a "no-nonsense" staff; while it "may be just the setting that makes one think it's all good", "it doesn't really matter" to fans who "can't wait to go back."

Peppone   25 | 21 | 23 | $51
11628 Barrington Ct. (Sunset Blvd.), Brentwood, 310-476-7379;
www.peppone.com
■ "Regulars are treated like long-lost family members" at this "clubby", "out-of-the-way" Brentwood Northern Italian where a "loyal clientele" is "hooked" on its "excellent", "not exactly healthy" cuisine, "award-winning" wine list and "old-world" charm; you're sure to "spot some stars hiding out" in the "classic, dark", windowless space complete with tiffany chandeliers, leather booths and "lots of autographed celebrity photos on the walls."

Petrelli's Steakhouse   15 | 14 | 18 | $28
5615 S. Sepulveda Blvd. (bet. Jefferson Blvd. & Slauson Ave.), Culver City, 310-397-1438
■ "Tender, juicy" steaks "overshadow everything else", including the "ok red-sauce Italian dishes", at this "classic" "neighborhood steakhouse" in Culver City run by the Petrelli family since 1931; the "'50s are alive" in the "kitschy" room with "red leather booths", where "retro waitresses" rule, and while some feel this "relic" could use an "overhaul", for fans it remains a "good old standby."

P.F. CHANG'S CHINA BISTRO   20 | 20 | 18 | $24
326 Wilshire Blvd. (4th St.), Santa Monica, 310-395-1912;
www.pfchangs.com
See review in LA/Hollywood/W. Hollywood Directory.

Pho Bac Huynh   ∇ 17 | 8 | 14 | $11
11819 Wilshire Blvd. (Westgate Ave.), West LA, 310-477-9379
■ For "delicious, reasonably priced" pho and other "simple, spicy" dishes on the Westside, this Vietnamese is "hard to beat", offering a "ton of bang for the buck" in a "casual", "friendly" setting; the signature dish also comes in "smaller sizes for smaller appetites"; there's also delivery service, and the food is "hot when it arrives."

Piccolo Paradiso 🗷   ∇ 19 | 16 | 17 | $40
150 S. Beverly Dr. (Wilshire Blvd.), Beverly Hills, 310-271-0030
◪ "Celestino's little brother [Giacomino] gets it right" at this "cozy" Drago family–owned Italian in Beverly Hills, offering "top-notch dining" "with lots of charm" in a "casual", "relaxing" setting; detractors dismiss it as a "poor imitation of Il Pastaio", its elder sibling located a few blocks north.

get updates at zagat.com   137

The Westside

| | F | D | S | C |

Pizzicotto
23 | 17 | 19 | $27

11758 San Vicente Blvd. (bet. Gorham & Montana Aves.), Brentwood, 310-442-7188

■ This "charming" Brentwood Italian "hole-in-the-wall" is "cramped and unbelievably tiny", but "no one seems to care", thanks to "masterfully prepared" dishes and an "excellent" wine list, served in an atmosphere that's like "Italy revisited"; the service is "attentive" and sidewalk tables "help" ease the crush, but it's still advisable to "make a reservation – and wear deodorant."

Polo Lounge ●
21 | 26 | 24 | $50

Beverly Hills Hotel, 9641 Sunset Blvd. (Beverly & Crescent Drs.), Beverly Hills, 310-276-2251; www.thebeverlyhillshotel.com

■ There's "Hollywood history in the air" at this "classy, old" Continental in the Beverly Hills Hotel where "celebrity sightings abound" and "deals get done", and the service is "impeccable"; while the Sunday brunch is "outstanding", the fare is "enjoyable at any meal", but it's still "not quite up to the scenery" on the "beautiful" outdoor patio where you feel like "you should see Gary Cooper or Fred Astaire."

Poquito Mas ●
21 | 9 | 15 | $10

2215 Westwood Blvd. (Olympic Blvd.), West LA, 310-474-1998; www.poquitomas.com

See review in LA/Hollywood/W. Hollywood Directory.

Porterhouse Bistro
21 | 17 | 19 | $43

8635 Wilshire Blvd. (bet. La Cienega & Robertson Blvds.), Beverly Hills, 310-659-1099

■ Carnivores clamor "sign me up" for the "terrific" $30 prix fixe at this "Beverly Hills bargain" steakhouse, a four-course feed that includes a "melt-in-your-mouth" porterhouse and a "real drink", but "what's with the cotton candy?"; à-la-cartesians find the "one-trick-pony" concept "boring", but cronies contend the "limited menu" ensures "everything is fresh and consistent"; the service is "friendly" but "could use some polish."

Prego
19 | 19 | 19 | $34

362 N. Camden Dr. (Brighton Way), Beverly Hills, 310-277-7346

See review in LA/Hollywood/W. Hollywood Directory.

Primitivo Wine Bistro
19 | 20 | 19 | $33

1025 Abbot Kinney Blvd. (bet. Main St. & Westminster Ave.), Venice, 310-396-5353

■ A "slice of Europe in funky Venice [CA]" awaits at this bacchic Cal-Med in the form of a "heady" (but "reasonably priced") wine list and "inventive" tapas made with "artisanal cheeses, handcrafted meats and Farmer's Market" produce, served in a "swanky" space with a "happening" vibe; the staff is "attentive and knowledgeable" and "tries hard to be your friend."

The Westside F | D | S | C

Rae's ∌   ▽ 15 | 14 | 16 | $11
2901 Pico Blvd. (29th St.), Santa Monica, 310-828-7937
■ "You'll get a big breakfast and a piece of Americana" and "pay next to nothing for them" at this Santa Monica "throwback to the '50s" serving "artery-clogging" American fare; "if you come on Sunday" get here "at 6 AM" or be prepared to wait.

Real Food Daily   19 | 15 | 17 | $20
242 S. Beverly Dr. (bet. Charleville Blvd. & Gregory Way), Beverly Hills, 310-858-0880
514 Santa Monica Blvd. (bet. 5th & 6th Sts.), Santa Monica, 310-451-7544
www.realfood.com
See review in LA/Hollywood/W. Hollywood Directory.

Rebecca's   14 | 16 | 15 | $26
101 Broadway (Ocean Ave.), Santa Monica, 310-260-1100; www.foodcowest.com
◪ "Drinks and appetizers are better than the mains" at this Nuevo Latino transplanted from Venice to a scenic spot on Santa Monica's Ocean Avenue, where insiders prefer to "sit outside" and watch "the sun sinking into the ocean" rather than in the room with "really bad acoustics"; foes find the fare "forgettable", but with "killer" margaritas and "chips and salsa this good", "who needs to eat?"

Reddi Chick BBQ ⌀∌   ▽ 21 | 7 | 14 | $10
Brentwood Country Mart, 225 26th St. (San Vicente Blvd.), Brentwood, 310-393-5238
■ "Absolutely habit-forming" is how fans describe the "always reliable" "rotisserie chicken and french fries" at this affordable Santa Monica "institution" in the retro Brentwood Country Mart, where you can "take the family to indulge" on birds "so good we even eat the bones" while "stargazing on the outside patio."

Red Moon Cafe ⌀   ▽ 21 | 14 | 18 | $17
Westdale Shopping Ctr., 11267 National Blvd. (Sawtelle Blvd.), West LA, 310-477-3177
■ The "crab is the reason to go" to this "inexpensive" West LA Chinese-Vietnamese located in a "hidden" mall under a freeway overpass, though fans also "love the crystal rolls" and other "light, flavorful" dishes; the staff is "friendly" even if service "can be a little trying sometimes", and the food is always "worth the wait."

Reel Inn   17 | 11 | 11 | $18
18661 PCH (Topanga Canyon Rd.), Malibu, 310-456-8221
1220 Third St. Promenade (Wilshire Ave.), Santa Monica, 310-395-5538
◪ Located on PCH in Malibu and Santa Monica's Third Street Promenade, these "no-frills" "shacks" serve "relatively

The Westside   F | D | S | C

inexpensive", "nice-sized portions" of "fresh seafood", in a "fun" setting peppered with "great fish-pun ads" ("trout on in", "just for the halibut") where you "order and pick up yourself", then "chill out on picnic benches."

REGENT BEVERLY WILSHIRE   25 | 27 | 26 | $56
Regent Beverly Wilshire, 9500 Wilshire Blvd. (Rodeo Dr.), Beverly Hills, 310-275-5200; www.regenthotels.com
■ "A dine-and-dancer's delight", this "civilized, refined" Beverly Hills hotel Cal-Med is an "elegant", "old world classic" with a lobby lounge, piano bar and "breathtaking" "neo-classical dining room", "exceptional" fare and a "professional" staff; be romanced with "cheek-to-cheek dancing on Friday nights" or just come for an "elegant" lunch and "celeb-sighting extravaganza" "at a window seat along Wilshire Boulevard."

Reign   21 | 24 | 21 | $42
180 N. Robertson Blvd. (bet. Clifton Way & Wilshire Blvd.), Beverly Hills, 310-273-4463
◪ There "are always Lakers" in the back room of this "haute Southern" spot on Robertson set in a stark white modernist space that "oozes cool" and fills up with "beautiful people" ("isn't that Lil' Kim in the corner?") who come for "simply delicious" fried chicken, "melt-in-your-mouth biscuits with honey and marmalade" and other "upscale", "down-home" delights; boo-birds say it's going "downhill" ever since gridiron standout Keyshawn Johnson sold his ownership.

RJ's the Rib Joint   15 | 15 | 17 | $28
252 N. Beverly Dr. (bet. Santa Monica & Wilshire Blvds.), Beverly Hills, 310-274-7427
◪ A huge appetite is required at this "old-school rib joint" in Beverly Hills where the portions are "more than enough for two", the "no-nonsense" salad bar reigns "supreme", the chocolate cake is served in "slabs" and the coffee "comes with whipped cream and chocolate chips on the side"; critics cool to the "new management" feel it's "not what it once was."

RÖCKENWAGNER ⓈⓂ   25 | 21 | 23 | $48
The Edgemar, 2435 Main St. (bet. Ocean Park & Pico Blvds.), Santa Monica, 310-399-6504; www.rockenwagner.com
■ This upscale Santa Monica "foodie mecca" now shares its "very cool", high-tech space with its more casual sibling, The Brasserie: the former offers "imaginative", "consistently well-prepared" Cal-Continental cuisine, including the "sublime" yearly asparagus festival and "wonderful" chocolate tart dessert, while the latter's weisswurst on a pretzel roll, moules frites and pretzel burger have fans wishing they "could eat there every night"; either is a "'röcken' choice for incredible food and great service."

The Westside | F | D | S | C |

Roll 'n Rye Deli | 17 | 10 | 17 | $15 |
Studio Village Shopping Ctr., 10990 W. Jefferson Blvd.
(Sawtelle Blvd.), Culver City, 310-390-3497
■ "It's another universe" once you leave the "strip mall outside" and enter this "funkier", yet "traditional" Culver City deli with a "fake bagel crashing through the ceiling", attracting a veritable "LA melting pot" with "big portions" of the "best matzo ball soup", "French dipped brisket of beef sandwich" and "tasty tongue sandwiches"; "friendly" service is a plus.

Rose Cafe | 18 | 17 | 15 | $19 |
220 Rose Ave. (Main St.), Venice, 310-399-0711
■ "Most are charmed enough to briefly put away their cell phones" at this "arty" "Venice Beach original" with a market and cafe that's "very European" and a spacious, "quintessential SoCal" patio reminiscent of a "friendly neighbor's backyard"; the moderately priced Cal menu is "great for breakfast or brunch", and the pastry case "seems to call my name the minute I walk in the door."

Rosti | 16 | 14 | 16 | $21 |
233 S. Beverly Dr. (bet. Olympic & Wilshire Blvds.), Beverly Hills, 310-275-3285
931 Montana Ave. (10th St.), Santa Monica, 310-393-3236
■ "Tasty Tuscan treats" and "friendly, not fancy" service in an indoor/outdoor "charming, country market setting" attract a steady following to this Northern Italian chain; "consistently good", "rustic" dishes such as "staple chicken and rosemary potatoes", "incredible handmade spinach ravioli" and "excellent grilled vegetable sandwiches" come in "ample portions" that make it a "good value."

Royal Star Seafood | 20 | 13 | 16 | $23 |
3001 Wilshire Blvd. (Stanford St.), Santa Monica, 310-828-8812
■ For a "taste of Monterey Park" ("at very Westside prices") in Santa Monica, Sinophiles get their "dim sum fix" at Ocean Star's sibling that's "always crowded" despite a reputation for "rude" service; "steaming hot, fresh seafood", "sautéed pea shoots" and pork buns that "make you cry with joy" may "tempt you to hijack" one of the "hot carts constantly patrolling the dining room."

Ruby's | 17 | 18 | 18 | $13 |
Villa Marina Mktpl., 13455 Maxella Ave., 2nd fl. (Frwy. 90), Marina del Rey, 310-574-7829; www.rubys.com
■ "Go back in time" at this "retro" American chain (the original is on the Balboa Pier) where "delicious" hamburgers and fries and "old-fashioned milkshakes (complete with the can)" are served at the same table as modern menu attractions such as fish tacos and veggie burgers; "parents love" this "kid-friendly" spot that's a "flashback" to "simpler days, simpler food."

get updates at zagat.com

The Westside

| | F | D | S | C |

RUTH'S CHRIS STEAK HOUSE   26 | 20 | 24 | $51

224 S. Beverly Dr. (bet. Olympic & Wilshire Blvds.), Beverly Hills, 310-859-8744; www.ruthschris.com

■ A "guilty pleasure" for "carnivores with impeccable taste", this "classic" chophouse chain is one of the "best of its class", where the "aroma of steak sizzling in butter" fills the air in the "boys' club" setting; in addition to "succulent" red meat, the "crab cakes are a must" and the "creamed spinach sparkles"; the staff may consist of "struggling actors", but the service is "attentive and unrushed."

Sandbag's Gourmet Sandwiches   17 | 8 | 15 | $10

9497 Santa Monica Blvd. (Rodeo Dr.), Beverly Hills, 310-786-7878
11640 San Vicente Blvd. (Barrington Ave.), Brentwood, 310-207-4888
1134 Westwood Blvd. (Wilshire Blvd.), Westwood, 310-208-1133 ⓢ

■ A "convenient" and "affordable" "lunch option for those chained to their desks" (i.e. "free delivery"), these "homemade quality sandwich" venues in Beverly Hills, Brentwood and Westwood are "what Subway dreams of becoming", serving "creative" combinations "with a free cookie" that'll make you "feel like you're five again."

San Gennaro Cafe   18 | 15 | 17 | $22

140 S. Barrington Pl. (Sunset Blvd.), Brentwood, 310-476-9696
9543 Culver Blvd. (Watseka Ave.), Culver City, 310-836-0400

■ "Regional favorites abound" at this "homestyle Italian" pair that remind *amici* of the "old neighborhood", where the "pizzas get rave reviews" and the "$10 bottles of wine" are just "the ticket"; at the Brentwood location the "to-go orders go flying out the door" while the more sedate Culver City branch has live music in the evenings – "a little Sinatra, a little ziti and . . . dance the night away."

Sawtelle Kitchen ⓢ   21 | 14 | 19 | $21

2024 Sawtelle Blvd. (bet. La Grange & Mississippi Aves.), West LA, 310-445-9288

■ "Simple western food prepared in a Japanese way" makes this "inexpensive", "imaginative Asian fusion" specialist a "great addition to the new J-Town" on the "Sawtelle strip"; it's "tiny" and "usually crowded", but "original" dishes such as "meatloaf to die for" and "melt-in-your-mouth lamb shank" are "worth the wait"; "make sure to BYO."

Schatzi on Main   14 | 15 | 15 | $35

3110 Main St. (bet. Marine & Navy Sts.), Santa Monica, 310-399-4800; www.schatzi-on-main.com

▣ Thanks to its association with the Running (for governor) Man, Arnold Schwarzenegger, this Santa Monica Cal-Austrian attracts a large contingent of *Terminator* fans,

The Westside | F | D | S | C |

who partake of "great happy-hour deals" and "good" Wiener schnitzel, while cigar aficionados can enjoy a stogie on the patio; but foes feel it's "gone downhill in all areas" and declare "I won't be back."

17th Street Cafe | 19 | 15 | 18 | $25 |
1610 Montana Ave. (16th St.), Santa Monica, 310-453-2771
■ "It's hard to go wrong" at this "swinging" New American, a "reliable neighborhood haunt" on the shopping strip of Montana Avenue, where a "pleasingly eclectic" menu that includes "great salads and salmon with balsamic sauce" and the "best sweet potato fries" is served in a casual cafe setting; "pleasant" service will help "lighten up your day."

Shabu 2 | - | - | - | M |
401 Santa Monica Blvd. (4th St.), Santa Monica, 310-576-7011
Shabu-shabu is one of the more appealing Japanese dining rituals, where diners cook their own food (usually beef) in tableside or counter hot pots; in this industrial-looking eatery, beef and chicken share a menu with Cal-influenced options like salmon, orange roughy, tiger shrimp, lobster tail, scallops and mussels.

Shack, The | 17 | 9 | 11 | $12 |
185 Culver Blvd. (Vista del Mar), Playa del Rey, 310-823-6222
2518 Wilshire Blvd. (26th St.), Santa Monica, 310-449-1171
■ You can "hang out with friends and play some pool" while "watching sporting events" at this "no-frills" American duo, whether at the Playa del Rey branch just steps from the sand or on Wilshire in Santa Monica; tucking into "solid" bar fare, including the signature Shackburger ("savory Louisiana sausage on a burger"), have many wishing they were "still in college" and didn't have to worry about the "cholesterol meter."

Shaherzad | ▽ 21 | 14 | 16 | $23 |
1422 Westwood Blvd. (bet. Santa Monica & Wilshire Blvds.), Westwood, 310-470-9131
■ "You don't need to be an expert on Persian cuisine" to appreciate this Westwood cafe that feels like a "nice place in Tehran" serving "huge piles of basmati rice with lamb or chicken on top", "sublime fessenjan" and the "best bread in the city" that's "made on the premises" and ideal for "mopping up the yummy sauces"; watch out, though, for "hurried" service that "never comes with a smile."

Sisley Italian Kitchen | 17 | 16 | 17 | $22 |
Westside Pavilion, 10800 W. Pico Blvd. (bet. Overland Ave. & Westwood Blvd.), West LA, 310-446-3030;
www.sisleykitchen.com
■ "For a relaxing fine meal after shopping", fans recommend this small chain of mall-based Cal-Italians for "warm bread

get updates at zagat.com

The Westside   F D S C

that'll melt anyone's heart", "creative chicken and pasta dishes", and "delicious salads", served by an "efficient" staff in a "basic" setting; it's a "solid value" "for the price."

Soleil Westwood M   ▽ 22 | 17 | 23 | $29

1386 Westwood Blvd. (Rochester Ave.), Westwood, 310-441-5384; www.soleilwestwood.com

■ A "casual, friendly" French "next door to Borders Books" in Westwood's Little Tehran, this bistro boasts an "extensive menu" that includes "a delicious Brie and grilled chicken sandwich" and "all the mussels and frites you can eat on Wednesday nights"; it's a "wonderful place to spend an evening", especially on the "sidewalk terrace."

Souplantation   15 | 10 | 12 | $11

11911 San Vicente Blvd. (Montana Ave.), Brentwood, 310-476-7080
Villa Marina Mktpl., 13455 Maxella Ave. (Lincoln Blvd.), Marina del Rey, 310-305-7669
www.souplantation.com
See review in LA/Hollywood/W. Hollywood Directory.

South Street   ▽ 24 | 14 | 18 | $10

1010 Broxton Ave. (Weyburn St.), Westwood, 310-443-9895

■ The "next best thing to a visit to the City of Brotherly Love", this Westwood Village American attracts Philly fanatics with "deliciously decadent", "authentic" cheese steaks, "not-for-the-novice spicy" fries and "even Tasty Cakes", served in a "cute", brick-walled room so evocative "you can almost hear the *Rocky* theme while you eat – oh, wait, they are playing it in the background."

SPAGO   26 | 25 | 24 | $63

176 N. Cañon Dr. (Wilshire Blvd.), Beverly Hills, 310-385-0880; www.wolfgangpuck.com

■ A "classic" that's "constantly evolving", this Beverly Hills "flagship of the Wolfgang Puck empire" is "synonymous with LA glamour and Californian cuisine", staying true to its culinary roots with chef Lee Hefter's "inventive" cuisine and pastry chef Sherry Yard's desserts that "continue to amaze"; fans "go for the foie gras three ways" without worry, since all the "cardiologists of BH are nearby", and "even a nobody is made to feel like somebody" in this "power hangout."

Sprazzo Cucina Italiana   21 | 19 | 20 | $26

1389 Westwood Blvd. (bet. Rochester & Wilkins Aves.), Westwood, 310-479-3337

■ Fans insist this "small, but comfortable" Westwood Village Italian "hasn't lost a step" "with a change in ownership", serving its specialty gnocchi that's still "the best", pizzas that come in "a close second" and "lovely" pastas with "freshly made sauces"; "warm", "friendly" service makes it a "delightful experience" for "grown-ups" and a "wonderful place to spend an evening with that special someone."

The Westside | F | D | S | C |

Stinking Rose | 17 | 20 | 17 | $29 |
55 N. La Cienega Blvd. (Wilshire Blvd.), Beverly Hills, 310-652-7673; www.thestinkingrose.com

■ "Worry about your breath later" after a visit to this La Cienega "garlic lover's paradise", a "theme park" with gift shop renowned for "aromatic dining", serving "redolent treats from the Garlic-tini to garlic ice cream" in a room graced with paintings of the eponymous root on the walls; "you won't run into any vampires here."

SUNNIN | 24 | 5 | 17 | $13 |
1779 Westwood Blvd. (Santa Monica Blvd.), Westwood, 310-477-2358

■ "Unapologetically low maintenance", this "tiny" Middle Easterner in Westwood is for "serious foodies" who "aren't deterred by lack of decor" and "don't mind waiting" for "family-recipe Lebanese" fare that "tastes like it came from my mother's kitchen", including the "mezzo plate of my dreams", a baba ghanoush worth crossing a desert for" and the best falafel I've ever had"; though it's "always crowded", the "staff is unfailingly gracious."

Sushi Masu M | ▽ 26 | 14 | 23 | $32 |
1911 Westwood Blvd. (bet. Olympic & Santa Monica Blvds.), West LA, 310-446-4368

■ What may be the "most unpretentious sushi bar in LA", this "secret" storefront Japanese on busy Westwood Boulevard is "not much to look at", but aficionados aver chef Hiroshi Masuko "knows his stuff", creating "awesome", "simple and carefully presented" dishes; "reasonable prices" and "incredibly friendly" service seal the deal.

SUSHI ROKU | 23 | 22 | 18 | $44 |
1401 Ocean Ave. (Santa Monica Blvd.), Santa Monica, 310-458-4771; www.sushiroku.com
See review in LA/Hollywood/W. Hollywood Directory.

SUSHI SASABUNE Ⓢ | 27 | 7 | 19 | $53 |
11300 Nebraska Ave. (Sawtelle Blvd.), West LA, 310-268-8380

■ "Don't even think about asking for what you want" at this Japanese "shack" on the unfashionable northern end of Sawtelle Boulevard in J-Town where you "ignore the decor" to feast on the "best of the best" sushi with "warm rice" (and "no rolls") at "prices as high as you get for raw fish in LA" (now that Ginza Sushi-Ko has left for New York); you "eat what the chef gives you", because the 'Trust Me' emblazoned on the waiters' aprons isn't a suggestion" – it's the law.

Swingers ☾ | 16 | 17 | 15 | $15 |
802 Broadway (Lincoln Blvd.), Santa Monica, 310-393-9793; www.swingersrestaurant.com
See review in LA/Hollywood/W. Hollywood Directory.

get updates at zagat.com

The Westside F | D | S | C

Taiko 22 | 17 | 20 | $23
Brentwood Gardens, 11677 San Vicente Blvd. (Barrington Ave.), Brentwood, 310-207-7782
■ The "decor is utilitarian, the service is simple, but the flavors burst through" at this Japanese duo where "you can get it all", from the "best noodles in LA" to "excellent sushi" to "fluffy, light tempura" to "melt-in-your-mouth" miso black cod; the Brentwood original is located in an upscale mall, while the South Bay branch boasts a sushi bar and outdoor patio, and both locations make you feel like you're in Tokyo's "Harajuku or Omotesando" neighborhoods.

Takao 25 | 12 | 20 | $48
11656 San Vicente Blvd. (bet. Barrington & Darlington Aves.), Brentwood, 310-207-8636
■ The storefront space is, well, a bit "ugly", but the "stuff on the plate is beautiful" at Takao Izumida's (ex Matsuhisa) "expensive", "tiny" Brentwood Japanese where the "unbelievable" sushi and "excellent" sashimi are so "fresh" the "fish are beheaded before you"; "fantastic" tempura and "adventurous" dishes also make it easy to overlook the "bland" digs, especially if you "put your fate in the chef's hands and order the omakase."

Talesai 23 | 18 | 19 | $27
9198 Olympic Blvd. (Oakhurst Dr.), Beverly Hills, 310-271-9345
See review in LA/Hollywood/W. Hollywood Directory.

Tanino 22 | 23 | 21 | $41
1043 Westwood Blvd. (bet. Kinross & Weyburn Aves.), Westwood, 310-208-0444; www.tanino.com
■ Brother Tanino Drago is a "wonderful host" who "knows how to cook" at his Westwood Village Southern Italian, housed in an "elegantly restored" historic space resembling a "Venetian palace", where "sexy", "energetic" waiters bring out "phenomenal" pastas and other "superb" dishes; it's "expensive", but "well worth it for a special evening."

TAVERNA TONY 23 | 21 | 21 | $29
Malibu Country Mart, 23410 Civic Center Way (Cross Creek Rd.), Malibu, 310-317-9667; www.tavernatony.com
■ "Festive frivolity", "fantastic" fare and "friendly" service make this Malibu Greek "worth the marathon-length drive"; out on the patio you can "smell the sea air" and feel like you're "dining on the Med", while inside it's "always a celebration" with "patrons dancing to live music" and "belly dancers" on weekends.

Tengu 22 | 22 | 18 | $39
10853 Lindbrook Dr. (Glendon Ave.), Westwood, 310-209-0071; www.tengu.cc
■ The sushi is "tremendously fresh" and the "flavored sakes are a must try" at this "sexy" (and "expensive") Westwood

The Westside

F | D | S | C

Village Japanese owned by a syndicate of CAA agents; a "beautiful" crowd congregates in the "darkly elegant" space with live DJs spinning "hip" tunes, although some could do with fewer "smarmy men in suits and their plastic-enhanced companions."

Thai Dishes   18 | 11 | 17 | $17

9901 Washington Blvd. (Hughes Ave.), Culver City, 310-559-0987
22333 PCH (bet. Carbon Canyon Rd. & Malibu Pier), Malibu, 310-456-6592
111 Santa Monica Blvd. (bet. Ocean Ave. & 2nd St.), Santa Monica, 310-394-6189
1910 Wilshire Blvd. (19th St.), Santa Monica, 310-828-5634

This Siamese chain is "convenient" as well as "cheap", and its "semi-authentic", "Americanized" fare is "tasty" and good for those "having Thai for the first time", but "be careful", because the "spicy" dishes can "clear out your sinuses"; the service is "quick", but the "Denny's-like" decor leads many to opt for "takeout or delivery."

TLAPAZOLA GRILL Ⓜ   24 | 13 | 23 | $23

11676 Gateway Blvd. (Barrington Blvd.), West LA, 310-477-1577

■ It "pays to stray from the traditional" at this "surprising, enlightening Oaxacan treat" and "nouvelle Mexican", a "strip-mall ringer" in West LA with a "healthy, interesting menu" featuring "well-prepared", "beautifully presented" seafood and "complex, delicious" moles; props to the "wonderful", "friendly" staff for keeping the storefront setting so "clean."

Tony P's Dockside Grill   18 | 19 | 17 | $23

4445 Admiralty Way (bet. Bali Way & Via Marina), Marina del Rey, 310-823-4534

■ "Sit on a nice deck and watch the boats" in the "marina right below you" from the patio at this "upscale" Marina del Rey sports bar and restaurant where an "incredible view follows" "once the game is over"; "reasonably priced", "reliable steaks, ribs and fish", "homemade pommes frites" and "no-bones-about-it spicy boneless wings" are served in a "relaxing, casual atmosphere."

Tony Roma's   16 | 13 | 15 | $22

50 N. La Cienega Blvd. (Wilshire Blvd.), Beverly Hills, 310-659-7427
Westside Pavilion, 10850 W. Pico Blvd. (Westwood Blvd.), West LA, 310-470-0737
www.tonyromas.com

For those who can't "wear Prada every day", this BBQ chain's "fall-off-the-bone" tender babyback ribs and "delicious" onion rings are "all you need" when the "mood for a Midwestern meal" strikes; there's "no atmosphere" and the service can be a "liability", but the "giant portions" come at "surprisingly reasonable prices"; just "bring an

get updates at zagat.com

The Westside F | D | S | C

extra artery in case one gets clogged", especially on "all-you-can-eat Mondays."

Torafuku — | — | — | M
10914 W. Pico Blvd. (Westwood Blvd.), West LA, 310-470-0014
Decorated to look like a modern shogun's palace, this is the first American branch of a Japanese chain specializing in rice, imported from Japan and cooked in a trio of samurai-helmeted pots; there's also a sushi bar and yakitori items.

Toscana 24 | 18 | 20 | $41
11633 San Vicente Blvd. (Darlington Ave.), Brentwood, 310-820-2448
■ "Hollywood's idea of the perfect little Italian restaurant" is this somewhat "expensive" "Tuscan mecca" in Brentwood where the fare is "fantastic", the staff will treat you "like you've made their day", there are "movie deals in the making" and "plenty of beautiful people to observe"; just "don't expect to be able to hear your dinner partner" in the "noisy" room with arguably the "worst acoustics in LA."

Trader Vic's 18 | 23 | 20 | $43
Beverly Hilton Hotel, 9876 Wilshire Blvd. (Santa Monica Blvd.), Beverly Hills, 310-276-6345; www.merv.com
■ A "favorite" for "as long as anyone can remember", this faux-Asian lodged in the Beverly Hilton is "one of the last real tiki bars", where the "pupu platter is still a must", the libations "take up a four-page menu" and the "Polynesian" decor "makes you feel like you were in Hawaii or Tahiti"; "be prepared to spend a lot" for one of its "deceptively strong" tropical drinks, and remember to "pace yourself."

Tra Di Noi 22 | 18 | 19 | $35
Malibu Country Mart, 3835 Cross Creek Rd. (PCH), Malibu, 310-456-0169
■ "You never know which famous Malibu resident you'll be seated next to" at this "romantic, charming" Italian trattoria that's a "home run for lunch or dinner", thanks to dishes such as "outstanding artichoke pizzas" and "creative lemon oil–infused salads", not to mention a "lovely patio" and "stargazing galore"; N.B. a recent chef change may outdate the above Food score.

Trastevere 18 | 18 | 17 | $26
1360 Third St. Promenade (Santa Monica Blvd.), Santa Monica, 310-319-1985; www.trastevereristorante.com
See review in LA/Hollywood/W. Hollywood Directory.

Trattoria Amici 22 | 16 | 20 | $33
Beverly Terrace Hotel, 469 N. Doheny Dr. (Santa Monica Blvd.), Beverly Hills, 310-858-0271; www.tamici.com
■ "Charming" and "intimate", this amiable Beverly Hills Northern Italian attracts a "cross-generational clientele" (including, reportedly, the "ladies from *Friends*") with "well-

The Westside | F | D | S | C |

prepared", "mouthwatering" fare and "wonderful" service; despite the "hard-to-find" location and "loud" room, the "homestyle atmosphere" makes it a "nice trip away from LA and its pretense."

Tsuji No Hana ⓜ | 22 | 12 | 21 | $29 |
4714 Lincoln Blvd. (Mindanao Way), Marina del Rey, 310-827-1433

■ "If it isn't fresh, fresh, fresh it isn't on the menu" at this Marina del Rey Japanese where "big portions" of "excellent sushi and sashimi", as well as "tasty dishes from the kitchen", at "reasonable prices" make it a "great value for the money"; you're certainly not paying for lavish decor in the "utilitarian" space, and there's no extra charge for the "consistently friendly" service.

2117 ⓜ | 23 | 13 | 19 | $34 |
2117 Sawtelle Blvd. (bet. Mississippi Ave. & Olympic Blvd.), West LA, 310-477-1617

■ Offering "stellar gourmet cuisine in a storefront setting", this Cal-Asian "gem" "may be the best quiet bargain in the city"; chef Hideo Mitsuno "continues to please" with his "consistently inventive", "artful" creations, served by a "warm, attentive" staff in an "intimate", "comfortable" setting that overcomes the "depressing" strip-mall locale.

26 Beach Café | 20 | 15 | 16 | $21 |
26 Washington Blvd. (Pacific Ave.), Marina del Rey, 310-821-8129
3100 Washington Blvd. (Yale Ave.), Venice, 310-823-7526

■ "Humongous" hamburgers on "awesome" homemade buns, "enormous" salads and brunches that are "every dream come true for French toast fans" loom large at this affordable Cal duo; people-watchers can espy the "funky Venice Beach crowd" from the patio at the Marina del Rey branch, located a short walk from the pier, while the Washington sibling is larger and boasts a somewhat "more appealing decor."

Typhoon | 21 | 21 | 19 | $34 |
Santa Monica Airport, 3221 Donald Douglas Loop S. (Centinela Ave.), Santa Monica, 310-390-6565; www.typhoon.biz

■ Perhaps the "inspiration for *Fear Factor*", this Pan-Asian set on the runway of private Santa Monica Airport is famous for serving the "best bugs in town", along with "big portions" of "less adventurous" but still "delicious" dishes and "awesome" tropical drinks; "huge windows" provide "sensational views" of "Jetstreams taking off and landing."

Union | 20 | 24 | 20 | $45 |
1413 Fifth St. (Santa Monica Blvd.), Santa Monica, 310-656-9688; www.unionsantamonica.com

◪ A "pleasant surprise in a site that's been death to others", this two-story Santa Monica New American wins praise

The Westside | F | D | S | C |

for its "cosmopolitan setting", highlighted by a "delightful" upstairs patio that "smacks of martinis, jazz and cigars"; critics carp over "inconsistent" cooking and "erratic" service, but boosters point out the "ambiance is really what you come here for."

U-Zen | 22 | 12 | 19 | $29 |
11951 Santa Monica Blvd. (Brockton St.), West LA, 310-477-1390

■ "Fantastic, fresh sushi without the pretense of high-end places" and "reasonable prices" make this Japanese "hole-in-the-wall" a "favorite of West LA locals" and one of the "best bangs for the buck" around; the "friendly" staff makes you feel "comfortable" in the "forgettable" space, and if you sit at the sushi bar, the "amicable" chefs will make you "specials if you're nice."

VALENTINO ☒ | 27 | 23 | 26 | $66 |
3115 Pico Blvd. (bet. 31st & 32nd Sts.), Santa Monica, 310-829-4313; www.welovewine.com

■ "You'll have the meal of a lifetime (and then spend a lifetime paying for it)" at this Santa Monica establishment, LA's No. 1 Italian in this *Survey*, a "legend" and "deservedly so" for a 3,500-label wine list that's "beyond hyperbole" and "consistently superior" cuisine, served in a "gorgeous" yet "comfortable" setting; Piero Selvaggio is the "consummate host", "so solicitous you can discuss your back problems with him", and regulars are happy to leave the menu to him and "sit back and be dazzled."

Versailles | 22 | 9 | 17 | $16 |
10319 Venice Blvd. (Motor Ave.), Palms, 310-558-3168
See review in LA/Hollywood/W. Hollywood Directory.

Via Veneto | ▽ 26 | 18 | 23 | $43 |
(fka Il Nido)
3009 Main St. (bet. Marine St. & Pier Ave.), Santa Monica, 310-399-1843

■ "Wonderful, authentic" Italian cuisine, a "fantastic" wine list, "attentive" service, a "cozy" space with "romantic lighting" and a "buzzing, chic European vibe" – this Santa Monica "restaurant has it all", including a "celebrity" co-owner (guitarist Warren Cuccurullo of Duran Duran and Missing Persons fame); it's "expensive", but just think of "the money you save on plane tickets to Italy."

Vincenti Ⓜ | 24 | 23 | 22 | $56 |
11930 San Vicente Blvd. (Montana Ave.), Brentwood, 310-207-0127

◪ This "upscale" "Brentwood institution" "keeps getting better" as chef Nicolo Mastronardi's "talents come out in full force" to create "inspired" Italian dishes that are paired with an "extensive wine list" and served in a "homey, beautiful" room by an "adorable", "friendly" staff; it's

The Westside   F | D | S | C

"wildly overpriced" wail wallet-watchers, who warn that service can vary "if you're not a regular or don't order big."

V.I.P. Harbor Seafood   20 | 13 | 16 | $22
11701 Wilshire Blvd. (Barrington Ave.), West LA, 310-979-3377

■ For some of the "best dim sum outside of Chinatown", Sinophiles gravitate to this reasonably priced West LA Chinese that also serves a full selection of seafood at night, when you can "choose your fish, crab or lobster from the tanks"; the service is "fast" and "businesslike", and the "large", "well-lit" space includes a "small party room for special occasions."

Vito   22 | 18 | 21 | $34
2807 Ocean Park Blvd. (28th St.), Santa Monica, 310-450-4999

■ Located directly across from Santa Monica Airport, this "comfortably traditional" Italian takes you back to a "bygone era" with "tuxedoed waiters and wine bottles" making up "part of the decor"; not to be overlooked are the "delectable pastas", seafood "so fresh it's still swimming" and "amazing" dishes prepared tableside; the 30-percent discount card for regulars is a "wonderful bonus" to an already "excellent value."

Vittorio Ⓜ   ▽ 19 | 12 | 18 | $23
16646 Marquez Ave. (Sunset Blvd.), Pacific Palisades, 310-459-9316

■ There are "garlic rolls for everyone" at this "down-to-earth" Pacific Palisades Southern Italian that's "popular with locals" for its "simple", "homestyle" red-sauce fare, "fast", "friendly" service and "cozy", "comfortable" room; "every meal is an experience" here – albeit a "noisy" one.

Wabi-Sabi   24 | 20 | 15 | $35
1635 Abbot Kinney Blvd. (Venice Blvd.), Venice, 310-314-2229

■ Though the name sounds a bit "silly" for such a "serious sushi bar", it "must mean 'wow' in Japanese" (it really means to genuflect) gush groupies of this "trendy" Venice spot that "doesn't feel trendy", popular with the local, "hip, arty crowd" for its "inventive menu" of "melt-in-your-mouth" raw fare and "equally great cooked food", served in a "cool bohemian" space; it's "a little pricey, but worth it."

Warszawa Ⓜ   22 | 18 | 22 | $33
1414 Lincoln Blvd. (Santa Monica Blvd.), Santa Monica, 310-393-8831

■ The "delicious", "homestyle" fare at this midpriced "heavy-duty old-world restaurant" in Santa Monica will "open your eyes to how good Polish food can be" exclaim enthusiasts enamored of the "perfect" pierogi and "splendid pea soup", as well as the "attentive" service; the "quaint" digs "look like someone's house" and boast a "great back patio" that's "far off the beaten path."

get updates at zagat.com

The Westside	F	D	S	C

Whist
21 | 21 | 18 | $60

Viceroy Hotel, 1819 Ocean Ave. (Pico Blvd.), Santa Monica, 310-451-8711; www.viceroysantamonica.com

■ Orange County stars Tim and Liza Goodell (Aubergine, Troquet) have created this "elegant, upscale" American "outpost" at Santa Monica's stylish Viceroy Hotel located a block from the ocean; the menu is "superbly" built around seasonal produce and served in a "mod", "campy" space with an outdoor dining area adjacent to the pool; the "exquisite" ambiance makes up for the "dicey" service.

Wolfgang Puck Cafe
17 | 15 | 16 | $22

1323 Montana Ave. (13th St.), Santa Monica, 310-393-0290; www.wolfgangpuck.com

See review in LA/Hollywood/W. Hollywood Directory.

Woo Lae Oak
21 | 20 | 18 | $32

170 N. La Cienega Blvd. (Clifton Way), Beverly Hills, 310-652-4187; www.woolaeoak.org

See review in LA/Hollywood/W. Hollywood Directory.

Xi'an
21 | 17 | 19 | $28

362 N. Cañon Dr. (bet. Brighton & Dayton Ways), Beverly Hills, 310-275-3345

■ "Healthy, filling" Chinese fare with a "bit of a Californian influence" and "moderate prices" make this "busy" Beverly Hills Sino spot a "favorite" choice of a "mix of residents" for lunch or dinner "before the theater on Cañon"; "everyone is treated like a regular" in the modern-looking space, which tends to get "crowded" and "noisy."

Yabu
23 | 15 | 19 | $26

11820 W. Pico Blvd. (bet. Barrington Ave. & Bundy Dr.), West LA, 310-473-9757

See review in LA/Hollywood/W. Hollywood Directory.

Ye Olde King's Head
17 | 19 | 17 | $21

116 Santa Monica Blvd. (bet. Ocean Ave. & 2nd St.), Santa Monica, 310-451-1402; www.yeoldekingshead.com

■ A "home away from home for rock stars" and "rowdy" "expats from the UK", this "authentic British pub just off the Promenade" in Santa Monica offers "outstanding bangers 'n' mash" and the "ultimate fish 'n' chips", with "many beers on tap" and dart games that never end in a "dark wood" tavern setting that transports you to "an English roadhouse."

Zax M
24 | 20 | 22 | $43

11604 San Vicente Blvd. (bet. Barrington & Federal Aves.), Brentwood, 310-571-3800; www.zaxrestaurant.com

■ Despite the departure of chef Brooke Williamson, this Brentwood New American remains a "mecca for foodies" who "aren't worried about price"; "attentive, wonderful" service helps create an ambiance that's "motherly yet trendy" in the "pleasant", "brick-walled" space.

The Westside

F | **D** | **S** | **C**

Zeidler's Café M
▽ 20 | 17 | 19 | $18

Skirball Cultural Ctr., 2701 S. Sepulveda Blvd. (Mulholland Dr.), Brentwood, 310-440-4515; www.skirball.org

■ "What a relief, a museum without prefab food!" exclaim visitors to Brentwood's Skirball Cultural Center, where a "trip isn't complete without a divine lunch" at this Cal-kosher lunch-only dairy cafe operated by cookbook author Judy Zeidler; "cool salads, great soups" and other "very nice" dishes make it a "good value for the money."

Zen Grill
21 | 15 | 17 | $22

9111 W. Olympic Blvd. (Doheny Dr.), Beverly Hills, 310-278-7773

See review in LA/Hollywood/W. Hollywood Directory.

The South Bay and Long Beach

Top Food

27 Christine
　 Gina Lee's Bistro
26 Frenchy's Bistro
　 Chez Melange
　 Fleming's Prime
24 Reed's
　 555 East
　 Depot, The
　 Christy's
　 Uncle Bill's Pancake

Top Decor

28 Madison, The
24 Kincaid's
　 Encounter
　 L'Opera
23 Christy's
　 Fleming's Prime
22 Depot, The
21 Lasher's
　 555 East
　 Chart House

Top Service

25 Christine
24 Reed's
　 Shenandoah Cafe
　 Chez Melange
23 Lasher's
　 Fleming's Prime
　 Mama D's
　 Christy's
　 Papadakis Tav.
22 555 East

Top Value

1. In-N-Out Burger
2. Noah's NY Bagels
3. Baja Fresh
4. Uncle Bill's Pancake
5. Jody Maroni's Sausage
6. Loft, The
7. La Salsa
8. Johnny Rockets
9. Ruby's
10. Martha's 22nd St.

By Location

El Segundo
26 Fleming's Prime
22 Taiko
20 P.F. Chang's
19 McCorm. & Schmick's
18 Thai Dishes

Long Beach
26 Frenchy's Bistro
24 555 East
　 Christy's
　 Shenandoah Cafe
22 Lasher's

Manhattan Beach
24 Reed's
　 Uncle Bill's Pancake
23 Cafe Pierre
22 Versailles
　 Michi

Redondo Beach
27 Gina Lee's Bistro
26 Chez Melange
23 Zazou
22 Kincaid's
21 Coyote Cantina

Torrance
27 Christine
24 Depot, The
22 Lucille's Smokehse.
21 BCD Tofu Hse.
20 Mishima

The South Bay and Long Beach Restaurant Directory

South Bay and Long Beach | F | D | S | C |

Addi's Tandoor ▽ 20 | 18 | 22 | $22
525 S. PCH (Ruby St.), Redondo Beach, 310-540-1616; www.addistandoor.com
■ Thanks to an engaging owner from Goa, this "glossy"-looking Indian newcomer in Redondo Beach has already won a loyal following among admirers who know that the "lunch buffet is a bargain" and that dinner offers a "varied menu with no losers"; not only is it a "vegetarian's paradise", but come weekends, the "sitar player and his bongo accompaniment add an excellent touch."

Aioli ⊠ 20 | 20 | 19 | $31
1261 Cabrillo Ave. (Torrance Blvd.), Torrance, 310-320-9200; www.aiolirestaurant.com
■ A prime "choice in Torrance for business lunches" (ok, "one of the few") among the honchos at the nearby Toyota and Honda corporate offices, this welcoming "oasis" features an "interesting fusion" of Cal-Med flavors; whether seated inside the modern dining room or out on the pleasant patio, boosters recommend preceding the "consistently good" entrees with selections from the tapas bar.

Alegria 19 | 20 | 17 | $28
115 Pine Ave. (bet. B'way & 1st St.), Long Beach, 562-436-3388; www.alegriacocinalatina.com
■ Not to be confused with the Italian trattoria Allegria in Malibu, this Long Beach Nuevo Latino fiesta looks like it could've been designed by Gaudí, with its mosaic tile floors and bold colors; it's a "fabulous" setting for nibbling on "authentic tapas" and "delicious paella" while taking in the nightly live entertainment ("foxy flamenco", salsa, jazz), so it's no wonder it's "packed on weekends with good-looking singles", both inside and out on the patio.

Alejo's 21 | 8 | 16 | $17
8343 Lincoln Blvd. (84th St.), Westchester, 310-670-6677
See review in Westside Directory.

Back Home in Lahaina 16 | 16 | 17 | $14
916 N. Sepulveda Blvd. (9th St.), Manhattan Beach, 310-374-0111
■ "Oh, brudda, you can't find more island style than this" sprawling Manhattan Beach Hawaiian offering a "taste of Hawaii the way the locals like it" – i.e. "huge portions" of "comfort food" such as fried chicken "just how my mom used to make" served by a "laid-back" staff in a "funky" room full of "aloha spirit."

BAJA FRESH MEXICAN GRILL ⊠ Ⓜ ⌀ 20 | 11 | 15 | $9
Los Altos Shopping Ctr., 2090 Bellflower Blvd. (bet. Abbeyfield St. & Britton Dr.), Long Beach, 562-596-9080; www.bajafresh.com
See review in LA/Hollywood/W. Hollywood Directory.

South Bay and Long Beach | F | D | S | C |

BCD Tofu House ⓪   21 | 12 | 14 | $13 |
1607 Sepulveda Blvd. (bet. Lockness & Western Aves.), Torrance, 310-534-3480
See review in LA/Hollywood/W. Hollywood Directory.

Belmont Brewing Co.   17 | 19 | 17 | $23 |
25 39th Pl. (bet. Allin & Midway Sts.), Long Beach, 562-433-3891; www.belmontbrewing.com

■ As "romantic" as a microbrewery can be, this Long Beach American offers "calming", "spectacular" vistas of the ocean and the Queen Mary from a "long outdoor patio" where you "can easily make a meal" of the appetizers that go with the "great ales and beers made on the premises"; so "come for the view and stay for a brew."

Benihana   19 | 18 | 21 | $32 |
21327 Hawthorne Blvd. (Fashion Way), Torrance, 310-316-7777; www.benihana.com
See review in Westside Directory.

Bistro Laramie   – | – | – | M |
18202 S. Western Ave. (182nd St.), Gardena, 310-532-6555
Chef Makoto Tanaka (Mako in Beverly Hills) quietly opened this minimalist Asian fusion cafe for lunch in the Japanese enclave of Gardena; he's now open for dinner, offering a variation on what you'd find at a Continental fusion eatery in Tokyo, meaning Asian-style crab cakes and beef rib and curry rice, all served at prices that are way down there.

BJ's ⓪   17 | 15 | 16 | $18 |
5258 E. Second St. (La Verne St.), Long Beach, 562-439-8181; www.bjsbrewhouse.com
See review in Westside Directory.

Blue Pacific   ▽ 23 | 20 | 24 | $27 |
201 Hermosa Ave. (2nd St.), Hermosa Beach, 310-406-8986

■ The "best-kept secret in the South Bay", this Cal-Asian offers a "myriad of creative dishes", from "fantastic" Vietnamese spring rolls to an "eclectic variety of sushi", at "modest prices"; "attentive" service and "cozy tables by the big windows" make it a "good date place", but it's "small", so be "sure you make reservations."

Bluewater Grill   19 | 17 | 18 | $29 |
King Harbor Marina, 665 N. Harbor Dr. (Beryl St.), Redondo Beach, 310-318-3474; www.bluewatergrill.com

■ There's "no nonsense" about this seafood chain with a New England theme, only "fresh, honest", "delicious fish, plain and simple", cooked "however you want it" from a "menu that changes daily"; the service is "friendly" and the decor "casual", with "fishing pictures on the walls", and "fabulous views of the marina" at the Redondo Beach and Newport Beach locations.

get updates at zagat.com

South Bay and Long Beach | F | D | S | C |

Bora Bora M ▽ 21 | 22 | 20 | $35
3505 Highland Ave. (35th St.), Manhattan Beach, 310-545-6464
■ A "true gem" "hidden in Manhattan Beach's north end", this "intimate" Cal-Asian is one of the area's "best-kept secrets", "tucked between a laundromat and a hair salon"; those who find it can expect "bold, delicious seafood combinations", "excellent soups" and other dishes in a "small" Trader Vic's–like room; "friendly" service and "comfy booths" make it a "great date" venue.

Brewski's 16 | 14 | 16 | $18
73 Pier Ave. (Hermosa Ave.), Hermosa Beach, 310-318-2666
■ For "home-brewed beer" and "simple" American fare "while taking in the beachgoers" from the patio, this "fun, loud" "classic California beach hangout" is "always a good call in Hermosa"; though there's "nothing exceptional", fans insist "you can't go wrong" with the "above-average" pub-grub menu.

Buca di Beppo 14 | 17 | 17 | $22
1670 S. PCH (Palos Verdes Blvd.), Redondo Beach, 310-540-3246; www.bucadibeppo.com
See review in Westside Directory.

Buggy Whip 18 | 16 | 20 | $29
7420 La Tijera Blvd. (74th St.), Westchester, 310-645-7131
■ "Old school all the way", this stalwart steakhouse in Westchester is the "kind of restaurant your parents used to go to when they were young", serving "wonderful" prime rib and other "traditional" fare in a "wood-and-leather"-decorated room; it's maybe one of the "last places in town with green goddess dressing" on its salads.

Cafe Pierre 23 | 20 | 21 | $36
317 Manhattan Beach Blvd. (bet. Highland Ave. & Morningside Dr.), Manhattan Beach, 310-545-5252
■ Where "bistro meets the beach", this "laidback coastal" French "only two blocks from the [Manhattan Beach] Pier" is where surfers and skateboarders head for one of the "best South Bay culinary experiences" – an "innovative" menu and "extensive" wine list served by a "friendly, efficient" staff in an understated room with doors that open wide to let in the sea breezes.

CALIFORNIA PIZZA KITCHEN 18 | 14 | 17 | $18
Manhattan Village Mall, 3280 N. Sepulveda Blvd. (Rosecrans Ave.), Manhattan Beach, 310-796-1233; www.cpk.com
See review in LA/Hollywood/W. Hollywood Directory.

Chart House 19 | 21 | 18 | $34
231 Yacht Club Way (bet. Harbor Dr. & Herondo St.), Redondo Beach, 310-372-3464; www.landrysrestaurants.com
See review in Westside Directory.

South Bay and Long Beach | F | D | S | C |

CHEESECAKE FACTORY 20 | 18 | 18 | $23
605 N. Harbor Dr. (190th St.), Redondo Beach, 310-376-0466;
www.thecheesecakefactory.com
See review in Westside Directory.

CHEZ MELANGE 26 | 17 | 24 | $35
Palos Verdes Inn, 1716 PCH (bet. Palos Verdes Blvd. & Prospect Ave.), Redondo Beach, 310-540-1222;
www.chezmelange.com
■ Chef/co-owner Robert Bell is back "cooking up a storm" and (co-)"owner par excellence" Michael Franks is "always at hand" at their Redondo Beach Eclectic, a "South Bay landmark" that's "aptly named" given the "extensive, inventive" daily-changing menu that ranges from sushi bar selections to Cajun meatloaf; "excellent" service helps add a little "*chi*" to the "cheesy" "hotel coffee shop setting."

CHRISTINE 27 | 21 | 25 | $36
Hillside Village, 24530 Hawthorne Blvd. (Via Valmonte), Torrance, 310-373-1952; www.restaurantchristine.com
■ The "jewel of the South Bay", "master" chef-owner Christine Brown's Torrance Cal-Med is the showcase for her "dazzlingly creative", "perfectly executed" dishes that "shine every time" and "keep one coming back"; the "friendly, efficient" staff "knows almost as much about the food as she does" and devotes "personal attention" to everyone in the "modest", "warm, hospitable" room that offers "people-viewing from the loft" and an "open window into the kitchen."

Christy's 24 | 23 | 23 | $38
3937 E. Broadway (Termino Ave.), Long Beach, 562-433-7133;
www.christysristorante.com
■ The beat goes on at Christy Bono's (daughter of the late Sonny Bono) "Long Beach favorite" offering "wonderful", "reliable" Italian fare complemented by a "fantastic wine list"; "romantic lighting" and "lovely ambiance" in the "cozy, warm" rooms (one of which boasts a wall of cascading water) make it a "perfect date" place.

Claim Jumper Restaurant 18 | 16 | 18 | $22
Marketplace Shopping Ctr., 6501 E. PCH (2nd St.), Long Beach, 562-431-1321
24301 Crenshaw Blvd. (Lomita Blvd.), Torrance, 310-517-1874
www.claimjumper.com
■ The "Jurassic"-sized portions ("big enough to qualify for humanitarian aid") at this popular suburban chain may offer an "interesting" glimpse into "American gluttony" "if you're a sociologist", but if you just want to "strap on a feedbag and binge", the meat-centric American fare can be "pretty tasty" and "reasonably priced"; the "wait is horrible" but "you never leave hungry."

get updates at zagat.com 161

South Bay and Long Beach | F | D | S | C |

Coyote Cantina | 21 | 18 | 21 | $25 |
King Harbor Ctr., 531 N. PCH (190th St.), Redondo Beach, 310-376-1066
■ Owner "Chaz Gaddie rules" and "makes everyone feel special" at his Redondo Beach mini-mall destination serving "inventive" Southwestern fare "with chutzpah" and the "South Bay's best margaritas" in a "neighborhood scene that's welcome to all"; it's "noisy", but "friendly" service helps make it a "memorable", "howling good time."

Cozymel's | 15 | 17 | 16 | $20 |
2171 Rosecrans Ave. (Continental Way), El Segundo, 310-606-5464
◪ In El Segundo, this popular "chain Mex" offers "yummy", "well-priced" south-of-the-border fare, including "fabulous guacamole and seafood that's quite respectable", and a "wide variety of margaritas" in a "fun and funky" setting for a "loud crowd"; detractors dismiss it as a "Taco Bell with nicer furniture" and a "forced festive vibe", but fans insist the "outside patio is perfect for happy hour."

Daily Grill | 17 | 16 | 17 | $25 |
2121 Rosecrans Ave. (Continental Way), El Segundo, 310-524-0700
LA Int'l Airport, Tom Bradley Terminal (Sepulveda Blvd.), LAX, 310-215-5180
www.dailygrill.com
See review in LA/Hollywood/W. Hollywood Directory.

Depot, The ⌧ | 24 | 22 | 22 | $36 |
1250 Cabrillo Ave. (Torrance Blvd.), Torrance, 310-787-7501; www.depotrestaurant.com
■ "Bravo" chef-owner Michael Shafer, who "always entertains with his food and his persona" at this Eclectic in the heart of Old Torrance, where he prepares "adventurous" dishes with a "Cal-Asian flair" when he's not "schmoozing tableside"; though it's popular with execs from nearby Honda and Toyota, it "serves for both business or pleasure" equally well, and fans "would love to station [themselves]" in the "restored train depot" where it's housed.

EL CHOLO | 18 | 18 | 17 | $21 |
LA Int'l Airport, Terminal 5, LAX, 310-417-1910; www.elcholo.com
See review in LA/Hollywood/W. Hollywood Directory.

El Pollo Inka | 18 | 11 | 15 | $15 |
Gateway Plaza, 1425 W. Artesia Blvd. (Normandie Ave.), Gardena, 310-516-7378
1100 PCH (Aviation Blvd.), Hermosa Beach, 310-372-1433
Lawndale Plaza, 15400 Hawthorne Blvd. (154th St.), Lawndale, 310-676-6665
23705 Hawthorne Blvd. (bet. Lomita Blvd. & PCH), Torrance, 310-373-0062
www.elpolloinka.com
See review in Westside Directory.

South Bay and Long Beach | F | D | S | C |

El Torito | 14 | 14 | 15 | $18 |
11855 S. Hawthorne Blvd. (bet. 118th & 119th Sts.), Hawthorne, 310-679-0233
6605 PCH (bet. 2nd St. & Westminster Ave.), Long Beach, 562-594-6917
100G Fisherman's Wharf (S. Catalina Ave.), Redondo Beach, 310-376-0547
www.eltorito.com
See review in Westside Directory.

El Torito Grill | 17 | 16 | 16 | $22 |
21321 Hawthorne Blvd. (Torrance Blvd.), Torrance, 310-543-1896; www.eltorito.com
See review in Westside Directory.

Encounter | 14 | 24 | 17 | $32 |
LA Int'l Airport, 209 World Way (bet. Terminals 1 & 2), LAX, 310-215-5151; www.encounterrestaurant.com

◾ That giant spider squatting in the middle of LAX is actually a Cal-Continental "space-age retro playground" with a Disney-designed decor, complete with lava lamps and laser light–emitting drink dispensers, that's straight out of the "*Jetsons*"; the fare is "not much better than airline food", but it's "fun to watch the planes come and go" in such a "trippy" setting; unfortunately, "most people in LA don't know it exists, and even those at the airport don't know how to get there."

555 East | 24 | 21 | 22 | $43 |
555 E. Ocean Blvd. (Linden St.), Long Beach, 562-437-0626; www.kingsseafood.com

◾ "Professionals created" this "dark, clubby steakhouse" in the heart of Long Beach, the granddaddy of the King's Seafood chain, "and it shows" in the "great steaks", "wonderful fish specials" and "intelligent wine list", as well as the "NY-style" setting "complete with surly yet accommodating waiters" and "big leather booths"; for meat eaters "it doesn't get any better than this."

FLEMING'S PRIME STEAKHOUSE & WINE BAR | 26 | 23 | 23 | $50 |
2301 Rosecrans Ave. (Aviation Blvd.), El Segundo, 310-643-6911; www.flemingssteakhouse.com
See review in Orange County Directory.

Fonz's | 21 | 17 | 20 | $34 |
1017 Manhattan Ave. (bet. 10th Pl. & 11th St.), Manhattan Beach, 310-376-1536

◾ Named after the father of co-owner and "beach volleyball champ" Mike Dodd, this "upscale" surf 'n' turf has a "laid-back approach" that's "just as it should be in Manhattan Beach"; the "food is off the page" – from "succulent" steaks to "decadently rich" lobster bisque – and the "people are

South Bay and Long Beach | F | D | S | C |

friendly", but wags quip that patrons "should be served olive oil since they cram us in like sardines."

Francesca M ▽ 20 | 18 | 21 | $32 |
1209 Highland Ave. (12th Pl.), Manhattan Beach, 310-545-3509
◪ This former take-out place in Manhattan Beach has won a "loyal following" with "creative", "delicious" Cal-Eclectic dishes in "just-right portions", served in a "cozy" room boasting a "funky" decor; critics find the fare "uneven", but fans argue it's "more hit than miss", with "great execution on simple favorites" such as the "best eggs Benedict for brunch", and "who can say no to mimosas in wine goblets?"

FRENCHY'S BISTRO M 26 | 15 | 21 | $38 |
4137 E. Anaheim St. (bet. Termino & Ximeno Aves.), Long Beach, 562-494-8787; www.frenchysbistro.com
■ A "spirited, very loyal local clientele" "thanks the culinary gods" for chef-owner Andre Angles' "fantastic" French bistro, an "unexpected gem" in an "iffy" part of Long Beach offering "superb" Gallic dishes, an "impressive" wine list "filled with bargains", and "exceptional" service in a "simple" storefront space.

Fritto Misto 21 | 11 | 19 | $19 |
316 Pier Ave. (Monterey Blvd.), Hermosa Beach, 310-318-6098
See review in Westside Directory.

GINA LEE'S BISTRO M 27 | 14 | 22 | $32 |
Riviera Plaza, 211 Palos Verdes Blvd. (bet. Catalina Ave. & PCH), Redondo Beach, 310-375-4462
■ "One of the top spots in the South Bay", this "hidden jewel" in Redondo Beach is "always off-the-hook busy" thanks to a "creative" menu of "stellar" Cal-Asian dishes that's "sure to make you a regular", and if it doesn't, the "graciousness of owners Scott and Gina Lee" just might; a "strip-mall location" and "poor acoustics" aren't enough to drive off a "loyal clientele", including many who would choose this spot for their "last meal on earth."

Green Field Churrascaria 18 | 15 | 19 | $28 |
5305 E. PCH (Anaheim St.), Long Beach, 562-597-0906; www.greenfieldchurrascaria.com
■ At this Brazilian "Meats-R-Us" duo in Long Beach and West Covina, outposts of the national churrascaria chain, "streams of charming waiters" come to your table with "abundant skewers" of flesh ranging from "filet mignon to rabbit" in an oversized "barnlike setting"; vegetarians, take heart: there's also a "magnificent" salad bar.

HOUSTON'S 21 | 19 | 20 | $29 |
Manhattan Mktpl., 1550 Rosecrans Ave. (bet. S. Sepulveda Blvd. & Village Dr.), Manhattan Beach, 310-643-7211; www.houstons.com
See review in Westside Directory.

South Bay and Long Beach | F | D | S | C |

Il Boccaccio ▽ 22 | 16 | 20 | $34
39 Pier Ave. (bet. Hermosa Ave. & The Strand), Hermosa Beach, 310-376-0211; www.ilboccaccio.com

■ Pros promise "you'll like what you find" at this Hermosa Beach Italian serving an "excellent selection" of "always impeccable" fare, including lasagna that's the "absolute best"; though it's the "most refined place" on a walking street replete with beer and margarita joints, appealing to "the older set", it can get surprisingly "noisy."

IL FORNAIO 20 | 19 | 19 | $29
Gateway Shopping Ctr., 1800 Rosecrans Ave. (bet. S. Sepulveda Blvd. & Village Dr.), Manhattan Beach, 310-725-9555; www.ilfornaio.com
See review in Westside Directory.

Inka Grill 19 | 13 | 17 | $17
Long Beach Town Ctr., 7563 Carson St. (west of Frwy. 605), Long Beach, 562-627-0087; www.inkagrill.com
See review in Orange County Directory.

IN-N-OUT BURGER ◐ 24 | 10 | 18 | $7
8767 Firestone Blvd. (I-5), Downey, 800-786-1000
5820 Bellflower Blvd. (South St.), Lakewood, 800-786-1000
7691 Carson St. (Frwy. 605), Long Beach, 800-786-1000
6391 E. PCH (Westminster Ave.), Long Beach, 800-786-1000
4600 Los Coyotes Diagonal (Rosade St.), Long Beach, 800-786-1000
3801 Inglewood Ave. (Marine Ave.), Redondo Beach, 800-786-1000
1090 N. Western Ave. (Capitol Dr.), San Pedro, 800-786-1000
24445 Crenshaw Blvd. (Lomita Blvd.), Torrance, 800-786-1000
730 W. Carson St. (Vermont Ave.), Torrance, 800-786-1000
9149 S. Sepulveda Blvd. (Westchester Pkwy.), Westchester, 800-786-1000
www.in-n-out.com
See review in LA/Hollywood/W. Hollywood Directory.

Islands 16 | 16 | 17 | $14
3200 Sepulveda Blvd. (bet. 30th & 33rd Sts.), Manhattan Beach, 310-546-4456
2647 PCH (Crenshaw Blvd.), Torrance, 310-530-5383
www.islandsrestaurants.com
See review in Westside Directory.

Jackson's Village Bistro ▽ 24 | 16 | 22 | $27
517 Pier Ave. (bet. Bard St. & Cypress Ave.), Hermosa Beach, 310-376-6714

■ Boosters of this "best-kept secret in the South Bay" praise its "wonderful", "good value" New American fare (like the "unparalleled lamb shank") as being a "great find in the land of so-so restaurants"; the "former storefront" setting is "quaint" but "cramped", so sitting outside on "balmy

South Bay and Long Beach | F | D | S | C |

summer evenings" "when all the beach bodies saunter by" is a bonus.

Jody Maroni's Sausage Kingdom | 19 | 6 | 13 | $9 |
LA Int'l Airport, Terminals 3 & 6 (Sepulveda Blvd.), LAX, 310-646-4455; www.jodymaroni.com
See review in Westside Directory.

Joe's Crab Shack | 15 | 17 | 16 | $23 |
6550 Marina Dr. (Studebaker Rd.), Long Beach, 562-594-6551
230 Portofino Way (Harbor Dr.), Redondo Beach, 310-406-1999
www.joescrabshack.com

■ There's "crazy decor and crazy stuff" at this "eclectic and eccentric" seafood chain that's "great for large groups and kids", where you "better be prepared to get messy" digging into trays of "garlic-flavored crabs", while digging the servers who "sing the night away"; be prepared to kill some time as well, for the "wait can be extensive."

JOHNNY REBS' | 22 | 16 | 20 | $19 |
SOUTHERN ROADHOUSE
16639 Bellflower Blvd. (Laurel St.), Bellflower, 562-866-6455
4663 Long Beach Blvd. (bet. 46th & 47th Sts.), Long Beach, 562-423-7327
www.johnnyrebs.com

■ "Where else in LA can you get fried okra and Brunswick stew?" except at these Bellflower and Long Beach Southern BBQ spots that also offer "authentic pulled pork" and "wonderful fried green tomatoes" served in a "roadhouse" setting with "peanut shells on the floor" that "looks like something out of the *Dukes of Hazzard*; be warned that you'll probably leave "wearing the food."

Johnny Rockets ● | 16 | 15 | 16 | $12 |
Pine Ct., 245 Pine Ave. (bet. B'way & 3rd St.), Long Beach, 562-983-1332
Manhattan Mktpl., 1550 Rosecrans Ave. (Sepulveda Blvd.), Manhattan Beach, 310-536-9464
www.johnnyrockets.com
See review in LA/Hollywood/W. Hollywood Directory.

Kamiyama | ▽ 22 | 6 | 20 | $24 |
2408 Lomita Blvd. (Pennsylvania Ave.), Lomita, 310-257-1363
3001 N. Sepulveda Blvd. (bet. Marine & Rosecrans Aves.), Manhattan Beach, 310-545-0554
www.kamiyamasushi.com

■ These cult favorite "solid" sushi specialists may "not be much to look at" (sit-down in Lomita, take-out in Manhattan Beach), "but the staff is friendly and the sushi is made to order"; surveyors single out the "very original rolls" with names like "Krunch and SLUR (Salmon Lover's Ultimate Roll)", because "once you've tried them, you're hooked."

South Bay and Long Beach F | D | S | C |

Khoury's ▽ 15 | 15 | 16 | $29 |
110 Marina Dr. (N. Studebaker Rd.), Long Beach, 562-598-6800; www.khourys.net

🔲 Proponents of this Long Beach Harbor Continental praise its Saturday night "all-you-can-eat seafood buffet", "best-deal" Sunday brunch and "romantic ocean views", but the less enthused crab about only "ok" food, "poor service" and the "banquet-hall feel" of the place.

Kincaid's 22 | 24 | 21 | $39 |
Redondo Beach Pier, 500 Fisherman's Wharf (Torrance Blvd.), Redondo Beach, 310-318-6080; www.kincaids.com

■ With the "best waterfront view in the South Bay", the Redondo Beach Pier branch of this steak-and-seafood chain is the "perfect place to take an out-of-town guest" "at sunset", for "tremendous margaritas" and "anything that's been applewood smoked", along with "good prime rib" and "very fresh seafood"; the "great bar" offers small, special dishes for those who want a casual evening watching a Lakers game on the water; it's "a bit pricey", but it "even pleases my father-in-law, who doesn't like anything."

King's Fish House/ King Crab Lounge 20 | 18 | 18 | $29 |
100 W. Broadway (Pine Ave.), Long Beach, 562-432-7463; www.kingsseafood.com

■ This sprawling seafood chain has found a niche as a "favorite" due to its "reasonably priced", "dependable" and "extremely wide selection of seafood" and "terrific oysters and chowder"; the main dining rooms have "classic" fish house decor with booths, while the funkier adjoining crab lounges resemble Louisiana fish shacks, serving up big portions of shrimp and crabs.

Koo Koo Roo 16 | 8 | 13 | $11 |
Manhattan Village Mall, 3294 Sepulveda Blvd. (Rosecrans Ave.), Manhattan Beach, 310-546-4500
415 Pacific Coast Hwy. (Carnelian St.), Redondo Beach, 310-372-7500
21300 Hawthorne Blvd. (bet. Carson St. & Torrance Blvd.), Torrance, 310-792-3900
www.kookooroo.com
See review in LA/Hollywood/W. Hollywood Directory.

La Brea Bakery Café – | – | – | M |
1430 PCH (Ave. F), Redondo Beach, 310-316-3131; www.labreabakery.com

The original bakery sits next to Campanile on La Brea, the first La Brea Bakery Cafe is in Downtown Disney and now comes this branch in the most southern of the Beach Cities; in a space that's part bakery and part well-lit cafe, the likes of grilled shrimp crostini, Sicilian tuna on rustic olive bread and panzanella salad with the best croutons

South Bay and Long Beach   F | D | S | C

imaginable are served at either indoor or outdoor tables or at a cozy counter ideal for single diners.

LA Food Show   – | – | – | M
Manhattan Village Mall, 3212 N. Sepulveda Blvd. (Rosecrans Ave.), Manhattan Beach, 310-546-5575
From the creators of California Pizza Kitchen (Larry Flax and Rick Rosenfield) comes this new Cal-American concept, which might be seen as CPK without the pizzas; there's a massive display kitchen, done in red, red and more red, and a family-friendly menu with the likes of avocado club rolls, babyback ribs and buttermilk-battered fried chicken; there's a full bar as well.

La Salsa   16 | 9 | 13 | $10
5325 E. Second St. (Pomona Ave.), Long Beach, 562-433-0221
2790 Manhattan Beach Blvd. (bet. Gibson Pl. & Inglewood Ave.), Redondo Beach, 310-793-9444
www.lasalsa.com
See review in LA/Hollywood/W. Hollywood Directory.

Lasher's M   22 | 21 | 23 | $38
3441 E. Broadway (bet. Newport & Redondo Aves.), Long Beach, 562-433-0153
■ "You'll feel like you just dropped in for dinner" at this "converted California bungalow" in Long Beach, a "warm", "homestyle gourmet" American with "attentive" service, "winning clam chowder and wonderful steaks"; it's "always consistent", and wallet-watchers note that "Thursday is wine lover's night and there are no corkage" fees.

Loft, The   19 | 16 | 18 | $13
23305 Hawthorne Blvd. (Lomita Blvd.), Torrance, 310-375-4051
■ "For those secret Spam lovers, it's the place to go" say surveyors about this South Bay Hawaiian serving "super-large portions" of "don't-miss island-style fried chicken", plate lunches and other "comfort food" at "cheap prices" in a "laid-back" atmosphere; "be prepared to leave with leftovers and a stuffed stomach."

L'Opera   22 | 24 | 22 | $42
101 Pine Ave. (1st St.), Long Beach, 562-491-0066; www.lopera.com
■ "My Italian mother makes excellent food", but nothing like the "ravioli stuffed with lobster" at this Downtown Long Beach establishment "in an old bank building"; "if you want to impress a date, bring them here" for a "fabulous dinner" served by a "friendly" staff in a "pretty" setting that also offers "live opera" on Saturday nights; the "wonderful" *vino* list is "extensive" and the wine cellar is in the vault, which is convenient because "you may need a loan" to pay the tab, but "it's worth it."

South Bay and Long Beach F | D | S | C |

Lucille's Smokehouse Bar-B-Que   22 | 19 | 19 | $23 |
7411 Carson St. (Nectar Ave.), Long Beach, 562-938-7427
4828 E. Second St. (St. Joseph Ave.), Long Beach, 562-434-7427
Del Amo Fashion Ctr., 21420 Hawthorne Blvd.
(Del Amo Circle Blvd.), Torrance, 310-370-7427
www.lucillesbbq.com

■ With four sprawling branches (one in OC), this Southern BBQ culinary theme park with a zany "roadhouse" feel dominates the South Bay when it comes to "great tasting ribs", the "best pulled-pork sandwich" and "real smoking", which is done in-house in a machine that looks like it was designed by Rube Goldberg; "ferociously long lines attest to the fact" that "this is what 'cue is all about."

MADISON, THE ⓈⒾ   21 | 28 | 21 | $48 |
102 Pine Ave. (1st St.), Long Beach, 562-628-8866;
www.themadisonrestaurant.com

■ Not just "another restaurant in a bank", this steak-and-seafood sibling of nearby L'Opera boasts a "spectacular, huge dining room" with a "high", "colorful vaulted ceiling" that makes it a "fabulous place to impress a date"; the steaks are "outstanding" and the staff is "friendly and competent", but the food and service "need to catch up with the decor", especially since, like a real financial institution, it takes "an interest in keeping a good chunk of your money."

Mama D's   21 | 12 | 23 | $20 |
1125 Manhattan Ave. (Manhattan Beach Blvd.),
Manhattan Beach, 310-546-1492

■ "You'll understand the line" at this "lively" Manhattan Beach Italian "a short walk from the Pier" after experiencing the "terrific", "honest" fare, "über-friendly" service and "warm homemade cookies at the end of the meal"; "even the wait is fun", thanks in part to the "killer" garlic bread served to those standing outside, and while the room is "cramped" and the "seating is NYC-tight", somehow that "adds to its charm."

Marcello Tuscany Room   ▽ 23 | 24 | 22 | $31 |
470 W. Seventh St. (S. Pacific Ave.), San Pedro,
310-519-7100

■ A "gem" "in the middle of downtown San Pedro", this "stylish" Northern Italian "promises to be a winner for our community", with a "wonderful", "breathtaking" space that "feels like Tuscany" and a chef who "makes food sing" ("superb" gnocchi, "dreamy risotto", "veal shank so tender it fell off the bone"); it's "expensive, but worth it" for a "great dining experience."

Marmalade Café   18 | 17 | 17 | $23 |
Ave. of the Peninsula Mall, 550 Deep Valley Dr. (Crossfield Dr.),
Rolling Hills, 310-544-6700
See review in Westside Directory.

South Bay and Long Beach | F | D | S | C |

Martha's 22nd St. Grill | 21 | 14 | 19 | $15 |
25 22nd St. (Hermosa Ave.), Hermosa Beach, 310-376-7786
■ "There's no better place to feel Californian than" this South Bay "cafe by the sea" that's "a must for breakfast, lunch or brunch", where "rollerbladers, skateboarders and dog walkers" gather "on the patio" to "enjoy the view of the ocean" over "eclectic New Age scrambles and omelets", a "wide variety of sandwiches" and more; "you'll have to wait", so just "think beach, sun, breezy clean air."

McCormick & Schmick's | 19 | 19 | 19 | $33 |
2101 Rosecrans Ave. (Continental Way), El Segundo, 310-416-1123; www.mccormickandschmicks.com
See review in LA/Hollywood/W. Hollywood Directory.

Michi | 22 | 21 | 19 | $40 |
903 Manhattan Ave. (9th St.), Manhattan Beach, 310-376-0613
■ For a taste of "West LA sophistication", the "beautiful people" of Manhattan Beach flock to this "lively bar and cozy restaurant" where you can grab a "meticulously mixed" martini and match it with "terrific" "Japanese-influenced" Asian fusion creations; while the "see-and-be-seen scene" can get "crowded and noisy", the crowd is "not pretentious" and the bartenders are "the best in the South Bay."

Mimi's Cafe | 18 | 17 | 18 | $18 |
12727 Towne Center Dr. (Bloomfield Ave.), Cerritos, 562-809-0510
8455 Firestone Blvd. (Brookshire Ave.), Downey, 562-862-2828
6670 E. PCH (N. Studebaker Rd.), Long Beach, 562-596-0831
25343 Crenshaw Blvd. (Airport Dr.), Torrance, 310-326-4477
www.mimiscafe.com
See review in LA/Hollywood/W. Hollywood Directory.

Mishima | 20 | 14 | 18 | $16 |
East Gate Plaza, 21605 S. Western Ave. (W. 216th St.), Torrance, 310-320-2089; www.mishima.com
See review in LA/Hollywood/W. Hollywood Directory.

Misto Caffe & Bakery | 20 | 14 | 20 | $20 |
Hillside Village, 24558 Hawthorne Blvd. (bet. Newton St. & Via Valmonte), Torrance, 310-375-3608; www.mistocaffe.com
■ "The secret on the hill" in Torrance is this "low-key" "local hangout", a cafe and bakery offering a "great simple menu" of "consistently good" Cal-American fare in a "cozy", "indoor/outdoor cafe" setting, with a "romantic ambiance" that "makes you forget you're in a mini-mall"; P.S. be sure to "save room for the desserts."

Momoyama | ▽ 21 | 22 | 22 | $36 |
1810 S. PCH (Palos Verdes Blvd.), Redondo Beach, 310-540-8211
■ A "welcome addition to the South Bay", this "upscale" Redondo Beach Japanese newcomer is turning heads

South Bay and Long Beach F | D | S | C

with a "dazzling" decor, "excellent presentations" of "tasty" sashimi and sushi and "accommodating" service; wallet-watchers take note of the "pricey" tabs as well.

Musha ▽ 25 | 20 | 22 | $25
1725 W. Carson St. (W. Western Ave.), Torrance, 310-787-7344
See review in Westside Directory.

Noah's New York Bagels 16 | 11 | 13 | $7
330 Manhattan Beach Blvd. (Morningside Dr.), Manhattan Beach, 310-937-2206; www.noahs.com
See review in LA/Hollywood/W. Hollywood Directory.

Olive Garden 11 | 12 | 14 | $18
11171 183rd St. (bet. Gridley & Studebaker Rds.), Cerritos, 562-860-8855
9253 Firestone Blvd. (bet. Lakewood Blvd. & Woodruff Ave.), Downey, 562-923-9773
2610 Sepulveda Blvd. (Marine Ave.), Manhattan Beach, 310-546-3341
23442 Hawthorne Blvd. (bet. Lomita Blvd. & PCH), Torrance, 310-373-0395
www.olivegarden.com
See review in Westside Directory.

O-Nami ▽ 18 | 13 | 15 | $23
1925 W. Carson St. (Cabrillo Ave.), Torrance, 310-787-1632; www.o-nami.com
■ Fans boast the all-you-can-eat spread at this clean, well-lighted Japanese chain is "what a buffet should be", offering "something for everyone", from "fresh" sushi to "succulent" baked lobster to an "extensive salad selection", and the service is "excellent, because you serve yourself"; purists pooh-pooh the fare as "fast food", most are "amazed" by the "quality", "given the amount they provide."

Outback Steakhouse 16 | 14 | 17 | $26
5305 Clark Ave. (Candlewood St.), Lakewood, 562-634-0353
Del Amo Fashion Ctr., 21880 Hawthorne Blvd. (Sepulveda Blvd.), Torrance, 310-793-5555
www.outbacksteakhouse.com
■ This "affordable" "beef-and-beer" chain serves "decent" "red meat for the masses" and other "good and filling" "middle-American" fare "with Aussie subtitles" ("two words: 'blooming onion'"); "g'day becomes g'night as you're waiting for a table", though, and cynics who find it "overrated" and "un–Down Under" "will never understand" why "people line up for hours to get in."

Paco's Tacos 19 | 14 | 17 | $16
6212 W. Manchester Ave. (Sepulveda Blvd.), Westchester, 310-645-8692; www.pacoscantina.com
See review in Westside Directory.

South Bay and Long Beach | F | D | S | C |

Papadakis Taverna — 22 | 17 | 23 | $35
301 W. Sixth St. (Centre St.), San Pedro, 310-548-1186;
www.papadakistaverna.com
■ A "grand experience" complete with "belly dancers", "singing waiters and broken crockery" awaits at this "fun", "upbeat" San Pedro Hellenic, where the "joyful" Papadakis brothers make you "feel like a guest in their home"; while fans "love the lamb loin in phyllo" and other "great" Greek dishes, it's "the spectacle that makes it worthwhile."

Pat & Oscar's — – | – | – | I |
Del Amo Mall, 21424 Hawthorne Blvd. (Del Amo Circle Blvd.), Torrance, 310-542-3020
A San Diego chain heads north to establish this large beachhead at the Del Amo Shopping Center, where lots of families order at the counter from a basic, inexpensive selection of Italian and barbecue items, complemented by oversized (and rather puffy) breadsticks served with a choice of three dipping sauces.

P.F. CHANG'S CHINA BISTRO — 20 | 20 | 18 | $24
2041 E. Rosecrans Ave. (Nash St.), El Segundo, 310-607-9062;
www.pfchangs.com
See review in LA/Hollywood/W. Hollywood Directory.

Ragin' Cajun Cafe M — 22 | 18 | 18 | $18
422 Pier Ave. (PCH), Hermosa Beach, 310-376-7878;
www.ragincajun.com
■ A "good beach bet" serving "tasty Cajun" and Creole fare listed on "paper bag menus", this duo in Hermosa Beach and Newport Beach will have you feeling "like you're in the heart of the bayou"; *amis* "would walk to New Orleans" for its "blackened rib-eye and crawfish", or "catfish on Fridays"; the "huge selection of hot sauces" leaves some wondering "how many can you take?"

Reed's — 24 | 18 | 24 | $32
Manhattan Village Mall, 2640 N. Sepulveda Blvd.
(bet. Marina & Rosecrans Aves.), Manhattan Beach,
310-546-3299; www.reedsrestaurant.com
■ You feel "like you're in another world" once you enter this Cal-French "piano-bar restaurant", a "hidden gem" in a Manhattan Beach strip mall with a "Ralphs next door", where "imaginative and well-priced" dishes are served by a "professional" staff in an "intimate", "romantic" setting; the "onion soup alone is worth the trip" to the South Bay.

Rock 'N Fish — 22 | 20 | 20 | $28
120 Manhattan Beach Blvd. (bet. Manhattan Ave. & Manhattan Beach), Manhattan Beach, 310-379-9900
■ The "sounds of martini glasses clinking are like a train depot at rush hour" at this appropriately named surf 'n' turf half a block from the Manhattan Beach pier serving "wood-

South Bay and Long Beach | F | D | S | C |

grilled specialties" and "excellent crab cakes" as well as the "best caramel apple martinis" and "Navy Grog that warms your stomach" from the "old-world mahogany bar"; a "bit on the loud side", it's nonetheless a "classy experience" just "yards from the ocean."

Romano's Macaroni Grill | 18 | 17 | 18 | $21 |
12875 Towne Center Dr. (bet. Bloomfield Ave. & 183rd St.), Cerritos, 562-916-7722
25352 Crenshaw Blvd. (Airport Dr.), Torrance, 310-534-1001
■ "Mass-produced Italian at its best" is how fans describe this "lively", "loud" chain where adults drink "Chianti by the honor system", "kids color on the paper tablecloths" and "serenading servers add to the fun"; "it's easy to fill up" on "design-it-yourself pasta dishes" and a "huge glass of house wine that's more than anyone needs"; there's even a bit of culture with "learn-to-speak Italian recordings playing in the bathroom."

Roscoe's House of Chicken 'n Waffles ◐ | 22 | 8 | 16 | $14 |
730 E. Broadway (Alamitos Ave.), Long Beach, 562-437-8355
See review in LA/Hollywood/W. Hollywood Directory.

Ruby's | 17 | 18 | 18 | $13 |
LA Int'l Airport, Terminal 6, LAX, 310-646-2480
245 N. Harbor Dr. (Beryl St.), Redondo Beach, 310-376-7829
The Ave. of the Peninsula, 550 Deep Valley Dr. (Hawthorne Blvd.), Rolling Hills, 310-544-7829
www.rubys.com
See review in Westside Directory.

Sea Empress | 21 | 14 | 15 | $21 |
Pacific Sq., 1636 W. Redondo Beach Blvd. (bet. Normandie & Western Aves.), Gardena, 310-538-6868
■ "So many choices, so little tummy" lament loyalists of this Gardena Chinese where you have to "come early to get your favorite" lunchtime dim sum selections at "ridiculously low" prices; "very fresh", more "upscale" seafood is the bill of fare at dinner, when the waiters act "like they'd rather be on Mars" serving "big gatherings and parties" in the "huge" series of rooms where "you can get lost."

SHENANDOAH CAFE | 24 | 17 | 24 | $35 |
4722 E. Second St. (Park Ave.), Long Beach, 562-434-3469; www.shenandoahcafe.com
■ This "romantic, Southern" Long Beach "getaway" with a "genteelly shabby" room takes your taste buds on an all-American road trip with "heavenly aromas" of "incredibly delicious" "regional eclectic" fare, such as fried green tomatoes and gumbo that are "well worth the trip"; the staff will "bend over backwards" to "make you feel at home."

| South Bay and Long Beach | F | D | S | C |

Sir Winston's
▽ 20 | 25 | 21 | $47

Queen Mary, 1126 Queen's Hwy. (south of Frwy. 710), Long Beach, 562-435-3511; www.queenmary.com

■ All aboard for a "special night out" of "first-class" Continental dining on the permanently anchored Queen Mary, from which you can "admire great views of the harbor" and "downtown Long Beach"; you'll want to "wear your Sunday best" in the dining room that'll make "you feel like you've gone back in time", while helping yourself to "well-made", "traditional, high-end" fare.

Sky Room, The ⑤
▽ 20 | 27 | 22 | $48

The Breakers, 40 S. Locust Ave. (Ocean Blvd.), Long Beach, 562-983-2703; www.theskyroom.com

■ You can "dance to live music" by a "delightful, smooth jazz band" at this "first-class" New American located atop the Breakers Hotel while you "step back in time" and take in "amazing 360-degree views of the city" from a "roaring '20s", "art deco" room; it's "expensive", but the "delicious" fare, "memorable" setting and "excellent" service make it a "place to splurge" on "special occasions."

Souplantation
15 | 10 | 12 | $11

4720 Candlewood St. (Faculty Ave.), Lakewood, 562-531-6778
21309 S. Hawthorne Blvd. (Village Ln.), Torrance, 310-540-4998
www.souplantation.com
See review in LA/Hollywood/W. Hollywood Directory.

Taiko
22 | 17 | 20 | $23

2041 Rosecrans Ave. (Sepulveda Blvd.), El Segundo, 310-647-3100
See review in Westside Directory.

Thai Dishes
18 | 11 | 17 | $17

150 S. Sepulveda Blvd. (El Segundo Blvd.), El Segundo, 310-416-1080 ⑤
1015 N. Sepulveda Blvd. (Manhattan Beach Blvd.), Manhattan Beach, 310-546-4147
2208 Artesia Blvd. (Hermosa Ave.), Redondo Beach, 310-798-4618
707 S. PCH (Knob Hill Ave.), Redondo Beach, 310-316-7739
See review in Westside Directory.

Todai
14 | 11 | 12 | $24

Cerritos Mall, 18425 Gridley Rd. (bet. 183rd & South Sts.), Cerritos, 562-467-1668; www.todai.com
See review in LA/Hollywood/W. Hollywood Directory.

Towne ⑤ Ⓜ
▽ 19 | 24 | 15 | $34

1142 Manhattan Ave. (Center Pl.), Manhattan Beach, 310-545-5405

◪ It helps to be "young, tan and wearing almost nothing" at this Manhattan Beach newcomer occupying the former

South Bay and Long Beach | F | D | S | C |

Soleil space, where the "beautiful people" of South Bay sojourn for the "sexy", "sophisticated" atmosphere and "happening bar", as much as for the "delicious, homestyle" New American cuisine; detractors, however, dismiss it as a "wanna-be Hollywood club scene", where "style is rewarded over substance."

Trio Mediterranean Grill ▽ 19 | 18 | 18 | $21
46B Peninsula Ctr. (Hawthorne Blvd.), Rolling Hills, 310-265-5577; www.triogrill.com

■ Aioli's Rolling Hills spin-off, a "reasonably priced" Cal-Med "tucked in the corner" of the Peninsula shopping center, is often "crowded and noisy" thanks to "tasty", "top-notch" fare that's "worth every $2 gallon of gas" it takes to drive there; although the "modern" decor is "pleasant", it clearly "needs more space."

Tsukiji ☒ ▽ 25 | 15 | 19 | $40
1745 W. Redondo Beach Blvd. (Western Ave.), Gardena, 310-323-4077

■ The clientele is "almost all Japanese" at this "expense-account" Gardena sushi specialist that's "not for those who like trendy rolls", serving instead "excellent" "traditional" raw fare and "cooked dishes that are just as good", made with the "freshest seafood this side of Tsukiji", Tokyo's famous fish market for which it's named; the digs are plain and "you may not be entertained" by the "friendly" chefs, but "you can count on awesome dining."

22nd St. Landing ▽ 15 | 17 | 13 | $26
141 W. 22nd St. (Harbor Blvd.), San Pedro, 310-548-4400

■ A "pleasant way to spend an afternoon" is lunch or drinks while "looking at the harbor" "when the sun gleams off the ocean" at this affordable San Pedro seafooder that's "big with the yachting crowd on weekends"; you "won't find chichi preparations of fish", just "generous portions" of "old-fashioned", "fresh" fin fare and "pleasant" service in a "quiet, relaxing" atmosphere.

Uncle Bill's Pancake House 24 | 14 | 18 | $12
1305 Highland Ave. (13th St.), Manhattan Beach, 310-545-5177

■ There's "always a wait on weekends" at this Manhattan Beach "institution", a "legend" among South Bay breakfast spots for its "phenomenal macadamia nut pancakes", the "best damn waffles in town" and "delicious" omelets, as well as an "incredible ocean view" from the "dog-friendly" patio; once you get in, don't expect to linger, for the staff is "not shy about rushing you out."

Versailles 22 | 9 | 17 | $16
1000 N. Sepulveda Blvd. (10th St.), Manhattan Beach, 310-937-6829
See review in LA/Hollywood/W. Hollywood Directory.

South Bay and Long Beach | F | D | S | C |

Whale & Ale ▽ 16 | 18 | 16 | $23 |
327 W. Seventh St. (bet. Centre & Mesa Sts.), San Pedro, 310-832-0363; www.whaleandale.com

◪ Fish and chips "worthy of a dousing of malt vinegar", "fantastic" soups and a "nice selection of beers and ales" attract Anglophiles and their "out-of-town guests" to this midpriced British pub in the heart of San Pedro's Restaurant Row; while fans find it all "very UK", naysayers knock the "non-authentic" fare and "theatrical atmosphere."

Yard House ◐ 19 | 18 | 18 | $24 |
401 Shoreline Village Dr. (Shoreline Dr.), Long Beach, 562-628-0455; www.yardhouse.com

■ The name refers to the 36-inch-tall glasses used for serving the "excellent selection" of 250 beers on tap at this suds-centric Cal-American trio in Long Beach and OC serving "surprisingly good" pub grub; it gets "crowded on weekends and most evenings", and "unless you're into the meet-market scene, avoid late nights" when it's "jumping with see-and-be-seen twentysomethings."

Zazou 23 | 19 | 21 | $36 |
1810 S. Catalina Ave. (bet. Ave. I & Vista Del Mar), Redondo Beach, 310-540-4884

■ Fans dub this Redondo Beach Mediterranean cafe (a casual spin-off of Manhattan Beach's Cafe Pierre) the "Cheers of the South Bay", where one can "sit at the bar and mingle with neighborhood folk" while tucking into "awesome tuna tartare" and other "eclectic" offerings from a "delightful", "imaginative" menu; it's usually "busy and noisy", but the service is always "friendly" and "helpful."

The San Fernando Valley and Burbank

Top Food

- 28 Katsu-ya
- 27 Sushi Nozawa
  Saddle Peak Lodge
- 26 Brent's Deli
  Brandywine
  Iroha
  Posto
- 25 Hirosuke
  Pinot Bistro
  Leila's

Top Decor

- 27 Saddle Peak Lodge
- 25 Firefly
  Bistro Gdn./Coldwater
- 24 Villa Piacere
- 23 Pinot Bistro
- 22 Castaway
  Posto
  Cha Cha Cha Encino
  Ca' del Sole
  Mistral

Top Service

- 25 Saddle Peak Lodge
  Posto
- 24 Mistral
  La Pergola
  Leila's
  Brandywine
  Spumante
- 23 Arnie Morton's
  Emmanuel
  Pinot Bistro

Top Value

1. In-N-Out Burger
2. Noah's NY Bagels
3. Baja Fresh
4. Poquito Mas
5. Jody Maroni's Sausage
6. Sharky's Mex.
7. California Ckn.
8. Zankou Chicken
9. La Salsa
10. Johnny Rockets

By Location

Burbank
- 25 Arnie Morton's
- 22 Picanha Churr.
- 21 Poquito Mas
- 20 Mi Piace
  Baja Fresh

Encino
- 25 Hirosuke
- 22 Mulberry St. Pizz.
  Versailles
- 21 Cha Cha Cha Encino
  Delmonico's Lobster

Northridge
- 26 Brent's Deli
- 21 Mandarin Deli
  California Ckn.
- 20 Wood Ranch BBQ
- 19 Sharky's Mex.

Sherman Oaks
- 26 Posto
- 24 Max Rest.
  La Pergola
  Mistral
- 23 Café Bizou

Studio City
- 28 Katsu-ya
- 27 Sushi Nozawa
- 26 Iroha
- 25 Pinot Bistro
  Emmanuel

Woodland Hills
- 26 Brandywine
- 23 Seashell
- 22 Monty's Steak.
- 20 Baja Fresh
  Cheesecake Factory

The San Fernando Valley and Burbank Restaurant Directory

San Fernando Valley/Burbank F | D | S | C

Arnie Morton's of Chicago 25 | 21 | 23 | $53
Pinnacle, 3400 W. Olive Ave. (Lima St.), Burbank, 818-238-0424
See review in LA/Hollywood/W. Hollywood Directory.

Art's Deli 19 | 10 | 16 | $18
12224 Ventura Blvd. (bet. Laurelgrove & Vantage Aves.), Studio City, 818-762-1221

◪ "Writing a screenplay? everyone is!" at this "real Jewish deli" in Studio City where "every sandwich is a work of Art" – Ginsburg, that is, a "mensch who serves huge portions with personality"; the space is merely functional and "you know when [the staff's] having a bad day", but with "such corned beef", "who could want more?"

Asanebo Ⓜ ▽ 28 | 16 | 23 | $49
11941 Ventura Blvd. (bet. Carpenter & Radford Aves.), Studio City, 818-760-3348

■ The "Valley's version of Matsuhisa" is what devotees dub this upscale Studio City production on the "sushi strip"; while it's best known for sashimi, especially the "seared toro", cognoscenti are happy to "break open the piggy bank, sit down and order" Tetsuya Nakao's "imaginative" omakase menu that represents "what Japanese should be"; the "plain" decor is "deceiving", for the service, like the food, is "top-notch."

August Chris Cafe ▽ 25 | 18 | 22 | $29
(fka Paul's Cafe)
13456 Ventura Blvd. (3 blocks east of Woodman Ave.), Sherman Oaks, 818-789-3575

■ This "cozy" Sherman Oaks cafe "does it right" with "good-to-excellent" French-accented Californian cuisine at "reasonable prices" (economizing oenophiles "love the $2 corkage"); co-owner and host August Nazzaro "greets you with warmth" and "makes you feel special", which is why it's the "favorite destination" of many to "celebrate even the smallest of occasions."

BAJA FRESH MEXICAN GRILL 20 | 11 | 15 | $9
Virgin Megastore Complex, 877 N. San Fernando Blvd. (Burbank Blvd.), Burbank, 818-841-4649
Bistro Ctr., 12930 Ventura Blvd. (Coldwater Canyon Ave.), Studio City, 818-995-4242
Winnetka Sq., 19960 Ventura Blvd. (bet. Lubao & Penfield Aves.), Woodland Hills, 818-888-3976
www.bajafresh.com
See review in LA/Hollywood/W. Hollywood Directory.

Bamboo Inn 22 | 17 | 19 | $22
14010 Ventura Blvd. (bet. Hazeltine & Woodman Aves.), Sherman Oaks, 818-788-0202

■ "No need to travel to Chinatown" boast boosters of this Sherman Oaks Chinese that "deserves the buzz" for its

San Fernando Valley/Burbank F | D | S | C |

"consistently" "fabulous" Middle Kingdom fare, including "addictive" sweet and pungent chicken; the room may be "too brightly lit" for some, but the atmosphere is "warm and hospitable" – just "don't expect to linger" on Sundays when it's "packed."

Barsac Brasserie ⑤ 22 | 20 | 22 | $35 |
4212 Lankershim Blvd. (bet. Acama St. & Valley Spring Ln.), North Hollywood, 818-760-7081; www.barsac.com

■ The setting for Larry David's fits in *Curb Your Enthusiasm*, this North Hollywood Cal-French is the "unofficial lunchroom for Technicolor and Universal execs", serving "martinis on steroids" and "rich", "upscale" fare that's "worth the calories and the cash", though it's "nicest if someone else is paying"; a "low-key" ambiance fills the "stylish" room, and the "hosts make everyone feel like regulars."

Benihana 19 | 18 | 21 | $32 |
16226 Ventura Blvd. (bet. Hayvenhurst & Woodley Aves.), Encino, 818-788-7121; www.benihana.com
See review in Westside Directory.

Billingsley's ⑤ Ⓜ – | – | – | I |
6550 Odessa Ave. (Victory Blvd.), Van Nuys, 818-785-7457
See review in Westside Directory.

Bistro Garden at Coldwater 22 | 25 | 22 | $44 |
12950 Ventura Blvd. (Coldwater Canyon Ave.), Studio City, 818-501-0202; www.bistrogarden.com

■ "Ladies who lunch" and a "smattering of show biz types" comprise the somewhat "older" crowd that frequents this "genteel" Studio City French-Continental for "dependably ok" fare and "adult" service in a "garden environment" that reminds some of a "hotel banquet room"; be sure to "save room for the trademark chocolate soufflé for dessert."

BJ's ● 17 | 15 | 16 | $18 |
107 S. First St. (Olive St.), Burbank, 818-557-0881
24320 Town Center Dr. (McBean Pkwy.), Valencia, 661-288-1299
6424 Canoga Ave. (Victory Blvd.), Woodland Hills, 818-340-1748
www.bjsbrewhouse.com
See review in Westside Directory.

BRANDYWINE ⑤ 26 | 20 | 24 | $52 |
22757 Ventura Blvd. (Fallbrook Ave.), Woodland Hills, 818-225-9114

■ The "place to go for amazing food" in the West Valley, this Woodland Hills Continental offers "old-world charm on a plate" along with a "terrific" wine list and "formal" service (the "maitre d' has an accent that'll weaken your knees") in a "lovely, intimate" space; "private booths with lace curtains" and a classical guitarist in the evenings contribute to the "romantic" atmosphere.

San Fernando Valley/Burbank F | D | S | C

BRENT'S DELI   26 | 12 | 20 | $18
19565 Parthenia St. (bet. Corbin & Shirley Aves.),
Northridge, 818-886-5679; www.brentsdeli.com
■ "Worth the trek" to Northridge, this *Survey*'s No. 1 deli "has everyone in (310) green with envy", "setting the standard" with "phenomenal" fare ("perfect corned beef", Reubens that'll "make a vegan switch teams"); there's "nuttin' fancy" about the decor, and though it's "always busy", the service is "prompt"; it almost makes some Westsiders "wish [they] lived in the Valley."

Buca di Beppo   14 | 17 | 17 | $22
17500 Ventura Blvd. (Encino Ave.), Encino, 818-995-3288
Universal CityWalk, 1000 Universal Center Dr. (off Frwy. 101),
Universal City, 818-509-9463
www.bucadibeppo.com
See review in Westside Directory.

Ca' del Sole   22 | 22 | 22 | $34
4100 Cahuenga Blvd. (Lankershim Blvd.), North Hollywood,
818-985-4669; www.cadelsole.com
■ You'll "keep your neck muscles well-trained" from all the "bigwig watching" at this North Hollywood "studio favorite" serving "real-deal" Northern Italian cuisine (including "osso buco that melts in your mouth") in a "warm, cozy" room or on one of the "prettiest patios in town"; the service is "attentive" – "even if you're a nobody."

CAFÉ BIZOU   23 | 19 | 21 | $29
14016 Ventura Blvd. (bet. Costello & Murietta Aves.),
Sherman Oaks, 818-788-3536; www.cafebizou.com
See review in Westside Directory.

Cafe '50s ●   14 | 17 | 16 | $13
4609 Van Nuys Blvd. (Hortense St.), Sherman Oaks,
818-906-1955; www.cafe50s.com
See review in Westside Directory.

Cafe Tu Tu Tango   17 | 20 | 18 | $23
Universal CityWalk, 1000 Universal Center Dr. (Frwy. 101),
Universal City, 818-766-4222; www.cafetututango.com
◪ It's an "art lover's dream" and "interesting dining experience" at this Eclectic duo in Universal City and Orange, outposts of a national chain, where you can watch artists at work in a loftlike space (the paintings are also for sale) while nibbling on "creative" small plates; cynics sneer "there's not a lot of substance" to this "pop-culture version of tapas", but aficionados insist it's a "great place to go with a big group" for "something different" and "fun."

Caioti Pizza Cafe   20 | 11 | 16 | $17
4346 Tujunga Ave. (Moorpark St.), Studio City, 818-761-3588
■ "Quintessential California pizza" "by the guy (Ed LaDou) who invented it" is the staple of this "cozy, casual" Studio

182   subscribe to zagat.com

San Fernando Valley/Burbank F | D | S | C

City storefront where the "large, flavorful" pies are "divine" and the garlic rolls are "dangerously delicious"; it's "not a scene at all" – i.e. "no attitude" or decor to speak of – which suits those on a "quiet, peaceful date" just fine.

California Chicken Cafe 21 | 9 | 15 | $10
15601 Ventura Blvd. (bet. Haskell Ave. & Sepulveda Blvd.), Encino, 818-789-8056
University Plaza, 18445 Nordhoff St. (Reseda Blvd.), Northridge, 818-700-9977
www.californiachickencafe.com
See review in LA/Hollywood/W. Hollywood Directory.

CALIFORNIA PIZZA KITCHEN 18 | 14 | 17 | $18
Media City Ctr., 601 N. San Fernando Blvd. (Burbank Blvd.), Burbank, 818-972-2589
12265 Ventura Blvd. (Laurel Grove St.), Studio City, 818-505-6437
www.cpk.com
See review in LA/Hollywood/W. Hollywood Directory.

California Wok 18 | 9 | 15 | $15
Encino Village, 16656 Ventura Blvd. (bet. Balboa Blvd. & Hayvenhurst Ave.), Encino, 818-386-0561
See review in LA/Hollywood/W. Hollywood Directory.

Carnival 21 | 8 | 13 | $16
4356 Woodman Ave. (bet. Moor Park & Ventura Blvd.), Sherman Oaks, 818-784-3469;
www.carnivalrestaurants.com
☑ "Generous portions" of "flavorful" Middle Eastern cuisine ("don't miss the hummus or chicken kebabs") keep this Sherman Oaks Lebanese "busy" in spite of "surly" service from an "understaffed" crew and "nonexistent" decor; pros promise the fare is "worth the wait", and make no mistake, "you will wait."

Casa Vega ● 18 | 16 | 18 | $19
13301 Ventura Blvd. (Fulton Ave.), Sherman Oaks, 818-788-4868;
www.casavega.com
☑ A "local legend", this "sexy" Sherman Oaks Mexican is the "place to dine without being seen", thanks to a "pitch-dark" room that's more "cavern" than "tavern", where "celebrities" occasionally come to "hide out"; "lethal" margaritas and "late-night conviviality" (it's open until 1 AM) make the "old-fashioned" south-of-the-border cuisine seem almost "inconsequential."

Castaway 16 | 22 | 18 | $30
1250 E. Harvard Rd. (Olive St.), Burbank, 818-848-6691
☑ "Spectacular views" from the "patio overlooking the SF Valley" make this Burbank Cal-American a "fantastic special-occasion place" that's "perfect on a warm summer night"; defenders insist the fare is "just marvy", with an

San Fernando Valley/Burbank F | D | S | C

"extensive" weekend brunch buffet and "abundant" salad bar, but most agree it's really "all about cocktail hour" "outside on the terrace."

Cha Cha Cha Encino   21 | 22 | 19 | $26
17499 Ventura Blvd. (bet. Balboa Blvd. & White Oak Ave.), Encino, 818-789-3600; www.chachachaencino.com
◪ A "fiesta of colors and flavors" awaits at this Encino Caribbean (no relation to Cha Cha Cha) where "huge" portions of "interesting" fare with "just the right spice level" occupy the palate and "lively" artwork "keeps the eyes busy"; a few "umbrella drinks" can help you "forget the noise" in the often "crowded" setting.

CHEESECAKE FACTORY   20 | 18 | 18 | $23
Sherman Oaks Galleria, 15301 Ventura Blvd. (Sepulveda Blvd.), Sherman Oaks, 818-906-0700
Thousand Oaks Mall, 442 W. Hillcrest Dr. (Lynn Rd.), Thousand Oaks, 805-371-9705
San Fernando Valley Warner Center Trillium, 6324 Canoga Ave. (Victory Blvd.), Woodland Hills, 818-883-9900
www.thecheesecakefactory.com
See review in Westside Directory.

Chevys   14 | 13 | 14 | $17
Media City Ctr., 701 N. San Fernando Blvd. (1st St.), Burbank, 818-846-6999
16705 Ventura Blvd. (bet. Balboa Blvd. & Hayvenhurst Ave.), Encino, 818-385-1905
www.chevys.com
◪ "Fresh" tortillas churned out by "El Machino" in "loud", "carefree" settings are the highlight of this "Americanized Mexican" chain, and while enemigos jeer the "standard", "mediocre" eats "ain't like they make it in Tijuana", the "complimentary chips are always warm, and the salsa good and smoky" at least; it's "fine for the kids" or as an occasional "guilty pleasure" for the young at heart.

Chili John's 🅂 🅼 ⌀   ▽ 20 | 10 | 19 | $10
2018 W. Burbank Blvd. (Keystone St.), Burbank, 818-846-3611
■ A "true Burbank institution" (circa 1946), this "classic roadside" "greasy spoon" with a "small hometown feel" serves "incredible chili" that makes a "perfect meal for the rare rainy day in LA", and "that's all they do, but they do it splendidly"; a few "don't understand" the appeal, but cronies crow "what other place can close for the summer [July–August] and still stay in business for 50 years?"

Chin Chin   17 | 13 | 16 | $20
16101 Ventura Blvd. (Woodley Ave.), Encino, 818-783-1717
12215 Ventura Blvd. (Laurel Canyon Blvd.), Studio City, 818-985-9090
www.chinchin.com
See review in LA/Hollywood/W. Hollywood Directory.

San Fernando Valley/Burbank F | D | S | C

Claim Jumper Restaurant 18 | 16 | 18 | $22
Northridge Mall, 9429 Tampa Ave. (Plummer St.), Northridge, 818-718-2882
25740 The Old Rd. (McBean Pkwy.), Valencia, 661-254-2628
www.claimjumper.com
See review in South Bay/Long Beach Directory.

Crocodile Café 16 | 15 | 17 | $21
201 N. San Fernando Blvd. (Orange Grove Ave.), Burbank, 818-843-7999; www.crocodilecafe.com
See review in Westside Directory.

Daily Grill 17 | 16 | 17 | $25
Burbank Hilton, 2500 Hollywood Way (Thornton Ave.), Burbank, 818-840-6464
Laurel Promenade, 12050 Ventura Blvd. (Laurel Canyon Blvd.), Studio City, 818-769-6336
Universal CityWalk, 1000 Universal Center Dr. (Frwy. 101), Universal City, 818-760-4448
www.dailygrill.com
See review in LA/Hollywood/W. Hollywood Directory.

D'Amore's Pizza Connection 20 | 7 | 15 | $14
7137 Winnetka Ave. (Sherman Way), Canoga Park, 818-348-5900
15928 Ventura Blvd. (bet. Haskell & Woodley Aves.), Encino, 818-907-9100
12910 Magnolia Blvd. (Coldwater Canyon Ave.), Sherman Oaks, 818-505-1111
14519 Ventura Blvd. (Van Nuys Blvd.), Sherman Oaks, 818-905-3377
2869 Thousand Oaks Blvd. (Hampshire Rd.), Thousand Oaks, 805-496-0030
See review in Westside Directory.

Delmonico's Lobster House 21 | 19 | 20 | $41
16358 Ventura Blvd. (Hayvenhurst Ave.), Encino, 818-986-0777
■ Though the Beverly Hills branch is no more, this Encino seafooder carries on with a menu featuring lobster "served different ways" and "imaginative" fin fare that'll "please the toughest critics", even if some find it a bit "overpriced"; the "gracious" setting includes "pleasant" booths where you can "be romantic or discuss business", or both.

DR. HOGLY WOGLY'S BBQ 22 | 7 | 17 | $18
8136 N. Sepulveda Blvd. (Roscoe Blvd.), Van Nuys, 818-780-6701
■ "Take your Lipitor", "bring extra wet wipes" and "leave the vegetarians at home" before moseying to this Texas-inspired BBQ "shrine" in Van Nuys for "large portions" of "the best ribs west of the Rio Grande", "wondrous" brisket that's a "reason to live" and other "mouthwatering" fare; it's "not much to look at", but for "meatlovers" it's "just what the doctor ordered."

get updates at zagat.com

San Fernando Valley/Burbank F | D | S | C |

Du-par's ◐   13 | 9 | 13 | $14 |
Studio City Plaza, 12036 Ventura Blvd. (Laurel Canyon Blvd.), Studio City, 818-766-4437
Thousand Oaks Inn, 75 W. Thousand Oaks Blvd. (bet. Frwy. 101 & Moorpark Rd.), Thousand Oaks, 805-373-8785
www.dupars.com
See review in LA/Hollywood/W. Hollywood Directory.

El Torito   14 | 14 | 15 | $18 |
4012 W. Riverside Dr. (Pass Ave.), Burbank, 818-848-4501
16817 Ventura Blvd. (Balboa Ave.), Encino, 818-784-5925
8855 Tampa Ave. (bet. Nordhoff & Parthenia Sts.), Northridge, 818-349-1607
18568 Ventura Blvd. (Reseda Blvd.), Tarzana, 818-343-7027
449 Moorpark Rd. (Thousand Oaks Blvd.), Thousand Oaks, 805-497-3952
6040 Canoga Ave. (Oxnard St.), Woodland Hills, 818-348-1767
www.eltorito.com
See review in Westside Directory.

Emmanuel Ⓜ   25 | 17 | 23 | $36 |
11929 Ventura Blvd. (Laurel Canyon Blvd.), Studio City, 818-766-3128; www.emmanuelcuisine.com
■ "They understand the art of hospitality" at this Studio City New American, an "unpretentious" "gem" on Ventura Boulevard offering "gourmet dining in a cozy room" that's "small enough so that they really care about making your experience an experience"; "maestro" chef-owner Tom Munoz "constantly amazes" with his "inventive", "unique dishes", and the "fab" prix fixe menus "delight the palate and wallet" alike.

Fab's Italian Kitchen   18 | 12 | 16 | $19 |
4336 Van Nuys Blvd. (Ventura Blvd.), Sherman Oaks, 818-995-2933
◪ This Sherman Oaks storefront Italian "lives up to its name" with "big portions" of "basic" fare, such as the "absolutely delicious chopped house salad", that "doesn't disappoint"; "everyone's a regular" in the "laid-back" setting, and though the service can be "lacking at times", it's always "friendly."

Fins   21 | 18 | 19 | $35 |
23504 Calabasas Rd. (Mulholland Dr.), Calabasas, 818-223-3467
West Lake Plaza, 982-8 S. Westlake Blvd. (bet. Agoura & Townsgate Rds.), Westlake Village, 805-494-8163
■ "Awesome seafood" like the "macadamia nut halibut to die for" and a "varied" Continental menu for "landlubbers" awaits at this West Valley fin fare pair; many prefer the Calabasas branch, which boasts a "creekside" location, "lovely garden patio" and the "best piano man around", over its Westlake Village counterpart located in a shopping mall.

San Fernando Valley/Burbank F | D | S | C

Firefly ●☒ — 19 | 25 | 17 | $35
11720 Ventura Blvd. (Colfax Ave.), Studio City, 818-762-1833
■ A "sexy, delicious" "wow of a restaurant", this Valley French-New American is a "hot scene" where "stars from the nearby CBS lot" and "industry types" gather in a "glass-ceilinged indoor/outdoor" room or "library-decorated" bar; the menu is "limited" but "enjoyable", while service from the "multi-dimensionally absent" staff "could sure use improvement"; P.S. "make sure you make reservations at least two weeks in advance."

Fromin's Restaurant & Deli — 15 | 9 | 16 | $16
17615 Ventura Blvd. (bet. Encino & White Oak Aves.), Encino, 818-990-6346
See review in Westside Directory.

Galletto — 20 | 16 | 16 | $31
Westlake Plaza, 982 S. Westlake Blvd. (Townsgate Rd.), Westlake Village, 805-449-4300
■ An "imaginative", "eclectic mix" of "mouthwatering flavors" and an "interesting, varied menu" with a "large selection of daily specials" make this "festive" Brazilian-Italian a "winner" in Westlake Village; on weekends the room gets "very loud" when live musical acts perform, but you can always "opt for the patio" outside.

Gaucho Grill — 18 | 15 | 16 | $21
12050 Ventura Blvd. (Laurel Canyon Blvd.), Studio City, 818-508-1030
6435 Canoga Ave. (Victory Blvd.), Woodland Hills, 818-992-6416
www.gauchogrillusa.com
See review in LA/Hollywood/W. Hollywood Directory.

Gladstone's Universal — 16 | 16 | 16 | $28
Universal CityWalk, 1000 Universal Studios Blvd. (Frwy. 101), Universal City, 818-622-3474; www.citywalkhollywood.com
◪ "Catering to tourists on Universal CityWalk", this landlocked surf specialist (no relation to the Pacific Palisades spot with the same name) offers "seafood for the masses", "people-watching" and "free peanuts"; the "themey" setting doesn't bother boosters, since "you're in a theme park already", but cold fish cavil "something seems to be missing – the beach!"

Gordon Biersch ● — 17 | 17 | 16 | $23
145 S. San Fernando Blvd. (Angeleno Ave.), Burbank, 818-569-5240; www.gordonbiersch.com
◪ A "lovely place to relax with the chaps", this "upscale brewpub" trio in Burbank, Pasadena and OC, links of a national chain, offers "better-than-average pub grub" "with some new twists" in a "modern setting" with a "see-or-be"-scene patio; for many, though, the "elevated bar

San Fernando Valley/Burbank F | D | S | C

food" comes in "second" to the "awesome" brews, with "slo-o-o-w", "distracted" service bringing up the rear.

Great Greek, The   21 | 16 | 20 | $27
13362 Ventura Blvd. (bet. Coldwater Canyon & Woodman Aves.), Sherman Oaks, 818-905-5250
◪ Have your "big fat Greek meal" (and "your Tylenol") at this "noisy", "fun-filled" Hellenic spot in Sherman Oaks where a "total party atmosphere" (lots of "loud" music and "amazing dancing" by "employees and customers") makes the "authentic, delicious" fare "taste even better"; the nine-course family style meal is "a must."

Hamburger Hamlet   15 | 13 | 15 | $18
29020 Agoura Rd. (Malibu Junction), Agoura Hills, 818-706-1393
4419 Van Nuys Blvd. (Ventura Blvd.), Sherman Oaks, 818-784-1183
27430 The Old Road (Magic Mountain Pkwy.), Valencia, 661-253-0888
www.hamburgerhamlet.com
See review in LA/Hollywood/W. Hollywood Directory.

Hard Rock Cafe   12 | 20 | 14 | $20
Universal Studios, 1000 Universal Center Dr. (Frwy. 101), Universal City, 818-622-7625; www.hardrock.com
See review in LA/Hollywood/W. Hollywood Directory.

Hirosuke   25 | 13 | 22 | $34
17237 Ventura Blvd. (Louise Ave.), Encino, 818-788-7548
■ "Reasonably priced", "unbelievable portions" of "phenomenal" sushi, including "fantastically inventive rolls" that are "hard to fit in your mouth", keep this Encino Japanese with a "minimalist" look "deservedly busy", even with so "many competitors on the boulevard"; though the crowds can be "daunting" and "loud", the "spunky" staff remains "friendly" and "attentive."

Hugo's   19 | 12 | 17 | $20
12851 Riverside Dr. (Coldwater Canyon Ave.), Studio City, 818-761-8985
See review in LA/Hollywood/W. Hollywood Directory.

India's Tandoori   19 | 11 | 18 | $18
Burbank Village, 142 N. San Fernando Blvd. (E. Olive Ave.), Burbank, 818-846-7500
Windsor Ctr., 19006 Ventura Blvd. (Donna Ave.), Tarzana, 818-342-9100
See review in LA/Hollywood/W. Hollywood Directory.

IN-N-OUT BURGER ◐   24 | 10 | 18 | $7
761 First St. (Burbank Blvd.), Burbank, 800-786-1000 ⊄
5864 Lankershim Blvd. (Burbank Blvd.), North Hollywood, 800-786-1000 ⊄
9858 Balboa Blvd. (Lassen St.), Northridge, 800-786-1000 ⊄

San Fernando Valley/Burbank F | D | S | C

(continued)
IN-N-OUT BURGER
26401 Bouquet Canyon Rd. (Newhall Ranch), Santa Clarita, 800-786-1000
28368 Sand Canyon Rd. (De Lone St.), Santa Clarita, 800-786-1000
4444 Van Nuys Blvd. (Moorpark St.), Sherman Oaks, 800-786-1000
7930 Van Nuys Blvd. (Blythe St.), Van Nuys, 800-786-1000
19920 Ventura Blvd. (Winnetka Ave.), Woodland Hills, 800-786-1000
www.in-n-out.com
See review in LA/Hollywood/W. Hollywood Directory.

IROHA ◐   26 | 19 | 21 | $30
12953 Ventura Blvd. (Coldwater Canyon Ave.), Studio City, 818-990-9559
■ Although its location "behind a less than stellar hotel" may seem fishy, this Japanese housed in a "magical little cottage" on the edge of the Studio City's Sushi Row is really a "celebrity hangout" that appeals to "those in the know" with "exquisite", "fresh" sushi and "excellent" cooked fare; "friendly, relaxed" service contributes to the "wonderful, cozy environment."

Islands   16 | 16 | 17 | $14
101 E. Orange Grove Ave. (N. 1st St.), Burbank, 818-566-7744
15927 Ventura Blvd. (Gloria Ave.), Encino, 818-385-1200
23397 Mulholland Dr. (Calabasas Rd.), Woodland Hills, 818-225-9839
www.islandsrestaurants.com
See review in Westside Directory.

Jinky's   21 | 10 | 16 | $13
14120 Ventura Blvd. (Hazeltine Ave.), Sherman Oaks, 818-981-2250
■ It's "1,000 percent worth the long lines you'll inevitably find" at this "awesome" Sherman Oaks American that "proves breakfast really is the best meal of the day" and that the lunches with Southwestern dishes like chili and burritos are "delicious"; "lots of studio people and hopefuls" feel the "how ya doin' honey attitude" only adds to the "hippest joint in the Valley" atmosphere; P.S. admirers exclaim "thank goodness" they just opened another location in Santa Monica.

Jody Maroni's Sausage Kingdom   19 | 6 | 13 | $9
Universal CityWalk, 1000 Universal Center Dr. (off Frwy. 101), Universal City, 818-622-5639; www.jodymaroni.com
See review in Westside Directory.

Johnnie's New York   18 | 11 | 15 | $15
Pizzeria & Caffe
14350 Ventura Blvd. (Beverly Glen Blvd.), Sherman Oaks, 818-905-3360
See review in LA/Hollywood/W. Hollywood Directory.

get updates at zagat.com

San Fernando Valley/Burbank F | D | S | C |

Johnny Rockets ⏺ 16 | 15 | 16 | $12
Media City Ctr., 201 E. Magnolia Blvd. (3rd St.), Burbank, 818-845-7055
16901 Ventura Blvd. (Balboa Blvd.), Encino, 818-981-5900
The Oaks, 322 W. Hillcrest Dr. (Lynn Rd.), Thousand Oaks, 805-778-0780
24425 Towne Center Dr. (bet. Magic Mtn. & McBean Pkwys.), Valencia, 661-291-2590
www.johnnyrockets.com
See review in LA/Hollywood/W. Hollywood Directory.

KATSU-YA 28 | 14 | 21 | $34
11680 Ventura Blvd. (Colfax Ave.), Studio City, 818-985-6976
■ "Fish so fresh it seems to have swum right onto your plate" is the lure at this "amazing" Japanese in Studio City that's an "industry favorite at lunchtime" despite its "humble" setting; it "can become expensive if you sample all the items on the menu, which you will"; it's tiny, "popular and crowded", so "making reservations means you only have to wait half as long."

Killer Shrimp 20 | 10 | 15 | $20
4000 Colfax Ave. (Ventura Blvd.), Studio City, 818-508-1570
See review in Westside Directory.

King's Fish House/ King Crab Lounge 20 | 18 | 18 | $29
The Commons, 4798 Commons Way (Calabasas Rd.), Calabasas, 818-225-1979; www.kingsseafood.com
See review in South Bay/Long Beach Directory.

Koo Koo Roo 16 | 8 | 13 | $11
Media City Ctr., 800 N. San Fernando Blvd. (bet. Burbank Blvd. & Grinnell Dr.), Burbank, 818-846-5100
17136 Ventura Blvd. (bet. Balboa Blvd. & Louise Ave.), Encino, 818-783-5576
12175 Ventura Blvd. (Laurel Canyon Blvd.), Studio City, 818-509-1600
10123 Riverside Dr. (bet. Mariota & Talofa Aves.), Toluca Lake, 818-985-7765
www.kookooroo.com
See review in LA/Hollywood/W. Hollywood Directory.

Kung Pao Chinese Bistro 17 | 13 | 17 | $17
15025 Ventura Blvd. (Lemona Ave.), Sherman Oaks, 818-788-1689
11838 Ventura Blvd. (bet. Colfax Ave. & Laurel Canyon Blvd.), Studio City, 818-766-8686
See review in LA/Hollywood/W. Hollywood Directory.

La Finestra Ⓜ ∇ 21 | 14 | 23 | $27
19647 Ventura Blvd. (bet. Corbin & Shirley Aves.), Tarzana, 818-342-2824
■ You'll find "lasagna like mama used to make" at this "accommodating" Tarzana Italian where "Mario and

San Fernando Valley/Burbank F | D | S | C

Fabrizio greet you like a long-lost relative", making it a "nice place to go even if you're eating alone"; it's an unassuming room in the middle of the SF Valley, but you never know who you'll see – "Kim Basinger has been sighted."

La Fondue Bourguignonne 18 | 16 | 17 | $33
13359 Ventura Blvd. (bet. Dixie Canyon & Fulton Aves.), Sherman Oaks, 818-788-8680

☑ "Step back into the '70s" at this Sherman Oaks spot for "fondue fanatics" that serves a four-course, dip-in-a-pot meal that ranges from cheese to chocolate in a space that's got a mile or three on it; but while fans find it "fun" for "both couples and large parties", those who don't melt at the thought of "cooking their own food" find it too "pricey for what it is."

La Frite 18 | 15 | 17 | $24
15013 Ventura Blvd. (Lemona Ave.), Sherman Oaks, 818-990-1791
22616 Ventura Blvd. (bet. Ponce & Sale Aves.), Woodland Hills, 818-225-1331

■ These "tried-and-true" "neighborhood" San Fernando Valley French bistros are "reliable" when it comes to classics like "delish pommes frites", omelets, onion soup, "huge salads" and "must-have chocolate soufflé", all at "reasonable prices"; they may not be "exciting", but "they're old favorites that haven't changed, thank God."

La Loggia ▽ 21 | 18 | 19 | $36
11814 Ventura Blvd. (bet. Colfax Ave. & Laurel Canyon Blvd.), Studio City, 818-985-9222

■ You'll have a "pleasant surprise" when you step through the door of this "reliable", chef-owned Ventura Boulevard Northern Italian for "homecooking that's always fresh" and where they'll "do anything to make you happy"; it can get "crowded", so the patio is an appealing alfresco option.

La Pergola 24 | 21 | 24 | $36
15005 Ventura Blvd. (Lemona Ave.), Sherman Oaks, 818-905-8402

■ Since this Northern Italian is best known as the SF Valley restaurant that "has its own gardens" out back, "before you order, ask Tino what he picked today" – that way you can dine with the seasons on herbs and "vegetables so fresh they're still vibrating", accompanied by "great" entrees; "excellent" service and "comfortable", "European-style decor" also add to the "romantic possibilities."

La Salsa 16 | 9 | 13 | $10
Sherman Oaks Fashion Sq., 14006 Riverside Dr. (Woodman Ave.), Sherman Oaks, 818-789-8587
12048 Ventura Blvd. (bet. Laurel Canyon Blvd. & Ventura Pl.), Studio City, 818-760-0797
www.lasalsa.com
See review in LA/Hollywood/W. Hollywood Directory.

San Fernando Valley/Burbank F | D | S | C

Le Chêne ▽ 22 | 18 | 21 | $41
12625 Sierra Hwy. (Sierra Vallejo Rd.), Saugus, 661-251-4315; www.lechene.com

☒ Truly "in the middle of nowhere", this Saugus French in an "old stone building" surrounded by "canyons and dust" features a "varied menu" with dishes like a "wonderful rabbit *moutarde*" backed up by a "vast wine list"; but critics counter that the food "isn't as good as it was in the past" and that "expansions over the years have changed the atmosphere from quaint" to common.

Leila's Ⓜ 25 | 19 | 24 | $37
Oak Park Plaza, 752 Lindero Canyon Rd. (Kanan Rd.), Oak Park, 818-707-6939

■ There's a "neighborhood feel but big city taste" at this "little treasure" in Conejo Valley; "well-prepared" New American fare, "attentive service" and a "comprehensive wine list" add up to a "wonderful evening" (there's live jazz at night in the separate adjacent bar).

Le Petit Bistro 20 | 19 | 18 | $32
13360 Ventura Blvd. (Fulton Ave.), Sherman Oaks, 818-501-7999; www.lepetitbistro.net
See review in LA/Hollywood/W. Hollywood Directory.

Les Sisters Southern Kitchen Ⓜ ▽ 23 | 8 | 19 | $20
21818 Devonshire St. (Topanga Canyon Blvd.), Chatsworth, 818-998-0755

■ The appeal of this Chatsworth Southern-Cajun is simple – "generous portions" of "excellent" cooking like "incredible fried chicken", "fantastic jambalaya" and "great buttermilk pie" at "reasonable prices"; it's "small" and there's a "wait at peak hours", but it's a "real keeper."

Louise's Trattoria 15 | 14 | 16 | $21
12050 Ventura Blvd. (Laurel Canyon Blvd.), Studio City, 818-762-2662; www.louises.com
See review in LA/Hollywood/W. Hollywood Directory.

MAGGIANO'S LITTLE ITALY 19 | 20 | 19 | $26
The Promenade at Woodland Hills, 6100 N. Topanga Canyon Rd. (bet. Erwin & Oxnard Sts.), Woodland Hills, 818-887-3777; www.maggianos.com
See review in LA/Hollywood/W. Hollywood Directory.

Mandarin Deli 21 | 9 | 13 | $13
9305 Reseda Blvd. (Prairie St.), Northridge, 818-993-0122
See review in LA/Hollywood/W. Hollywood Directory.

Mandevilla 22 | 19 | 21 | $31
951 S. Westlake Blvd. (Hampshire Rd.), Westlake Village, 805-497-8482; www.mandevillarestaurant.com

■ You can "go again and again and not be bored" at this Westlake Village Continental that has "something to

San Fernando Valley/Burbank F | D | S | C

please everyone" on its "varied menu" of "interesting, well-presented" dishes; the "well-trained" staff is "always helpful", and the "European" setting is highlighted by a "lovely", "sedate" outdoor patio.

Maria's Italian Kitchen 17 | 13 | 17 | $18

29035 Thousand Oaks Blvd. (Kanan Rd.), Agoura Hills, 818-865-8999
16608 Ventura Blvd. (Rubio Ave.), Encino, 818-783-2920
9161 Reseda Blvd. (Nordhoff St.), Northridge, 818-341-5114
13353 Ventura Blvd. (bet. Dixie Canyon & Fulton Aves.), Sherman Oaks, 818-906-0783
23460 Cinema Dr. (Valencia Blvd.), Valencia, 661-287-3773
El Camino Shopping Ctr., 23331 Mulholland Dr. (Calabasas Rd.), Woodland Hills, 818-225-0586
www.mariasitaliankitchen.com

■ Want "Hoboken Italian with a New Jersey attitude"? – this "reliable" chain "has it down", dishing out "honest red-sauce comfort food" in a "friendly, family-type" setting that "looks like grandma's kitchen"; as the service can vary from "attentive to invisible", many opt for the "fast delivery."

Market City Caffe 19 | 18 | 15 | $23

164 E. Palm Ave. (San Fernando Blvd.), Burbank, 818-840-7036; www.marketcitycaffe.com

■ The all-you-can-eat "antipasti bar can't be beat" at this "casual" Burbank Cal-Italian, though the "heavenly breadsticks", "pasta with sausage and red peppers" and many other dishes with "unpronounceable" names give it a run for the money; "fun people-watching" on the outdoor patio and "chamber music on Sundays" add allure.

Marmalade Café 18 | 17 | 17 | $23

The Commons, 4783 Commons Way (Calabasas Rd.), Calabasas, 818-225-9092
14910 Ventura Blvd. (Kester Ave.), Sherman Oaks, 818-905-8872
Promenade at Westlake, 140 Promenade Way (Thousand Oaks Blvd.), Westlake Village, 805-370-1331
See review in Westside Directory.

Marrakesh ▽ 21 | 21 | 20 | $35

13003 Ventura Blvd. (Coldwater Canyon Ave.), Studio City, 818-788-6354; www.marrakeshrestaurant.com

■ An "unforgettable" "dining adventure, complete with belly dancing" awaits at this Studio City Moroccan where you enter a "colorful" "casbah" furnished with "couches and tiny seats" where you dine on "authentic, delicious" cuisine; it's a "great place to go with a group."

Matterhorn Chef Ⓜ ▽ 21 | 20 | 22 | $29

13726 Oxnard St. (Woodman Ave.), Van Nuys, 818-781-4330; www.matterhornchef.com

■ "All that's missing is Heidi" at this "kitschy" "gem" "lost" in Van Nuys offering "delectable" German-Swiss–centric

get updates at zagat.com

San Fernando Valley/Burbank F | D | S | C

Continental fare and "great" Deutsch beer; it's a "colorful", "old-fashioned" place with a keyboardist/accordionist who has 'Edelweiss' down pat.

Max Restaurant 24 | 18 | 20 | $38
13355 Ventura Blvd. (bet. Dixie Canyon & Nagle Aves.), Sherman Oaks, 818-784-2915; www.maxrestaurant.com
■ Chef Andre Guerrero's son should be pleased to be lending his name to this "Cal-Asian jewel" in Sherman Oaks attracting a "hip Valley crowd" with a "sophisticated" menu of "attractively presented" dishes and some of the "best desserts" around; it's "way too loud" in the "tiny" room, and the service can be "unprofessional" at times, but most all's "forgiven when the food arrives."

Mazzarino's 18 | 10 | 15 | $20
12920½ Riverside Dr. (Coldwater Canyon Ave.), Sherman Oaks, 818-788-5050
11946 Ventura Blvd. (bet. Carpenter & Radford Aves.), Studio City, 818-761-8808
■ Since 1947, fans in Sherman Oaks have been flocking to this "mom-and-pop Southern Italian pizzeria" for "fabulous" free garlic bread, "fresh clam–and–garlic pizzas" and "meatball subs right out of Jersey" in a "classic red-and-white checker tablecloth" setting; the atmosphere is "lacking", but it's "always busy", and "deservedly so"; N.B. the Studio City spin-off is more of a take-out place.

Mel's Drive-In ● 15 | 17 | 16 | $14
14846 Ventura Blvd. (Kester Ave.), Sherman Oaks, 818-990-6357; www.melsdrive-in.com
See review in LA/Hollywood/W. Hollywood Directory.

Mexicali ● 16 | 16 | 14 | $20
12161 Ventura Blvd. (Laurel Canyon Blvd.), Studio City, 818-985-1744
■ With "so many choices of tequila", ordering a margarita can be an "adventure" at this "trendy" Cal-Mex that fans tout as "Studio City's top hang out" for "big stars and wanna-be actors"; most agree it's the "atmosphere, not the food", that "keeps this place packed", as long as "you don't mind shouting over your fajitas" in a din that "makes Times Square seem quiet."

Miceli's 15 | 19 | 19 | $23
3655 Cahuenga Blvd. W. (Regal Pl.), Universal City, 323-851-3345
See review in LA/Hollywood/W. Hollywood Directory.

Mimi's Cafe 18 | 17 | 18 | $18
19710 Nordhoff Pl. (Corbin Ave.), Chatsworth, 818-717-8334
24201 W. Magic Mtn. Pkwy. (Valencia Blvd.), Santa Clarita, 661-255-5520
www.mimiscafe.com
See review in LA/Hollywood/W. Hollywood Directory.

San Fernando Valley/Burbank F | D | S | C

Mi Piace 20 | 17 | 17 | $27
801 N. San Fernando Blvd. (Burbank Blvd.), Burbank, 818-843-1111
The Commons, 4799 Commons Way (Calabasas Rd.), Calabasas, 818-591-8822
■ At this "reliable" chain of "casual Cal-Italians", "everyone will find something on the menu", from "carbonara to die for" to "yummy" lasagna to "perfect stuffed French toast that could brighten any morning" (on weekends); there's "always a wait" and the service is "iffy", but they're "wildly popular" nonetheless.

Mistral 24 | 22 | 24 | $40
13422 Ventura Blvd. (bet. Dixie Canyon & Greenbush Aves.), Sherman Oaks, 818-981-6650; www.mistralrestaurant.com
■ This "authentic French bistro" in Sherman Oaks "does everything right", with "excellent", "elegant" Gallic dishes, including "amazing steak tartare" and the "best frites in town", an "outstanding, well-priced" wine list, "wonderful" service and a "dark", "beautiful room"; the atmosphere is "warm and friendly", though it can get "terribly noisy."

Monty's Steakhouse 22 | 18 | 22 | $38
5371 Topanga Canyon Blvd. (Ventura Blvd.), Woodland Hills, 818-716-9736
■ "Step back in time" at this "old-school" steakhouse duo in Woodland Hills and Pasadena serving "Flintstone"-size portions of beef "cooked to perfection", "baked potatoes as big as footballs" and other "eat-till-you-drop" fare in an "old-fashioned", "leather-boothed" room; the service is "friendly" and "not at all pretentious", and there's a "busy bar scene for the over-40 crowd."

Mo's 19 | 13 | 17 | $18
4301 Riverside Dr. (bet. N. Rose & N. Valley Sts.), Burbank, 818-845-3009; www.eatatmos.com
■ The de facto "lunchtime cafeteria" of "Disney, Warner Brothers and NBC", this Burbank American "does the job" with "amazing hamburger choices" with "fresh fixings" from a condiment bar, "massive" salads and a "standout" Sunday champagne brunch; while "everyone at lunch is scanning the room for industry players", it's also a "family-friendly" "neighborhood hang."

Mr. Cecil's California Ribs 20 | 11 | 16 | $21
13625 Ventura Blvd. (Woodman Ave.), Sherman Oaks, 818-905-8400
See review in Westside Directory.

Mulberry Street Pizzeria 22 | 10 | 15 | $13
17040 Ventura Blvd. (Oak Park Ave.), Encino, 818-906-8881
See review in Westside Directory.

get updates at zagat.com

San Fernando Valley/Burbank F | D | S | C |

Nicola's Kitchen   20 | 12 | 19 | $19 |
French Qtr., 20969 Ventura Blvd. (bet. Canoga & De Soto Aves.), Woodland Hills, 818-883-9477
■ For "Italian at its natural best", this "casual" spot in Woodland Hills gets high marks "for the bread alone", though the rest of the menu is "impeccable" and "elegantly served" by a "friendly staff" that's "always willing to help"; it's the "favorite standby" of many for lunch or a "last-minute dinner out."

Noah's New York Bagels   16 | 11 | 13 | $7 |
14622 Ventura Blvd. (Van Nuys Blvd.), Sherman Oaks, 818-907-9570; www.noahs.com
See review in LA/Hollywood/W. Hollywood Directory.

Odyssey   ▽ 14 | 20 | 15 | $27 |
15600 Odyssey Dr. (Rinaldi St.), Granada Hills, 818-366-6444
◪ It's best to "dine at sunset" "on a clear day" at this Granada Hills Continental seafooder "overlooking the whole San Fernando Valley", where a "drink on the patio is a nice romantic way to end a week", and the lunchtime buffet is a "wonderful way to do a group meeting"; still, "nothing can beat the view" – "including the food."

Olive Garden   11 | 12 | 14 | $18 |
1741 N. Victory Pl. (Empire Ave.), Burbank, 818-559-3640
19724 Nordhoff Pl. (Corbin Ave.), Chatsworth, 818-772-6090
www.olivegarden.com
See review in Westside Directory.

Omino Sushi   ▽ 26 | 14 | 20 | $28 |
20957 Devonshire St. (De Soto Ave.), Chatsworth, 818-709-8822; www.ominosushi.com
■ An "oasis at the far end of the San Fernando Valley", this Japanese "gem" in Chatsworth is "nothing fancy or pretentious", just a "small-town sushi bar" offering a "fabulous selection" of "fresh", "consistent" fare that finatics "never get tired of"; it's tiny, so "don't tell anyone."

Outback Steakhouse   16 | 14 | 17 | $26 |
Empire Ctr., 1761 N. Victory Pl. (W. Empire Ave.), Burbank, 818-567-2717
18711 Devonshire St. (Reseda Blvd.), Northridge, 818-366-2341
25261 N. The Old Rd. (Frwy. 5), Santa Clarita, 661-287-9630
137 E. Thousand Oaks Blvd. (Moorpark Rd.), Thousand Oaks, 805-381-1590
www.outbacksteakhouse.com
See review in South Bay/Long Beach Directory.

Out Take Cafe   21 | 14 | 18 | $24 |
12159 Ventura Blvd. (Laurel Canyon Blvd.), Studio City, 818-760-1111
■ "Potstickers and borscht make a great combo" swear fans of the "eclectic", "Asian-French-American" Cal menu

subscribe to zagat.com

San Fernando Valley/Burbank F | D | S | C

at this storefront "industry hangout" in Studio City that's the "bargain of the century when it comes to creative dishes"; the portions are "big", "like mom would give you", but "if you made as much noise as the diners do here" in the "convivial, crowded", "itty-bitty" room, she might give you "a spanking."

Padri 21 | 20 | 18 | $31
29008 Agoura Rd. (Kanan Rd.), Agoura Hills, 818-865-3700; www.padrirestaurant.com

■ Sunday night "family-style specials" and a martini bar that "rocks with the singles set" (mostly "middle-aged" "yuppies") on weekends make for a mixed crowd at this "cozy", "upscale" Agoura Hills Italian housed in a "homey" "California-style bungalow" that's "comfortable any night of the week"; "generous portions" of "better-than-average" cuisine and "plenty of people-watching" contribute to the "overall enjoyable experience."

Paul's Cafe 21 | 17 | 20 | $29
18588 Ventura Blvd. (Reseda Blvd.), Tarzana, 818-343-8588

■ Now separate from the original Paul's Cafe in Sherman Oaks (nka August Chris Cafe), this "very un-Valley" Cal-French in Tarzana has "cloned the Cafe Bizou formula" and run with it (i.e. $1 soup or salad, and $2 corkage); it's "city dining at Valley prices" with "excellent" service and an "intimate space" where "even the bathrooms are lit by candlelight."

P.F. CHANG'S CHINA BISTRO 20 | 20 | 18 | $24
Sherman Oaks Galleria, 15301 Ventura Blvd. (Sepulveda Blvd.), Sherman Oaks, 818-784-1694
The Promenade at Woodland Hills, 21821 Oxnard St. (Topanga Canyon Blvd.), Woodland Hills, 818-340-0491
www.pfchangs.com

See review in LA/Hollywood/W. Hollywood Directory.

Piatti 21 | 20 | 20 | $30
101 S. Westlake Blvd. (Thousand Oaks Blvd.), Thousand Oaks, 805-371-5600; www.piatti.com

■ This Thousand Oaks outpost of a statewide Italian syndicate is a "refreshing change from the larger chains", with "delectable pasta dishes that are worth every carb" and a "classy, warm atmosphere" that's "a little fancy, but not stuffy"; "convenient for lunch meetings", it's also a "reliable" destination for a "relaxed dinner with friends"; P.S. insiders hint "try to get a table next to the fireplace."

Picanha Churrascaria 22 | 16 | 20 | $30
269 E. Palm Ave. (bet. San Fernando Blvd. & 3rd St.), Burbank, 818-972-2100; www.picanharestaurant.com

■ It's a "carnivore's carnival" at this Burbank Brazilian BBQ where "succulent meats arrive at your table for as long as you can keep eating", "sliced from skewers" by

get updates at zagat.com

San Fernando Valley/Burbank F | D | S | C

"hot" servers dressed as gauchos in a cavernous space with a South American look; "extreme" meat eaters "ignore the salad bar and sides, and leave the plate free" for the "namesake steak" that's "worth a second helping."

Pinot Bistro   25 | 23 | 23 | $44
12969 Ventura Blvd. (½ block west of Coldwater Canyon Ave.), Studio City, 818-990-0500; www.patinagroup.com

■ The original Pinot, and still "the best", Joachim Splichal's Studio City Cal-French bistro is an "aristocratic experience", featuring "consistently outstanding", "well-prepared" cuisine with "flashes of brilliance", a "cozy, upscale" setting with "French country elegance" and "real waiters without attitude"; popular among "entertainment people" from the nearby studios, it also appeals to a "senior crowd."

Poquito Mas ●   21 | 9 | 15 | $10
2635 W. Olive Ave. (Buena Vista St.), Burbank, 818-563-2252
10651 Magnolia Blvd. (Cartwright Ave.), North Hollywood, 818-994-8226
3701 Cahuenga Blvd. W. (bet. Barham & Lankershim Blvds.), Studio City, 818-760-8226
Valencia Town Ctr., 24405 Town Center Dr. (McBean Pkwy.), Valencia, 661-255-7555
www.poquitomas.com
See review in LA/Hollywood/W. Hollywood Directory.

Posto ☒   26 | 22 | 25 | $46
14928 Ventura Blvd. (Kester Ave.), Sherman Oaks, 818-784-4400; www.welovewine.com

■ Piero Selvaggio's "junior version of Valentino" in the Valley is a "class act" in its own right, serving "excellent", "upscale" Italian cuisine (including "fabulous" tasting menus) and an "outstanding" wine list in an "elegant, yet relaxed" setting; with a "personal touch" and an "enthusiasm that just won't quit", the staff "treats [you] graciously", even if you come in "looking like a slob."

Prego   19 | 19 | 19 | $34
Sherman Oaks Galleria, 15301 Ventura Blvd. (Sepulveda Blvd.), Sherman Oaks, 818-905-7004
See review in LA/Hollywood/W. Hollywood Directory.

Ribs USA   20 | 8 | 16 | $18
2711 W. Olive Ave. (bet. Buena Vista & Florence Sts.), Burbank, 818-841-8872; www.ribsusa.com

■ You'll find "serious BBQ" but "no attitude" at this "hole-in-the-wall" in the middle of Burbank's "media district", where the "messy" babybacks have a "good smoky flavor", the chicken is "wonderful" and the "backyard bacon burger is everything you ever wanted"; there are "unlimited peanuts" to go along with "beer, beef and a ballgame on the big screen" – just "be sure to throw your shells on the floor", and "dig that sawdust!"

San Fernando Valley/Burbank F | D | S | C

Rive Gauche Cafe M   21 | 22 | 19 | $33
14106 Ventura Blvd. (Hazeltine Ave.), Sherman Oaks, 818-990-3573

■ "A quiet jewel" tucked away on busy Ventura Boulevard in Sherman Oaks, this "tried-and-true" bistro offers "classic" Gallic fare that harkens "back to the days when sauces and butter were in" at prices that "won't break you"; the "charming outdoor patio" is "wonderful in the summer" and "perfect for Sunday brunch", and for a bit of "romance" you can retreat to the lounge "with fireplace."

Romano's Macaroni Grill   18 | 17 | 18 | $21
19400 Plummer St. (Tampa Ave.), Northridge, 818-725-2620
25720 N. The Old Road (McBean Pkwy.), Santa Clarita, 661-284-1850
Promenade Shopping Ctr., 4000 E. Thousand Oaks Blvd. (Westlake Blvd.), Thousand Oaks, 805-370-1133
See review in South Bay/Long Beach Directory.

Roma via Paris S   ▽ 25 | 20 | 20 | $32
3413 Cahuenga Blvd. W. (bet. Barham & Lankershim Blvds.), Universal City, 323-882-6965

■ "You feel like you're in Europe" at this "charming" BYO Franco-Italian "hideaway" in Universal City where "you can chat with the chef" as he prepares "can't-lose entrees" "such as "incredible sun-dried tomato–and–olive crusted salmon" featured on a "menu that changes regularly"; the room is "cozy" enough for a "romantic dinner" with "ample" space for a "party of 10."

Rosti   16 | 14 | 16 | $21
Encino Mktpl., 16403 Ventura Blvd. (Hayvenhurst Ave.), Encino, 818-995-7179
Promenade at Westlake, 160 Promenade Way (Thousand Oaks Blvd.), Westlake Village, 805-370-1939
See review in Westside Directory.

Ruby's   17 | 18 | 18 | $13
The Promenade at Woodland Hills, 6100 Topanga Canyon Blvd. (Oxnard Blvd.), Woodland Hills, 818-340-7829; www.rubys.com
See review in Westside Directory.

SADDLE PEAK LODGE M   27 | 27 | 25 | $55
419 Cold Canyon Rd. (Piuma Rd.), Calabasas, 818-222-3888; www.saddlepeaklodge.com

■ A "carnivore's carnival" awaits at this New American set in a "secluded" "mountaintop" "hunting lodge" with a "roaring fireplace" just a short drive from Malibu; you can "savor the Santa Monicas at sunset" while you dine on "exotic" game "cooked to perfection", including "must-try elk", "excellent" steaks and "absolutely exquisite" salmon; it's "not for those on a budget", but "if you have an appetite for game", it's well "worth the buck."

get updates at zagat.com

San Fernando Valley/Burbank F | D | S | C |

Salt Creek Grille
19 | 20 | 18 | $30 |

Valencia Town Ctr., 24415 Town Center Dr. (McBean Pkwy.), Valencia, 661-222-9999; www.saltcreekgrille.com

■ This "popular" American steakhouse duo in Valencia and Dana Point is "ideal for dining alfresco on a summer evening", where you can "cuddle up to your loved one by the outdoor fire pit" or mingle with "older singles" at the bar; design doyens can imagine "Frank Lloyd Wright sitting near the open fireplace" in the "Craftsman-style" interior where meat eaters can tuck into prime NY steak "grilled to perfection" and "tasty" blue-cheese burgers.

Seashell
23 | 20 | 21 | $34 |

19723 Ventura Blvd. (Corbin Ave.), Woodland Hills, 818-884-6500; www.theseashellrestaurant.com

■ After 30 years, this "upscale", "old-school classic" Continental in Woodland Hills is still serving "excellent seafood", and the "service is enhanced by the presence of the owners" who "treat you as an old friend even if it's your first time"; a "pleasing" decor and an "elegant atmosphere" help make it a "lovely place" for "special occasions."

Señor Fred
– | – | – | M |

13730 Ventura Blvd. (Woodman Ave.), Sherman Oaks, 818-789-3200; www.senorfred.com

Less than a year after he opened Max just a few blocks east in Sherman Oaks, Andre Guerrero strikes again (once more naming a restaurant for a son) with a colorful spot with modern Mexican decor and the Guadalajaran cuisine of chef Raphael Solorzano; choices include tamalitos in pumpkin-seed sauce and *caldo siete mares* (Mexican bouillabaisse).

Sharky's Mexican Grill
19 | 12 | 15 | $11 |

9250 Reseda Blvd. (bet. Nordhoff & Plummer Sts.), Northridge, 818-772-2203
13238 Burbank Blvd. (Fulton Ave.), Sherman Oaks, 818-785-2533
5511 Reseda Blvd. (Ventura Blvd.), Tarzana, 818-881-8760
111 S. Westlake Blvd. (Thousand Oaks Blvd.), Westlake Village, 805-370-3701
6219 Topanga Canyon Blvd. (Erwin St.), Woodland Hills, 818-887-6963
www.sharkys.com

See review in LA/Hollywood/W. Hollywood Directory.

Sisley Italian Kitchen
17 | 16 | 17 | $22 |

15300 Ventura Blvd. (Sepulveda Blvd.), Sherman Oaks, 818-905-8444
The Oaks Mall, 446 W. Hillcrest Dr. (bet. Lynn Rd. & McCloud Ave.), Thousand Oaks, 805-777-7511
Valencia Town Ctr., 24201 Valencia Blvd. (McBean Pkwy.), Valencia, 661-287-4444
www.sisleykitchen.com

See review in Westside Directory.

San Fernando Valley/Burbank F | D | S | C

Smoke House 19 | 16 | 19 | $32
4420 Lakeside Dr. (Barham Blvd.), Burbank, 818-845-3731
■ "One of the last of the red-leather steakhouses", this "old studio standby" in Burbank may be a "bit dated and frayed around the edges", but it's still a "classic" where "Hollywood meets the Chicago stockyards", with "tasty Day-Glo garlic cheese bread" that's matched by the "cheesy" lounge setting, a popular haunt of "stars of daytime soaps" and "TV execs" "who appreciate a great martini."

Souplantation 15 | 10 | 12 | $11
19801 Rinaldi St. (Corbin Ave.), Northridge, 818-363-3027; www.souplantation.com
See review in LA/Hollywood/W. Hollywood Directory.

Spark Woodfire Cooking 20 | 19 | 19 | $27
11801 Ventura Blvd. (bet. Carpenter & Colfax Aves.), Studio City, 818-623-8883; www.sparkwoodfirecooking.com
■ Staying true to its name, nearly every dish is "wood-fire grilled" at this rustic Italian duo in Studio City and Huntington Beach that earns raves for its "thin-crust pizzas", "planked salmon", "grilled artichokes and meats"; as a bonus, "you can't beat the view at sunset" at the OC branch.

Spumante ☒ 24 | 18 | 24 | $29
12650 Ventura Blvd. (bet. Coldwater Canyon & Whitsett Aves.), Studio City, 818-980-0734
■ "Everyone feels welcome" at this Studio City Cal-Italian where the "owner greets people as if they were close friends", and the "giant Hawaiian shrimp is the favorite of regulars, which seems to be everyone"; "excellent pastas", "top-notch" service and a "romantic patio" all help make this the "perfect neighborhood" trattoria.

Stanley's 18 | 16 | 17 | $21
13817 Ventura Blvd. (bet. Hazeltine & Woodman Aves.), Sherman Oaks, 818-986-4623; www.stanleys83.com
■ This "neighborhood American bistro" has "stood the test of time" as a "reliable standby for casual Californian cuisine" in the SF Valley where you can order everything from "hamburgers and fries" to "wonderful Chinese chicken salad" while you relax in the "spacious" room or "garden" patio; it's a "great place to meet someone new" especially with a "happening bar scene on Friday nights."

Stevie's Creole Cafe – | – | – | M
16911 Ventura Blvd. (Balboa Blvd.), Encino, 818-528-3500
For a taste of N'Awlins in the San Fernando Valley, this moderately priced Encino Creole cafe-cum-nightclub dishes out big portions of gumbo, jambalaya, shrimp and crawfish étouffée, Louisiana hot links and more along with exotic cocktails in a down-home setting that's hoppin' on weekends with live entertainment.

get updates at zagat.com

San Fernando Valley/Burbank F | D | S | C

SUSHI NOZAWA 27 | 7 | 16 | $48
11288 Ventura Blvd. (Main St.), Studio City, 818-508-7017
■ "Let Mr. Trust Me [aka chef Kazunori Nozawa] take care of it" at this decor-challenged storefront Japanese in Studio City, a perennial top-ten contender for Food renowned for its omakase menu of "sublime" sushi that's "tailored to American tastes"; while some are growing tired of his "Sushi Nazi" "shtick", you still have to "arrive early" or else join the "line stretching down the street."

Talesai 23 | 18 | 19 | $27
11744 Ventura Blvd. (bet. Colfax Ave. & Laurel Canyon Blvd.), Studio City, 818-753-1001
See review in LA/Hollywood/W. Hollywood Directory.

Tama Sushi ▽ 25 | 21 | 23 | $29
11920 Ventura Blvd. (bet. Carpenter Ave. & Laurel Canyon Blvd.), Studio City, 818-760-4585
■ "Still undiscovered" by the general public, "talented" chef Katsu Michite's Studio City Japanese (fka Katsu) has recovered from a fire two years ago to serve "outstanding" sushi that is "unmatched", even in "NY or Tokyo", as well as other "creative" dishes; "friendly service" and a "Zen-like setting" also help make it an "incredible find."

Tempo 19 | 15 | 16 | $23
16610 Ventura Blvd. (bet. Balboa Blvd. & Hayvenhurst Ave.), Encino, 818-905-5855; www.temporestaurant.com
■ "You can make a meal out of the appetizers" at this "lively" Encino Middle Easterner serving "savory" fare "with a definite zing"; "if you hate noise, avoid weekends" when the "vocal crowds" and "music" get "wa-a-a-y too loud", but if you're a devout diner, the "Friday night Shabbat dinners are special."

Teru Sushi ▽ 22 | 19 | 21 | $40
11940 Ventura Blvd. (Laurel Canyon Blvd.), Studio City, 818-763-6201; www.terusushi.com
■ A "solid go-to place for the industry crowd", this Studio City sushi stalwart was the "first to introduce" many to the joys of raw fish, and while some feel it's being "outshone by some of its more inventive counterparts", it's still an "upbeat" scene that's "always packed", with plenty of "famous faces" for stargazers to espy; one question, though – "how do you say 'overpriced' in Japanese?"

Todai 14 | 11 | 12 | $24
Studio City Pl., 11239 Ventura Blvd. (bet. Tonga & Vineland Aves.), Studio City, 818-762-8311
20401 Ventura Blvd. (bet. De Soto & Winnetka Aves.), Woodland Hills, 818-883-8082
www.todai.com
See review in LA/Hollywood/W. Hollywood Directory.

San Fernando Valley/Burbank F | D | S | C

Tony Roma's 16 | 13 | 15 | $22
220 N. San Fernando Rd. (Orange Grove Ave.), Burbank, 818-557-7427
1901 Daily Dr. (Carmen Ave.), Camarillo, 805-987-4939
16575 Ventura Blvd. (Hayvenhurst Ave.), Encino, 818-461-8400
Universal CityWalk, 1000 Universal Studios Blvd. (off Frwy. 101), Universal City, 818-763-7674
www.tonyromas.com
See review in Westside Directory.

Tournesol 23 | 20 | 19 | $30
13251 Ventura Blvd. (Longridge Ave.), Studio City, 818-986-3190; www.tournesolbistro.com
■ Providing a "touch of Provence in the Valley", this Studio City French bistro beckons budget-conscious bec fins with "fabulous food at fantastic prices", with notable specials such as Lobster Night Mondays and Steak Night Wednesdays that are "real bargains"; the setting is "intimate and not stuffy", and the staff is "friendly", although the service can be "uneven"; P.S. "don't miss the chocolate sunflower for dessert."

Tuscany II Ristorante ⑤ 24 | 21 | 23 | $44
Westlake Plaza Ctr., 968 S. Westlake Blvd. (Townsgate Rd.), Westlake Village, 805-495-2768
■ "Take someone important" to this "expense-account" Italian establishment in Westlake Village, an "oasis of excellent food in the Conejo Valley" and a "favorite" destination for "special occasions"; the "upscale" cuisine is "always delicious", the service "outstanding" and the decor truly "lovely"; some may grouse about having to make the "long drive from downtown LA", but most agree it's "worth a repeat trip."

2087 An American Bistro ⑤ 20 | 21 | 18 | $43
2087 E. Thousand Oaks Blvd. (bet. Hampshire & Rancho Rds.), Thousand Oaks, 805-374-2087
◪ "If the produce were any fresher, you'd have to brush the soil off your shoes" at this contemporary, upscale New American bistro situated "conveniently close" to the Thousand Oaks Civic Arts Plaza, where the "tasty fare" is "prepared with care", and the atmosphere is "pure casual elegance" in the "lovely", "inviting" room; "overrated and overpriced" howl hecklers who are unimpressed by the "country-club" setting.

Versailles 22 | 9 | 17 | $16
17410 Ventura Blvd. (bet. Louise & White Oak Aves.), Encino, 818-906-0756
Universal CityWalk, 1000 Universal Center Dr. (off Frwy. 101), Universal City, 818-505-0093
See review in LA/Hollywood/W. Hollywood Directory.

San Fernando Valley/Burbank | F | D | S | C |

Villa Piacere | 19 | 24 | 19 | $31 |
22160 Ventura Blvd. (bet. Shoup Ave. &
Topanga Canyon Blvd.), Woodland Hills, 818-704-1185;
www.villapiacere.com

■ While it garners accolades for serving "reliable", "nicely presented" Italian cuisine, this establishment in Woodland Hills is better known for its "beautiful garden patio" that makes it the "place to go in the Valley for special events in the summer"; the service "varies", but "when it's on, it's very good."

Vitello's | 14 | 15 | 16 | $23 |
4349 Tujunga Ave. (Moorpark St.), Studio City, 818-769-0905;
www.vitellosrestaurant.com

◪ "Before Robert Blake made it infamous", this pizza and pasta house in Studio City was known simply as an "old-fashioned Italian-American" serving "dependable" "standard" fare, including "thin-crust pizzas" that "make me homesick for Brooklyn", with "opera in the back room" four nights a week; boosters grouse there's "too much noise about the shooting" and wish people would "pay more attention to the food."

Wine Bistro ⌾ | 20 | 19 | 20 | $38 |
11915 Ventura Blvd. (Laurel Canyon Blvd.), Studio City,
818-766-6233; www.winebistrorestaurant.com

■ A "great little find" in Studio City, this "pretty and romantic" French bistro next to CBS offers "authentic, delicious" Gallic fare in a "high-class" setting where you might see "Brando at his table in the rear"; frugal Francophiles applaud the "prix fixe that's an absolute steal" (you can order "anything off the menu, as long as you order an appetizer, entree and dessert").

Wolfgang Puck Cafe | 17 | 15 | 16 | $22 |
Universal CityWalk, 1000 Universal Center Dr. (off Frwy. 101),
Universal City, 818-985-9653
The Promenade at Woodland Hills, 6100 Topanga Canyon Blvd.
(Oxnard St.), Woodland Hills, 818-710-9653
www.wolfgangpuck.com
See review in LA/Hollywood/W. Hollywood Directory.

WOOD RANCH BBQ & GRILL | 20 | 16 | 18 | $23 |
Whizins Plaza, 5050 Cornell Rd. (Roadside Dr.), Agoura Hills,
818-597-8900
1101 Daily Dr. (Lantana St.), Camarillo, 805-482-1202
540 New Los Angeles Ave. (bet. Science Dr. & Spring Rd.),
Moorpark, 805-523-7253
Northridge Fashion Mall, 9301 Tampa Ave. (bet. Nordhoff &
Plummer Sts.), Northridge, 818-886-6464
25580 The Old Road (Lyons Ave.), Valencia, 661-222-9494
www.woodranch.com
See review in LA/Hollywood/W. Hollywood Directory.

San Fernando Valley/Burbank   F | D | S | C

Yang Chow   24 | 11 | 18 | $21
*6443 Topanga Canyon Blvd. (Victory Blvd.), Canoga Park,
818-347-2610*
See review in LA/Hollywood/W. Hollywood Directory.

ZANKOU CHICKEN ●⊄   23 | 5 | 12 | $10
*5658 Sepulveda Blvd. (Burbank Blvd.), Van Nuys,
818-781-0615*
See review in LA/Hollywood/W. Hollywood Directory.

The San Gabriel Valley and Pasadena/Glendale

Top Food

27 Derek's
Bistro 45
26 Shiro
Yujean Kang's
Julienne

25 Cinnabar
Maison Akira
Arroyo Chop Hse.
Parkway Grill
Tre Venezie

Top Decor

27 Ritz-Carlton Hunt.
24 Bistro 45
Nonya
Raymond, The
Parkway Grill

Arroyo Chop Hse.
23 Maison Akira
22 Sushi Roku
Halie
Cinnabar

Top Service

26 Bistro 45
25 Ritz-Carlton Hunt.
Derek's
24 Shiro
23 Parkway Grill

Cinnabar
Dal Rae
Maison Akira
22 Raymond, The
Derby, The

Top Value

1. In-N-Out Burger
2. Noah's NY Bagels
3. Baja Fresh
4. Astro Burger
5. El Tepeyac
6. Zankou Chicken
7. Pie 'N Burger
8. Johnny Rockets
9. Ruby's
10. Pho 79

By Location

Arcadia
22 Derby, The
17 BJ's
Carmine's
16 Outback Steakhse.
Tony Roma's

Glendale
25 Cinnabar
23 Zankou Chicken
Far Niente
22 Carousel
19 Panda Inn

Monterey Park/Alhambra
23 Ocean Star
El Tepeyac
NBC Seafood
21 Mandarin Deli
20 Pho 79

Pasadena
27 Derek's
Bistro 45
26 Yujean Kang's
25 Maison Akira
Arroyo Chop Hse.

The San Gabriel Valley and Pasadena/Glendale Restaurant Directory

SG Valley/Pasadena/Glendale F | D | S | C

Akbar Cuisine of India 22 | 14 | 20 | $24
One Colorado, 44 N. Fair Oaks Ave. (Union St.), Pasadena, 626-577-9916; www.akbarcuisineofindia.com
See review in Westside Directory.

All India Café 21 | 13 | 17 | $19
39 S. Fair Oaks Ave. (bet. Colorado Blvd. & Green St.), Pasadena, 626-440-0309; www.allindiacafe.com
See review in Westside Directory.

Arroyo Chop House 25 | 24 | 22 | $48
536 S. Arroyo Pkwy. (bet. California & Del Mar Blvds.), Pasadena, 626-577-7463
■ This "pricey" "meat-eaters' paradise", a spin-off of the adjacent Parkway Grill, is the "place to go in Pasadena" for "awesome" steaks and other "formidable" "meat-and-potato" fare, served in a "loud, boisterous" "old boys'–club" setting complete with "dark woods and leather booths"; a few find the service "challenged", but most credit the staff for making the place feel like a "second home."

Astro Burger ◐⌀ 19 | 9 | 15 | $9
3421 W. Beverly Blvd. (Bradshawe St.), Montebello, 323-724-3995
See review in LA/Hollywood/W. Hollywood Directory.

Babita Mexicuisine Ⓜ ▽ 25 | 15 | 23 | $28
1823 S. San Gabriel Blvd. (Norwood Pl.), San Gabriel, 626-288-7265
■ A "surprising find" in an "unlikely neighborhood", this "haute" San Gabriel Mexican serves "unique", "impossibly delicious" Yucatan cuisine with "amazingly complex flavors" in an "unpretentious", "intimate" space; it's a "labor of love" for the "well-trained, creative" chef-owner, whose "passion for food" and "pride show through."

BAJA FRESH MEXICAN GRILL 20 | 11 | 15 | $9
899 E. Del Mar Blvd. (Lake Ave.), Pasadena, 626-792-0446; www.bajafresh.com
See review in LA/Hollywood/W. Hollywood Directory.

Bayou ▽ 20 | 19 | 18 | $26
10 N. First St. (Main St.), Alhambra, 626-943-9901
◪ "Not for the faint of heart when it comes to spices", this Alhambra Cajun will set "your tongue on fire" with "big portions" of "tasty", hot fare, but critics charge that "its attempt to be modern and cool" (witness the "way-too-dark" lighting) "overshadows the cuisine", which is "not the most authentic", anyway.

Beckham Grill 17 | 18 | 19 | $31
77 W. Walnut St. (Fair Oaks Ave.), Pasadena, 626-796-3399; www.beckhamgrill.com
◪ "If creamed corn is your thing", cognoscenti recommend this "poor man's Lawry's" in Pasadena offering "tasty

SG Valley/Pasadena/Glendale   F | D | S | C

enough" prime rib and other "predictable" Traditional American and English dishes, as well as "friendly" service, in "pleasant", "throwback" "pub surroundings"; skeptics sniff "it's seen better days."

Benihana   19 | 18 | 21 | $32
17877 Gale Ave. (Fullerton Rd.), City of Industry, 626-912-8784; www.benihana.com
See review in Westside Directory.

Bice ⓜ   19 | 19 | 19 | $37
Paseo Colorado, 266 E. Colorado Blvd. (Marengo Ave.), Pasadena, 626-793-0468; www.biceristorante.com
See review in LA/Hollywood/W. Hollywood Directory.

Big Mama's Rib Shack ⓜ   ▽ 16 | 13 | 13 | $19
1453 N. Lake Ave. (Rio Grande St.), Pasadena, 626-797-1792; www.bigmamasribshack.com
◪ The "sauce is boss" at this BBQ import from Las Vegas (?) situated high up the hill from Old Town Pasadena, where "wonderful" ribs, chicken, beef and pork are "not too sweet with just enough kick"; "big on ordinary" is how detractors describe the fare, combined with "service that needs improvement" and an "oddly decorated" room.

BISTRO 45 ⓜ   27 | 24 | 26 | $49
45 S. Mentor Ave. (bet. Colorado Blvd. & Green St.), Pasadena, 626-795-2478; www.bistro45.com
■ Tops in Pasadena, this "old world" Cal-French "leaves you with that warm pampered feeling", starting with a "wonderful" welcome from "ever-charming" owner Robert Simon, the "créme de la crème of restaurateurs", who makes you "feel like a friend after one visit"; "seasonal menus" of "inventive", "excellent" fare and a wine list that's "other-worldly" are served by a "gracious", "friendly" staff in a retro-modern "art deco" setting; no wonder it remains a "longtime favorite" after more than a decade.

BJ's ☻   17 | 15 | 16 | $18
400 E. Huntington Dr. (Gateway Dr.), Arcadia, 626-462-1494
Eastland Shopping Ctr., 2917 Eastland Center Dr. (Barranca St.), West Covina, 626-858-0054
www.bjsbrewhouse.com
See review in Westside Directory.

Blue Pyramid ⓢ   ▽ 24 | 21 | 22 | $27
1000 E. Broadway (Belmont St.), Glendale, 818-548-1000; www.bluepyramidrestaurant.com
■ The "bread alone is worth a visit" to this "charming Mediterranean getaway" in Glendale, but "don't fill up" lest you miss out on "delicious, exuberantly seasoned" dishes like the "amazing spanakopita" and "special house pizza"; the "friendly staff" "makes you feel welcome", and the "eye-popping" trompe l'oeil decor is "enjoyable."

get updates at zagat.com

SG Valley/Pasadena/Glendale F | D | S | C

BORDER GRILL 21 | 19 | 19 | $30
*Paseo Colorado, 260 E. Colorado Blvd. (Marengo Ave.),
Pasadena, 626-844-8988; www.bordergrill.com*
See review in Westside Directory.

Bric ☒ ▽ 22 | 13 | 15 | $29
*2833 Honolulu Ave. (Pleasure Way), Montrose,
818-248-0009*
◪ A "funky gem in Montrose", this Italian is operated by Vincenti's former sommelier and his wife, who "make great recommendations"; a "wonderful wine list" complements the "authentic" fare better than the decor, which recalls the previous tenant, a Mexican restaurant, and just "doesn't fit"; the performance is still "a bit rough around the edges", but *amici* are glad to "give it more time to get organized."

Buca di Beppo 14 | 17 | 17 | $22
*505 W. Foothill Blvd. (Indian Hill Blvd.), Claremont,
909-399-3287
80 W. Green St. (De Lacey Ave.), Pasadena,
626-792-7272
www.bucadibeppo.com*
See review in Westside Directory.

Burger Continental 17 | 10 | 15 | $16
*535 S. Lake Ave. (California Blvd.), Pasadena, 626-792-6634;
www.burgercontinental.com*
◪ At this "versatile" Pasadena Eclectic-Mediterranean, a "wonderful mix of many cultures" is represented on the "varied" menu, from "burgers" to "stuffed grape leaves", all served in "huge portions"; on weekends, live music and belly dancers enliven the "cheesy", "shabby chic" room and "sprawling" outdoor patio, which get "so crowded you'll be forced to make new friends."

Cafe Atlantic ▽ 20 | 16 | 18 | $21
*53 E. Union St. (Raymond Ave.), Pasadena, 626-796-7350;
www.cafeatlantic.com*
■ Just around the corner from its elder sibling Xiomara in Old Pasadena, this Cuban neophyte offers "large portions" of "creative", "authentic" fare that reflect chef-owner Xiomara Ardolina's "unerring taste for flavor and quality" in a more "casual" setting; amigos aver "if I lived in Pasadena, I'd eat here once a week."

CAFÉ BIZOU 23 | 19 | 21 | $29
*91 N. Raymond Ave. (Holly St.), Pasadena, 626-792-9923;
www.cafebizou.com*
See review in Westside Directory.

Café Med 17 | 16 | 16 | $25
*Paseo Colorado, 260 E. Colorado Blvd. (Marengo Ave.),
Pasadena, 626-793-0600*
See review in LA/Hollywood/W. Hollywood Directory.

SG Valley/Pasadena/Glendale F | D | S | C |

Café Mundial Ⓜ ▽ 23 | 21 | 20 | $29 |
516 S. Myrtle Ave. (Colorado Blvd.), Monrovia, 626-303-2233; www.cafemundial.net
■ A "terrific value in the San Gabriel Valley's fastest growing hot spot", this "unpretentious" "little gem" plays a big role in putting Old Town Monrovia on the culinary map with a "creative" though "limited" menu of "rich" Cal-Med fare; while the service can be "spotty" at times, the staff is usually "friendly."

Cafe Santorini 19 | 19 | 18 | $29 |
64-70 W. Union St. (Fair Oaks Ave.), Pasadena, 626-564-4200; www.cafesantorini.com
☑ Expect a "long wait on weekends" at this Old Town Pasadena Mediterranean, where those in the know prefer the "beautiful outdoor patio"/balcony to the "funky" room; the scene "can be loud, but it's worth it" for the "fun, energetic" vibe, as well as "standbys" like "authentic hummus and baba ghanoush" and "outstanding lamb."

Caffe Citron 22 | 18 | 20 | $35 |
110 E. Lemon Ave. (Myrtle Ave.), Monrovia, 626-358-1908
■ A "gem" in Old Town Monrovia, "or anywhere", this "sexy little" Cal–Northern Italian is a "great neighborhood spot" that's "also worth a drive", serving "earthy" dishes along with an "affordable", "interesting wine list" in a "comfortable, sophisticated" setting with sidewalk and patio seating; the service is "always pleasant" and "attentive."

CALIFORNIA PIZZA KITCHEN 18 | 14 | 17 | $18 |
Plaza Las Fuentes, 99 N. Los Robles Ave. (Union St.), Pasadena, 626-585-9020; www.cpk.com
See review in LA/Hollywood/W. Hollywood Directory.

Camilo's Ⓜ ▽ 22 | 21 | 23 | $25 |
2128 Colorado Blvd. (Caspar St.), Eagle Rock, 323-478-2644
■ A "welcome addition" to Eagle Rock, an "up-and-coming hipster area" ("who would've thought?"), this "classy" Californian offers a "moderately priced menu" of "delicious" fare ("truly outstanding" filet mignon) in a "charming", multi-hued interior; N.B. it now has a liquor license, though you can still BYO.

Carmine's 17 | 13 | 18 | $20 |
311 E. Live Oak Ave. (bet. 3rd & 4th Sts.), Arcadia, 626-445-4726
424 Fair Oaks Ave. (bet. Columbia St. & Frwy. 110), South Pasadena, 626-799-2266
☑ It's like taking a "trip back to New Jersey" at this Italian duo in Arcadia and South Pasadena serving "great pizzas" and "comfy mounds" of "dependable red-sauce" fare with "minimal foo foo" at "affordable" prices; N.B. live music at the South Pasadena branch on Fridays and Saturdays.

get updates at zagat.com

SG Valley/Pasadena/Glendale F | D | S | C |

Carousel M   22 | 16 | 20 | $23
304 N. Brand Blvd. (California St.), Glendale, 818-246-7775;
www.carouselrestaurant.com
See review in LA/Hollywood/W. Hollywood Directory.

CASA BIANCA ⑤ M ⇨   24 | 12 | 17 | $15
1650 Colorado Blvd. (Vincent Ave.), Eagle Rock, 323-256-9617
■ Pie-zanos proclaim this "friendly" family-run Italian in Eagle Rock "the only place for real pizza in LA", and regular "long lines" seem to bear them out; in addition to "incredible" thin-crust pies, "homestyle" red-sauce fare is also served in a "glitz-challenged", "'50s time-warp" room; "bring cash [no plastic], and be prepared to wait"; N.B. closed Sunday and Monday.

Celestino ⑤   24 | 19 | 21 | $36
141 S. Lake Ave. (bet. Cordova & Green Sts.), Pasadena,
626-795-4006; www.celestinopasadena.com
■ There's "no pretense" at this Pasadena "outpost of the Drago empire", just "superb, consistent" Italian cuisine, "friendly" service and a quietly elegant space with an outdoor patio: "high-class" and "highly recommended", it's a "delight" "after the movies or almost anytime."

CHEESECAKE FACTORY   20 | 18 | 18 | $23
2 W. Colorado Blvd. (Fair Oaks Ave.), Pasadena, 626-584-6000;
www.thecheesecakefactory.com
See review in Westside Directory.

Chevys   14 | 13 | 14 | $17
Ontario Mills Mall, 4551 Mills Circle (4th St.), Ontario, 909-481-4846
100 S. California Ave. (W. Garvey Ave. S.), West Covina,
626-851-9400
101 N. Brand Blvd. (B'way), Glendale, 818-291-9555
www.chevys.com
See review in San Fernando Valley/Burbank Directory.

Cinnabar M   25 | 22 | 23 | $41
933 S. Brand Blvd. (Chevy Chase Dr.), Glendale, 818-551-1155
■ A "true genius", chef Damon Bruner "shines" with his "fresh, exhilarating" Cal-Asian cuisine that's even "worth a trip from NY" to this "classy" spot housed in a former warehouse "hidden among the car dealers" of Glendale; each dish on the seasonal menu is "lovingly prepared and beautifully presented" while "attentive" service and a "hip, cozy" setting add to the experience; the "funky, old" bar, "rescued" from an old dive in Chinatown and manned by "some of the best bartenders around", "cinches it" for many.

Claim Jumper Restaurant   18 | 16 | 18 | $22
18061 Gale Ave. (Fullerton Rd.), City of Industry, 626-964-1157
820 W. Huntington Dr. (Frwy. 210), Monrovia, 626-359-0463
www.claimjumper.com
See review in South Bay/Long Beach Directory.

SG Valley/Pasadena/Glendale F | D | S | C

Crocodile Café 16 | 15 | 17 | $21
140 S. Lake St. (Cordova St.), Pasadena, 626-449-9900
626 N. Central Ave. (Doran St.), Glendale, 818-241-1114
88 W. Colorado Blvd. (S. De Lacey Ave.), Pasadena, 626-568-9310
www.crocodilecafe.com
See review in Westside Directory.

Cuban Bistro Ⓜ ▽ 18 | 20 | 18 | $22
28 W. Main St. (Garfield Ave.), Alhambra, 626-308-3350;
www.cubanbistro.com
■ The "best mojitos in LA will get you in a romantic mood" at this "lively" Alhambra Cuban with a "happening" bar, where "people get up and dance" when live music is played on weekend nights; not to be overlooked are "tasty", "exotic" dishes served in "large portions that'll fill any aching stomach."

Dal Rae 24 | 20 | 23 | $41
9023 E. Washington Blvd. (Rosemead Blvd.), Pico Rivera, 562-949-2444; www.dalrae.com
☑ "Industrialists and the people who love them" get their "fill of cholesterol" at this Pico Rivera Continental, a "gentlemen's style" "throwback" to the "days of three-martini lunches" where "solid", "old-school" dishes such as oysters Rockefeller and pepper steak (with "tableside preparation of many dishes") are served in a "retro" room complete with "leather banquettes" and a piano bar.

Damon's Steakhouse Ⓜ 18 | 17 | 19 | $25
317 N. Brand Blvd. (bet. California Ave. & Lexington Dr.), Glendale, 818-507-1510
☑ "Tacky tiki decor at its best" and "lethal mai tais" will transport you to "*Fantasy Island* at this stalwart steakhouse (circa 1937) offering a "bit of the South Seas in Glendale" along with the "plain good" "slabs of meat" at "prices that won't break the bank."

De Lacey's Club 41 18 | 20 | 19 | $30
41 S. De Lacey Ave. (bet. Colorado Blvd. & Green St.), Pasadena, 626-795-4141; www.delaceysclub41.com
■ An "old-time chophouse" in Old Town Pasadena, this "speakeasylike" "meat-lover's haven" is a "throwback" to a "simpler time", with "lots of red meat and martinis straight up", and a "yummy Caesar salad made tableside", served in a "clubby" setting of "dark woods and comfy seats" and a "great mahogany bar"; "friendly" service also helps "make for a pleasurable meal."

Delmonico's Seafood Grille ◐ 20 | 17 | 19 | $35
Paseo Colorado, 260 E. Colorado Blvd. (Green St.), Pasadena, 626-844-7700;
www.delmonicosseafoodgrille.com
See review in LA/Hollywood/W. Hollywood Directory.

SG Valley/Pasadena/Glendale F | D | S | C |

Derby, The 22 | 21 | 22 | $33 |
233 E. Huntington Dr. (bet. Gateway Dr. & 2nd Ave.), Arcadia, 626-447-2430; www.thederbyarcadia.com

■ A "thoroughbred throwback", this "classic" steakhouse across the street from Santa Anita racetrack is the "'in' place for the race horse crowd and old-time Arcadians" who come for "bacon-wrapped fillets" and "great prime ribs", served in a "warm, cozy" room that "looks unchanged from the '50s", graced with "old pictures of movie stars and jockeys"; the service is "professional" ("nobody's trying to be an actor or screenwriter").

DEREK'S ⓈⓂ 27 | 22 | 25 | $51 |
181 E. Glenarm St. (Marengo Ave.), Pasadena, 626-799-5252; www.dereks.com

■ A "diamond in the rough, behind the dry cleaners" and a "large potted plant" in a Pasadena mini-mall, "charming" host-owner Derek Dickerson's "hard-to-find" "oasis" is "worth wandering off the beaten path" for "excellent" Californian cuisine, including a "fantastic" tasting menu with "perfect pairings of wines", "impeccable" service by an "enthusiastic" staff and an "unpretentious yet elegant" interior with a "soothing" decor.

Diner on Main ⊄ – | – | – | I |
201 W. Main St. (2nd St.), Alhambra, 626-281-3488

For years now, the City of Alhambra has declared that its Main Street will be the next Old Town Pasadena, and with the opening of this wildly popular retro American diner, they may be right; done up in chrome and Formica with Schwinn bicycles hanging from the walls, along with photos of James Dean, its menu naturally focuses on items like hot dogs and burgers; imbibers will like the cocktail lounge where drinks have names like 'Old Blue Eyes.'

Dino's Italian Inn ∇ 19 | 14 | 21 | $20 |
2055 E. Colorado Blvd. (bet. Allen Ave. & Sierra Madre Blvd.), Pasadena, 626-449-8823

■ There's "no California-Nouveau" at this Pasadena stalwart (circa 1949), just "true traditional Italian" "comfort food" served in a "comfy" interior of dark wood, low lights and red banquettes; "large-portioned entrees" (that come with soup, salad, antipasto and pasta) at "bargain prices" and "helpful" service are a few reasons why it's "still going strong" after more than half a century.

Dish 16 | 16 | 15 | $19 |
734 Foothill Blvd. (Walnut St.), La Cañada Flintridge, 818-790-5355; www.dishbreakfastlunchanddinner.com

☒ "Shabby chic meets grandma's ol' time favorites" at this Traditional American "country cafe" in La Cañada Flintridge, where the menu includes dishes such as "old-fashioned" johnny cakes, "great" gingersnap-crusted ham and mac 'n'

SG Valley/Pasadena/Glendale F | D | S | C |

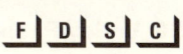

cheese that'll "fill you up and weigh you down"; though the service is "less than professional", the "sun-filled" room is "pleasant" and "relaxing."

EL CHOLO   18 | 18 | 17 | $21 |
958 S. Fair Oaks Ave. (bet. California Blvd. & Glenarm St.), Pasadena, 626-441-4353
See review in LA/Hollywood/W. Hollywood Directory.

El Pollo Inka   18 | 11 | 15 | $15 |
1938 E. Rd. 66 (Lone Hill Ave.), Glendora, 626-963-1044
See review in Westside Directory.

EL TEPEYAC M ⇄   23 | 9 | 17 | $12 |
1965 Potrero Grande Dr. (Arroyo Dr.), Monterey Park, 626-573-4607
See review in LA/Hollywood/W. Hollywood Directory.

El Torito   14 | 14 | 15 | $18 |
3333 Foothill Blvd. (Madre St.), Pasadena, 626-351-8995; www.eltorito.com
See review in Westside Directory.

Empress Harbor   ▽ 22 | 17 | 16 | $22 |
Atlantic Plaza, 111 N. Atlantic Blvd. (Garvey Ave.), Monterey Park, 626-300-8833; www.empressharbor.com

■ "Bring the gang" to this "Hong Kong–style dim sum house" in the heart of Monterey Park for the "best shrimp dumplings" and other small bites in "large portions" during the day, and a full selection of Cantonese seafood at night; "fine" "antiques" grace the "giant dining room", but don't diminish the "bustle" that makes "this place so much fun."

Far Niente   23 | 19 | 22 | $32 |
204½ N. Brand Blvd. (Wilson Ave.), Glendale, 818-242-3835

■ "If this was on the Westside it would be a shrine" declare loyalists of this Glendale bistro offering "sophisticated", "elegant" Northern Italian cuisine at "reasonable prices" including "a tuna carpaccio to die for", the "best mussel soup in L.A." and "fabulous fish entrees"; "top-notch" service and a convenient location make it "perfect for dinner before or after the Alex Theater."

Firefly Bistro M   20 | 19 | 20 | $33 |
1009 El Centro St. (Meridian Ave.), South Pasadena, 626-441-2443

■ A "wonderful outdoor experience" even on a "steamy evening", this South Pasadena New American newcomer is a "romantic open-air bistro" that "feels like an upscale picnic", where you tuck into "delicious" dishes from an "exciting" menu under a "sturdy tent"; "friendly" service contributes to a scene that "really buzzes"; N.B. no relation to Firefly in Studio City.

get updates at zagat.com

SG Valley/Pasadena/Glendale   F | D | S | C |

Five Sixty-One ☒   ▽ 22 | 18 | 20 | $36 |
Southern CA School of Culinary Arts, 561 E. Green St. (Madison Ave.), Pasadena, 626-405-1561; www.calchef.com

■ The inmates are running the asylum at this "lovely" Cal-French operated by the California School of Culinary Arts in Pasadena, where students prepare and serve an "ever-changing menu" of "flavorful, eye-appealing" dishes; it can be "inconsistent" as they're "still learning", but it's "wonderful to watch people so thrilled by the idea of food" putting forth such an "honest effort"; P.S. "try their cafe next door for something less fancy and more affordable."

Fresco Ristorante ☒   ▽ 25 | 19 | 25 | $41 |
514 S. Brand Blvd. (Colorado St.), Glendale, 818-247-5541

■ "High-brow food without high-brow prices or Westside attitude" can be found amid the "tire shops and car lots" on "Glendale's Auto Row" at this "romantic" "jewel" of a "cozy, old-style Italian" where "excellent chef-owner" Antonio Orlando and his "incredible" staff provide "sublime service without being pushy", which helps make it easy to overlook the "strange" decor.

Fu-Shing   ▽ 22 | 16 | 19 | $20 |
2960 E. Colorado Blvd. (El Nido Ave.), Pasadena, 626-792-8898

■ "Be ready for the Szechuan spiciness" at this Pasadena Chinese that's "worth the extra mile for takeout" or a "spectacular" lunch for "amazing" Middle Kingdom fare made with "delicate, flavorful sauces"; "cheerful decor" and "quick", "friendly" service are additional reasons it's a spot "worth experiencing."

Gaucho Grill   18 | 15 | 16 | $21 |
121 W. Colorado Blvd. (De Lacey Ave.), Pasadena, 626-683-3580; www.gauchogrillusa.com

See review in LA/Hollywood/W. Hollywood Directory.

Gennaro's Ristorante ☒   – | – | – | E |
1109 N. Brand Blvd. (Dryden St.), Glendale, 818-243-6231

Tucked away in an unobtrusive location in Glendale, this Northern Italian is a long-standing local favorite, thanks to a stellar wine list and classic Northern Italian cuisine, served by a professional staff in an elegant, sophisticated setting; cronies complain it's been "overlooked too long", but those who value its intimate, soothing atmosphere may not mind so much.

Golden Deli ⌿   ▽ 24 | 9 | 15 | $10 |
815 W. Las Tunas Dr. (Mission Dr.), San Gabriel, 626-308-0803

■ Pho sure, you have to be "crazy" about this San Gabriel Vietnamese to "take a number" and "wait in the inevitable

SG Valley/Pasadena/Glendale | F | D | S | C |

long lines" to dine in a "small", somewhat "tacky" space, but an "extensive" menu of "excellent, authentic" fare at "very reasonable prices" makes it all worthwhile.

Gordon Biersch ●   17 | 17 | 16 | $23 |
41 Hugus Alley (bet. Colorado Blvd. & Union St.), Pasadena, 626-449-0052; www.gordonbiersch.com
See review in San Fernando Valley/Burbank Directory.

Greco's   19 | 16 | 17 | $26 |
1065 E. Green St. (bet. Catalina & Wilson Sts.), Pasadena, 626-795-9615
◪ While the "food remains special" at this Pasadena Italian, some longtime loyalists lament "it's not the same experience since the move" to its present location; although the room is "prettier" and the ambiance "more upscale" than the previous site, critics contend it's also "a bit stuffier" and "out of sync with the red-tablecloth, classic" cuisine.

Green Field Churrascaria   18 | 15 | 19 | $28 |
381 N. Azusa Ave. (Workman Ave.), West Covina, 626-966-2300; www.greenfieldbbq.com
See review in South Bay/Long Beach Directory.

Halie Ⓜ   21 | 22 | 19 | $43 |
Cheesewright Bldg., 1030 E. Green St. (Catalina Ave.), Pasadena, 626-440-7067; www.restauranthalie.com
■ Housed in a "well-renovated" historic structure, a former top-secret research facility, this "sultry", "sophisticated" Pasadena Californian impresses with an "eye-grabbing" decor, "fabulous and ever-changing" cuisine and "friendly" service; a "frenetic" bar scene and DJs on the weekends help to attract a "young, hip" crowd.

Hamburger Hamlet   15 | 13 | 15 | $18 |
214 S. Lake Ave. (bet. E. Colorado & E. Del Mar Blvds.), Pasadena, 626-449-8520; www.hamburgerhamlet.com
See review in LA/Hollywood/W. Hollywood Directory.

Hayakawa Ⓜ   ∇ 24 | 13 | 20 | $37 |
750 Terrado Plaza (bet. Citrus & Workman Aves.), Covina, 626-332-8288
■ "Just say 'omakase' and enjoy" the "chef's choice" of "sophisticated sushi" and "new-style sashimi" "excellently prepared" by toque Kazuhiko Hayakawa at this Covina Japanese; the "spartan" digs look "due for a remodel", and it's ensconced in a "depressing" mini-mall (which may explain why it's "rarely very busy"), but finatics insist it's "worth a pilgrimage."

HOUSTON'S   21 | 19 | 20 | $29 |
320 S. Arroyo Pkwy. (Del Mar Blvd.), Pasadena, 626-577-6001; www.houstons.com
See review in Westside Directory.

get updates at zagat.com

SG Valley/Pasadena/Glendale F | D | S | C

IL FORNAIO   20 | 19 | 19 | $29
One Colorado Shopping Plaza, 1 W. Colorado St. (Fair Oaks Ave.), Pasadena, 626-683-9797; www.ilfornaio.com
See review in Westside Directory.

IN-N-OUT BURGER ●⇗   24 | 10 | 18 | $7
1210 N. Atlantic Blvd. (Huntington Dr.), Alhambra, 800-786-1000
119 Brand Ave. (B'way), Glendale, 800-786-1000
420 N. Santa Anita Ave. (Colorado Blvd.), Arcadia, 800-786-1000
310 N. Harvey Dr. (Rte. 134), Glendale, 800-786-1000
324 S. Azusa Ave. (Gladstone St.), Azusa, 800-786-1000
15259 E. Amar Rd. (Hacienda Blvd.), City of Industry, 800-786-1000
17849 E. Colima Rd. (Stoner Creek Rd.), City of Industry, 800-786-1000
1371 Grand Ave. (Arrow Hwy.), Covina, 800-786-1000
1261 S. Lone Hill (210 Frwy.), Glendora, 800-786-1000
2114 E. Foothill Blvd. (Craig St.), Pasadena, 800-786-1000
9070 Whittier Blvd. (Rosemead Blvd.), Pico Rivera, 800-786-1000
4242 N. Rosemead Blvd. (Mission Dr.), Rosemead, 800-786-1000
Additional locations throughout the San Gabriel Valley/Pasadena/Glendale area.
www.in-n-out.com
See review in LA/Hollywood/W. Hollywood Directory.

Islands   16 | 16 | 17 | $14
3533 E. Foothill Blvd. (Rosemead Blvd.), Pasadena, 626-351-6543
117 W. Broadway (Orange St.), Glendale, 818-545-3555
www.islandsrestaurants.com
See review in Westside Directory.

Johnny Rockets ●   16 | 15 | 16 | $12
One Colorado, 52 Hugus Alley (Fair Oaks Ave.), Pasadena, 626-793-6570; www.johnnyrockets.com
See review in LA/Hollywood/W. Hollywood Directory.

JULIENNE ⌧   26 | 22 | 21 | $22
2649 Mission St. (bet. El Molino & Los Robles Aves.), San Marino, 626-441-2299; www.juliennetogo.com
■ You'll swear you were "sidewalk dining in Paris" at this French bistro/gourmet market, a "culinary oasis in the middle of a quiet residential community" that's "worth the drive from the Westside" to the Eastside enclave of moneyed San Marino, where "upper-class patrons" gather for the "best breakfasts and luscious lunching" on the likes of "fabulous rosemary bread and salads."

Koo Koo Roo   16 | 8 | 13 | $11
915 W. Huntington Dr. (5th Ave.), Monrovia, 626-359-6768
238 S. Lake Ave. (bet. Cordova St. & E. Del Mar Blvd.), Pasadena, 626-683-9600
www.kookooroo.com
See review in LA/Hollywood/W. Hollywood Directory.

SG Valley/Pasadena/Glendale F | D | S | C |

Lake Spring Shanghai   ▽ 22 | 8 | 12 | $19 |
219 E. Garvey Ave. (Lincoln Ave.), Monterey Park, 626-280-3571
■ "If you don't care about clogged arteries", head for this Monterey Park BYO Chinese for the "renowned pork pump", an "oddly named", "meltingly tender" "fatty hock" that's the "stuff of legendary memories" for locals; just note as the scores indicate, decor and service can't compete with the signature dish, which hogs the show.

La Parisienne   ▽ 23 | 17 | 22 | $41 |
1101 E. Huntington Dr. (bet. Buena Vista & Mountain Aves.), Monrovia, 626-357-3359;
www.laparisiennerestaurant.com
◨ Since 1972, the "gracious", "old-world" staff at this Monrovia stalwart has been serving "well-prepared", unabashedly "Classic French" fare like braised sweetbreads and salmon in champagne sauce; but while nostalgists are pleased that it's "just as it was when my husband proposed to me over 30 years ago", progressives pout it's "pricey" and "past its prime."

Louise's Trattoria   15 | 14 | 16 | $21 |
2-8 E. Colorado Blvd. (Fair Oaks Ave.), Pasadena, 626-568-3030;
www.louises.com
See review in LA/Hollywood/W. Hollywood Directory.

Madre's Ⓜ   13 | 21 | 15 | $39 |
897 Granite Dr. (Lake Ave.), Pasadena, 626-744-0900
◨ Surveyors are split over "J.Lo's joint" in Pasadena – to fans and "wanna-bes" it's a "sexy" "dining delight", with a "beautiful, romantic", "shabby chic" decor and "wonderful, flavorful" Caribbean-Latino cuisine; foes flog the "prissy" room, "average", "expensive" eats and a "staff that truly doesn't care", suggesting it's best left to "tourists on the prowl" for its famous owner.

Magalys Ⓜ   – | – | – | M |
7051 Greenleaf Ave. (bet. Philadelphia & Wardman Sts.), Whittier, 562-464-2626
This BYO Cal-French newcomer is the "ambitious effort" of the "former chef at Devon" and gives Whittier "what it's needed for years" – "slow, thoughtful dining" "worthy of a Westside restaurant"; early reports indicate dishes such as the "red pepper soup, elk in sage red wine sauce and mango crème brûlée" are "all excellent" and "reasonably priced."

Maison Akira Ⓜ   25 | 23 | 23 | $46 |
713 E. Green St. (bet. El Molino & Oak Knoll Aves.), Pasadena, 626-796-9501; www.maisonakira.com
■ An "excellent place to forget a bad play" at the nearby Pasadena Playhouse, Akira Hirose's "fantastique" Franco-Japanese offers "nicely balanced, cross-cultural" "fusion that's not fussy"; "the bar is raised every time you go" and

get updates at zagat.com

SG Valley/Pasadena/Glendale   F | D | S | C

there's "never a dull feast", as "artistically presented" dishes such as "irresistible" Chilean sea bass with miso are served in an "elegant" room by an "attentive" staff.

Mandarin Deli ⌀   21 | 9 | 13 | $13
701 W. Garvey Ave. (Atlantic Blvd.), Monterey Park, 626-570-9795
See review in LA/Hollywood/W. Hollywood Directory.

Maria's Italian Kitchen   17 | 13 | 17 | $18
Hastings Ranch Shopping Ctr., 3537 E. Foothill Blvd. (bet. Rosemead Blvd. & Sierra Madre Villa Ave.), Pasadena, 626-351-2080; www.mariasitaliankitchen.com
See review in San Fernando Valley/Burbank Directory.

Marston's   23 | 17 | 19 | $18
151 E. Walnut St. (bet. N. Marengo & N. Raymond Aves.), Pasadena, 626-796-2459; www.marstonsrestaurant.com
■ Having established itself as Pasadena's "favorite breakfast place" (that's also "great for lunch"), with "excellent" blueberry pancakes, "heavenly" salads and other "creative comfort foods", this venerable American now serves dinner every night; the "cozy, homey" cottage is "very, very small" and "there's always a line before it even opens", but for fans it's "worth it."

McCormick & Schmick's   19 | 19 | 19 | $33
111 N. Los Robles Ave. (Union St.), Pasadena, 626-405-0064; www.mccormickandschmicks.com
See review in LA/Hollywood/W. Hollywood Directory.

Mimi's Cafe   18 | 17 | 18 | $18
17919 Gale Ave. (S. Azusa Ave.), City of Industry, 626-912-3350
500 Huntington Dr. (S. Mayflower Ave.), Monrovia, 626-359-9191
15436 E. Whittier Blvd. (Santa Gertrudes Ave.), Whittier, 562-947-0339
www.mimiscafe.com
See review in LA/Hollywood/W. Hollywood Directory.

Mi Piace   20 | 17 | 17 | $27
25 E. Colorado Blvd. (bet. Fair Oaks & Raymond Aves.), Pasadena, 626-795-3131
See review in San Fernando Valley/Burbank Directory.

Monty's Steakhouse   22 | 18 | 22 | $38
592 S. Fair Oaks Ave. (California Blvd.), Pasadena, 626-792-7776
See review in San Fernando Valley/Burbank Directory.

Mountain View Sushi M   – | – | – | M
24 W. Sierra Madre Blvd. (Baldwin Ave.), Sierra Madre, 626-355-1324
In a space that was recently home to a Cajun restaurant owned by jockey Kent Desormeaux comes this casual sushi bar with an extensive specialty-roll menu with names (i.e.

SG Valley/Pasadena/Glendale F | D | S | C

'Godzilla in NY', 'Captain Kark') that defy interpretation; whatever their meaning, the fish is fresh, the place is clean and prices are lower than most.

NBC SEAFOOD 23 | 13 | 15 | $20
404 S. Atlantic Blvd. (bet. Harding & Newmark Aves.), Monterey Park, 626-282-2323
"Excellent" "Hong Kong–style" dim sum and "well-priced specials" keep this "bustling", "bellweather" Sino seafooder in Monterey Park "crazy busy" at lunch and especially on weekends, when you might see "a big fat Chinese wedding party" or two, while in the evening, "fresh", "fantastic" fin fare rules; the staff "acts as if they're doing you a favor" unless you can "speak Cantonese."

Noah's New York Bagels 16 | 11 | 13 | $7
Hastings Ranch Shopping Ctr., 3711 E. Foothill Blvd. (Rosemead Blvd.), Pasadena, 626-351-0352
605 S. Lake Ave. (E. California Blvd.), Pasadena, 626-449-6415
www.noahs.com
See review in LA/Hollywood/W. Hollywood Directory.

Nonya 23 | 24 | 20 | $34
61 N. Raymond Ave. (Union St.), Pasadena, 626-583-8398; www.nonyarestaurant.com
There's "bamboo everywhere" at this "sleek", "gorgeous" "Asian getaway" in the heart of Old Pasadena, where you'll find "delicious, intriguing" Chinese-Malaysian offerings that are "beyond ambitious", served by a "friendly", "helpful" staff; "don't let the prices scare you", for the "portions are generous" and "big enough to share."

OCEAN STAR 23 | 15 | 14 | $21
145 N. Atlantic Blvd. (bet. Emerson & Garvey Aves.), Monterey Park, 626-308-2128
At lunch the lines are "longer than at Magic Mountain" for the "best dim sum this side of Hong Kong" at this Monterey Park Chinese where "angry" "cart-ladies" look as if they might "run you over" in the "crowded, noisy" room that's as "vast" as a "football field"; by night, it serves "impeccable" seafood "so fresh it swims to your plate."

Olive Garden 11 | 12 | 14 | $18
430 E. Huntington Dr. (bet. 2nd & 5th Aves.), Arcadia, 626-821-0636
13500 Whittier Blvd. (Painter Ave.), Whittier, 562-693-5999
101 N. Brand Blvd. (bet. B'way & Wilson Ave.), Glendale, 818-240-7119
www.olivegarden.com
See review in Westside Directory.

O-Nami ▽ 18 | 13 | 15 | $23
West Covina Plaza, 1526 Plaza Dr. (Vincent Ave.), West Covina, 626-962-8110; www.o-nami.com
See review in South Bay/Long Beach Directory.

SG Valley/Pasadena/Glendale | F | D | S | C |

Outback Steakhouse | 16 | 14 | 17 | $26 |
166 E. Huntington Dr. (2nd Ave.), Arcadia, 626-447-6435
1418 Azusa Ave. (Frwy. 60), City of Industry, 626-810-6765
1476 N. Azusa Ave. (Arrow Hwy.), Covina, 626-812-0488
www.outbacksteakhouse.com
See review in South Bay/Long Beach Directory.

Panda Inn | 19 | 16 | 17 | $21 |
111 E. Wilson Ave. (Maryland Ave.), Glendale,
818-502-1234
3488 E. Foothill Blvd. (Rosemead Blvd.), Pasadena,
626-793-7300
www.pandainn.com
◪ Though the cuisine may be "more American than Chinese", this "reliable" veteran Sino duo in Glendale and Pasadena "continues to impress" with "consistently" "satisfying, tasty" fare and one of the "best buffets in SoCal" that includes all-you-can-drink mai tais; with "fast" service and a "pretty" "Asian-inspired" decor to boot, "who needs a fancy restaurant?"

PARKWAY GRILL | 25 | 24 | 23 | $43 |
510 S. Arroyo Pkwy. (bet. California & Del Mar Blvds.),
Pasadena, 626-795-1001
■ A "Pasadena landmark", this "cornerstone of the Smith brothers mini-empire" (Arroyo Chop House, Crocodile Café, Smitty's) provides a "reference point for Cal cuisine" with its "diverse menu" of "wonderfully prepared" dishes, and "everything tastes fresh because it is", featuring produce grown in its own garden; a "classy", "inviting" space, "friendly, prompt" service and "good jazz on weekends" all help to make it a "fabulous setting for a special event."

P.F. CHANG'S CHINA BISTRO | 20 | 20 | 18 | $24 |
Paseo Colorado, 260 E. Colorado Blvd. (Garfield Ave.),
Pasadena, 626-356-9760; www.pfchangs.com
See review in LA/Hollywood/W. Hollywood Directory.

Pho 79 | 20 | 7 | 12 | $10 |
29 S. Garfield Ave. (Main St.), Alhambra, 626-289-0239
535 W. Valley Blvd. (New Ave.), San Gabriel, 626-289-0657 ⇗
See review in LA/Hollywood/W. Hollywood Directory.

Pie 'N Burger ⇗ | 20 | 10 | 17 | $12 |
913 E. California Blvd. (bet. S. Lake & S. Mentor Aves.),
Pasadena, 626-795-1123; www.pienburger.com
■ A "Pasadena institution" and a "favorite of Cal Tech denizens" since 1963, this "tiny" American "dive" "lives up to its name", serving the "best pies in LA bar none" and "burgers that are bliss" in a "'50s" setting complete with "sit-down counter" and soda fountain; the breakfasts are "exceptional" as well, and on weekend mornings the line "stretches out the door and down the block."

224 subscribe to zagat.com

SG Valley/Pasadena/Glendale F | D | S | C |

Radhika's ▽ 21 | 15 | 20 | $22 |
140 Shoppers Ln. (Cordova Ave.), Pasadena, 626-744-0994; www.radhikas.com

■ "Creative", "bold, flavorful" Indian dishes, including "excellent chicken and lamb dishes with lovely sauces", can be found at this inconspicuous spot "tucked behind an office building, next to a parking structure" in the middle of Pasadena; the "tasty buffet lunch" is a big draw.

Raymond, The ⓜ 24 | 24 | 22 | $42 |
1250 S. Fair Oaks Ave. (Columbia St.), Pasadena, 626-441-3136; www.theraymond.com

■ Set in a "cozy Craftsman-style home" (formerly the groundskeeper's cottage of the long-gone Raymond Hotel), this Pasadena "hideaway" is a fine locale for "intimate dinners" and "special occasions" with a "romantic fireplace" and "lovely outdoor patio", and a "quiet" setting in which "you can actually have a conversation"; "reliable" Cal-Continental cuisine and a staff that "will go to any length to please the customer" add allure.

Restaurant Devon ⓜ 24 | 19 | 22 | $45 |
109 E. Lemon Ave. (Myrtle Ave.), Monrovia, 626-305-0013

■ While some say a place offering such "adventurous dining" "has no business being in Monrovia", others call this "creative" Cal-French a local "treasure" "worth schlepping to", thanks to "unique", "well-executed" dishes served by a "gracious" staff; the "idiosyncratic", "eclectic" room with a "techno-cave" atmosphere is "quiet" and "soothing", "perfect for a romantic date."

RITZ-CARLTON HUNTINGTON ⓈⓂ 24 | 27 | 25 | $54 |
Ritz-Carlton Huntington Hotel & Spa, 1401 S. Oak Knoll Ave. (Huntington Dr.), Pasadena, 626-577-2867; www.ritzcarlton.com

■ As "solid as the name implies", this hotel "classic" in Pasadena is "the place" to go "if you need to impress someone" with a "magnificent" dining room blessed with "stunning vistas" and the "incredible" New American cuisine of "enthusiastic, creative" chef Craig Strong; whether you come for a "relaxing lunch on the patio", "world-class" high tea or the "extravagant" Sunday brunch, it's "worth the splurge" and "makes one feel all is right with the world."

Robin's Woodfire BBQ & Grill ▽ 16 | 13 | 16 | $20 |
395 N. Rosemead Blvd. (Foothill Blvd.), Pasadena, 626-351-8885; www.robinsbbq.com

■ Robin Salzer is the "witty friend you had in high school with the collection of stolen street signs", and his "informal", inexpensive rib joint in Pasadena is "well worth the drive even from the Pacific Palisades", thanks to "down-home

SG Valley/Pasadena/Glendale   F | D | S | C

cooking" highlighted by "killer BBQ sauce" and the favorite appetizer "served on a garbage can lid"; "go hungry, because the portions are huge."

Romano's Macaroni Grill   18 | 17 | 18 | $21
945 W. Huntington Dr. (5th St.), Monrovia, 626-256-7969
See review in South Bay/Long Beach Directory.

Roscoe's House of   22 | 8 | 16 | $14
Chicken 'n Waffles ●
830 N. Lake Ave. (Orange Grove Blvd.), Pasadena, 626-791-4890
See review in LA/Hollywood/W. Hollywood Directory.

Ruby's   17 | 18 | 18 | $13
45 S. Fair Oaks Ave. (bet. Colorado Blvd. & Green St.), Pasadena, 626-796-7829
Whittwood Mall, 10109 Whittwood Ln. (Whittier Blvd.), Whittier, 562-947-7829
www.rubys.com
See review in Westside Directory.

Russell's Burgers   17 | 11 | 15 | $13
30 N. Fair Oaks Ave. (Union St.), Pasadena, 626-578-1404
■ "Reminiscent of days gone by", this "affordable" "diner-type" "burger 'n' shake" spot in the heart of Old Pasadena is a place to "indulge in comfort food", including "great chili cheese fries", "always good onion rings" and "peanut-butter pie", "at old-fashioned prices" in a "blessedly old-fashioned setting"; just "leave the calorie counter at home."

SALADANG   24 | 20 | 20 | $22
363 S. Fair Oaks Ave. (bet. California & Del Mar Blvds.), Pasadena, 626-793-8123
383 S. Fair Oaks Ave. (bet. California & Del Mar Blvds.), Pasadena, 626-793-5200
■ Locals refer to these "side-by-side" Siamese twins just south of Old Pasadena as a "benchmark for all new Thai excursions", with the original offering more traditional cuisine in a "beautiful" orchid-filled setting, while Song ('number two') is set in a "modern", "warehouse" location with a large patio, where "you can go wild trying new things" and the "wait is substantially shorter"; either one is a "pick for picky eaters."

Scampi   ▽ 25 | 17 | 20 | $34
40 N. Mentor St. (bet. Colorado & Union Blvds.), Pasadena, 626-568-4959; www.restaurantscampi.com
■ "Low-key but excellent", the Simental brothers' "gem" in Pasadena sparkles with chef Pedro's (ex Shiro) Cal-French cuisine, the "food that moans are made of", including "divine melt-in-your-mouth red snapper" and "surprise touches like mint sorbet between courses"; the "warm, friendly" setting is "perfect when you want to hear the voice of your date", and the staff is "enthusiastic" and "helpful."

SG Valley/Pasadena/Glendale F | D | S | C

Sea Harbour ▽ 22 | 15 | 17 | $38
3939 N. Rosemead Blvd. (Valley Blvd.), Rosemead, 626-288-3939
■ At this Rosemead outpost of Vancouver's most famous Cantonese seafooder, plenty of brass and marble have transformed a former ice cream parlor into an "expensive" "new standard" for Chinese fish houses; "outstanding" Hong Kong fare is listed on a trio of menus that "require familiarity with the cuisine", and cognoscenti counsel you "order carefully", since the "cost of dinner ranges greatly."

SHIRO Ⓜ 26 | 18 | 24 | $41
1505 Mission St. (Fair Oaks Ave.), South Pasadena, 626-799-4774; www.restaurantshiro.com
■ This South Pasadena "perennial" "favorite" proves that sometimes the "hype can be true" with "excellent", "innovative", "reasonably priced" Cal-Asian cuisine that's "as good as it gets"; dishes such as the "famous" catfish with ginger and ponzu sauce are served by a "friendly" staff that's "not overbearing" in a "stark", "mellow" space where "East meets West" in a "gracious" way.

Smitty's Grill 21 | 20 | 19 | $33
110 S. Lake Ave. (bet. Cordova & Green Sts.), Pasadena, 626-792-9999
■ A "good treatment of the basics" earns applause for the Smith brothers' (Arroyo Chop House, Crocodile Café, Parkway Grill) Pasadena American serving "cornbread that makes you think you've died and awoke in the South", "great ribs and swordfish" and other comfort fare; the setting is "casual" and "homey", and for a "much quieter" experience, the patio is "just what the doctor ordered to unwind on a Friday night."

SolyAzul ▽ 18 | 21 | 19 | $21
20 E. Colorado Blvd. (Fair Oaks Ave.), Pasadena, 626-796-0919; www.solyazul.com
■ "Tucked away in a back alley of Old Town" Pasadena, this "undiscovered" Mexican is luring locals "tired of the same old menu" with a "refreshing" cuisine full of "complex flavors", served in a decidedly "cool" setting; for "upscale fare at downscale prices", it's a "true winner."

Souplantation 15 | 10 | 12 | $11
2131 W. Commonwealth Ave. (bet. Date & Palm Aves.), Alhambra, 626-458-1173
301 E. Huntington Dr. (bet. Gateway Dr. & 2nd Ave.), Arcadia, 626-446-4248
Puente Hills Mall, 17411 Colima Rd. (Asuza Ave.), City of Industry, 626-810-5756
201 S. Lake Ave. (bet. Cordova St. & Del Mar Blvd.), Pasadena, 626-577-4798
www.souplantation.com
See review in LA/Hollywood/W. Hollywood Directory.

SG Valley/Pasadena/Glendale F | D | S | C

SUSHI ROKU 23 | 22 | 18 | $44
33 Miller Alley (bet. De Lacey & Fair Oaks Aves.), Pasadena, 626-683-3000; www.sushiroku.com
See review in LA/Hollywood/W. Hollywood Directory.

Taste of Manila M – | – | – | I
417 W. Main St. (bet. 4th & 5th Sts.), Alhambra, 626-570-4340
Despite a sizable Filipino population, LA has a dearth of restaurants serving the country's cuisine, a point that's partly corrected by this handsome, warmly decorated cafe across from the Alhambra Public Library in the heart of Main Street's Restaurant Row; the menu boasts a selection of can't-miss faves (fried lumpia, chicken adobo, flan).

Taylor's Prime Steaks 21 | 16 | 19 | $32
901 Foothill Blvd. (Angeles Crest Hwy.), La Cañada Flintridge, 818-790-7668; www.taylorssteakhouse.com
See review in LA/Hollywood/W. Hollywood Directory.

Thai Dishes 18 | 11 | 17 | $17
239 E. Colorado Blvd. (bet. Garfield & Marengo Sts.), Pasadena, 626-304-9975
See review in Westside Directory.

Tibet Nepal House ∇ 20 | 17 | 21 | $19
36 E. Holly St. (N. Fair Oaks Ave.), Pasadena, 626-585-9955
■ A "one-of-a-kind restaurant" in Pasadena, this Tibetan-Nepalese specialist is a "nice change for the palate", serving "exotic" dishes that resemble a "blend of Thai and Indian flavors", "described in painstaking detail" by an "attentive" staff; there's "such tranquility" here, where the ambiance "just makes you breath deeply and relax."

Tidal Wave M – | – | – | M
414 S. Myrtle Ave. (Lemon St.), Monrovia, 626-303-7338
Chef Juan Mercado, of the old Columbia Bar & Grill, returns with a seafood-intensive cafe in the heart of Monrovia's Restaurant Row; the long room is adorned with stylized fish murals that go from one end to the other, and the menu is just as piscatorially focused; the handsome bar doesn't yet offer any alcoholic beverages, but for those in the mood for tuna and salmon tartare, drunken shrimp and pistachio-crusted whitefish, this is the place of the moment in town.

Todai 14 | 11 | 12 | $24
Santa Anita Fashion Plaza, 400 S. Baldwin Ave. (Huntington Dr.), Arcadia, 626-445-6155
Glendale Galleria, 50 W. Broadway (Orange St.), Glendale, 818-247-8499
Puente Hills Mall, 1600 S. Azusa Ave. (Colima Rd.), City of Industry, 626-913-8530
www.todai.com
See review in LA/Hollywood/W. Hollywood Directory.

SG Valley/Pasadena/Glendale F | D | S | C

Tony Roma's 16 | 13 | 15 | $22
333 E. Huntington Dr. (2nd St.), Arcadia, 626-445-3595
9335 Monte Vista Ave. (Frwy. 10), Montclair, 909-626-3391
126 N. Maryland Ave. (Wilson Ave.), Glendale, 818-244-7427
www.tonyromas.com
See review in Westside Directory.

Tre Venezie Ⓜ 25 | 21 | 21 | $49
119 W. Green St. (bet. De Lacey & Pasadena Aves.), Pasadena, 626-795-4455
■ "If money isn't an issue", this "rare" Venetian "jewel" "on the outskirts of Old Pasadena" is an "excellent choice for a special, romantic occasion", with an "adventuresome menu" that's the "next best thing to eating in Venice", "knowledgeable" staff and "charming" atmosphere; while neophytes find the fare "a little too authentic", aficionados "couldn't ask for a more complete dining experience."

Trio Ristorante Ⓜ ∇ 22 | 21 | 20 | $41
932 Huntington Dr. (Oak Knoll Ave.), San Marino, 626-588-2627;
www.trytrio.com
■ A "hidden gem in the suburbs", this "outrageously good" Italian run by "trendy Europeans" in "gourmet-challenged San Marino" attracts "upscale yet laid-back families" with "tremendous" osso buco, "outstanding" risottos and other "excellent, unusual, well-prepared" dishes, "served elegantly" in a warm, woodsy room; it's a "pricey" but nonetheless "lovely experience."

Tulipano Ⓜ ∇ 23 | 14 | 21 | $25
530 S. Citrus Ave. (Gladstone St.), Azusa, 626-967-6670
■ "If only the setting could match the polenta" of this "charming, small Italian" "lost in a run-down mall" in Asuza, serving a "wide selection of specialties" from the Boot-shaped country, including "great pastas and bruschetta"; an "attentive" staff takes its cue from the "super-friendly", "hand-kissing" owner, who "makes the customers feel special"; N.B. reservations are required on weekends.

Tung Lai Shun ∇ 21 | 8 | 14 | $20
San Gabriel Sq., 140 W. Valley Blvd. (Del Mar Ave.), San Gabriel, 626-288-6588
■ "Not the usual" Sino spot, this "Islamic Chinese" in the San Gabriel Square Mall is a "wonderful culinary adventure" offering "superlative Hunan lamb", "steamy sesame bread" and "wonderful hot pots" in a "hospitable" setting; there's "no pork" on the premises, but "beer is available."

Twin Palms 16 | 21 | 17 | $34
101 W. Green St. (De Lacey Ave.), Pasadena, 626-577-2567
☑ The "open-air environment can't be beat" at this Old Pasadena Californian where "elegant, comfy dining" "under a big tent" is enlivened by "live music" to dance to, and a

get updates at zagat.com 229

SG Valley/Pasadena/Glendale F | D | S | C

"beautiful" crowd graces the "loud" room; foes, though, fume at the "inconsistent" fare, "slow" service and "meet-market" scene for "30-plus divorcées."

Wahib's Middle East ▽ 19 | 13 | 17 | $17
910 E. Main St. (bet. Garfield Ave. & Mission Dr.), Alhambra, 626-576-1048; www.wahibsmiddleeast.com

■ It's best to "pace yourself" at this "reasonably priced" storefront Middle Easterner in Alhambra that'll "stuff you like no other" with "huge servings" of the "best kebabs around", as well as "endless bowls of hummus and warm pita, pickled turnips and spicy peppers", served by "nutty waiters who won't leave you alone"; it's a "favorite for lunch" for many, especially those who "love garlic."

XIOMARA 24 | 20 | 21 | $41
69 N. Raymond Ave. (bet. Colorado Blvd. & Walnut St.), Pasadena, 626-796-2520; www.xiomararestaurant.com

■ "Bartender, more mojitos please!" is a popular refrain at Xiomara Ardolina's Nuevo Latino in Old Pasadena where "sophisticated" "Cuban-influenced" dishes are served by "cute" waiters in a somewhat "conservative" setting that exudes "charm and taste"; to make the "wonderful" signature drink, they "press the sugarcane right in front of you", and the result is "so good you might not even notice the food is great, too."

Yang Chow 24 | 11 | 18 | $21
3777 E. Colorado Blvd. (Rosemead Blvd.), Pasadena, 626-432-6868
See review in LA/Hollywood/W. Hollywood Directory.

Yoshida ⊠ ▽ 20 | 13 | 18 | $40
2026 Huntington Dr. (San Marino Ave.), San Marino, 626-281-9292

■ "Keep this place a secret" plead fans of this "small", upscale San Marino Japanese, for it's "hard enough to get a seat" at the sushi bar; "meticulous" chef Yoshi Okatomi and his "crew" "will be sure to take care of you", and the combination of the "freshest fish in town" plus his "skill and personality" have earned this spot a following that's almost "too large."

YUJEAN KANG'S 26 | 18 | 22 | $34
67 N. Raymond Ave. (bet. Holly & Union Sts.), Pasadena, 626-585-0855

■ Groupies gush that it's "worth the schlep to Pasadena" "no matter where you live" to "eat and educate yourself" at Yujean Kang's midpriced "flagship of adventurous Asian cooking" where his "splendid", "inventive" Chinese cuisine "bends all the rules" and "will have you scratching your head with wonder"; with a staff of "real waiters, not wanna-bes", the service is the "essence of welcome"; P.S. it's a "bargain for lunch."

SG Valley/Pasadena/Glendale F | D | S | C

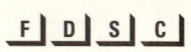

ZANKOU CHICKEN ●⊄ 23 | 5 | 12 | $10
1296 E. Colorado Blvd. (Hill Ave.), Pasadena, 626-405-1502
1415 E. Colorado Blvd. (Verdugo Rd.), Glendale,
818-244-1937
See review in LA/Hollywood/W. Hollywood Directory.

Zeke's Smokehouse ▽ 20 | 13 | 19 | $20
2209 Honolulu Ave. (Verdugo Blvd.), Montrose,
818-957-7045; www.zekessmokehouse.com
■ After spending months "researching throughout the U.S.", chefs Leonard Schwartz (ex Maple Drive) and Michael Rosen (ex Reign) have joined forces to create this casual Montrose BBQ spot that serves "properly smoked meats", the "best meatloaf in SoCal" and other "impressive" eats in a small, "stark" space; though some find the "small portions" "overpriced", partisans swear you really "get what you pay for."

Orange County

Top Food

- **28** Ramos House
  Napa Rose
- **27** Basilic
  Riviera/Fireside
  Aubergine
- **26** Pavilion
  Gustaf Anders
  Back Pocket
  Picayo*
  Black Sheep Bistro

Top Decor

- **27** Splashes
  Ritz-Carlton Lag. Nig.
- **26** Pavilion
  Ritz Rest.
- **25** Napa Rose
  Pinot Provence
  Aqua
  Woody's/Beach
  Claes
  Cat & Custard Cup

Top Service

- **28** Riviera/Fireside
- **27** Pavilion
  Basilic
  Ritz-Carlton Lag. Nig.*
- **26** Napa Rose
  Woody's/Beach
  Hobbit, The
- **25** Ritz Rest.
  Mr. Stox
  Back Pocket
  Picayo*
- **24** Pascal

Top Value

1. In-N-Out Burger
2. Baja Fresh
3. Taco Mesa
4. Original Pancake
5. Jody Maroni's Sausage
6. Zankou Chicken
7. La Salsa
8. Ruby's
9. Pho 79
10. Taco Loco

By Location

Anaheim
- **28** Napa Rose
- **26** Mr. Stox
- **24** Rosine's
  Original Pancake
- **23** Zankou Chicken

Corona Del Mar
- **25** Mayur
- **24** Bungalow
  Oysters
  Rothschild's
- **22** Five Crowns

Costa Mesa
- **26** Pinot Provence
  Troquet
- **25** Plums Cafe
  Golden Truffle
- **24** Taco Mesa

Irvine
- **26** Ruth's Chris
- **24** Taiko Jap.
  Bistango
- **22** Vessia Rist.
  Chanteclair

Laguna Beach
- **26** Picayo
- **25** Woody's/Beach
  Cafe Zoolu
  230 Forest
- **24** Five Feet

Newport Beach
- **27** Basilic
  Aubergine
- **26** Pavilion
  Fleming's Prime
- **25** Abe

Orange County Restaurant Directory

| Orange County | F | D | S | C |

Abe
25 | 16 | 21 | $43

2900 Newport Blvd. (29th St.), Newport Beach, 949-675-1739

■ Disciples of "wonderfully inventive" "gourmet sushi" trek to "Abe-san, the master" for "unbelievably delicious" "indulgent stuff" like live uni, not to mention cooked items like sea bass with foie gras; yes, the Newport peninsula location is "out of the way" and the "lackluster" digs "could stand an upgrade", but there's "no one better" in OC for this type of food; tip: insiders swear the "$25 omakase is a steal at lunch."

Accents
▽ 22 | 20 | 21 | $41

Sutton Place Hotel, 4500 MacArthur Blvd. (bet. Birch St. & Von Karman Ave.), Newport Beach, 949-476-2001; www.suttonplace.com

◪ Often cited as a "favorite for a [buffet-style] Sunday brunch", this three-meal-a-day, airport-adjacent dining venue also turns out "high-quality" French-accented Californian fare, complemented by a "great" wine list (over 20 by the glass); its indoor atrium is dotted with market umbrellas and manned by a "friendly, grape-knowledgeable staff" that'll get you to your plane on time.

Amazon Churrascaria
– | – | – | M

1445 S. Lemon St. (Durst St.), Fullerton, 714-447-1200

"The sights, the smells, the inexpensive eats" instantly transport diners "to South America" at this new Fullerton foray into the sizzling world of "delicious", Brazilian-style all-you-can-eat feasting, where "various types of meats" are served off long, gleaming blades by a "very enthusiastic staff"; while definitely "not for vegetarians", meat mavens "hope it'll be around a long, long time."

Anaheim White House
23 | 23 | 24 | $46

887 S. Anaheim Blvd. (Vermont Ave.), Anaheim, 714-772-1381

◪ Located in a "not-so-beautiful part of Anaheim", a short ride from Disneyland, this "glamorous" "converted manor house" is an "OC tradition" for "romantic", "big-occasion" meals of "marvelous" Northern Italian cuisine brought by a staff that gives "reliable VIP service" even if you're not one; "creative desserts" are "worth saving room for" too, especially the "other-worldly Grand Marnier soufflé."

Antonello ⊠
23 | 25 | 23 | $47

South Coast Plaza Village, 3800 Plaza Dr. (Sunflower Ave.), Santa Ana, 714-751-7153; www.antonello.com

◪ South Coast movers and shakers gather inside this "warm", "glorious" faux villa for "classic" Italian dishes and "big chairs, big tables and big smiles" from "solicitous" "professional waiters"; while protesters find it "overpriced" and "pretentious", loyalists insist it's "worth it" for a

Orange County   F | D | S | C

"dynamite" repast that feels like a visit to "another country"; P.S. "don't miss the greens with pear and Gorgonzola" or the veal chop and crème brûlée.

AQUA   23 | 25 | 22 | $64
St. Regis Monarch Beach Resort & Spa, 1 Monarch Beach Resort Dr. (Niguel Rd.), Dana Point, 949-234-3325; www.stregismonarchbeach.com

◪ For "sophisticated dining" in a "romantic" Dana Point resort look no further than this "sumptuously elegant" seafooder where the many "creative" concoctions include a "lobster pot pie that's a must", "delicious" tuna tartare and "the best desserts" like the signature root beer float; apostates note "tiny portions" and "way-out-of-line prices", but plenty more deem it "worth a visit for a memorable occasion" "if your credit card can take it."

Arches ●   20 | 16 | 20 | $45
3334 W. PCH (Newport Blvd.), Newport Beach, 949-645-7077

◪ "It's fun to dine with the old guard" at this Newport Continental "landmark" where the surf 'n' turf "standards" are "tasty" and "doting waiters" still prepare "tableside" classics like Caesar salad, coffee Diablo and "lovely bananas Foster"; yes, some might find the tab "pricey" and the setting "a tad long in the tooth" (think "red-leather booths", "campy paintings"), but others wax nostalgic over "John Wayne's favorite hangout."

AUBERGINE Ⓜ   27 | 24 | 23 | $79
508 29th St. (Newport Blvd.), Newport Beach, 949-723-4150

◪ "SoCal's answer to the French Laundry" might be this "superb", "prix fixe–only" Newport Beach Cal-French destination where Tim Goodell prepares "spectacular", "creative" dishes "with the utmost care" and "presents them like art" in a "jewel box" of a "lovely beach cottage"; critics find it "extraordinarily overpriced" with "an air of arrogance", but acolytes insist "this isn't dinner, it's an event"; P.S. if you've got very "deep pockets", consider the "private room" "overlooking the kitchen", or on a budget opt for the less expensive four-course Sunday night deal.

BACK POCKET Ⓜ   26 | 20 | 25 | $35
South Coast Plaza Village, 3851 S. Bear St. (Sunflower Ave.), Santa Ana, 714-668-1737; www.gustaf-anders.com

■ "What could be better than Gustaf Anders at half the price?" declare supporters of this "laid-back" Santa Ana adjunct to the "world-class" Swedish fave; expect to have "fun with herring", "spectacular potato salad" and "yummy meatballs" in roomy quarters that "actually allow for private conversation"; the staff, moreover, "takes the food and service seriously", and the South Coast location works for a "fine" "pre-performance" dinner.

Orange County | F | D | S | C |

BAJA FRESH MEXICAN GRILL | 20 | 11 | 15 | $9 |
5781 E. Santa Ana Canyon Rd. (Imperial Hwy.), Aliso Viejo, 714-685-9386
2445 Imperial Hwy. (Kraemer Blvd.), Brea, 714-671-9992
171 E. 17th St. (bet. Fullerton & Orange Aves.), Costa Mesa, 949-722-2994
7101 Yorktown Ave. (Goldenwest St.), Huntington Beach, 714-374-7450
Market Pl., 13248 Jamboree Rd. (Irvine Blvd.), Irvine, 714-508-7777
2540 Main St. (Sky Park S.), Irvine, 949-261-2214 ☒
26548 Moulton Pkwy. (La Paz Rd.), Laguna Hills, 949-360-4222
30231 Golden Lantern St. (bet. Crystal Cay & Martinique St.), Laguna Niguel, 949-249-0488
2220 E. 17th St. (Tustin Ave.), Santa Ana, 714-973-1943
Main Place Mall, 2800 N. Main St. (Town & Country Rd.), Santa Ana, 714-541-3202
www.bajafresh.com
See review in LA/Hollywood/W. Hollywood Directory.

Bandera | 21 | 20 | 20 | $29 |
3201 E. PCH (Marguerite Ave.), Corona Del Mar, 949-673-3524
See review in Westside Directory.

Bangkok Four | 22 | 19 | 20 | $28 |
South Coast Plaza, 3333 S. Bear St. (Sunflower Ave.), Costa Mesa, 714-540-7661
■ Don't be put off by the "mall setting" because this "upscale Thai" on the top floor at South Coast Plaza is a "slick", "minimalist" spot for "toothsome" options like the "best crispy duck in OC" and the signature deep-fried catfish; keep a visit in mind for a "refreshing" lunch "after shopping" or as a "quiet" option for a date overlooking the Bridge of Gardens.

BASILIC Ⓜ | 27 | 22 | 27 | $48 |
217 Marine Ave. (Park Ave.), Newport Beach, 949-673-0570
■ "It's a find" rave the many admirers of this "cozy" 24-seat Balboa Island "hideaway" that "feels like Europe" thanks to "personalized service" "with charm" and a "devoted chef-owner" who's "hands on in all phases of the business" and turns out "consistently first-rate", "thoughtfully put together" Swiss-French fare; in sum, "a quiet rendezvous" that leaves you "warm and happy inside."

Bayside | 24 | 24 | 22 | $43 |
900 Bayside Dr. (Jamboree Rd.), Newport Beach, 949-721-1222; www.baysiderestaurant.com
■ "There's always something new" on the "interesting" Contemporary American menu at this waterfront-adjacent Newport hot spot that manages to be both "very romantic and hip at the same time", all while attracting a spirited "over-40 crowd" at the "comfortable bar scene"; "great"

Orange County | F | D | S | C |

rotating artwork, Asian decorative influences, live nightly music, informal wine tastings and a "refreshing" terrace are other inducements.

BeachFire ▽ 18 | 22 | 20 | $34
204 Avenida Del Mar (N. Ola Vista), San Clemente, 949-366-3232; www.beachfirebarandgrill.com

☑ "The site of the old Coronet store" in downtown San Clemente "has been redone" as a "hip, flashy" Mission-style" bar and Contemporary American grill with "interesting artwork" like carved woods, "innovative live music" and curious eats such as ginger-pepper ahi and s'mores made from scratch; N.B. be sure to check out the wine rack made of recycled campground tables.

Benihana 19 | 18 | 21 | $32
2100 E. Ball Rd. (State College Blvd.), Anaheim, 714-774-4940
4250 Birch St. (Dove St.), Newport Beach, 949-955-0822
www.benihana.com
See review in Westside Directory.

Bistango 24 | 23 | 21 | $40
19100 Von Karman Ave. (bet. Campus Dr. & Martin St.), Irvine, 949-752-5222; www.bistango.com

■ "Revolving artwork" from around the world and a "high-caliber" New American menu that changes just as often are the highlights at this "solid performer" "hidden away" in a "pretty atrium" in Irvine's business district; whether you're coming for "great power lunches", "dancing on weekends" with the "40-plus" crowd or "cocktail hour fun on the patio", most feel it's "memorable in every way."

BLACK SHEEP BISTRO ⌀ Ⓜ 26 | 18 | 24 | $37
303 El Camino Real (3rd St.), Tustin, 714-544-6060; www.blacksheepbistro.com

■ What a "little gem" sigh the smitten of Old Town Tustin's "quaint", "European-style" spot for "innovative" French and Spanish offerings often graced with "divine sauces"; an "excellent cheese tray", a "good wine program", "discreet service", "friendly owners" and "new alfresco seating" are more reasons to seek out this "hidden treasure."

Bluewater Grill 19 | 17 | 18 | $29
630 Lido Park Dr. (Lafayette St.), Newport Beach, 949-675-3474
South Coast Plaza Village, 1621 W. Sunflower Ave. (bet. Bear & Bristol Sts.), Santa Ana, 714-546-3474
www.bluewatergrill.com
See review in South Bay/Long Beach Directory.

Britta's Café ▽ 23 | 20 | 21 | $31
4237 Campus Dr. (Stanford Ct.), Irvine, 949-509-1211; www.brittascafe.com

■ "Love it" declare admirers of this "offbeat", three-meal-a-day "little secret" "close to UCI" that serves "hearty"

get updates at zagat.com

Orange County   F | D | S | C

American "seasonal faves" like "comfy short ribs", along with foreign favorites like "the best bratwurst and spaetzle"; the "clean, attractive" quarters are enlivened by blue-and-white checked tablecloths, flower arrangements made daily by the "friendly" owner's mom and a "delightful patio."

Bungalow, The   24 | 22 | 22 | $44
2441 E. Coast Hwy. (MacArthur Blvd.), Corona Del Mar, 949-673-6585; www.thebungalowrestaurant.com
■ Wiggle past the "uptown beach singles" clutching "killer cocktails" at the "mobbed bar" of this Corona Del Mar "'in' spot" and you'll find "yummy" surf 'n' turf like bone-in rib-eye and hazelnut-crusted sea bass, "professional" service and a "lovely owner who remembers everyone by name"; P.S. the "charming patio" is a quiet hideaway.

Cafe El Cholo   19 | 16 | 17 | $19
840 E. Whittier Blvd. (Harbor Blvd.), La Habra, 562-691-4618; www.elcholo.com
◪ For icy pitchers of "great margaritas" and "rather old-fashioned Mexican food" like the "cheesiest nachos" and "succulent sweet green tamales" fans can't get enough of this "noisy, fun" choice in a sprawling faux hacienda in La Habra; the less enthralled call the cooking "Americanized to suit gringos", but hey, prices are "modest", and there's "always hot sauce for purists"; N.B. Monday–Wednesday, select items are offered at reduced prices.

Cafe Pascal   21 | 17 | 18 | $30
South Coast Plaza, 3333 Bristol St. (Sunflower Ave.), Costa Mesa, 714-751-4911; www.pascalnewportbeach.com
■ This sleek veranda sidewalk spot at the base of South Coast Plaza's footbridge makes a "fabulous stop" for a "relaxing" French lunch of "scrumptious" sandwiches, salads and crêpes, or just a "glass of wine on a beautiful summer day" "after shopping", in between "stealing kisses from your loved one"; N.B. it's only open weather-permitting.

Cafe Plaka   ▽ 20 | 17 | 21 | $21
18633 Brookhurst St. (Ellis Ave.), Fountain Valley, 714-963-4999; www.cafeplaka.com
■ Don't let the ho-hum Huntington Beach strip mall mislead you because inside this "fun", "energetic Greek" venue diners are "dancing with waiters" and chowing down on classics like "divine egg-lemon soup" and "fine slow-cooked lamb shanks"; the decor strikes some as "a bit cheesy", but the "warm service" (led by the new owner) and "reasonable prices" stir fans to confess "if all of Greece is like this, I want to move there."

Cafe Tu Tu Tango   17 | 20 | 18 | $23
The Block at Orange, 20 City Blvd. W. (Chapman Ave.), Orange, 714-769-2222; www.cafetututango.com
See review in San Fernando Valley/Burbank Directory.

Orange County

F | **D** | **S** | **C**

Cafe Zoolu M 25 | 13 | 20 | $36
860 Glenneyre St. (bet. St. Anne's Dr. & Thalia St.), Laguna Beach, 949-494-6825
■ Since it's located "away from the tourist zoo" in Laguna, "mainly locals" crowd this "tiny" "wonderful dive" where the "so-little" kitchen cranks out "huge portions" of "high-class home cookin'" like the "best ahi this side of Maui" and "superb blackened swordfish" that "will curl your tongue with delight"; "funky" tiki kitsch decor, a "laid-back" attitude and "cute surfer waiters" add to the appeal of this "dimly lit" option in an "off-the-beaten-path" location.

Californian, The – | – | – | VE
Hyatt Huntington Beach, 21500 PCH (Beach Blvd.), Huntington Beach, 714-698-1234; www.hyatt.com
Recent efforts to transform this Surf City hotel into a big-ticket resort include the addition of this signature dining room inspired by the cuisine and the lush life SoCal provides for those whose wallets can take the hit; choices like ahi tuna and risotto find their match on an impressive list of boutique wines, both well-suited to the gracious space off a lush courtyard that overlooks the sun-splashed Pacific.

CALIFORNIA PIZZA KITCHEN 18 | 14 | 17 | $18
Brea Mall, 1065 Brea Mall (N. State College Blvd.), Brea, 714-672-0407
South Coast Plaza, 3333 Bear St. (W. Sunflower Ave.), Costa Mesa, 714-557-1279
Park Pl., 2957 Michelson Dr. (Jamboree Rd.), Irvine, 949-975-1585
Laguna Hills Mall, 24155 Laguna Hills Mall (bet. El Toro Rd. & Regional Ct.), Laguna Hills, 949-458-9600
25513 Marguerite Pkwy. (La Paz Rd.), Mission Viejo, 949-951-5026
Fashion Island, 1511 Newport Center Dr. (bet. Corporate Plaza & Farallon Drs.), Newport Beach, 949-759-5543
Santa Ana Main Pl., 2800 N. Main St. (Town & Country Rd.), Santa Ana, 714-479-0604
Market Pl., 3001 El Camino Real (Jamboree Rd.), Tustin, 714-838-5083 S M
www.cpk.com
See review in LA/Hollywood/W. Hollywood Directory.

Cannery Seafood of the Pacific 20 | 25 | 19 | $34
3010 Lafayette Rd. (30th St.), Newport Beach, 949-566-0060; www.cannerynewport.com
☑ "Wow", what a "beautiful" "transformation of a great old landmark" declare surveyors commenting on this "recently remodeled", newly "trendy" Newport channel waterfront entry that satisfies fin fans with "well-prepared" seafood downstairs and "great sushi upstairs" amid "cool living-room seating"; "for singles", the bar (also on the second floor) is the "place to be scene", so expect a "noisy and hectic" vibe after dark.

---

get updates at zagat.com 241

Orange County F | D | S | C

Capriccio ▽ 19 | 17 | 19 | $25
Village Center Shopping Ctr., 25380 Marguerite Pkwy. (La Paz Dr.), Mission Viejo, 949-855-6866
■ "Excellent for south county" where "chains dominate", is one way to look at this Mission Viejo shopping center Italian, which garners kudos for "amazing pastas" and "great specials" served in a bistro-type setting that includes original artwork and a full bar; yes, it's a "good value" year-round, but insiders know to mob the joint each spring during the annual 'Pasta Festival', when deals abound.

Catal Restaurant & Uva Bar 22 | 22 | 19 | $37
Downtown Disney Shops, 1580 Disneyland Dr. (Ball Rd.), Anaheim, 714-774-4442; www.patinagroup.com
◪ Downtown Disney visitors call this "sophisticated" Mediterranean a nice "respite from its sugar-coated environs"; street level is a "noisy", "crowded" circular bar with lots of wines by the glass, while upstairs, "high above", is a "relaxing", "casually elegant" spot for items like "wonderful ahi tuna salad"; detractors sniff that it "needs work to become top-drawer", even if it is "a nice alternative to amusement-park fare."

CAT & THE CUSTARD CUP 24 | 25 | 24 | $42
800 E. Whittier Blvd. (Harbor Blvd.), La Habra, 562-694-3812; www.elcholo.com
■ "Warm, inviting" "British pub" quarters makes it feel like a "trip to London" at this La Habra "oldie but goodie" that has an "upscale" menu of "delectable" Contemporary American cuisine and a "mind-blowing" selection of wines served by "professional" staffers; regulars say "arrive early" for the "best martinis" and "live piano music" in the "romantic bar", which is especially "cozy" by the "divine" fireplace.

Catch, The ▽ 17 | 21 | 17 | $39
1929 S. State College Blvd. (Katella Ave.), Anaheim, 714-935-0101
◪ "Can't beat the atmosphere, especially during the season" when you can "rub elbows with Angels players after the game", rave sports fans commenting on this Anaheim arena- and stadium-adjacent standby that's "reopened" under "new ownership" with a clubby "big city restaurant feel"; cheerleaders find the American surf 'n' turf menu "pretty darn good", while boo-birds blare that the cooking and service are "inconsistent."

Cedar Creek Inn 19 | 20 | 19 | $28
20 Pointe Dr. (Lambert Rd.), Brea, 714-255-5600
384 Forest Ave. (3rd St.), Laguna Beach, 949-497-8696
26860 Ortega Hwy. (El Camino Real), San Juan Capistrano, 949-240-2229
www.cedarcreekinn.com
■ This "good local chain" pleases fans with its "homey", "relaxed" settings and large American menu ("variety at

Orange County   F | D | S | C

its best") that's served all day and also in the bar; whether for "drinks and jazz" or "burgers and salads" these are "friendly", "dependable" spots in their neighborhoods.

Cellar, The ⓈⓂ   23 | 21 | 21 | $49
Villa del Sol, 305 N. Harbor Blvd. (Wilshire Ave.), Fullerton, 714-525-5682
■ "When you want to impress your girlfriend's parents", put on a jacket (suggested, not required) and head to this "dark", basement "downtown Fullerton" option for "traditional" French dining where lobster bisque and Dover sole are teamed up with "well-priced older wines"; detractors claim it's "running on its reputation", but partisans opine that it still has "romantic", "special-occasion" cachet.

Chanteclair Ⓢ   22 | 22 | 23 | $42
18912 MacArthur Blvd. (Douglass St.), Irvine, 949-752-8001
■ "Quiet", with "delicious" French-Belgian cooking and "anticipatory" service is the word on this "beautiful" spot with "five different rooms" and fireplaces and a south-coast-of-France vibe; while some find the menu "tired", there's now a new chef and owner, and the consensus is that it's "still a treat" for a "business lunch", "relaxing evening out to celebrate" or "traveler's arrival" (it's across from John Wayne Airport in Irvine).

Chart House   19 | 21 | 18 | $34
34442 St. of the Green Lantern (PCH), Dana Point, 949-493-1183
2801 W. PCH (Riverside Ave.), Newport Beach, 949-548-5889
www.chart-house.com
See review in Westside Directory.

CHEESECAKE FACTORY   20 | 18 | 18 | $23
Irvine Spectrum Ctr., 71 Fortune Dr. (Pacifica), Irvine, 949-788-9998
42 The Shops at Mission Viejo (I-5), Mission Viejo, 949-364-6200
Fashion Island, 1141 Newport Center Dr. (Santa Barbara Dr.), Newport Beach, 949-720-8333
www.thecheesecakefactory.com
See review in Westside Directory.

Chevys   14 | 13 | 14 | $17
8200 E. Santa Ana Canyon Rd. (Weir Canyon Rd.), Anaheim Hills, 714-974-6703
18727 Brookhurst St. (bet. Ellis & Garfield Aves.), Fountain Valley, 714-963-3008
4700 Barranca Pkwy. (bet. Creek & Lake Rds.), Irvine, 949-559-5808
32431 Golden Lantern St. (Camino Del Avion), Laguna Niguel, 949-489-5511
www.chevys.com
See review in San Fernando Valley/Burbank Directory.

get updates at zagat.com

Orange County F | D | S | C

Chimayo at the Beach   19 | 21 | 19 | $28
315 PCH (Main St.), Huntington Beach, 714-374-7273; www.culinaryadventures.com

An enviable location "on the beach at the pier" lures salt-air seekers to this seafood-focused Southwestern in Huntington where the "eclectic", "spicy and novel" fare gets milder praise than the 200-seat patio with fire pit and "wonderful sunset views"; at a minimum it's a must for "a post-volleyball drink" while "people-watching."

Citrus City Grille ⊠   22 | 20 | 19 | $28
122 N. Glassell St. (Chapman Ave.), Orange, 714-639-9600; www.citruscitygrille.com

As "upbeat" and "trendy" as when it first opened, this Old Towne Californian also continues to score well for its "creative" menu choices and "cool decor" (though "bad acoustics" mean you'll have to "shout to be heard"); malcontents mumble that it "sometimes lacks consistency" but others recommend a visit "after antiquing" for a "charming patio lunch" topped off by "homemade desserts" ("you'll love the soufflés").

CLAES   20 | 25 | 19 | $41
Hotel Laguna, 425 S. PCH (Laguna Ave.), Laguna Beach, 949-376-9283; www.claesrestaurant.com

"On a clear day you can see Catalina" thanks to a "killer" "panoramic ocean view" at this seafooder in a historic hotel overlooking Laguna's busy Main Beach; those not distracted by the surroundings assert that the "Euro-inspired" dishes are "surprisingly great" and "well-matched with excellent wines"; of course, "the vista is so beautiful, it hardly matters what the food tastes like."

Claim Jumper Restaurant   18 | 16 | 18 | $22
190 S. State College Blvd. (Birch St.), Brea, 714-529-9061
South Coast Plaza, 7971 Beach Blvd. (La Palma Ave.), Buena Park, 714-523-3227
3333 Bristol St. (Anton Blvd.), Costa Mesa, 714-434-8479
18050 Brookhurst St. (Talbert Ave.), Fountain Valley, 714-963-6711
3935 Alton Pkwy. (Culver Dr.), Irvine, 949-851-5085
25322 McIntyre St. (La Paz Rd.), Laguna Hills, 949-768-0662
27845 Santa Margarita Pkwy. (Marguerite Pkwy.), Mission Viejo, 949-461-7170
2250 E. 17th St. (Tustin Ave.), Santa Ana, 714-836-6658
www.claimjumper.com
See review in South Bay/Long Beach Directory.

Cottage, The   15 | 15 | 14 | $19
308 N. PCH (Aster St.), Laguna Beach, 949-494-3023; www.thecottagerestaurant.com

A bit of a "tourist trap, but still ok for breakfast", concede Laguna locals of this Traditional American in a "historic"

Orange County | F | D | S | C |

house "close to the beach"; as "a happening" in the morning, expect an especially "long wait on weekends" before you get a chance to dig into omelets, pancakes and "the best French toast" under the trees on the "nice patio"; "dinner is marginal."

Crab Cooker, The | 20 | 11 | 16 | $23 |
2200 Newport Blvd. (22nd St.), Newport Beach, 949-673-0100
Enderle Ctr., 17260 E. 17th St. (Yorba St.), Tustin, 714-573-1077
www.crabcooker.com

☑ "If you don't mind paper and plastic" and "campy", "no-frills" decor, you can get "killer clam chowder", a "fun crab and lobster fix" and other "seafood right off the boat that day" at this wildly popular nautical duo; doubters dis it as "overpriced", "very average" and "touristy", so to beat the "long lines in summer", consider the Tustin branch, which offers the "same quality without the scent of suntan oil."

Daily Grill | 17 | 16 | 17 | $25 |
Jamboree Promenade, 2636 Dupont Dr. (Via Nicola), Irvine, 949-474-2223
Fashion Island Shopping Ctr., 957 Newport Center Dr. (Santa Barbara Dr.), Newport Beach, 949-644-2223
www.dailygrill.com
See review in LA/Hollywood/W. Hollywood Directory.

Darya | 24 | 21 | 20 | $27 |
South Coast Plaza Village, 1611 Sunflower Ave.
(bet. Greenville St. & Smalley Rd.), Santa Ana, 714-557-6600

■ A "treat for the taste buds" awaits visitors to this "fancy" (some say "ostentatious") South Coast Plaza Persian where "aromatic rices", "tender kebabs" and the signature filet mignon are a "taste adventure" that makes you "want to fly to Iran for dessert"; but don't do that without first having a drink on the patio or taking in the weekend music.

Dexter's Ⓜ | – | – | – | M |
2892 S. PCH (Nyes Pl.), Laguna Beach, 949-497-8912
Hidden in plain sight on busy PCH at Laguna's southern edge is chef-owner Scott Savoy's tiny, stylish Californian, which has a counter-wrapped cooking area that makes patrons feel "like they're eating in a friend's kitchen", albeit one where the "good, innovative" fare can include the likes of pepper-crusted salmon and curry-marinated pork.

Dizz's as Is Ⓜ | 23 | 19 | 22 | $41 |
2794 S. Coast Hwy. (Nyes Pl.), Laguna Beach, 949-494-5250

■ "Only the locals know" about this "romantic, nostalgic wonderland" in Laguna with "familiar", but "delicious" Continental cuisine (like rack of lamb and chocolate crème brûlée), "cozy" art deco environs "straight out of the '40s" and quirky touches like "mismatched plates and silverware"; while undeniably a "great little hole-in-the-wall" where

get updates at zagat.com

Orange County | F | D | S | C |

the staff "works hard to ensure your evening is special", be prepared to wait at the "small bar" because it can get cramped due to the "no-reservations" policy.

Dolce ▽ 18 | 18 | 18 | $44 |
800 W. PCH (Dover Dr.), Newport Beach, 949-631-4334
◪ It "has some interesting elements" say commentators on this Newport Italian on PCH that boasts "chic" furnishings like a "cigar-friendly" "outdoor room", a dramatic fireplace in the bar and "beautiful" display wine cellar; maybe "no one is reinventing cuisine here" but admirers insist the food is still "good"; clean-air advocates decry "drifting smoke from stogies."

Duke's Malibu/Huntington Beach 16 | 20 | 18 | $28 |
317 PCH (Main St.), Huntington Beach, 714-374-6446; www.hulapie.com
See review in Westside Directory.

EL CHOLO 18 | 18 | 17 | $21 |
Alton Sq., 5465 Alton Pkwy. (Jeffrey Rd.), Irvine, 949-451-0044; www.elcholo.com
See review in LA/Hollywood/W. Hollywood Directory.

El Torito Grill 17 | 16 | 16 | $22 |
555 Pointe Dr. (Lambert Rd.), Brea, 714-990-2411
633 Anton Blvd. (Bristol St.), Costa Mesa, 714-662-2672
1910 Main St. (MacArthur Blvd.), Irvine, 949-975-1220
Kaleidoscope at Mission Viejo, 27741 Crown Valley Pkwy. (I-5), Mission Viejo, 949-367-1567
Fashion Island, 951 Newport Center Dr. (Santa Barbara Dr.), Newport Beach, 949-640-2875
www.eltorito.com
See review in Westside Directory.

Fish Market, The 19 | 15 | 15 | $27 |
Irvine Spectrum Ctr., 85 Fortune Dr. (Pacifica), Irvine, 949-727-3474; www.thefishmarket.com
◪ New to the Irvine Spectrum is this "casual", "family-oriented" New England–style "seafood house" that features a retail market, exhibition kitchen and vintage photographs; it wins praise for a "tremendous selection" of "inexpensive" aquatic offerings, though surveyors find the "noisy" settings best for schools of "large groups" who don't mind "cell phones going off all the time."

Fitness Pizza/Grill 19 | 15 | 18 | $17 |
103 W. Imperial Hwy. (Brea Blvd.), Brea, 714-672-0911; www.fitnessgrill.com
Yorba Linda Station, 18246 Imperial Hwy. (bet. Lemon Dr. & Yorba Linda Blvd.), Yorba Linda, 714-993-5421; www.fitnesspizza.com
■ "Hard to believe healthy can be so good" say disciples of these north county Mediterranean siblings known for

246 subscribe to zagat.com

Orange County | F | D | S | C |

"tasty", "eclectic" pizzas, wraps, salads and such that boast "a lot of flavor without a lot of fat" (the menus include "nutritional breakdowns for each item"); the Brea site offers a slightly larger lineup that includes grilled meats and fish, but both are "stylish" "little spots for a casual meal" with "caring service."

Five Crowns | 22 | 23 | 23 | $42 |

3801 E. PCH (Poppy St.), Corona Del Mar, 949-760-0331; www.lawrysonline.com

■ The enduring "grand dame" of Corona Del Mar dining, this ivy-covered "English Tudor landmark" still lures "special occasion" and "holiday" diners with "tradition, class and professionalism" plus the "best prime rib imaginable" (after all it's "owned by Lawry's"); a few wonder if the "nostalgic" "olde English ambiance" complete with "silly wench costumes on waitresses" is "perhaps a bit passé", but scores more can't resist this "consistently fine" "classic" for family celebrations and "Christmas dinner."

Five Feet | 24 | 18 | 20 | $43 |

Anaheim Marriott Stes., 12017 Harbor Blvd. (Chapman Ave.), Garden Grove, 714-383-6000
328 Glenneyre St. (bet. Forest Ave. & Mermaid St.), Laguna Beach, 949-497-4955

■ "SoCal's original Asian fusion" entry still delights thanks to celeb chef Michael Kang's "always amazing" Chinese-French creations ("the best catfish on either coast") further enhanced by "food-savvy", "wine-knowledgeable" servers working from the "finest list on the coast"; the "fun, funky" Laguna branch can get "cramped and loud", while the new mid-county outpost is more serene; detractors maintain that "time has passed" this concept by.

FLEMING'S PRIME | 26 | 23 | 23 | $50 |
STEAKHOUSE & WINE BAR

Fashion Island, 455 Newport Center Dr. (San Miguel Dr.), Newport Beach, 949-720-9633; www.flemingssteakhouse.com

■ Where meat eaters go "to be seen and have fun" at Fashion Island, this "classic" high-end steakhouse is praised for "fat" cuts of prime beef, plus chops, seafood and "amazing sides" like "the best onion rings"; the "dark", "modern" space feels "warm and comfortable" thanks to "fabulous" service and an "extensive" wine cellar that includes an "incredible variety by the glass" (over 100); N.B. there's a new branch in El Segundo.

Fox Sports Grill | – | – | – | M |

Irvine Spectrum, 31 Fortune Dr. (Pacifica), Irvine, 949-753-1369; www.foxsportsgrill.com

In keeping with the namesake network's rep for razzle-dazzle, this colossal upscale sports bar at the Spectrum

Orange County | F | D | S | C |

has a sleek, snazzy lounge abuzz with screens monitoring every form of athletic action; upstairs houses a handsome (and TV-free) Contemporary American wood-fired-grill restaurant complete with waterfall walls, fire pit and wine room; for those who would prefer to do, rather than to watch, there's an outdoor putting green, indoor billiards and duck-pin bowling.

French 75 | 22 | 25 | 23 | $50 |
1464 S. PCH (Mountain St.), Laguna Beach, 949-494-8444
◪ This Laguna "hot spot" for "intimate celebrations" seduces romantics with "dark", "sexy '40s Paris bistro decor", a "great champagne bar", "classic French" fare ("the chocolate soufflé is amazing"), "live jazz" and a "composed" "staff who allow you to enjoy your privacy"; detractors deem it "pricey" and "overrated."

Gemmell's | ▽ 21 | 15 | 17 | $34 |
34471 Golden Lantern St. (Dana Point Harbor Dr.), Dana Point, 949-234-0064; www.gemmellsrestaurant.com
◪ Loyalist say veteran chef-owner Byron Gemmell's latest enterprise at the Dana Point marina is a "best-kept secret" for "pretty good" French-Continental dishes like lobster with tarragon or banana-rum duck; though tough-love types say "it could be better because they have the talent", at any rate, the airy, country casual room is a "nice local place" for lunch or brunch near the water.

Golden Truffle, The Ⓢ Ⓜ | 25 | 15 | 22 | $42 |
1767 Newport Blvd. (bet. 17th & 18th Sts.), Costa Mesa, 949-645-9858
■ Culinary brave hearts head to this Cost Mesa French-Caribbean "storefront in the middle of nowhere" for Alan Greeley's "unusual way with old standbys", which have "as much flavor as the chef has personality"; with so many "surprising combinations" and up to 20 nightly specials "diners should take waiters' recommendations" or "just let Greeley cook what he likes for you."

Gordon Biersch ◐ | 17 | 17 | 16 | $23 |
Laguna Hills Mall, 24032 El Toro Rd. (Paseo de Valencia), Laguna Hills, 949-770-0123; www.gordonbiersch.com
See review in San Fernando Valley/Burbank Directory.

Grill at Pelican Hill, The | – | – | – | E |
Pelican Hill Golf Club, 22651 Pelican Hill Rd. (PCH), Newport Coast, 949-717-6000; www.fourseasons.com
Known best by Newport Coast golfers as a luxe wrap-up to a day on the links, this cordial clubhouse is also open to the public for leisurely dining amid stately palms and soaring windows overlooking the 18th hole and its panoramic ocean vista; the compact Californian menu changes seasonally, but consistent high standards from the kitchen and staff are a given since this is a Four Seasons operation.

Orange County   F | D | S | C

Gulfstream   21 | 21 | 20 | $33
850 Avocado Ave. (bet. MacArthur Blvd. & PCH), Newport Beach, 949-718-0187; www.houstons.com
◪ Fashion Island's "hip hangout" for "Porsche-driving singles" cruising an "overcrowded plastic scene" with "huge glasses of wine" in hand also works for "relaxing" dining on American favorites like "ribs that fall off the bone" and the "best ahi burger on the coast"; high approval is heaped on the "nice patio" where you can "chill by the fire under the trees" in a "big Adirondack chair."

Gulliver's   21 | 18 | 19 | $36
18482 MacArthur Blvd. (Michelson Ave.), Irvine, 949-833-8411; www.gulliversrestaurant.com
■ "Close your eyes and you're in England" (and not John Wayne Airport) at this "reliable", "always busy" source for "Brobdingnagian portions" of "delicious creamed corn", the "best prime rib" and "awesome trifle"; the "kitschy", fireplace-filled, "publike" environs make for a "popular" "fun place for celebrations", especially when "beautifully decorated at Christmas time."

GUSTAF ANDERS Ⓜ   26 | 22 | 23 | $49
South Coast Plaza Village, 3851 S. Bear St. (Sunflower Ave.), Santa Ana, 714-668-1737
◪ "Better than Stockholm" is a visit to this "top-league" Santa Ana Scandinavian that "never falters" for lovers of "housemade gravlax", "herring buffets", "crawfish feasts" and a "myriad of aquavits"; the "sleek", "stylish" interior, moreover, is filled with "minimalist art", the atmosphere is so "serene" "you can hear yourself talk" and the "generally excellent" service pleases as well; P.S. do not miss the "unforgettable" Christmas smorgasbord.

Gypsy Den   ∇ 18 | 16 | 14 | $12
The Anti-Mall, 2930 Bristol St. (bet. Baker St. & Randolph Ave.), Costa Mesa, 714-549-7012
125 N. Broadway (1st St.), Santa Ana, 714-835-8840
www.gypsyden.com
■ These "interesting", "comfy" "old-school" coffeehouse siblings dish up "surprisingly good" "sandwiches and salads" to an "eclectic crowd" that ranges from "lots of hippies" to a "charming grandpa sipping iced tea"; all said, they're a "relaxed" choice when you need to get "away from the mall rats."

Habana   19 | 20 | 17 | $27
The Lab, 2930 Bristol St. (bet. Baker St. & Randolph Ave.), Costa Mesa, 714-556-0176; www.restauranthabana.com
◪ The "aura of old Havana lives" at this "dark", "sexy" Cuban in the Anti-Mall that "stands out in a world of sameness", luring fans via a "gorgeous patio" aglow with "flickering candles", flamenco dancers and "surprisingly

Orange County

F D S C

good" renditions like "excellent chicken encrusted with plantains"; live music and "great martinis" bring in the "young", "hip" crowd late at night, but beware, "a few of their mojitos and you'll be off to Cuba without a plane."

Heroes Bar & Grill ● 19 | 18 | 16 | $17
125 W. Santa Fe Ave. (N. Harbor Blvd.), Fullerton, 714-738-4356

■ "Fullerton's answer to *Cheers*" is "just a fun ol' place" where "peanut shells crunch underfoot" as "groups of friends" "watch the game" while filling up "so many beers on tap" (almost 120) and "consistent" pub grub served on "plates the size of trash can lids"; the new location is "larger" but "harder to find" than its predecessor.

Hibachi Steak House ▽ 24 | 17 | 20 | $23
108 S. Fairmont Blvd. (Santa Ana Canyon Rd.), Anaheim, 714-998-4110

■ "No matter what day of the week, prepare to wait" for a seat beside the grill at this Anaheim Hills Japanese where the "best lobster and filet mignon combo" is sizzled and sliced before your eyes by knife-twirling chefs; the "show with your food" is "not overdone", making this low-key "neighborhood" mini-maller a "fun place for a nice dinner."

HOBBIT, THE Ⓜ 25 | 24 | 26 | $74
2932 E. Chapman Ave. (Malena Dr.), Orange, 714-997-1972; www.hobbitrestaurant.com

■ "Reservations can be hard to get" but they're "worth the effort" for a "once-in-a-lifetime", "special-occasion" dining experience at this French-Continental in a "converted hacienda" in Orange; the evening begins with hot and cold hors d'oeuvres and "bubbly in the wine cellar", followed upstairs by a "splendid fixed menu" of "many gourmet courses" (seven) served in such an "unhurried" manner that guests are allotted time to tour the kitchen and grounds.

HOUSTON'S 21 | 19 | 20 | $29
Park Plaza, 2991 Michelson Dr. (Jamboree Rd.), Irvine, 949-833-0977; www.houstons.com
See review in Westside Directory.

Ichibiri Japanese Restaurant ▽ 19 | 13 | 18 | $29
16 Monarch Bay Plaza (Crown Valley Pkwy.), Dana Point, 949-661-1544

◪ "Good teppan grill eats" ("try the fried shrimp tails") and "basic sushi" are the call at this unfussy veteran Dana Point Japanese joint where it's better to "go for the food, not the ambiance", though blade-whirling chefs compensate a little ("who can't have fun with teppanyaki?").

IL FORNAIO 20 | 19 | 19 | $29
Lakeshore Tower, 18051 Von Karman Ave. (bet. Main St. & Michelson Dr.), Irvine, 949-261-1444; www.ilfornaio.com
See review in Westside Directory.

Orange County F | D | S | C |

Inka Grill 19 | 13 | 17 | $17 |
260 Bristol St. (Red Hill Ave.), Costa Mesa, 714-444-4652
301 Main St. (Olive Ave.), Huntington Beach, 714-374-3399
23600 Rockfield Blvd. (Lake Forest Dr.), Lake Forest, 949-587-9008
www.inkagrill.com

■ With four branches in OC and one in Long Beach, this Peruvian chain is a "nice change from margarita bars and sushi places", offering "big platters" of "exquisite" dishes; it gets "noisy" when it's "packed", but otherwise the ambiance is "pleasant."

IN-N-OUT BURGER ● 24 | 10 | 18 | $7 |
600 S. Brookhurst St. (W. Orange Ave.), Anaheim, 800-786-1000
7926 Valley View St. (La Palma Ave.), Buena Park, 800-786-1000
594 W. 19th St. (Anaheim Ave.), Costa Mesa, 800-786-1000
26482 Towne Centre Dr. (Alton Pkwy.), Foothill Ranch, 800-786-1000
1180 S. Harbor Blvd. (Orangethorpe Ave.), Fullerton, 800-786-1000
9032 Trask Ave. (Magnolia St.), Garden Grove, 800-786-1000
4115 Campus Dr. (Bridge Rd.), Irvine, 800-786-1000
24001 Avenida de la Carlota (El Toro Rd.), Laguna Hills, 800-786-1000
28782 Camino Capistrano (Junipero Serra Rd.), Laguna Niguel, 800-786-1000
27380 La Paz Rd. (Avenida Breve), Laguna Niguel, 800-786-1000
Additional locations throughout Orange County.
www.in-n-out.com
See review in LA/Hollywood/W. Hollywood Directory.

Islands 16 | 16 | 17 | $14 |
250 S. State College Blvd. (E. Birch St.), Brea, 714-256-1666
26582 Towne Center Dr. (bet. Alton & Bake Pkwys.), Foothill Ranch, 949-588-0086
18621 Brookhurst St. (bet. Ellis & Garfield Aves.), Fountain Valley, 714-962-0966
2201 W. Malvern Ave. (N. Gilbert St.), Fullerton, 714-992-6685
4020 Barranca Pkwy. (Culver Dr.), Irvine, 949-552-1888
24321 Avenida de la Carlota (bet. El Toro Rd. & Los Alisos Blvd.), Laguna Hills, 949-458-6338
Kaleidoscope Mall, 27741 Crown Valley Pkwy. (I-5), Mission Viejo, 949-582-2221
550 N. Tustin St. (Walnut Ave.), Orange, 714-997-4085
www.islandsrestaurants.com
See review in Westside Directory.

Iva Lee's ∇ 20 | 20 | 22 | $34 |
555 N. El Camino Real (bet. Avenida Palizada & Marquita), San Clemente, 949-361-2855

■ "To-die-for" creative martinis in the lounge are a "fun, spirited" way to begin the evening at this San Clemente

Orange County   F | D | S | C |

Cajun-Creole outpost where the "tasty cooking" like New Orleans–style BBQ shrimp is "like grandmother never made"; there's also "innovative" offerings like chipotle-crusted scallops, making this an "absolutely fabulous" addition to the town's lean dining scene.

JackShrimp   18 | 11 | 14 | $22 |
26705 Aliso Creek Rd. (Enterprise St.), Aliso Viejo, 949-448-0085
Park Pl., 3041 Michelson Dr. (Jamboree Rd.), Irvine, 949-252-1023
2400 W. PCH (Tustin Ave.), Newport Beach, 949-650-5577
www.jackshrimp.com

◪ "Messy eating", peel 'n' eat Gulf shrimp dripping in a broth that "will make you breath deep" and reach for some "excellent French bread" is the signature item at this "small, simple", "down-home" Cajun trio; critics say it "needs a more interesting setting" ("a tad generic") and has a "limited menu."

Javier's   23 | 19 | 19 | $27 |
480 S. PCH (Laguna Ave.), Laguna Beach, 949-494-1239

■ It "feels like you're on vacation in Mexico" rave revelers of this "airy", "high-energy" "Laguna Beach hangout" where the "upscale" fare "with a twist" is "better than it needs to be" (the "crab enchiladas are divine", "try the queso fundido steak"), and ferried by a "friendly staff"; not surprisingly, there's "always a long wait", but the "vibrant bar scene" (a "meat *mercado*") keeps many occupied.

Jody Maroni's Sausage Kingdom   19 | 6 | 13 | $9 |
The Block at Orange, 20 City Dr. (Frwy. 22), Orange, 714-769-3754;
www.jodymaroni.com
See review in Westside Directory.

Joe's Crab Shack   15 | 17 | 16 | $23 |
2607 W. PCH (Tustin Ave.), Newport Beach, 949-650-1818;
www.joescrabshack.com
See review in South Bay/Long Beach Directory.

King's Fish House/   20 | 18 | 18 | $29 |
King Crab Lounge
24001 Avenida de la Carlota (El Toro St.), Laguna Hills, 949-586-1515
1521 W. Katella Ave. (Main St.), Orange, 714-771-6655
www.kingsseafood.com
See review in South Bay/Long Beach Directory.

Koo Koo Roo   16 | 8 | 13 | $11 |
212 E. 17th St. (bet. Orange & Westminster Aves.), Costa Mesa, 949-631-1800
2963A Michelson Dr. (Jamboree Rd.), Irvine, 949-263-8880
www.kookooroo.com
See review in LA/Hollywood/W. Hollywood Directory.

Orange County

F | D | S | C

La Cave ⓈZ
▽ 19 | 15 | 20 | $38
1695 Irvine Ave. (17th St.), Costa Mesa, 949-646-7944;
www.lacaverestaurant.com

■ "Watch for vampires as the steaks are rare and the room is dark" at this enduring subterranean surf 'n' turfer in Costa Mesa, an "old-timer's spot" with a "'60s" vibe, to-die-for cheese bread" and a "melt-in-your-mouth filet"; it's even catching on with an "ultrahip twentysomething crowd", which often "rolls in late" " for the kitsch of yesteryear" plus drinks and "good live jazz on weekends"; P.S. "if allowed, this would be a smoke-filled room."

La Salsa
16 | 9 | 13 | $10
730 E. Imperial Hwy. (Laurel Ave.), Brea, 714-529-5006
3850 Barranca Pkwy. (Culver Dr.), Irvine, 949-786-7692
Fashion Island Mall, 401 Newport Center Dr. (San Miguel Dr.), Newport Beach, 949-640-4289
3930 S. Bristol St. (Sunflower Ave.), Santa Ana, 714-549-9974
www.lasalsa.com
See review in LA/Hollywood/W. Hollywood Directory.

Las Brisas
14 | 21 | 15 | $33
361 Cliff Dr. (PCH), Laguna Beach, 949-497-5434;
www.lasbrisaslagunabeach.com

■ A "phenomenal ocean view" complete with "dolphins" is why this Mexican seafooder is Laguna's most popular destination with "thousands who come to watch the sun sink into the Pacific" over "great drinks" beside the "outdoor patio fireplace"; yet, the "ridiculously priced" menu and "nonexistent" service lead cynics to call it "a tourist trap."

La Vie en Rose ⓈZ
22 | 25 | 24 | $42
240 S. State College Blvd. (E. Birch St.), Brea, 714-529-8333;
www.lavnrose.com

☑ "Despite the mall location" "next to three banks", this "intimate" Gallic-Belgian entry actually feels like a "little bit of France" thanks to a faux farmhouse look, "excellent" items such as filet mignon with béarnaise sauce, an "extensive wine list" and an "unbelievable dessert cart"; the staff "makes you feel like a personal guest", meaning this is "unique enough to survive the competition."

Lawry's Carvery
21 | 14 | 13 | $18
South Coast Plaza, 3333 Bristol St. (Anton Blvd.), Costa Mesa, 714-434-7788; www.lawrysonline.com

☑ "Like a four-star meal on a bun" insist fans extolling the "awesome prime rib" and carved turkey sandwiches served at this South Coast Plaza "new restaurant concept" from the people at Lawry's; despite a tab that's "overpriced" relative to the "no-frills", "cafeteria-style" setup, it's "always packed at lunch" for those desiring a "quick", "quality" meal; P.S. don't overlook the "luscious salads."

Orange County F | D | S | C

L'Hirondelle Ⓜ ▽ 22 | 18 | 23 | $35
31631 Camino Capistrano (Ortega Hwy.), San Juan Capistrano, 949-661-0425

■ Loyalists of this "quaint" Mission-adjacent French-Belgian in San Juan Capistrano speak up for its "great comfort food" served by "attentive, helpful" staffers "devoid of the snobbiness of typical" places in the genre; the "classic cafelike surroundings" make for a "lovely lunch" or "fantastic evening" meal, and the "nice patio in summer" works for a champagne brunch; transportation tip: it's located near the train station and is a "quick jaunt away from the Ritz-Carlton" in Dana Point.

Lodge, The ⓢ ▽ 18 | 16 | 16 | $32
The Camp, 2937 Bristol St. (bet. Baker & Bear Sts.), Costa Mesa, 714-751-1700

◪ Surveyors are divided on this "trendy" American from the Goodell's (Aubergine, Troquet, Whist): hipsters like the "hearty", "upscale" "comfort food" ("try the chicken pot pie" and "best meatloaf") and dig the "'70s ski lodge decor"; naysayers find the service "too casual", the acoustics "painfully noisy" and say that overall it's "not up to the owners' other places."

Luciana's ▽ 21 | 20 | 20 | $35
24312 Del Prado Ave. (bet. Blue Lantern & Ruby Lantern Sts.), Dana Point, 949-661-6500; www.lucianas.com

■ "Cozy" surroundings that include a "relaxing fireplace" "make it all the more inviting, particularly on a foggy evening", note devotees weighing in on this "comfortable" Dana Point choice for "authentic", "solid Italian by the shore"; P.S. in warm weather the patio beckons.

Lucille's Smokehouse Bar-B-Que 22 | 19 | 19 | $23
1639 E. Imperial Hwy. (Rte. 57), Brea, 714-990-4944; www.lucillesbbq.com
See review in South Bay/Long Beach Directory.

MAGGIANO'S LITTLE ITALY 19 | 20 | 19 | $26
South Coast Plaza, 3333 Bristol St. (Sunflower Ave.), Costa Mesa, 714-546-9550; www.maggianos.com
See review in LA/Hollywood/W. Hollywood Directory.

Mama Rose ⓢ Ⓜ ▽ 23 | 19 | 18 | $27
2346 Newport Blvd. (Wilson St.), Costa Mesa, 949-650-1949

■ A "best-kept secret on Newport Boulevard" in Costa Mesa, this "always reliable" Italian is a "very sweet place" where "locals love" the "classic" Italian dishes ("the chicken Gorgonzola is wonderful") and owners Elaine and Richard, who are "full of smiles" and "treat you like family"; sure, it's a bit "hard to find" but it's "worth the search", especially because prices "won't break the bank."

subscribe to zagat.com

Orange County

| F | D | S | C |

Mascarpone's Ⓜ
▽ 23 | 15 | 23 | $24

1446 E. Katella Ave. (bet. N. California St. & Tustin Ave.), Orange, 714-633-0101

■ Gracious owners who "greet you by name after a visit or two" are part of the appeal of this "neighborhood icon" situated in an unlikely Orange office strip center; once seated in the "quiet, cozy" room prepare for "excellent" Northern Italian dishes like homemade gnocchi, "specials that do not disappoint" and "to-die-for cheesecake."

Mayur
25 | 17 | 22 | $33

2931 E. Coast Hwy. (bet. Heliotrope & Iris Aves.), Corona Del Mar, 949-675-6622

■ "You can smell the curry" as you enter this "tranquil peacock-hued" Corona del Mar Indian that makes a "fast trip to a foreign land" for "subtly flavored" dishes that are "spiced to perfection"; grumbles about the "pricey" tab are diminished by applause for the "smiling", "unobtrusive" staff; N.B. there's a champagne brunch on Sundays.

McCormick & Schmick's
19 | 19 | 19 | $33

2000 Main St. (Sky Park S.), Irvine, 949-756-0505; www.mccormickandschmick.com

See review in LA/Hollywood/W. Hollywood Directory.

Melting Pot, The
▽ 22 | 22 | 20 | $36

2646 Dupont Dr. (bet. Jamboree Rd. & Teller Ave.), Irvine, 949-955-3242; www.meltingpot.com

■ "Wow, a fondue flashback!" cry boomers over corporate Irvine's new "out-of-the-ordinary" spot for "do-it-yourself" full meals dipping into "rich" cheeses, broths and "sinful" chocolate; it's a "great date" or "party place", but wallet watchers think prices "should be cheaper since you're the cook"; P.S. "carve out a good three hours" to dine here.

Memphis
20 | 13 | 16 | $25

2920 Bristol St. (Randolph Ave.), Costa Mesa, 714-432-7685
201 N. Broadway (2nd St.), Santa Ana, 714-564-1064 ✉
www.memphiscafe.com

■ These "very groovy" twins are "reasonably priced" choices for "imaginative", "down-home, Southern-esque" fare and "arty soul food", backed by a "boutique-y wine list" and "fantastic music"; the original Costa Mesa site attracts a "too-cool-for-you crowd" ideal for "people-watching" while the Santa Ana artist's district branch delivers a "more citified feel" with "'50s moderne decor."

Mimi's Cafe
18 | 17 | 18 | $18

1240 N. Euclid Ave. (W. Romneya Dr.), Anaheim, 714-535-1552
1400 S. Harbor Blvd. (S. Manchester Ave.), Anaheim, 714-956-2223

(continued)

Orange County F D S C

(continued)
Mimi's Cafe
1835 Newport Blvd. (Harbor Blvd.), Costa Mesa, 949-722-6722
18461 Brookhurst St. (Ellis Ave.), Fountain Valley, 714-964-2533
4030 Barranca Pkwy. (Culver Dr.), Irvine, 949-559-8840
27430 La Paz Rd. (Avila Rd.), Laguna Niguel, 949-643-0206
22651 Lake Forest Dr. (Muirlands Blvd.), Lake Forest, 949-457-1052
17231 E. 17th St. (I-55), Tustin, 714-544-5522
18342 Imperial Hwy. (Yorba Linda Blvd.), Yorba Linda, 714-996-3650
www.mimiscafe.com
See review in LA/Hollywood/W. Hollywood Directory.

Mirabeau   – | – | – | E
17 Monarch Bay Plaza (Crown Valley Pkwy.), Monarch Beach, 949-234-1679; www.mirabeaubistro.com
A neighborhood Dana Point shopping plaza is the unlikely site for this new *trés* Francais effort specializing in bistro standards like bouillabaisse, coq au vin and steak frites at diplomatic prices; a compact wine list includes franc-pinching bulk Rhone wines served by the carafe; tile floors, ochre walls and imposing wood bar lend a Provençal air, better yet, the roomy patio offers a view of the Pacific standing in for the Mediterranean.

Morton's, The Steakhouse   25 | 21 | 22 | $54
South Coast Plaza Village, 1641 W. Sunflower Ave. (bet. Bear & Bristol Sts.), Santa Ana, 714-444-4834; www.mortons.com
■ "Huge portions" of "fabulous prime beef" ("the filet will melt in your mouth") abetted by "delicious sides", a winning Godiva chocolate cake and an "unparalleled" wine selection have a "noisy", "upscale" crowd excited about this South Coast Plaza steakhouse temple of "decadence"; just "bring the deed to your house" to cover the tab.

Motif   – | – | – | E
St. Regis Monarch Beach Resort & Spa, 1 Monarch Beach Resort (PCH), Dana Point, 949-234-3200; www.stregismb.com
Not content to be the resort's overlooked stepchild to high-profile Aqua, this airy dining room has undergone a major retooling to emerge as a trendy purveyor of flavor-intense small plates (barely the size of appetizers) from the world over (think lobster martini, foie gras BLT, tandoori lamb chops) plus mini-wine flights to match; the Romanesque terrace with a view of formal gardens and the sea beyond supplies the beguiling setting.

Mrs. Knott's Chicken Dinner   20 | 14 | 18 | $18
California Market Pl., 8039 Beach Blvd. (La Palma Ave.), Buena Park, 714-220-5080; www.knotts.com
■ Buena Park's famous berry farm is home to this "very old-fashioned" "tradition" where hordes of locals and

Orange County

F | **D** | **S** | **C**

tourists chow down on the "best biscuits on earth", "big servings" of "fabulous", "tender, moist" fried chicken and "excellent" boysenberry pie; if you don't "get there early" you should expect "long lines" amid "screaming kids", but purists say that's a small price to pay for the "charm of grandma's place" and a menu that "hasn't changed since Mrs. Knott ran the place."

MR. STOX ◐

26 | **23** | **25** | **$43**

1105 E. Katella Ave. (bet. Lewis St. & State College Blvd.), Anaheim, 714-634-2994; www.mrstox.com

■ This "Anaheim landmark" is a "reliable" "OC institution" among the "over-40 crowd", who come for "outstanding" New American and "classic Continental" cuisine enhanced by a vast wine selection that's "one of the best anywhere" and "reasonably priced" to boot; the "first-rate" hospitality is part of the overall "attention to detail", and the "gorgeous, upscale" decor (complete with live piano music) creates an air of "old-time glamour" ideal for "business lunches" and "special occasions."

Mulberry Street Ristorante

▽ **22** | **18** | **21** | **$27**

114 W. Wilshire Ave. (Harbor Blvd.), Fullerton, 714-525-1056

■ "Consistently good" "old-fashioned Italian the way you remember it" back in "New York's Little Italy" is the draw at this "hidden gem" of a "locals' place" in "atmospheric old Fullerton"; "perfect treatment" by the staff and a "good" wine selection by the glass only ups the appeal of this "happy standout in the downtown scene."

Muldoons Irish Pub Ⓜ

17 | **18** | **18** | **$25**

202 Newport Center Dr. (Anacapa Dr.), Newport Beach, 949-640-4110

■ "As Irish as Newport gets" declare Celtic-aholics who say this "always fun" pub "knows how to pour a proper Guinness" and delivers "old-world hospitality" along with "fine whiskeys", "authentic shepherd's pie" and "live music on the patio without the annoying barely legal crowd"; it's also "perfect for a pint after work" or "a night out with friends" next to the "roaring fireplace."

NAPA ROSE

28 | **25** | **26** | **$57**

Grand Californian Hotel, 1600 S. Disneyland Dr. (Katella Ave.), Anaheim, 714-300-7170

■ "Mickey has made his mark on the area's culinary scene" with this Disney hotel site for "over-the-top dining" on "enthralling" Californian creations by chef Andrew Sutton, a "creative genius" who "brings the wine country to OC" with "gastronomic marvels" that "reflect the bounty of the season" all "presented with panache" by an "intelligent", "highly trained" staff that "knows and loves the cellar" (GM/sommelier "Michael Jordan's selection will astound"); the "cavernous" room is like a "Frank Lloyd Wright heaven."

Orange County

F | **D** | **S** | **C**

Naples Ristorante e Pizzeria   19 | 19 | 18 | $26
1550 S. Disneyland Dr. (Katella Ave.), Anaheim, 714-776-6200;
www.patinagroup.com

◪ "Disney does [Southern] Italian" via the Patina Group at this "real find" that's "surprisingly good" for "family meals" of "flavorful" pastas and "high-quality" pizzas and calzones from a wood-fired oven, enjoyed in "big booths" that are "comfy after trekking around all day"; detractors sneer that it's "all concept, no substance", but for many, this is "a top choice" along the resort's no-admission retail row.

Natraj   ▽ 20 | 12 | 18 | $17
Food Festival Ct., 26612 Towne Center Dr. (bet. Alton & Bake Pkwys.), Foothill Ranch, 949-830-2015
24861 Alicia Pkwy. (Hon Ave.), Laguna Hills, 949-581-4200

■ Spice buffs say these sibling cafes serving the "best Indian food this side of Bombay" are a "must-go" for "delicious" standards like garlic naan and "sumptuous chicken tikka"; their "great lunch buffet" is not only a bargain, "it beats most competitors' dinner entrees."

Nieuport 17   20 | 22 | 21 | $37
13051 Newport Ave. (Irvine Blvd.), Tustin, 714-731-5130

◪ "Popular with the old-money set" ("the lot is a showcase of fancy cars"), this enduring Tustin Continental reminds some of "a men's club that's somehow survived into this century" thanks to wood-and-leather hunting-lodge decor festooned with aviation mementos; the "all-inclusive" meals garner less praise than the "attentive", "experienced" staff and "dark, cozy bar" with "fireplace and pianist."

Olde Ship, The   ▽ 21 | 19 | 19 | $19
709 N. Harbor Blvd. (bet. Chapman & Union Aves.), Fullerton, 714-871-7447
1120 W. 17th St. (bet. Bristol St. & Flower Ave.), Santa Ana, 714-550-6700
www.theoldeship.com

■ "Filled to the rafters with Anglophiles" sporting "fun accents" and "local blokes sipping black-and-tans" (or one of the 20 imports on tap), this "friendly" duo of nautically themed English pubs is a "trencherman's delight" offering basics like "tender, flaky fish 'n' chips" and bangers 'n' mash "prepared in the true British way."

Old Spaghetti Factory, The   15 | 18 | 17 | $15
110 E. Santa Fe Ave. (S. Harbor Blvd.), Fullerton, 714-526-6801
2110 Newport Blvd. (21st St.), Newport Beach, 949-675-8654
www.osf.com

◪ Despite grumbles over "long waits" and "marginal" eats, these Italian twins in "landmark locations" fill a niche "for families" and "teen dates" looking for "cheap", "no-nonsense pastas" and "ostentatious" surroundings.

Orange County | F | D | S | C |

O-Nami | 18 | 13 | 15 | $23 |
Laguna Hills Mall, 24155 Laguna Hills Mall (El Toro Rd.), Laguna Hills, 949-768-0500; www.o-nami.com
See review in South Bay/Long Beach Directory.

Opah | 22 | 20 | 19 | $34 |
Aliso Viejo, 26851 Aliso Creek Rd. (Enterprise St.), Aliso Viejo, 949-360-8822
22332 El Paseo (El Corazon), Rancho Santa Margarita, 949-766-9988
www.opahrestaurant.com
■ These "trendy", "sleek" siblings ooze "urban energy" and attract "single minglers" and other "beautiful people" of the suburbs in search of "artfully prepared" Cal cuisine from a "varied, creative menu" that, given the name, of course includes "sumptuous seafood"; "oversized martinis" keep the mood "lively and bustling" (read: "deafening"), so try the "heated patio" for a refuge from the "packed bar."

Original Fish Co. | 23 | 19 | 20 | $31 |
11061 Los Alamitos Blvd. (Katella Ave.), Los Alamitos, 714-960-2229; www.originalfishcompany.com
■ Afishionados "drive for miles to dine" at Los Alamitos' "popular" standby for "large amounts of fabulous seafood" ("the chowder will make you wonder why people bother living in Boston") all served in upscale coffee-shop quarters; "get there early or prepare to wait" but if "long lines" are a turnoff, pick up a take-out order at the market counter.

Original Pancake House | 24 | 11 | 18 | $12 |
1418 E. Lincoln Ave. (bet. East St. & State College Blvd.), Anaheim, 714-535-9815
18453 Yorba Linda Blvd. (bet. Imperial Hwy. & Lakeview Ave.), Yorba Linda, 714-693-1390
www.originalpancakehouse.com
■ "It doesn't get any better" claim morning mavens pining for this mini-chain's "hearty breakfast" lineup of "out-of-this-world" pancakes, "scrumptious omelets" and crêpes washed down with "freshly ground coffee"; on weekends it helps to "go early to beat the church crowd."

Outback Steakhouse | 16 | 14 | 17 | $26 |
402 Pointe Dr. (Lambert Rd.), Brea, 714-990-8100
7575 Beach Blvd. (91 Frwy.), Buena Park, 714-523-5788
1670 Newport Blvd. (17th St.), Costa Mesa, 949-631-8377
26652 Portola Pkwy. (bet. Alton & Bake Pkwys.), Foothill Ranch, 949-455-4158
12001 Harbor Blvd. (Chapman Ave.), Garden Grove, 714-663-1107
15433 Culver Dr. (Irvine Center Dr.), Irvine, 949-651-8760
25322 Cabot Rd. (bet. La Paz Rd. & Oso Pkwy.), Laguna Hills, 949-829-0683
www.outbacksteakhouse.com
See review in South Bay/Long Beach Directory.

| **Orange County** | F | D | S | C |

Oysters   24 | 18 | 21 | $39
2515 E. Coast Hwy. (MacArthur Blvd.), Corona Del Mar, 949-675-7411; www.oystersrestaurant.com
■ Corona Del Mar villagers and the "beautiful people" claim that "everybody knows your name" at this "neighborhood mainstay" for "incredibly innovative" Cal-Asian cuisine (especially "the best kung pao calimari ever" and "jumpin' fresh seafood"), bolstered by a "tantalizing wine selection" and service that's "attentive and intelligent"; "live jazz" nightly and a "great crew behind the bar" keep this joint "bustling" ("go for a drink after work to meet chicks"), so "ask for the garden room" to avoid the "high noise levels."

Paolo's Ristorante Ⓜ   ▽ 25 | 20 | 24 | $27
Old World Int'l Village, 7561 Center Ave. (Huntington Village Ln.), Huntington Beach, 714-373-5399
■ Maybe the Germanic Old World Village is an incongruous site for dining on "solid, unpretentious" Northern Italian fare, but "don't let the odd location put you off" insist advocates of chef-owner Paolo Pestarino's "cozy, romantic" "gem" serving "wonderful pastas" and "excellent" specials like sea bass balsamico; you're treated "like family", so it's no wonder the faithful "keep coming back."

PASCAL Ⓢ   25 | 21 | 24 | $52
1000 N. Bristol St. (Jamboree Rd.), Newport Beach, 949-752-0107; www.pascalnewportbeach.com
◪ Pascal Olhats prepares "amazing" "traditional" French "cooking with flair" at this Newport Beach venue in an "unassuming strip mall" that belies the restaurant's "quaint", "feminine" room a-bloom with "fresh roses"; foes quibble about "snippy" service and "tired decor", but *amis* insist "if you can't get to France", this is a "must-eat in OC"; P.S. if dinner looks "too tough on the wallet", "lunch is more reasonable", as is the next door épicerie.

PAVILION   26 | 26 | 27 | $58
Four Seasons Hotel, 690 Newport Center Dr. (Santa Cruz Dr.), Newport Beach, 949-760-4920; www.fourseasons.com
■ "A joyful experience" awaits at this "serene" Fashion Island "crown jewel" for "pampered, high-class dining" complete with "extraordinarily graceful, thoughtful" service, an "elegant, but unstuffy room" and "exquisite", "artfully presented" seasonal Cal-Med creations including a prix fixe menu that's "a steal"; of course, "perfection is the norm" at the Four Seasons, that's why this "special-occasion" destination "simply outclasses its neighbors."

Pei Wei Asian Diner   ▽ 17 | 15 | 16 | $15
Oak Creek Village, 5781 Alton Pkwy. (bet. Jeffrey Rd. & Royal Oak), Irvine, 949-857-8700; www.peiwei.com
◪ Owned by P.F. Chang's, this "loud", "busy" new chainlet is a "casual" spot for "cheap" Pan-Asian dishes prepared

Orange County | F | D | S | C |

with "blazing" speed; some of the open kitchen's offerings will "light up your mouth" while others, such as the lettuce wraps, are "soothing", still critics deem the fare "mediocre" and the mood "sterile" ("takeout is frequently preferable").

Peppino's | 18 | 12 | 16 | $19 |

26952 La Paz Rd. (Pacific Pkwy.), Aliso Viejo, 949-643-1355
31371 Niguel Rd. (Clubhouse Dr.), Laguna Niguel, 949-661-1250
23600 Rockfield Blvd. (Lake Forest Dr.), Lake Forest, 949-951-2611
27782 Vista del Lago (Marguerite Pkwy.), Mission Viejo, 949-859-9556
665 N. Tustin St. (bet. Collins & Walnut Aves.), Orange, 714-289-2838
651 E. First St. (Newport Blvd.), Tustin, 714-573-9904
www.peppinosonline.com

"Consistent", "heavy-on-the-garlic", "traditional red-sauce" cooking in "portions fit for a king" is the appeal of this "family-run" regional chain that's "good for any occasion and attire"; the settings have a "local pizzeria flavor", so expect "lots of kids and noise" early in the evening, otherwise "go later" for an "adults-only dinner."

Pescadou Bistro Ⓜ | ∇ 19 | 11 | 16 | $30 |

3325 Newport Blvd. (bet. Finley Ave. & 32nd St.), Newport Beach, 949-675-6990

"Delish and a great deal" rave devotees of this Newport French bistro whose prix fixe (only) four-course meals of "authentic" fare are served with "open hearts and smiles" in a color-splashed, "hole-in-the-wall" space that recalls "a backstreet Parisian bistro"; some feel "inconsistency" plagues the kitchen, but "on the plus side, at least the wines are plentiful and affordable."

P.F. CHANG'S CHINA BISTRO | 20 | 20 | 18 | $24 |

Irvine Spectrum Ctr., 61 Fortune Dr. (Irvine Center Dr.), Huntington Beach, 949-453-1211
800 The Shops at Mission Viejo (Crown Valley Pkwy.), Mission Viejo, 949-364-6661
1145 Newport Center Dr. (Santa Barbara St.), Newport Beach, 949-759-9007
www.pfchangs.com
See review in LA/Hollywood/W. Hollywood Directory.

Pho 79 | 20 | 7 | 12 | $10 |

9941 Hazard Ave. (Brookhurst St.), Garden Grove, 714-531-2490
9200 Bolsa Ave. (bet. Bushard & Magnolia Sts.), Westminster, 714-893-1883
See review in LA/Hollywood/W. Hollywood Directory.

PICAYO Ⓜ | 26 | 21 | 25 | $45 |

610 N. PCH (Boat Canyon Dr.), Laguna Beach, 949-497-5051; www.picayorestaurant.com

"What a jewel" sigh the smitten about this tiny, "low-key" Med-French tucked away in a North Laguna "shopping

Orange County F | D | S | C

center"; despite its location (hey, at least there's "lots of parking"), chef-partner Laurent Brazier is "serious about the quality of his food", turning out "inspired, flawless" dishes ("the lobster bisque with orange zest is excellent") that are served in an "inviting" room bedecked with Mediterranean landscapes, and enhanced by an "outstanding" staff that's "friendly and knowledgeable."

PINOT PROVENCE   26 | 25 | 24 | $49
Westin South Coast Plaza Hotel, 686 Anton Blvd. (Bristol St.), Costa Mesa, 714-444-5900; www.patinagroup.com
■ "Probably the best of Splichal's Pinots" is the word on this South Coast Plaza "Grand Cru" choice for "refined" Provençal cuisine from "creative genius" chef Florent Marneau, whose "memorable selections" include "foie gras recipes that are always home runs"; "soft lighting and French antiques" make the "spacious but warm space" "feel like a real getaway", factor in "refined service" and "charisma and heart" and the result is a "great place before the theater" and a "regular haunt for those in the know."

Plums Cafe & Catering   25 | 17 | 19 | $19
Westport Square Shopping Ctr., 369 E. 17th St. (Tustin Ave.), Costa Mesa, 949-548-7586; www.plumscafe.com
■ Set in a "hard-to-find" strip mall in Costa Mesa, this AM destination's "lovely" patio is a place where locals "dine alfresco" on the "best breakfasts in town" and "tantalizing lunch plates" of "imaginative", "delicious" American eats with a "Northwestern twist" (think smoked salmon hash, sautéed trout and wild berry tarts); most agree "it's a shame they aren't open in the evening", but it's surely a "great way to spend a weekend morning."

Prego   19 | 19 | 19 | $34
18420 Von Karman Ave. (Michelson Dr.), Huntington Beach, 949-553-1333; www.pregoirvine.com
See review in LA/Hollywood/W. Hollywood Directory.

Ragin' Cajun Cafe Ⓜ   22 | 18 | 18 | $18
3012 Newport Ave. (PCH), Newport Beach, 949-566-9099; www.ragincajun.com
See review in South Bay/Long Beach Directory.

Ralph Brennan's Jazz Kitchen   20 | 23 | 20 | $33
1590 S. Disneyland Dr. (Magic Way), Anaheim, 714-776-5200; www.rbjazzkitchen.com
◪ You'll find an "idealized version of New Orleans" at this "beautifully decorated", "amazing space" in Downtown Disney, which earns more applause for its "neat setting" ("you feel as if you've just stepped off Bourbon Street"), "live jazz nightly" and "perfect mint juleps" than for the "pretty darn good" (if "overpriced" and "small-portioned") Louisiana cooking; tip: insiders recommend the "excellent gumbo" and bread pudding.

Orange County F | D | S | C |

RAMOS HOUSE CAFE ⓜ 28 | 19 | 22 | $24 |
31752 Los Rios St. (Del Obispo St.), San Juan Capistrano, 949-443-1342

■ Despite an "out-of-the-way" location down a "small country road" "near the tracks" in San Juan Capistrano, decor no fancier than a rustic patio beneath a giant mulberry tree and a kitchen that puts on the breaks before dark, this "cool" "whistle-stop cafe" ranks No. 1 for Food in the OC *Survey*; the reason: chef-owner John Humphries wows diners with "unique", "amazing" New and Southern American brunch and lunch fare like "perfect scrambles", "superb crab cakes" and "interesting Bloody Mary's" that are a "meal in themselves."

Red Pearl Kitchen 21 | 21 | 18 | $32 |
412 Walnut Ave. (bet. 5th & Main Sts.), Huntington Beach, 714-969-0224

☑ Tim and Liza Goodell (Aubergine, Troquet) are the force behind this "very hip" Surf City spot where "big-flavored", "inventive Pan-Asian food" complements the "funky" proto-Shanghai decor (and "Japanese monster movies at the bar"); critics politely label it "a great place for a drink", but give "high marks for people-watching", highlighted by "bare-all young ladies showing off tattoos."

Rembrandt's Beautiful Food – | – | – | M |
Stonewood Ctr., 909 E. Yorba Linda Blvd. (McCormack Ln.), Placentia, 714-528-6222

Reopened after a renovation, Placentia's "throwback to the '60s" is once again serving "old-fashioned" Continental fare to loyalists who like their service personalized ("owner Bernie Gordon is a gem") and their "good steaks" served with "potatoes topped with buckets of chives, sour cream and cheese sauce"; the "great wine list, fairly priced" too, only adds to the allure of this "step back in time."

Ristorante Mamma Gina 19 | 18 | 21 | $37 |
251 E. PCH (Bayside Dr.), Newport Beach, 949-673-9500; www.mammagina.com

☑ Opinions conflict on this Newport bay-front choice for "traditional, high-end" Northern Italian": supporters give the thumbs up to "warm, hearty" fare like "the best lamb chops in all of OC", a "serene, romantic" room and "super-professional" service; "too much schmaltz, too little food quality", counter naysayers, who concede they stick around for the "live jazz" in the "fantastic bar" after dark.

RITZ-CARLTON 26 | 27 | 27 | $60 |
LAGUNA NIGUEL ⓈⓂ
Ritz-Carlton Laguna Niguel, 1 Ritz-Carlton Dr. (PCH), Dana Point, 949-240-5008; www.ritzcarlton.com

■ "Close to paradise" for "a special occasion or wonderful night out", the Dining Room at Laguna Niguel's "best resort"

Orange County F | D | S | C

is the "classy" option for "superb, if pricey" French fare in an "elegant" space with marble fireplace and banquettes; voters also tout the Grill Room for supper club "dining and dancing", the open-air Terrace for "unbelievable Friday night seafood buffets" and "sinful Sunday brunches", and the Lobby Lounge for "breathtaking views" at sunset.

RITZ RESTAURANT & GARDEN, THE   25 | 26 | 25 | $54
Fashion Island, 880 Newport Center Dr. (Santa Barbara Ave.), Newport Beach, 949-720-1800; www.ritzrestaurant.com
■ "Always the grande dame", this Fashion Island choice for "classy" Continental dining "consistently delivers quality" on all counts; look for a "world-class bar", "big leather booths", "impeccable" service and a menu of "terrific" classics; a few grumble that it's "losing its luster" "since (former owner) Hans Prager retired", but for now Newport's "good old boys" still gather here "when the deal closes."

RIVIERA AT THE FIRESIDE ⊠   27 | 24 | 28 | $41
13950 Springdale Ave. (Frwy. 405), Westminster, 714-897-0477; www.rivierarestaurant.net
■ Expect an "oasis of pampered comfort" at this "clubby" Westminster "old-line" Continental dinner house that's "reminiscent of a '50s supper club" complete with "elegant service" (No. 1 in the OC *Survey*) from "tuxedoed waiters" who "remember your name and drink" and "prepare flaming entrees and desserts tableside"; it's a "rich, outstanding" "retro meal" that loyalists insist "matches up to any hot-shot nouvelle palace of fine dining."

Rosine's   24 | 14 | 19 | $19
721 S. Weir Canyon Rd. (Serrano Ave.), Anaheim, 714-283-5141; www.rosines.com
■ This easygoing "Mediterranean winner" in an east Anaheim Hills shopping center is "worth seeking" out for "fantastic", "bargain-priced" Armenian faves like "superb rotisserie chicken" and "the best kebabs"; the "surprising selection of wines" at "extraordinarily fair prices" is another bonus, making this cafe an "absolute gem" that sparkles "when everyone's too tired to cook" or just looking for "a delightful alternative to chains."

Rothschild's   24 | 22 | 23 | $43
2407 E. PCH (MacArthur Blvd.), Corona Del Mar, 949-673-3750; www.rothschildscdm.com
■ "One of the most romantic rooms in town" swoon Corona Del Mar locals of this "always reliable" village center "haunt" with "incredibly good" Continental cuisine served in an "intimate" space "imbued with old-world charm"; "outstanding" service ups the appeal of this "dinner for two or a cozy get together with friends" "favorite" that's "the kind of place you want to keep as a secret."

Orange County | F | D | S | C |

Royal Khyber ▽ 22 | 22 | 21 | $34 |
South Coast Plaza Village, 1621 W. Sunflower Ave. (Plaza Dr.), Santa Ana, 714-436-1010; www.royalkhyber.com

◪ Judgments differ widely on this upscale South Coast Plaza Village bistro serving a broad menu of North Indian fare: supporters say it's a "pleasant place" for "fine", "reasonably priced" cooking ("the naans and tandoor items are terrific") boosted by "attentive" service; gripers find the tariff "pricey" and are less than smitten with the staff.

Royal Thai Cuisine ▽ 18 | 14 | 15 | $22 |
1750 S. Coast Hwy. (bet. Agate & Pearl Sts.), Laguna Beach, 949-494-8424

◪ South Laguna's durable pick for "multicourse feasts" of "tasty" if "not original" Thai cuisine strikes fans as a "local gem"; grumblers sneer that the fare is "average" and "won't appeal to those who've eaten in Thailand", but still return to "the cute patio for casual dinners" time and again.

Roy's 24 | 21 | 22 | $46 |
Fashion Island, 453 Newport Center Dr. (San Miguel Dr.), Newport Beach, 949-640-7697; www.roys-restaurants.com

◪ "All the flavors of Hawaii" lure the "beautiful people" of Newport Beach to this "stylish" Fashion Island outpost for celeb chef Roy Yamaguchi's "very imaginative" cuisine marked by "yummy fish" and stellar sauces ("if you love them, this is the place"); yes, since it's "packed" and "sooo loud", it's "bustling, not relaxing", but for most, it's "always a treat" from "drinks to dessert" ("save room" for the "amazing chocolate soufflé").

Ruby's 17 | 18 | 18 | $13 |
1 Balboa Pier (Palm Ave.), Balboa, 949-675-7829
2305 E. PCH (bet. Avocado Ave. & MacArthur Blvd.), Corona Del Mar, 949-673-7829
428 E. 17th St. (bet. Irvine & Tustin Aves.), Costa Mesa, 949-646-7829
Huntington Beach Pier, 1 Main St. (PCH), Huntington Beach, 714-969-7829
4602 Barranca Pkwy. (Lake Rd.), Irvine, 949-552-7829
30622 S. PCH (Wesley Dr.), Laguna Beach, 949-497-7829
Mission Viejo Mall, 27000 Crown Valley Pkwy. (Frwy. 5), Mission Viejo, 949-481-7829
Seal Beach Pier (Ocean Ave.), Seal Beach, 562-431-7829
13102 Newport Ave. (Irvine Blvd.), Tustin, 714-838-7829
www.rubys.com
See review in Westside Directory.

Rusty Pelican 20 | 21 | 19 | $35 |
2735 W. Coast Hwy. (bet. Riverside & Tustin Aves.), Newport Beach, 949-642-3431; www.rustypelican.com

■ "The kitchen knows how to do fish" at this enduring Newport seafooder whose "great location" sports an

get updates at zagat.com 265

Orange County   F | D | S | C

"outstanding harbor view"; it's a "nice place for a date" by a "window watching the sunset" "while munching on excellent oysters" and "yummy garlic bread", and don't forget the lively upstairs bar, "the place to be for happy hour", when "half-price apps and drinks" are consumed from a scenic crow's nest.

RUTH'S CHRIS STEAK HOUSE   26 | 20 | 24 | $51
2961 Michaelson Dr. (Carlson Ave.), Irvine, 949-252-8848; www.ruthschris.com
See review in Westside Directory.

Sage   25 | 19 | 22 | $36
Eastbluff Ctr., 2531 Eastbluff Dr. (Vista del Sol), Newport Beach, 949-718-9650; www.sagerestaurant.com
■ Disciples of "very talented" chef-owner Rich Mead swear their "taste buds dance in elation" over his "delicious", "inventive" American bistro cuisine ("I love the duck", "excellent grilled seafood") served in a "candlelit" space with a "pretty" outdoor garden patio; first-timers will have to search for this "little secret" since it's "isolated" in an "ordinary" Newport bluffs "shopping plaza", but as "a hidden treasure in a town known for restaurants", it's worth the effort.

Salt Creek Grille   19 | 20 | 18 | $30
32802 PCH (Crown Valley Pkwy.), Dana Point, 949-661-7799; www.saltcreekgrille.com
See review in San Fernando Valley/Burbank Directory.

Sam Woo's   21 | 10 | 15 | $18
Metro Pointe Shopping Ctr., 901C S. Coast Dr. (bet. Bear St. & Fairview Ave.), Costa Mesa, 714-668-0800
54068 Walnut Ave. (Jeffrey Rd.), Huntington Beach, 949-262-0128
15333 Culver Dr. (Irvine Center Dr.), Irvine, 949-262-0688
■ This trio of "authentic" Cantonese joints "stands out from their ubiquitous Chinese competition" by virtue of "awesome dim sum served all day" plus a "wide array" of "quick, tasty", "affordable dishes" like fresh fish "right from the tank" and "the best BBQ duck around"; the decor tends toward "sterile", the service can be "rushed and surly" and English is the second language of lots of patrons, so you'll definitely "think you're in Hong Kong."

Savannah Chop House   21 | 21 | 22 | $39
32441 Golden Lantern St. (Camino del Avion), Laguna Niguel, 949-493-7107; www.culinaryadventures.com
☑ Locals call this "very beautiful" Laguna Niguel dinner house an "all around good dining" choice based on its "leather banquettes" ("sinking into them is heavenly after a long week"), stone fireplaces, "delicious" surf 'n' turf fare, "experienced staff" and "great patio overlooking the ocean"; it may be "pricey, but is well worth the extra cost

Orange County F | D | S | C |

for an intimate evening" that might begin with "tasty munchies" and "decent single malts" at the bar.

Savoury's ⓈⓂ ▽ 24 | 21 | 21 | $50 |
Hotel La Casa Del Camino, 1287 S. Coast Hwy. (Cress St.), Laguna Beach, 949-376-9718; www.savourys.com
■ Based in a historic Laguna hotel, this "gorgeous" dinner spot has "European atmosphere" and a "sumptuous menu" of "complex", "artfully designed" dishes that "mix great flavors" from France and the Pacific Rim, resulting in cuisine deemed "delicious", if "somewhat overworked"; "for the hefty price there should be an ocean view", but it's "charming just the same", and management is "trying hard to make its mark"; tip: for a peek at the Pacific, "take your drinks and appetizers to the incredible rooftop."

Scott's Seafood 21 | 21 | 21 | $38 |
3300 Bristol St. (Anton Blvd.), Costa Mesa, 714-979-2400
27321 La Paz Rd. (Pacific Park Dr.), Laguna Niguel, 949-389-0055
www.scottsseafood.com
◪ These "classy" fish houses with a "bright ambiance" and "very accommodating" hospitality earn praise for the "freshest fish" "simply prepared" and "well-presented", plus a broad menu (including "wonderful steaks") that includes "something for everyone"; the Costa Mesa site is particularly "popular before attending OCPAC and SCR" since "they do a great job getting diners in and out" prior to curtain time.

Seafood Paradise ▽ 20 | 12 | 12 | $21 |
8602 Westminster Blvd. (bet. Magnolia & Newland Sts.), Westminster, 714-893-6066
■ Westminster's Little Saigon is the home of this "cheap find for foodies" boasting "excellent dim sum every day", "fabulous" "live tank seafood" and a kitchen "capable of amazing things"; the "plain" banquet hall digs don't offer "much glamour or sophistication", but that doesn't deter adventurous types who advise "be fearless, try anything."

Sensasian – | – | – | M |
Irvine Mktpl., 13290 Jamboree Rd. (Bryan Ave.), Irvine, 714-368-3330
Longtime media darling Martin Yan brings his name, cookbooks and take on healthy, wokwise cuisine from all over Asia to OC with this sprawling, stylish debut in the Tustin Market Place; the freestanding space is sure to attract suburbanites of all sorts since the seating is group- and family-friendly and the bar (specializing in exotic cocktails) offers early and late happy hours for the kid-less crowd.

Side Street Cafe ⇸ ▽ 23 | 10 | 18 | $12 |
1799 Newport Blvd. (18th St.), Costa Mesa, 949-650-1986
■ For a "wonderful daytime eating experience" insiders head to this "charming", "homey" strip-mall joint in Costa

Orange County F | D | S | C

Mesa that's a "favorite among locals" for "excellent", "inexpensive" Traditional American "comfort food" at breakfast and lunch; factor in "sidewalk seating" and "lots of personality" ("hand written menus", "family photos of the owners") and the result is "a wait every weekend."

Sorrento Grille 23 | 20 | 21 | $38
370 Glenneyre St. (Mermaid St.), Laguna Beach, 949-494-8686
■ Downtown Laguna's "happening local hangout" is a "trendy spot" for scene-makers sipping "fabulous martinis" and noshing on "scrumptious" Cal-Med creations that are "inventive but not overly creative"; the "atmosphere is sexy" but "terribly noisy" so it can be "difficult to communicate over the din" unless you "eat upstairs above the maddening crowd"; a "solid performer" overall if you believe "your hearing will be back to normal in 12–24 hours."

Spaghettini 19 | 20 | 19 | $33
3005 Old Ranch Pkwy. (bet. 405 Frwy. & Seal Beach Blvd.), Seal Beach, 562-596-2199; www.spaghettini.com
◪ A "freeway-convenient" site and nightly "live jazz" of all flavors (cool, Latin, traditional) attract a "dressy, upscale crowd" from "all over OC and LA" to this Seal Beach Italian; while some find the fare "uninspired" relative to the "expensive" tab, others pipe up for the Sunday brunch ("the best!"), and recommend the bar as "an after-work watering hole"; P.S. "make reservations" or "you'll collect your pension before being seated."

Spark Woodfire Cooking 20 | 19 | 19 | $27
300 PCH (Main St.), Huntington Beach, 714-960-0996; www.sparkwoodfirecooking.com
See review in San Fernando Valley/Burbank Directory.

SPLASHES 21 | 27 | 21 | $44
Surf & Sand Hotel, 1555 S. PCH (Bluebird Canyon Dr.), Laguna Beach, 949-497-4477; www.jcresorts.com
■ With tables "practically on the sand", "waves crashing 20 yards away from you" and "stunning views of the ocean", it's no surprise that "what is already good [Mediterranean] food tastes even better" at this three-meal-a-day Laguna Beach destination rated No. 1 for Decor in the OC *Survey*; "go before dark" to best enjoy the sunsets, and "better yet, get a room" at the hotel, provided you're not about to do anything you'll later regret ("you'll start feeling romantic about your clients" here).

Steelhead Brewing Co. 17 | 15 | 17 | $19
University Ctr., 4175 Campus Dr. (Bridge Rd.), Irvine, 949-856-2227; www.steelheadbrewingco.com
■ "Popular with UCI folk and nearby residents", this handsome campus-close brewpub features "very tasty, fresh suds" and "large portions" of "decent" American

Orange County   F | D | S | C

grub like "a nice selection of wood-fired pizzas" and "good burgers"; the "atmosphere is student-y, but not loud" and "slouchy couches" promote "good conversation"; keep it in mind "after a movie" or even for a "casual business lunch."

Studio Ⓜ   – | – | – | VE
Montage Resort & Spa, 30801 S. Coast Hwy. (Montage Dr.), Laguna Beach, 949-715-6420; www.montagelagunabeach.com

Laguna's newest (and maybe poshest) luxury coastal resort is the home of this serene dining space that crowns an oceanfront bluff and has wraparound windows that maximize its sweeping views; chef James Boyce is the artist-in-residence behind the distinctive, ever-changing Mediterranean cuisine that accentuates local, artisanal ingredients; early reports of "superb meals" even go so far as to contend it's "by far the best in OC", but "bring along your banker" if you care to partake of the "extensive" wines, displayed in large vaults that flank the bar.

Summit House   24 | 24 | 24 | $38
2000 E. Bastanchury Rd. (State College Blvd.), Fullerton, 714-671-4111; www.summithouse.net

◪ North countians celebrating "special occasions of any kind" head to this Fullerton hilltop where a "lodgelike" Tudor-style manse boasts a "breathtaking" "view of the city lights", a backdrop for "service the way it should be" and repasts of "flavorful" Continental standards like "excellent prime rib" and "to-die-for" John Dory; some gripe about "lack of change" on the "pedestrian menu", but most agree this is a "gracious place for a relaxing, well-presented meal"; P.S. nature lovers should "get a window seat" to view "rabbits on the lawn."

Table Ten   – | – | – | M
124 W. Commonwealth Ave. (N. Harbor Blvd.), Fullerton, 714-526-3210

Formerly located in a drab Placentia strip mall, this friendly independent operation has taken its eclectic American menu to larger, more urbane digs in semi-hip downtown Fullerton, which accommodate a full bar and room for weekend entertainment; the move adds a bit of panache to dining on an interesting selection of dishes that range from chimichurri steak to corned beef tacos.

Taco Loco ☽   21 | 8 | 13 | $12
640 S. PCH (bet. Cleo & Legion Sts.), Laguna Beach, 949-497-1635

■ Surfer dudes and window shoppers agree that this perennial "beach shack" on a busy "PCH sidewalk" in Laguna "can't be beat" for "awesome" "New Age Mexican" grub like "to-die-for blackened shrimp tacos" and "tofu mushroom burgers" that are a "vegetarian's dream come

Orange County

F | **D** | **S** | **C**

true" and "cheap, cheap, cheap" to boot; "dining on resin chairs" keeps thing "very casual", but at least "you can hear the waves crashing" across the street.

Taco Mesa 24 | 8 | 15 | $10
647 W. 19th St. (bet. Harbor Blvd. & Placentia Ave.), Costa Mesa, 949-642-0629
22922 Los Alisos Blvd. (Trabuco Rd.), Mission Viejo, 949-472-3144
Saddleback Shopping Ctr., 3533 E. Chapman Ave. (Prospect St.), Orange, 714-633-3922
www.tacomesa.net

■ "Hands down the best Mexican in OC" declare disciples of these "friendly" family-run triplets known for "always fabulous" seafood tacos, "outstanding burritos" and "very creative" "whiteboard specials" "you would expect to find in a top-tier restaurant", ideal choices for those "late-night munchies"; despite their "ugly" "fast-food settings" and "loud, bright" ambiance, these are "irreplaceable" options in their genre that "need to open up more locations."

Taiko Japanese Restaurant 24 | 15 | 17 | $26
14775 Jeffrey Rd. (Walnut Ave.), Irvine, 949-559-7190

◪ "An amazing following" of locals "lines up around the building" "before the restaurant opens" at this Irvine mecca for "flawless", "amazing sushi" and cooked Japanese dishes served in "large portions for the money"; skeptics feel it "doesn't warrant the crowds it gets", but worshipers feel it's "definitely worth the wait."

Tangata Ⓜ ▽ 21 | 21 | 17 | $27
Bowers Museum, 2002 N. Main St. (bet. Santa Ana Frwy. & 17th St.), Santa Ana, 714-550-0906; www.patinagroup.com

■ Another of the Patina gang, this "very peaceful" museum cafe in an "old California" courtyard is a "lovely" stop for "lunch while visiting the Bowers" "for a day of mind expansion"; a "small" but "varied menu" with seasonal regional dishes like "outstanding pumpkin ravioli" and "generous salads" boasting "first-rate ingredients" makes for "terrific" noshing at what fans call "probably the best museum restaurant in SoCal."

Taps 23 | 22 | 20 | $30
101 E. Imperial Hwy. (Brea Blvd.), Brea, 714-257-0101; www.tapsbrea.com

■ Located in rehabbed downtown Brea, this source for "fresh" "seafood far from the sea" and eight "beers brewed on the premises" is "hopping every night" with a crowd of "all ages and types" partaking in "huge portions" of "tasty" Traditional American fare brought by "energetic" staffers "bearing smiles"; the large, "open" warehouse space with "terrific" decor also has room enough for lots of fireplaces, a raw bar, "great patio" and large bar where you can listen to live music.

Orange County | F | D | S | C |

Thaifoon | 19 | 24 | 18 | $27 |
Irvine Spectrum Ctr., 85 Fortune Dr. (Pacifica), Irvine, 949-585-0022
Fashion Island, 857 Newport Center Dr. (bet. Corporate Plaza & Farallon Dr.), Newport Beach, 949-644-0133; www.thaifoon.com
◨ "Waterfall walls", "slick decor" and an "atmosphere of Eurasian cool" give these "upscale" siblings an "exotic" flavor "perfect for a date"; while some speak up for the "excellent variety" of dishes at "reasonable prices", others feel that despite the name the "heavily modified" Thai fare is "Pan-Asian at most" and might "disappoint" purists.

Thai This | ▽ 20 | 15 | 19 | $23 |
24501 Del Prado (Amber Lantern St.), Dana Point, 949-240-7944; www.thaithis.com
■ "Just Thai this one and you won't be sorry" assure regulars at this "serene", modest (it's "little more than a shack") Dana Point joint where the prices are "excellent" on "surprisingly good" fare; for those in a hurry at lunch, it's a "good, fast" choice (the "mean pad Thai comes quicker than you can say the name"), while at dinner, it's a "fine, neighborhood" locale for a "friendly" "casual" meal.

Thanh My ● | ▽ 23 | 9 | 15 | $14 |
9553 Bolsa Ave. (Bushard St.), Westminster, 714-531-9540
■ Its "mini-mall" interior may be "nondescript", but this "late-night" Westminster Vietnamese's dishes are "all above average" ("some are excellent"); "pho is recommended" as are the "superlative spring rolls and rice plates", just be prepared to solicit the "staff's expert advice" in trying to navigate the "huge", "wonderful and varied menu."

Ti Amo | 22 | 20 | 21 | $40 |
31727 S. PCH (3rd St.), South Laguna Beach, 949-499-5350
◨ South Laguna's "romantic hideaway" compensates for having "no view" by offering a "charming" "maze of dining rooms" "heavy on the cherubs", "servers with fantastic memories" and "tasty, well-prepared" Ital-Med cooking, which diners sometimes "don't notice" because they're "so busy gazing into each other's eyes"; cynics find the decor "cheesy", but it's still a popular "place to take a date when you want to sweep her off her feet."

Tommy Bahama's Tropical Cafe | 18 | 22 | 18 | $33 |
854 Avocado Ave. (bet. MacArthur Blvd. & PCH), Newport Beach, 949-760-8686; www.tommybahama.com
◨ Prepare for a "two-hour trip to the tropics" at this Caribbean-themed chainlet located in a "hip" Newport Beach mini-mall; described as the "essence of ease", it attracts "Jimmy Buffet wanna-bes" with its "beautiful patio", "good music", "deluxe drinks" and "pseudo island fare" that's "like the company's clothes – slightly better than average and puts a hole in your wallet" ("browse the store next door and you'll leave $250 lighter").

Orange County

| | F | D | S | C |

Tony Roma's 16 | 13 | 15 | $22
1300 S. Harbor Blvd. (Puente St.), Fullerton, 714-871-4000
7862 Warner Ave. (Beach Blvd.), Huntington Beach, 714-841-7427
3642 Katella Ave. (Los Alamitos Blvd.), Los Alamitos, 562-598-0401
17245 17th St. (Yorba St.), Tustin, 714-669-0121
www.tonyromas.com
See review in Westside Directory.

Tortilla Flats ▽ 14 | 17 | 13 | $21
27792 Vista Del Lago (Marguerite Pkwy.), Mission Viejo, 949-830-9980; www.tacotuesday.com
■ Mission Viejans "sit outside when the weather is nice and watch the ducks" from this waterfront Mexican's terraced patio where the "views are great" but the "food looks tired and tastes mediocre"; though some deem it "barely passable overall", this "genial" spot still attracts "lots of families on weekends."

Trabuco Oaks ▽ 20 | 16 | 17 | $26
20782 Trabuco Oaks Rd. (Live Oak Canyon Rd.), Trabuco Canyon, 949-586-0722; www.trabucooakssteakhouse.com
◪ "Don't wear a good tie" because the staff will snip it off at this "funky", "rustic" Trabuco Canyon outpost where "superior" "mesquite-grilled steaks" and an "old West" vibe are the lure for beef lovers who say this operation has "more soul than other steakhouses in town"; "inexpensive to moderate" tariffs, including "great prices on wine", heighten the appeal of this "fun place" and "south county tradition" off a winding road.

Troquet ☒ 26 | 23 | 22 | $52
South Coast Plaza, 3333 Bristol St. (Town Center Dr.), Costa Mesa, 714-708-6865
◪ An "obscure" location within South Coast Plaza is part of why this high-achiever from Tim Goodell (Aubergine, Red Pearl Kitchen) is "an unexpected respite from the hurly-burly" of its mall surroundings; other reasons include "incredible French fare" like sweetbreads and truffle-crusted filet mignon that "would make Jacques Pepin proud" and an "elegant, yet unpretentious" space; despite gripes about "pricey", "tiny portions" and "lack of attention" by ownership, more think it "hits all the marks."

Turner New Zealand ▽ 21 | 17 | 20 | $51
650 Anton Blvd. (Park Center Dr.), Costa Mesa, 714-668-0880; www.turnernewzealand.com
◪ An all-Kiwi menu is the "unique concept" behind this Costa Mesa curiosity from Noel Turner, an established purveyor of New Zealand goods, who brings in "wonderful wines", mussels, "awesome" lamb and venison (this is a "great spot for carnivores") from the country; naysayers find the food "boring" and "overpriced", but concede the

Orange County | F | D | S | C |

"intimate space" adjacent to SCR and OCPAC is "good for pre-theater" dining.

Tutto Fresco ▽ 20 | 15 | 19 | $19
30642 Santa Margarita Pkwy. (El Paseo), Rancho Santa Margarita, 949-858-3360
■ This "south county's version of a neighborhood Italian" "where the owners care", the service is "friendly" and the "food is very good" is "incongruously located" in a strip mall beside the local megaplex; the basic pasta lineup is mostly Northern Italian and "reasonably priced"; despite being "always busy" and "very noisy", it somehow manages to feel "cozy and fit for a family dinner."

Tutto Mare 18 | 19 | 18 | $35
Fashion Island, 545 Newport Center Dr. (Santa Rosa Dr.), Newport Beach, 949-640-6333
☑ "Likable" and "consistent" are two fair ways to describe this "trendy" Fashion Island Italian that stands out by "focusing on seafood" ("the crab salad will knock your socks off") and "great risottos", served in a handsome space to a "trendy crowd"; cynics say it's "losing its edge" and "promises more than it delivers" at "skyrocketing prices", but fans swear it "can be trusted" and note "Sunday brunch is a bargain" with "something for everyone."

21 Oceanfront 23 | 23 | 23 | $50
2100 W. Oceanfront (21st St.), Newport Beach, 949-673-2100; www.21oceanfront.com
☑ Based near a pier "right across from the ocean", this Newport Beach seafooder is a "romantic favorite" where the "upscale setting" and "million-dollar view" earn as many kudos as the crab legs, lobster and "great abalone" ("if you're prepared to mortgage the house"); a few claim it's "just ok for the price" but others insist it's where to go to "live like a king" while "watching the sun descend behind Catalina Island."

230 Forest 25 | 19 | 20 | $36
230 Forest Ave. (PCH), Laguna Beach, 949-494-2545; www.230forestavenue.com
■ Smack in the "heart of Laguna", this art-filled seafood-focused Californian is a "hip, vibrant" magnet for "trendy pretty people" to sip "superb" martinis and chow down on "unparalleled seared ahi" and other "creative creations"; "tight quarters" mean you may want to stretch your legs with an "after-dinner walk on Main Beach."

Vessia Ristorante 22 | 18 | 20 | $29
Crossroads Shopping Ctr., 3966 Barranca Pkwy. (Culver Dr.), Irvine, 949-654-1155; www.vessia.com
☑ An "unexpected find" and "touch of elegance" in an "unassuming shopping center" in Irvine, this Southern Italian surprises with "very tasty", "authentic" dishes like

Orange County

F | D | S | C

the "highly recommended 'Di Mare salad'", "awesome broccoli rabe" and "the best braciole around"; in sum, a "reasonably priced" "neighborhood mainstay" that's a "step up from the usual."

Villa Nova ◐ — 19 | 22 | 20 | $37
3131 W. PCH (Newport Blvd.), Newport Beach, 949-642-7880; www.villanovarestaurant.com

◪ Luring "old-timers" with its "spectacular" "view of Newport Harbor" is this "bayside institution" for Italian cooking along the town's Restaurant Row; reactions to the food range from "excellent" ("no one can top their veal Milanese") to "unremarkable", but "polished" service from "professional waiters who memorize your order", "terrific early-birds specials" and a "fun piano bar" that's a "good scene for the over-40 set" weigh in its favor.

Walt's Wharf — 24 | 17 | 21 | $31
201 Main St. (PCH), Seal Beach, 562-598-4433; www.waltswharf.com

■ A "small-town feel and uptown food" describes this "cozy" Seal Beach "landmark" for "scrumptious seafood" like "unbelievable caramelized salmon" enhanced by wood-grilling and "delicious sauces and glazes"; factor in an "impressive", "fairly priced" selection of wines (the proprietors own a winery) and "courteous" service and no wonder you should "expect to wait eons" (no reservations are taken) for a weekend table.

Wasa — – | – | – | M
Market Pl., 13124 Jamboree Rd. (Irvine Blvd.), Irvine, 714-665-3338

Expect a "wide variety" of "extremely fresh and creative sushi" at "very reasonable prices", plus "traditional" Japanese dishes "with a twist", on the "hip menu" of this sleek, "cool" storefront newcomer in the growing retail megalopolis that straddles Tustin and Irvine.

Wild Artichoke, The ⌧ — ▽ 24 | 18 | 24 | $32
4973 Yorba Ranch Rd. (Yorba Linda Blvd.), Yorba Linda, 714-777-9646

■ Fans of "rising star" chef-owner James D'Aquila's "quality" Cal-Med cooking venture way out east to a "nondescript shopping center" in Yorba Linda to dine off his "limited but inventive menu" that's "not your typical north county stuff"; meals start with a "delicious artichoke dip" and can include "fabulous wines by the glass" and "outstanding soups and desserts"; the "cute", "simple" quarters awash in dusty green "don't have many tables", so "make reservations on weekends."

Wolfgang Puck Cafe — 17 | 15 | 16 | $22
South Coast Plaza Mall, 3333 Bristol St. (Bear St.), Costa Mesa, 714-546-9653
Irvine Spectrum Ctr., 55 Fortune Dr. (Pacifica), Irvine, 949-453-9393

Orange County | F | D | S | C |

(continued)
Wolfgang Puck Cafe
*Fashion Island, 841 Newport Center Dr. (Santa Cruz Dr.),
Newport Beach, 949-720-9653*
*The Block at Orange, 20 City Blvd. W. (City Dr.), Orange,
714-634-9653*
www.wolfgangpuck.com
See review in LA/Hollywood/W. Hollywood Directory.

WOOD RANCH BBQ & GRILL | 20 | 16 | 18 | $23 |
*8022 E. Santa Ana Canyon Rd. (Weir Canyon Rd.), Anaheim Hills,
714-974-6660; www.woodranch.com*
See review in LA/Hollywood/W. Hollywood Directory.

WOODY'S AT THE BEACH Ⓜ | 25 | 25 | 26 | $33 |
*1305 S. PCH (Cress St.), Laguna Beach, 949-376-8809;
www.woodysatthebeach.com*
■ You'll find "class not crass" and a "diverse crowd" at this "gay-owned", "straight-friendly" spot on Laguna's PCH; "caring management" and a "great-looking, attentive staff" set the scene for "festive" meals of "incredible" Cal fare (with an occasional French twist); for an "ocean view", the "outdoor deck is a piece of paradise."

Yard House ⏺ | 19 | 18 | 18 | $24 |
*Triangle Square Shopping Mall, 1875 Newport Blvd.
(bet. Harbor Blvd. & 19th St.), Costa Mesa, 949-642-0090*
*Irvine Spectrum Ctr., 71 Fortune Dr. (bet. Frwy. 405 & I-5),
Irvine, 949-753-9373*
www.yardhouse.com
See review in South Bay/Long Beach Directory.

Yi Dynasty Restaurant Ⓢ | 22 | 6 | 14 | $22 |
*1701 Corinthian Way (Martingale Way), Newport Beach,
949-797-9292*
See review of Soot Bull Jeep in LA/Hollywood/
W. Hollywood Directory.

Yujean Kang's Asian Bistro | ▽ 16 | 13 | 15 | $28 |
*South Coast Plaza, 3333 Bristol St. (Frwy. 405), Costa Mesa,
714-662-1098*
◪ South Coast Plaza shoppers agree this OC outpost of the Kang empire makes a "good stab at attacking bland mall food" by dishing up "enjoyable" Asian fare with a Chinese spin, but the "sterile concrete" space has "no ambiance"; voters in the know concede it's a "major disappointment considering its lineage" and suggest "take the drive to Pasadena to sample the food at the mother house."

Yves' Bistro | ▽ 23 | 16 | 22 | $31 |
*5753 E. Santa Ana Canyon Rd. (bet. Imperial Hwy. & Via Cortez),
Anaheim Hills, 714-637-3733*
■ "Hard to find" but "always dependable" is this "fine neighborhood bistro" in Anaheim Hills where locals tuck

Orange County

F | **D** | **S** | **C**

into "delightful" French-Italian classics while being served by a "young, enthusiastic staff"; the "quaint", "cozy" surroundings are "very comfortable" for lingering over "incredible" soufflés, and the "friendly owner makes you feel like coming back."

ZANKOU CHICKEN ●∌   23 | 5 | 12 | $10
2424 W. Ball Rd. (Roanne St.), Anaheim, 714-229-2060
See review in LA/Hollywood/W. Hollywood Directory.

Zinc Cafe & Market   21 | 16 | 12 | $15
350 Ocean Ave. (Beach St.), Laguna Beach, 949-494-6302; www.zinccafe.com

■ Laguna's "*très* popular" daytime "sidewalk cafe" is a "locals' hangout" for the "artistic New Age crowd", who bring along their "pooches" and newspapers as they nosh on "fresh, healthy, bursting-with-flavor" Californian morning and midday dishes that include "requisite vegetarian" choices; the patio beneath "flowing bougainvillea" may be "adorable" but it's also "constantly packed", so "go early" to get your serving of "great people-watching."

Zov's Bistro & Bakery Cafe Ⓢ   25 | 19 | 22 | $32
Enderle Ctr., 17440 E. 17th St. (Yorba St.), Tustin, 714-838-8855; www.zovs.com

■ Fans of "gracious hosts" Zov and Gary Karamardian "can't stop raving" about the "fabulous flavor in every bite" of their "creative", "exotic" Mediterranean fare (tip: "any lamb choice is a good one") and "amazing assortment of desserts" "worth breaking a diet for"; the "casual, elegant" space (much of it covered patio) is a "charming" "favorite whether you're in jeans or out for a nice night"; "don't forget" the "unique" "bakery/cafe out back" for "less expensive, but still high-quality", light meals.

Z'tejas   17 | 15 | 18 | $23
South Coast Plaza, 3333 Bristol St. (Anton St.), Costa Mesa, 714-979-7469; www.ztejas.com

◪ Advocates of "fine Southwestern dining" say this "bustling", "very casual" South Coast Plaza newcomer decorated with rawhide lampshades and colorful walls charms with "creatively prepared" New American fare that's "oh-so-tasty" (the "skillet cornbread is yummy"); detractors deem the fare "unstellar" "mall food" and suggest "sitting in the bar" for "happy-hour" "margaritas, martinis and appetizers."

Indexes

CUISINES
LOCATIONS
SPECIAL FEATURES

Indexes list the best of many within each category.

Restaurant locations are indicated by the following abbreviations: Los Angeles/Hollywood=LA; The Westside=W; The South Bay and Long Beach=SB; The San Fernando Valley and Burbank=SF; The San Gabriel Valley and Pasadena/Glendale=SG; Orange County=OC.

† Multiple locations in the Los Angeles area.

Cuisine Index

CUISINES

American (New)
Amuse Café/W
Avenue/W
Bayside/OC
BeachFire/OC
Beach House/W
Bistango/OC
Bliss/LA
Brentwood Rest./W
Cadillac Cafe/LA
Caffe Latte/LA
Cat & Custard/OC
Cinespace/LA
EM Bistro/LA
Emmanuel/SF
Firefly/SF
Firefly Bistro/SG
Formosa Cafe/LA
Four Oaks/W
Fox Sports Grill/OC
G. Garvin's/LA
Globe Venice Bch./W
Grace/LA
Grand Lux/LA
Hal's B&G/W
Hollywood Canteen/LA
House, The/LA
Hugo's†
Ivy/LA
Ivy/ Shore/W
Jaan/W
Jackson's Village/SB
Jimmy's Tavern/W
John O'Groats/W
Jones Hollywood/LA
Josie Rest./W
Leila's/SF
Lola's/LA
Mélisse/W
Michael's/W
Moonshadows/W
Morton's/LA
Mr. Stox/OC
Nic's/W
Noé/LA
One Pico/W
Pete's Cafe/LA
Ramos House/OC
Ritz-Carlton Hunt./SG
Saddle Peak/SF
17th St. Cafe/W
Sky Room/SB
Spark Woodfire/OC
Tangata/OC

Towne/SB
Traxx/LA
2087 Amer. Bistro/SF
Union/W
Urth Caffé/LA
Zax/W
Z'tejas/OC

American (Traditional)
Airstream Diner/W
Apple Pan/W
Authentic Cafe/LA
A Votre Sante/W
Bandera†
Beckham Grill/SG
Belmont Brew./SB
Billingsley's†
Blue on Blue/W
Bob Morris'/W
Brewski's/SB
Britta's Café/OC
Buffalo Club/W
Cafe '50s†
California Ckn.†
Castaway/SF
Catch/OC
Cedar Creek/OC
Cheesecake Fact.†
Chili John's/SF
Claim Jumper†
Clementine/W
Cole's P.E. Buffet/LA
Cottage/OC
Cynthia's/LA
Daily Grill†
Diner on Main/SG
Dish/SG
Doughboys/LA
Du-par's†
Edendale Grill/LA
Engine Co. No. 28/LA
555 East/SB
Griddle Cafe/LA
Grill/W
Grill on Hollywood/LA
Gulfstream/OC
Hamburger Hamlet†
Hard Rock Cafe†
Houston's†
In-N-Out Burger†
James' Beach/W
JAR/LA
Jinky's†
Kate Mantilini/W
King's Road Cafe/LA

278 subscribe to zagat.com

Cuisine Index

Kitchen/LA
Koo Koo Roo†
LA Food Show/SB
Lasher's/SB
Lawry's Carvery/OC
Lobster/W
Lodge/OC
Maple Drive/W
Marmalade Café†
Marston's/SG
Martha's 22nd St./SB
Maxwell's Cafe/W
Mimi's Cafe†
Misto Caffe/SB
Mo's/SF
Mrs. Knott's/OC
Musso & Frank/LA
Original Pancake Hse./OC
Original Pantry Bak./LA
Original Pantry Cafe/LA
Patrick's Road./W
Pie 'N Burger/SG
Plums Cafe/OC
Rae's/W
Ruby's†
Russell's Burgers/SG
Sage/OC
Shack/W
Shenandoah Cafe/SB
Side Street/OC
Smitty's Grill/SG
Souplantation†
South Street/W
Stanley's/SF
Steelhead Brew. Co./OC
Swingers†
Table Ten/OC
Tam O'Shanter/LA
Taps/OC
Toast Bakery/LA
Tony P's Dockside/W
Uncle Bill's Pancake/SB
Whist/W
Yard House†

Argentinean
Carlito's Gardel/LA
Gaucho Grill†

Armenian
Carousel†
Marouch/LA
Rosine's/OC
Zankou Ckn.†

Asian
Blue Pacific/SB
Bora Bora/SB
Chaya Brass./LA
Chaya Venice/W
Chinois/Main/W
Cinnabar/SG
Feast from East/W
Fenix/Argyle/LA
Gina Lee's/SB
Koi/LA
Mako/W
Max Rest./SF
Oysters/OC
Sensasian/OC
Shiro/SG
Trader Vic's/W
2117/W
White Lotus/LA
Yamashiro/LA
Yujean Kang's Asian/OC

Asian Fusion
Asia de Cuba/LA
Bistro Laramie/SB
Fat Fish/LA
Five Feet/OC
Michi/SB
Sawtelle Kit./W

Austrian
Schatzi on Main/W

Bakeries
Campanile/LA
Il Fornaio†
La Brea Bakery/SB
Le Pain Quot.†
Mäni's Bakery†

Barbecue
Amazon Churr./OC
Benny's BBQ/W
Big Mama's Rib/SG
Dr. Hogly Wogly's/SF
Green Field Churr.†
Gyu-kaku/W
Johnny Rebs'/SB
JR's BBQ/W
La Korea/LA
Lucille's†
Manna/LA
Mr. Cecil's†
Nak Won/LA
Pat & Oscar's/SB
Picanha Churr./SF
Pig, The/LA
Reddi Chick/W
Ribs USA/SF
RJ's Rib Joint/W
Robin's Woodfire/SG
Seoul Jung/LA

Cuisine Index

Soot Bull Jeep/LA
Tony Roma's†
Wood Ranch BBQ†
Woo Lae Oak†
Yi Dynasty/OC
Zeke's Smokehse./SG

Belgian

Chanteclair/OC
La Vie en Rose/OC
L'Hirondelle/OC

Brazilian

Amazon Churr./OC
Cafe Brasil/W
Galletto/SF
Green Field Churr.†
Picanha Churr./SF

Cajun

Bayou/SG
Bourbon St.†
Gumbo Pot/LA
Harold & Belle's/LA
House of Blues/LA
Iva Lee's/OC
JackShrimp/OC
Les Sisters/SF
Ragin' Cajun†

Californian

Accents/OC
Aioli/SB
Alex/LA
Ammo/LA
A.O.C./LA
Aubergine/OC
August Chris/SF
Axe/W
Babalu/W
Back on the Bch./W
Barbara's/Brew./LA
Barefoot B&G/LA
Barfly/LA
Barsac Brasserie/SF
Basix Cafe/LA
Bel-Air B&G/W
Bel-Air Hotel/W
Belly/LA
Belvedere/W
Bistro 45/SG
Bistro 31/W
Blue Pacific/SB
Bora Bora/SB
Breeze/W
Café Bizou†
Cafe Montana/W
Café Mundial/SG
Cafe Pinot/LA

Cafe Zoolu/OC
Caffe Citron/SG
Caioti Pizza/SF
Californian/OC
California Piz. Kit.†
Camilo's/SG
Campanile/LA
Castaway/SF
Cézanne/W
Chaya Venice/W
Checkers/LA
Chloe/W
Christine/SB
Cinnabar/SG
Citrus City/OC
Coral Tree/W
Cravings/LA
Crocodile Café†
Derek's/SG
Dexter's/OC
Encounter/SB
Farm of Bev. Hills†
Feinstein's/LA
Fenix/Argyle/LA
Five Sixty-One/SG
Flora Kitchen/LA
410 Boyd/LA
Francesca/SB
Fritto Misto†
Gardens/W
Gardens/Glendon/W
Geoffrey's/W
Getty Ctr./W
Gina Lee's/SB
Granita/W
Grill at Pelican Hill/OC
Halie/SG
Hamasaku/W
Impresario/LA
Inn/Seventh Ray/W
Jack Sprat's/W
JiRaffe/W
Joe's/W
Kokomo Cafe/LA
La Boheme/LA
L.A. Farm/W
LA Food Show/SB
Linq/LA
Louise's Tratt.†
Lucques/LA
Magalys/SG
Market City/SF
Marmalade Café†
Max Rest./SF
Mexicali/SF
Milky Way/LA
Mi Piace†

280   subscribe to zagat.com

Cuisine Index

Mirabelle/LA
Misto Caffe/SB
Morton's/LA
Napa Rose/OC
Napa Valley Grille/W
Oceanfront/W
Off Vine/LA
Opah/OC
Opaline/LA
Otto's/LA
Out Take Cafe/SF
Oysters/OC
Pace/LA
Palomino/W
Parkway Grill/SG
Patina/LA
Pat's/LA
Paul's Cafe/SF
Pavilion/OC
Pedals/W
Pinot Bistro/SF
Pinot Hollywood/LA
Primitivo Wine/W
Raymond/SG
Reed's/SB
Reg. Bev. Wilshire/W
Rest. Devon/SG
Röckenwagner/W
Rose Cafe/W
Scampi/SG
Schatzi on Main/W
Shiro/SG
Sisley Ital. Kit.†
Sorrento Grille/OC
Spago/W
Spumante/SF
Stanley's/SF
Sunset Room/LA
Surya India/LA
Tommy Tang's/LA
Trio Med. Grill/SB
2117/W
26 Beach Café/W
Twin Palms/SG
230 Forest/OC
vermont/LA
White Lotus/LA
Wild Artichoke/OC
Windows/LA
Wolfgang Pk. Cafe†
Woody's/Beach/OC
Yamashiro/LA
Yard House†
Zeidler's Café/W
Zinc Cafe/OC

Caribbean
Asia de Cuba/LA
Babalu/W
Bamboo/W
Cha Cha Cha/LA
Cha Cha Cha Encino/SF
Cha Cha Ckn./W
Golden Truffle/OC
Madre's/SG
Prado/LA
Tommy Bahama's/OC

Chinese
(* dim sum specialist)
ABC Seafood/LA*
Asian Noodles/LA
Bamboo Inn/SF
California Wok†
Chi Dynasty/LA
Chin Chin†*
Chow Fun/LA
Chung King/W
Empress Harbor/SG*
Empress Pavilion/LA*
Eurochow/W
Five Feet/OC
Formosa Cafe/LA
Fu-Shing/SG
Genghis Cohen/LA
Hop Li†
Hop Woo/W
Hu's Szechwan/W
JR Seafood/W
Kabob & Chinese†
Kung Pao†
Lake Spring/SG
Madame Wu's/LA*
Mandarette/LA
Mandarin/W
Mandarin Deli†
Manhattan Wonton/W
Mon Kee's/LA
Mr. Chow/W
NBC Seafood/SG*
Nonya/SG
Ocean Seafood/LA*
Ocean Star/SG*
Panda Inn/SG
P.F. Chang's†
Red Moon Cafe/W
Royal Star/W*
Sam Woo's/OC*
Sea Empress/SB*
Seafood Paradise/OC*
Sea Harbour/SG
Tung Lai Shun/SG
V.I.P. Harbor/W*

get updates at zagat.com 281

Cuisine Index

Wokcano/LA
Xi'an/W
Yang Chow†
Yujean Kang's/SG

Coffeehouses
Gypsy Den/OC
Urth Caffé/LA

Coffee Shops/Diners
Apple Pan/W
Blueberry/W
Brighton Coffee/W
Cafe '50s†
Cora's Coffee/W
Diner on Main/SG
Duke's Coffee/LA
Du-par's†
Fred 62/LA
Hollywood Hills/LA
Jan's/LA
Johnnie's Pastrami/W
Johnny Rockets†
Kate Mantilini/W
Mel's Drive-In†
Original Pantry Bak./LA
Original Pantry Cafe/LA
Patrick's Road./W
Rae's/W
Russell's Burgers/SG
Standard/LA
Sweet Lady Jane/LA
Swingers†

Continental
Arches/OC
Bistro Gdn./Coldwtr./SF
Brandywine/SF
Checkers/LA
Dal Rae/SG
Dizz's as Is/OC
Encounter/SB
Fins/SF
Gemmell's/OC
Gray Whale/W
Hobbit/OC
Jimmy's Tavern/W
Khoury's/SB
Mandevilla/SF
Matterhorn Chef/SF
Mr. Stox/OC
Nieuport 17/OC
Odyssey/SF
Patinette Cafe/LA
Pentimento/LA
Pig 'n' Whistle/LA
Polo Lounge/W
Raymond/SG

Rembrandt's/OC
Ritz Rest./OC
Riviera/Fireside/OC
Röckenwagner/W
Rothschild's/OC
Seashell/SF
Sir Winston's/SB
Summit House/OC

Creole
Bourbon St.†
Gumbo Pot/LA
Harold & Belle's/LA
Iva Lee's/OC
Ragin' Cajun†
Stevie's Creole/SF

Cuban
Cafe Atlantic/SG
Cuban Bistro/SG
Habana/OC
Paladar/LA
Versailles†

Delis
Art's Deli/SF
Barney Greengrass/W
Brent's Deli/SF
Broadway Deli/W
Canter's/LA
Factor's Deli/LA
Fromin's Rest.†
Greenblatt's Deli/LA
Junior's/W
La Bottega Marino†
Langer's Deli/LA
Mort's Deli/W
Nate 'n Al's/W
Roll 'n Rye Deli/W

Dessert
Babalu/W
Cheesecake Fact.†
Clementine/W
EM Bistro/LA
Grand Lux/LA
Il Fornaio†
La Dijonaise/W
Le Pain Quot.†
Mäni's Bakery†
Moustache Café†
Real Food Daily†
RJ's Rib Joint/W
Rose Cafe/W
Spago/W
Sweet Lady Jane/LA

Eclectic
Authentic Cafe/LA
Barbara's/Brew./LA

282 subscribe to zagat.com

Cuisine Index

Broadway Deli/W
Burger Contin./SG
Cafe Tu Tu†
Canal Club/W
Chaya Brass./LA
Cheesecake Fact.†
Chez Melange/SB
Depot/SB
5 Dudley/W
Francesca/SB
Fred 62/LA
Literati Café/W
Motif/OC
Newsroom Café†

English
Beckham Grill/SG
Five Crowns/OC
Gulliver's/OC
Olde Ship/OC
Whale & Ale/SB
Ye Olde King's/W

Ethiopian
Nyala Ethiopian/LA

Filipino
Taste of Manila/SG

Fondue
La Fondue/SF
Melting Pot/OC

French
Alex/LA
Aubergine/OC
Barfly/LA
Bar Marmont/LA
Barsac Brasserie/SF
Basilic/OC
Bastide/LA
Bel-Air Hotel/W
Bistro 45/SG
Bistro Gdn./Coldwtr./SF
Bistro 21/LA
Black Sheep/OC
Café Bizou†
Cafe Blanc/W
Cafe Pinot/LA
Cafe Stella/LA
Casbah Cafe/LA
Cellar/OC
Cézanne/W
Chameau/LA
Chanteclair/OC
Chez Mimi/W
Diaghilev/LA
Encore/W
Feinstein's/LA
Firefly/SF
Five Feet/OC
Five Sixty-One/SG
Gemmell's/OC
Golden Truffle/OC
Hobbit/OC
La Boheme/LA
La Cachette/W
L.A. Farm/W
La Parisienne/SG
La Vie en Rose/OC
Le Chêne/SF
Les Deux Cafés/LA
L'Hirondelle/OC
Little Door/LA
L'Orangerie/LA
Lucques/LA
Lunaria/W
Magalys/SG
Maison Akira/SG
Marguerite/W
Michelia/LA
Morels French/LA
Pascal/OC
Patina/LA
Patinette Cafe/LA
Paul's Cafe/SF
Picayo/OC
Pinot Provence/OC
Reed's/SB
Rest. Devon/SG
Ritz-Carlton Lag. Nig./OC
Roma via Paris/SF
Savoury's/OC
Scampi/SG
Taix French/LA
Troquet/OC
Yves' Bistro/OC

French (Bistro)
A La Tarte/W
Angelique Cafe/LA
Cafe des Artistes/LA
Cafe Pascal/OC
Cafe Pierre/SB
Cafe Tartine/LA
Clafoutis/LA
French Country/W
French 75/OC
Frenchy's Bistro/SB
Julienne/SG
La Dijonaise/W
La Frite/SF
Le Marmiton/W
Le Petit Bistro†
Le Petit Café/W
Le Petit Four/LA

get updates at zagat.com   283

Cuisine Index

Lilly's French Cafe/W
Mimosa/LA
Mirabeau/OC
Mistral/SF
Monsieur Marcel/LA
Morels First Floor/LA
Moustache Café†
Pastis/LA
Pescadou/OC
Pinot Bistro/SF
Pinot Hollywood/LA
Rive Gauche/SF
Soleil Westwood/W
Tournesol/SF
Vert/LA
Wine Bistro/SF

French (Brasserie)
Brass. des Artistes/W
Figaro Brass./LA

French (New)
Jaan/W
Sona/LA

Fusion
Roy's/OC

German
Knoll's Black Forest/W

Greek
Cafe Plaka/OC
Delphi Greek/W
Great Greek/SF
Le Petit Greek/LA
Papa Cristo's/LA
Papadakis Tav./SB
Sofi/LA
Taverna Tony/W
Ulysses Voyage/LA

Hamburgers
Apple Pan/W
Astro Burger†
Barney's Hamburger/W
Burger Contin./SG
Cassell's/LA
Father's Office/W
Hamburger Hamlet†
In-N-Out Burger†
Islands†
Johnny Rockets†
Mel's Drive-In†
Mo's/SF
Outlaws B&G/W
Pie 'N Burger/SG
Ruby's†
Russell's Burgers/SG
Shack/W

Tommy's/LA
26 Beach Café/W

Hawaiian
Back Home/Lahaina/SB
Duke's Mal./Hunt.†
Loft/SB
Roy's/OC

Health Food
A Votre Sante/W
Inn/Seventh Ray/W
Jack Sprat's/W
Juliano's Raw/W
Kinara Cafe/LA
Literati Café/W
Mäni's Bakery†
Newsroom Café†
Toast Bakery/LA
Urth Caffé/LA

Hot Dogs
Pink's Chili Dogs/LA

Indian
Addi's Tandoor/SB
Akbar†
All India Café†
Anarkali/LA
Bombay Bite/W
Bombay Cafe/W
Bombay Palace/W
Clay Pit/W
Electric Lotus/LA
Flavor of India/LA
Gate of India/W
India's Oven†
India's Tandoori†
Mayur/OC
Natraj/OC
Nawab of India/W
Nizam/W
Radhika's/SG
Royal Khyber/OC
Surya India/LA
Tantra/LA

Indonesian
Indo Cafe/W

Irish
Muldoons Irish/OC
Tom Bergin's/LA

Italian
(N=Northern; S=Southern)
Ago/LA (N)
Alejo's†
Alessi Rist./LA (N)
Allegria/W

Cuisine Index

Alto Palato/LA
Anaheim White/OC (N)
Angeli Caffe/LA
Angelini Osteria/LA
Anna's/W (S)
Antica Pizz./W
Antonello/OC
Basix Cafe/LA
Berri's Pizza†
Bice†
Bravo Cucina/W
Bric/SG
Buca di Beppo†(S)
Ca'Brea/LA (N)
Ca' del Sole/SF (N)
Café Med†
Cafe Misto/W
Caffe Citron/SG (N)
Caffe Delfini/W
Caffe Pinguini/W (N)
C & O Tratt./W (S)
Capo/W
Capriccio/OC
Carmine's/SG (S)
Casa Bianca/SG (S)
Celestino/SG
Celestino Ital./LA
Chianti/LA (N)
Chianti Cucina/LA (N)
Christy's/SB
Ciao Tratt./LA (N)
Cicada/LA (N)
Coral Tree/W
Dan Tana's/LA
Da Pasquale/W (N)
De Mori/W
Dino's Italian/SG
Di Stefano/W
Divino/W (N)
Dolce/OC
Dolce Enoteca/LA
Drago/W
Eurochow/W
Fabiolus Café/LA
Fab's Italian/SF
Farfalla Tratt./LA
Far Niente/SG (N)
Fresco Rist./SG
Fritto Misto†
Galletto/SF
Gennaro's Rist./SG (N)
Giorgio Baldi/W (N)
Girasole/LA (N)
Greco's/SG
Guido's/W (N)
i Cugini/W
Il Boccaccio/SB

Il Buco/W
Il Capriccio/LA
Il Cielo/W
Il Fornaio†
Il Forno/W
Il Grano/W
Il Moro/W (N)
Il Pastaio/W
Impresario/LA
Jacopo's†
Johnnie's NY Pizz.†
Jones Hollywood/LA
La Bottega Marino†
La Bruschetta/W
La Finestra/SF
La Loggia/SF (N)
La Luna/LA (N)
La Pergola/SF (N)
La Scala/W (N)
La Scala Presto/W
La Vecchia/W (N)
Locanda del Lago/W (N)
Locanda Veneta/LA (N)
L'Opera/SB
Louise's Tratt.†
Luciana's/OC
Lunaria/W
Madeo/LA (N)
Maggiano's†(S)
Mama D's/SB
Mama Rose/OC
Marcello Tusc./SB (N)
Maria's Italian†(S)
Marino/LA
Market City/SF
Mascarpone's/OC (N)
Matteo's/W
Matteo's Hoboken/W (S)
Mazzarino's/SF (S)
Miceli's†
Mi Piace†
Mulberry St. Rist./OC
Naples Rist./OC (S)
Nicola's Kitchen/SF
Old Spag. Factory/OC
Olive Garden†
Orso/LA (N)
Osteria Nonni/LA (S)
Pace/LA
Padri/SF
Palermo/LA (S)
Pammolli/W (N)
Pane e Vino/LA (N)
Paolo's Rist./OC (N)
Pastina/W
Pat & Oscar's/SB
Pat's/LA

get updates at zagat.com

Cuisine Index

Pedals/W
Peppino's/OC
Peppone/W (N)
Petrelli's Steakhse./W
Piatti/SF
Piccolo Paradiso/W
Pizzicotto/W
Posto/SF
Pregot(N)
Prizzi's Piazza/LA
Rist. Mamma Gina/OC (N)
Romano's†
Roma via Paris/SF
Rosti†(N)
San Gennaro/W
Sisley Ital. Kit.†
Spaghettini/OC
Spark Woodfire†
Sprazzo Cuc. Ital./W
Spumante/SF
Stinking Rose/W
Tanino/W (S)
Tesoro Tratt./LA (N)
Ti Amo/OC
Toscana/W (N)
Tra Di Noi/W
Trastevere†(S)
Trattoria Amici/W (N)
Tre Venezie/SG (N)
Trio Rist./SG
Tulipano/SG
Tuscany II Rist./SF
Tutto Fresco/OC (N)
Tutto Mare/OC
Valentino/W
Vessia Rist./OC (S)
Via Veneto/W
Villa Nova/OC
Villa Piacere/SF
Vincenti/W
Vitello's/SF
Vito/W
Vittorio/W (S)
Yves' Bistro/OC
Zita Tratt./LA
Zucca/LA

Japanese
(* sushi specialist)

Abe/OC*
Asahi Ramen/W
Asakuma/W*
Asanebo/SF*
Asuka/W*
Benihana†
Bistro 21/LA
Cafe Sushi/LA*
Crazy Fish/W*
Gyu-kaku/W
Hamasaku/W*
Hama Sushi/W*
Hayakawa/SG*
Hibachi Steak/OC
Hide Sushi/W*
Hirosuke/SF*
Hirozen/LA*
Hump, The/W*
Ichibiri/OC*
Iroha/SF*
Ita-Cho/LA*
Kamiyama/SB*
Katana/LA*
Katsu-ya/SF*
Madame Wu's/LA*
Maison Akira/SG
Matsuhisa/W*
Mishima†*
Miyagi's/LA*
Momoyama/SB*
Mori Sushi/W*
Mountain View/SG*
Musha†*
Nishimura/LA*
Nobu Malibu/W*
Omino Sushi/SF*
O-Nami†*
Pearl Dragon/W*
R-23/LA*
Sawtelle Kit./W
Shabu Shabu/LA
Shabu 2/W
Sushi Masu/W*
Sushi Mon/LA*
Sushi Nozawa/SF*
Sushi Roku†*
Sushi Sasabune/W*
Taiko†*
Taiko Jap./OC*
Takao/W*
Tama Sushi/SF*
Tengu/W*
Teru Sushi/SF*
Thousand Cranes/LA*
Todai†*
Torafuku/W*
Tsuji No Hana/W*
Tsukiji/SB*
Ubon/LA
U-Zen/W*
Wabi-Sabi/W*
Wasa/OC*
Wokcano/LA*
Yabu†*
Yoshida/SG*

Cuisine Index

Korean
BCD Tofu Hse.†
Gyu-kaku/W
La Korea/LA
Manna/LA
Nak Won/LA
Seoul Jung/LA
Soot Bull Jeep/LA
Woo Lae Oak†
Yi Dynasty/OC

Lebanese
Carnival/SF
Marouch/LA

Malaysian
Nonya/SG

Mediterranean
Aioli/SB
A.O.C./LA
Beau Rivage/W
Berri's Pizza†
Blue Pyramid/SG
Burger Contin./SG
Café Mundial/SG
Cafe Santorini/SG
Campanile/LA
Catal Rest./OC
Christine/SB
Cravings/LA
Fitness Pizza/OC
Flora Kitchen/LA
Gardens/W
Granita/W
Lavande/W
Opaline/LA
Palomino/W
Pavilion/OC
Picayo/OC
Primitivo Wine/W
Reg. Bev. Wilshire/W
Rosine's/OC
Sorrento Grille/OC
Splashes/OC
Studio/OC
Sunset Room/LA
Ti Amo/OC
Trio Med. Grill/SB
Wild Artichoke/OC
Zazou/SB
Zov's Bistro/OC

Mexican
Antonio's/LA
Babita/SG
Baja Fresh†
Border Grill†
Cafe El Cholo/OC
Casa Antigua/W
Casablanca/W
Casa Vega/SF
Chevys†
Cozymel's/SB
El Cholo†
El Coyote/LA
El Dorado/W
El Tepeyac†
El Texate/W
El Torito†
El Torito Grill†
Guelaguetza/W
Javier's/OC
Kay 'n Dave's/W
La Parrilla/LA
La Salsa†
Las Brisas/OC
La Serenata/Garibaldi†
La Serenata Gourmet/W
Lotería! Grill/LA
Mexicali/SF
Mexico City/LA
Mi Ranchito/W
Monte Alban/W
Pacifico's/W
Paco's Tacos†
Poquito Mas†
Señor Fred/SF
Sharky's Mex. Grill†
SolyAzul/SG
Spanish Kitchen/LA
Taco Loco/OC
Taco Mesa/OC
Tlapazola Grill/W
Tortilla Flats/OC

Middle Eastern
Falafel King/W
Moishe's/LA
Noura Cafe/LA
Sunnin/W
Tempo/SF
Wahib's/SG

Moroccan
Casbah Cafe/LA
Chameau/LA
Dar Maghreb/LA
Koutoubia/W
Marrakesh/SF

Nepalese
Tibet Nepal/SG

New Zealand
Turner New Zeal./OC

get updates at zagat.com

Cuisine Index

Noodle Shops
Asahi Ramen/W
Mandarin Deli†
Mishima†
Pho Café/LA
Pho 79†
Ubon/LA
Yabu†

Nuevo Latino
Alegria/SB
Ciudad/LA
La Boca del Conga/LA
Mojo/W
Rebecca's/W
Xiomara/SG

Pacific Rim
Cafe Blanc/W
Cafe Del Rey/W
Savoury's/OC

Pan-Asian
Buddha's Belly/LA
Monsoon Cafe/W
Pei Wei Asian/OC
Red Pearl Kit./OC
Sensasian/OC
Thaifoon/OC
Typhoon/W
Wokcano/LA
Zen Grill†

Persian
Darya/OC
Javan/W
Kabob & Chinese†
Shaherzad/W

Peruvian
El Pollo Inka†
Inka Grill†
Mario's Peruvian/LA

Pizza
Abbot's Pizza/W
Allegria/W
Alto Palato/LA
Antica Pizz./W
Berri's Pizza†
BJ's†
Bravo Cucina/W
Caioti Pizza/SF
California Piz. Kit.†
Carmine's/SG
Casa Bianca/SG
Cheebo/LA
D'Amore's Pizza†
Farfalla Tratt./LA
Frankie & Johnnie's†
Granita/W
Jacopo's†
Johnnie's NY Pizz.†
Lamonica's Pizza/W
La Scala Presto/W
Mazzarino's/SF
Mulberry St. Pizz.†
Naples Rist./OC
Orso/LA
Palermo/LA
Parkway Grill/SG
Peppino's/OC
Prizzi's Piazza/LA
Spago/W
Spark Woodfire/SF
Steelhead Brew. Co./OC
Tra Di Noi/W
Village Pizz./LA
Vitello's/SF
Wolfgang Pk. Cafe†

Polish
Warszawa/W

Pub Food
Belmont Brew./SB
Brewski's/SB
Father's Office/W
Gordon Biersch†
Heroes B&G/OC
Olde Ship/OC
Outlaws B&G/W
Steelhead Brew. Co./OC
Tom Bergin's/LA
Whale & Ale/SB
Ye Olde King's/W

Russian
Diaghilev/LA

Sandwiches
Art's Deli/SF
Barney Greengrass/W
Brent's Deli/SF
Canter's/LA
Factor's Deli/LA
Greenblatt's Deli/LA
Jody Maroni's†
Johnnie's Pastrami/W
Junior's/W
Langer's Deli/LA
Lawry's Carvery/OC
Nate 'n Al's/W
Noah's NY Bagels†
Philippe/Original/LA
Roll 'n Rye Deli/W
Sandbag's/W

Cuisine Index

Seafood
ABC Seafood/LA
Aqua/OC
Arches/OC
Balboa/LA
Ballona Fish/W
Bluewater Grill†
Bungalow/OC
Cannery Sea./OC
Casablanca/W
Catch/OC
Chart House†
Chez Jay/W
Chimayo/Beach/OC
Claes/OC
Crab Cooker/OC
Delmonico's Lobster/SF
Delmonico's Sea.†
Empress Harbor/SG
Enterprise Fish/W
Fins/SF
Fish Market/OC
Fonz's/SB
Galley/W
Gladstone's Malibu/W
Gladstone's Univ./SF
Gulfstream/OC
Gulfstream/W
Hop Woo/W
i Cugini/W
Joe's Crab Shack†
JR Seafood/W
Khoury's/SB
Killer Shrimp†
Kincaid's/SB
King's Fish Hse.†
La Cave/OC
Las Brisas/OC
Lobster/W
Madison/SB
Malibu Seafood/W
McCorm. & Schmick's†
Menemsha/W
Mon Kee's/LA
NBC Seafood/SG
Neptune's Net/W
Ocean Ave./W
Ocean Seafood/LA
Odyssey/SF
Opah/OC
Original Fish Co./OC
Pacifico's/W
Reel Inn/W
Rock 'N Fish/SB
Royal Star/W
Rusty Pelican/OC
Savannah Chop/OC
Scott's Seafood/OC
Sea Empress/SB
Seafood Paradise/OC
Sea Harbour/SG
Seashell/SF
Sharky's Mex. Grill†
Tidal Wave/SG
Tutto Mare/OC
21 Oceanfront/OC
22nd St. Landing/SB
230 Forest/OC
V.I.P. Harbor/W
Walt's Wharf/OC
Water Grill/LA

Soul Food
Memphis/OC
Roscoe's Hse.†

Southern
Aunt Kizzy's/W
House of Blues/LA
Johnny Rebs'/SB
Kokomo Cafe/LA
Les Sisters/SF
Lucille's†
Memphis/OC
Pig, The/LA
Ralph Brennan's/OC
Ramos House/OC
Reign/W
Roscoe's Hse.†
Shenandoah Cafe/SB

Southwestern
Authentic Cafe/LA
Chimayo/Beach/OC
Coyote Cantina/SB
Jinky's†
Sonora Cafe/LA

Spanish
(* tapas specialist)
Black Sheep/OC
Cobra Lily/W*
Cobras & Matadors/LA*
La Paella/LA*

Steakhouses
Arches/OC
Arnie Morton's†
Arroyo Chop/SG
Balboa/LA
Benihana†
Buggy Whip/SB
Bungalow/OC
Carlito's Gardel/LA
Catch/OC

get updates at zagat.com 289

Cuisine Index

Celestino Ital./LA
Chart House†
Chez Jay/W
Damon's Steak./SG
De Lacey's Club/SG
Delmonico's Sea.†
Derby/SG
555 East/SB
Fleming's Prime†
Fonz's/SB
Galley/W
Hibachi Steak/OC
Hillmont/LA
Kincaid's/SB
La Cave/OC
Lawry's/W
Madison/SB
Mastro's Steak./W
Monty's Steak.†
Morels French/LA
Morton's Steak./OC
Nick & Stef's/LA
Outback Steakhse.†
Pacific Din. Car†
Palm/LA
Petrelli's Steakhse./W
Porterhouse/W
Rock 'N Fish/SB
Ruth's Chris†
Saddle Ranch/LA
Salt Creek†
Savannah Chop/OC
Smoke House/SF
Taylor's Prime†
Trabuco Oaks/OC

Swedish
Back Pocket/OC
Gustaf Anders/OC

Swiss
Basilic/OC

Tex-Mex
Marix Tex Mex†

Thai
Bangkok Four/OC
Chan Dara†
Chao Krung/LA
Cholada/W
Jitlada/LA
Menjin/LA
Natalee/W
Palms Thai/LA
Rambutan Thai/LA
Royal Thai/OC
Saladang/SG
Talesai†
Thai Dishes†
Thaifoon/OC
Thai This/OC
Tommy Tang's/LA
Tuk Tuk Thai/LA

Tibetan
Tibet Nepal/SG

Tunisian
Moun of Tunis/LA

Uzebekistani
Uzbekistan/LA

Vegan
Juliano's Raw/W

Vegetarian
Astro Burger†
Juliano's Raw/W
Kung Pao†
Real Food Daily†

Vietnamese
Crustacean/W
Golden Deli/SG
Le Saigon/W
Michelia/LA
Pho Bac Huynh/W
Pho Café/LA
Pho 79†
Red Moon Cafe/W
Thanh My/OC

Yemenite
Magic Carpet/LA

Location Index

LOCATIONS

LOS ANGELES/HOLLYWOOD/WEST HOLLYWOOD

Atwater Village
Osteria Nonni
Tam O'Shanter

Beverly Center
Arnie Morton's
California Piz. Kit.
Grand Lux
Hard Rock Cafe
Hirozen
Ivy
Jan's
JAR
King's Road Cafe
Newsroom Café
P.F. Chang's
Real Food Daily
Sushi Mon
Todai
Ubon

Beverlywood/ Pico-Robertson
Delmonico's Sea.
Factor's Deli
Kabob & Chinese
Louise's Tratt.
Magic Carpet
Mäni's Bakery
Milky Way
Pat's
Tuk Tuk Thai

Boyle Heights
La Serenata/Garibaldi

Chinatown
ABC Seafood
Asian Noodles
Chow Fun
Empress Pavilion
Hop Li
Mandarin Deli
Mon Kee's
Ocean Seafood
Philippe/Original
Pho 79
Yang Chow

Downtown
Angelique Cafe
Arnie Morton's
Barbara's/Brew.
BCD Tofu Hse.
Cafe Pinot
California Piz. Kit.
Checkers
Ciao Tratt.
Cicada
Ciudad
Cole's P.E. Buffet
Engine Co. No. 28
410 Boyd
Impresario
Johnnie's NY Pizz.
Koo Koo Roo
Langer's Deli
La Parrilla
La Salsa
McCorm. & Schmick's
Nick & Stef's
Noé
Original Pantry Bak.
Original Pantry Cafe
Otto's
Pacific Din. Car
Palm
Patinette Cafe
Pete's Cafe
Prego
R-23
Seoul Jung
Standard
Tesoro Tratt.
Traxx
Water Grill
Windows
Wokcano
Zita Tratt.
Zucca

East LA
El Tepeyac
La Parrilla

Echo Park/Silver Lake
Casbah Cafe
Chameau
Edendale Grill
Kitchen
Mimi's Cafe
Pho Café
Rambutan Thai
Taix French
Tantra
Tommy's

Fairfax
Authentic Cafe
Buddha's Belly

get updates at zagat.com

Location Index

Cafe Sushi
Cafe Tartine
California Ckn.
Canter's
Chao Krung
Cobras & Matadors
Du-par's
El Coyote
EM Bistro
Farm of Bev. Hills
Genghis Cohen
Grace
Gumbo Pot
India's Oven
Ita-Cho
Johnnie's NY Pizz.
Johnny Rockets
Kokomo Cafe
La Korea
Lotería! Grill
Madame Wu's
Maggiano's
Menjin
Mimosa
Moishe's
Monsieur Marcel
Morels First Floor
Morels French
Opaline
Pane e Vino
Pastis
Swingers
Ulysses Voyage
Wokcano
Wood Ranch BBQ

Hancock Park

Chan Dara
Girasole
Koo Koo Roo
La Bottega Marino
La Luna
Le Petit Greek
Louise's Tratt.
Noah's NY Bagels
Prado
Village Pizz.

Hollywood

Ammo
Bice
Cafe des Artistes
California Piz. Kit.
Carousel
Chan Dara
Cheebo
Cinespace
Dar Maghreb
Dolce Enoteca
Fabiolus Café
Feinstein's
Greenblatt's Deli
Griddle Cafe
Grill on Hollywood
Hamburger Hamlet
Hillmont
Hollywood Canteen
Hollywood Hills
House, The
In-N-Out Burger
Jitlada
Johnny Rockets
Les Deux Cafés
Marino
Mario's Peruvian
Marouch
Mel's Drive-In
Miceli's
Moun of Tunis
Musso & Frank
Off Vine
Paladar
Palms Thai
Patina
Pig 'n' Whistle
Pinot Hollywood
Prizzi's Piazza
Roscoe's Hse.
Sharky's Mex. Grill
Sunset Room
Trastevere
Uzbekistan
Vert
White Lotus
Yamashiro
Zankou Ckn.

Koreatown

BCD Tofu Hse.
Cassell's
El Cholo
Manna
Nak Won
Papa Cristo's
Soot Bull Jeep
Taylor's Prime
Woo Lae Oak

La Brea

Angelini Osteria
Ca'Brea
Campanile
Flora Kitchen
Pig, The
Pink's Chili Dogs
Sonora Cafe

Location Index

La Cienega/Robertson
Baja Fresh
Daily Grill
Johnny Rockets

Little Tokyo
Mandarin Deli
Shabu Shabu
Thousand Cranes

Los Feliz
Cafe Stella
Cha Cha Cha
Chi Dynasty
Electric Lotus
Farfalla Tratt.
Figaro Brass.
Fred 62
Il Capriccio
La Parrilla
Louise's Tratt.
Mexico City
Palermo
vermont

Melrose
Alessi Rist.
Alex
Anarkali
Angeli Caffe
Antonio's
Carlito's Gardel
Chianti
Chianti Cucina
Fabiolus Café
Johnny Rockets
Louise's Tratt.
Moustache Café
Tommy Tang's

Mid-City
Harold & Belle's
India's Tandoori
Koo Koo Roo
Nyala Ethiopian
Roscoe's Hse.
Versailles

Mid-Wilshire
La Boca del Conga

Miracle Mile
Caffe Latte
Pentimento
Toast Bakery
Tom Bergin's

Third Street (bet. Robertson & La Brea)
A.O.C.
Barefoot B&G
Berri's Pizza
California Wok
Cynthia's
Doughboys
G. Garvin's
Linq
Little Door
Locanda Veneta
Michelia
Mishima
Orso
Sofi
Souplantation
Surya India
Sushi Roku
Zen Grill

West Hollywood
Ago
Alto Palato
Asia de Cuba
Astro Burger
Balboa
Barfly
Bar Marmont
Basix Cafe
Bastide
Belly
Bistro 21
Bliss
Bourbon St.
Cadillac Cafe
Café Med
Celestino Ital.
Chaya Brass.
Chin Chin
Clafoutis
Cravings
Dan Tana's
Diaghilev
Duke's Coffee
Du-par's
Fat Fish
Fenix/Argyle
Flavor of India
Formosa Cafe
Frankie & Johnnie's
Gaucho Grill
Hamburger Hamlet
House of Blues
Hugo's
Jacopo's
Jones Hollywood

Location Index

Katana
Kinara Cafe
Koi
Koo Koo Roo
Kung Pao
La Boheme
La Paella
Le Pain Quot.
Le Petit Bistro
Le Petit Four
Lola's
L'Orangerie
Lucques
Madeo
Mandarette
Marix Tex Mex
Mel's Drive-In

Mirabelle
Miyagi's
Morton's
Nishimura
Noura Cafe
Pace
Palm
Poquito Mas
Saddle Ranch
Sona
Spanish Kitchen
Standard
Sweet Lady Jane
Talesai
Urth Caffé
Wolfgang Pk. Cafe
Yabu

THE WESTSIDE

Bel Air
Bel-Air B&G
Bel-Air Hotel
Four Oaks

Beverly Hills
Airstream Diner
Asakuma
Avenue
Baja Fresh
Barney Greengrass
Belvedere
Benihana
Berri's Pizza
Blue on Blue
Bombay Palace
Brass. des Artistes
Brighton Coffee
Cafe Blanc
California Piz. Kit.
Cheesecake Fact.
Chin Chin
Cobra Lily
Crazy Fish
Crustacean
Da Pasquale
De Mori
El Torito Grill
Farm of Bev. Hills
Frankie & Johnnie's
French Country
Gardens
Grill
Hamburger Hamlet
Il Buco
Il Cielo
Il Fornaio
Il Pastaio

Islands
Jaan
Jacopo's
Johnnie's NY Pizz.
Johnny Rockets
Kate Mantilini
Koo Koo Roo
La Salsa
La Scala
Lawry's
Le Pain Quot.
Mako
Mandarin
Manhattan Wonton
Maple Drive
Mastro's Steak.
Matsuhisa
McCorm. & Schmick's
Mr. Chow
Mulberry St. Pizz.
Natalee
Nate 'n Al's
Nic's
Pammolli
Piccolo Paradiso
Polo Lounge
Porterhouse
Prego
Real Food Daily
Reg. Bev. Wilshire
Reign
RJ's Rib Joint
Rosti
Ruth's Chris
Sandbag's
Spago
Stinking Rose

Location Index

Talesai
Tony Roma's
Trader Vic's
Trattoria Amici
Woo Lae Oak
Xi'an
Zen Grill

Brentwood

A Votre Sante
Baja Fresh
Barney's Hamburger
Brentwood Rest.
Cheesecake Fact.
Chin Chin
Clay Pit
Coral Tree
Daily Grill
Divino
El Dorado
Gaucho Grill
Getty Ctr.
Hamburger Hamlet
Koo Koo Roo
La Salsa
La Scala Presto
Le Pain Quot.
Louise's Tratt.
Noah's NY Bagels
Peppone
Pizzicotto
Reddi Chick
Sandbag's
San Gennaro
Souplantation
Taiko
Takao
Toscana
Vincenti
Zax
Zeidler's Café

Century City

Breeze
Clementine
Encore
Gulfstream
Houston's
Jody Maroni's
Johnnie's NY Pizz.
Johnny Rockets
La Cachette
Lunaria

Culver City

In-N-Out Burger
Jody Maroni's
Johnnie's Pastrami
Johnny Rockets
JR's BBQ
La Dijonaise
Mi Ranchito
Pacifico's
Petrelli's Steakhse.
Roll 'n Rye Deli
San Gennaro
Thai Dishes

Malibu

Allegria
Beau Rivage
Bob Morris'
Chart House
Cholada
D'Amore's Pizza
Duke's Mal./Hunt.
Geoffrey's
Granita
Gray Whale
Guido's
Johnnie's NY Pizz.
Malibu Seafood
Marmalade Café
Moonshadows
Neptune's Net
Nobu Malibu
Reel Inn
Taverna Tony
Thai Dishes
Tra Di Noi

Marina del Rey

Akbar
Alejo's
Antica Pizz.
Asakuma
Aunt Kizzy's
Baja Fresh
Ballona Fish
Benny's BBQ
Cafe Del Rey
C & O Tratt.
Chan Dara
Chart House
Cheesecake Fact.
Chin Chin
El Torito
Islands
Johnnie's NY Pizz.
Killer Shrimp
Marguerite
Noah's NY Bagels
Ruby's
Souplantation
Tony P's Dockside

get updates at zagat.com 295

Location Index

Tsuji No Hana
26 Beach Café

Mar Vista
Paco's Tacos

Pacific Palisades
A La Tarte
Cafe Misto
Gladstone's Malibu
Jacopo's
Kay 'n Dave's
Mort's Deli
Pearl Dragon
Vittorio

Palms
Bamboo
Cafe Brasil
Guelaguetza
Hu's Szechwan
Indo Cafe
Natalee
Versailles

Playa del Rey
Berri's Pizza
Caffe Pinguini
Chloe
Outlaws B&G
Shack

Rancho Park
John O'Groats

Santa Monica
Abbot's Pizza
Akbar
Babalu
Back on the Bch.
Beach House
Benihana
Bistro 31
Blueberry
Border Grill
Bravo Cucina
Broadway Deli
Buca di Beppo
Buffalo Club
Café Bizou
Cafe Montana
Caffe Delfini
California Ckn.
California Piz. Kit.
Capo
Cézanne
Cha Cha Ckn.
Chez Jay
Chez Mimi
Chinois/Main
Cora's Coffee
Crocodile Café
Drago
El Cholo
El Texate
Enterprise Fish
Falafel King
Father's Office
Fritto Misto
Fromin's Rest.
Galley
Gate of India
Gaucho Grill
Giorgio Baldi
Houston's
Hump, The
i Cugini
Il Fornaio
Il Forno
Ivy/ Shore
Jinky's
JiRaffe
Johnnie's NY Pizz.
Johnny Rockets
Josie Rest.
Juliano's Raw
Kay 'n Dave's
Knoll's Black Forest
Koo Koo Roo
L.A. Farm
La Salsa
La Serenata/Garibaldi
Lavande
La Vecchia
Le Marmiton
Le Petit Café
Lobster
Locanda del Lago
Louise's Tratt.
Mäni's Bakery
Marix Tex Mex
Marmalade Café
Mélisse
Michael's
Monsoon Cafe
Musha
Nawab of India
Newsroom Café
Noah's NY Bagels
Ocean Ave.
Oceanfront
One Pico
Pacific Din. Car
Patrick's Road.
Pedals
P.F. Chang's
Rae's

subscribe to zagat.com

Location Index

Real Food Daily
Rebecca's
Reel Inn
Röckenwagner
Rosti
Royal Star
Schatzi on Main
17th St. Cafe
Shabu 2
Shack
Sushi Roku
Swingers
Thai Dishes
Trastevere
Typhoon
Union
Valentino
Via Veneto
Vito
Warszawa
Whist
Wolfgang Pk. Cafe
Ye Olde King's

Topanga
Inn/Seventh Ray

Venice
Abbot's Pizza
Amuse Café
Axe
Cafe '50s
Canal Club
Casablanca
Chaya Venice
5 Dudley
Globe Venice Bch.
Hal's B&G
Hama Sushi
James' Beach
Jody Maroni's
Joe's
Koo Koo Roo
Lilly's French Cafe
Maxwell's Cafe
Menemsha
Primitivo Wine
Rose Cafe
26 Beach Café
Wabi-Sabi

West LA
All India Café
Anna's
Apple Pan
Asahi Ramen
Asakuma
Bandera
Billingsley's
Bombay Cafe
Bourbon St.
Cafe '50s
California Ckn.
California Wok
Casa Antigua
Chan Dara
Chung King
El Pollo Inka
Feast from East
Gardens/Glendon
Guido's
Gyu-kaku
Hamasaku
Hamburger Hamlet
Hide Sushi
Hop Li
Hop Woo
Il Grano
Il Moro
India's Oven
India's Tandoori
Islands
Jack Sprat's
Jacopo's
Javan
Jimmy's Tavern
Johnnie's NY Pizz.
JR Seafood
Junior's
Kabob & Chinese
Koo Koo Roo
Koutoubia
La Bottega Marino
La Salsa
La Serenata Gourmet
Le Petit Bistro
Le Saigon
Literati Café
Matteo's
Matteo's Hoboken
Mishima
Monte Alban
Mori Sushi
Mr. Cecil's
Nizam
Olive Garden
Pastina
Pho Bac Huynh
Poquito Mas
Red Moon Cafe
Sawtelle Kit.
Sisley Ital. Kit.
Sushi Masu
Sushi Sasabune
Tlapazola Grill

get updates at zagat.com

Location Index

Tony Roma's
Torafuku
2117
U-Zen
V.I.P. Harbor
Yabu

Westwood
Asuka
Baja Fresh
BJ's
Bombay Bite
California Piz. Kit.
Delphi Greek
Di Stefano
Eurochow
Falafel King
In-N-Out Burger
La Bruschetta
Lamonica's Pizza
La Salsa
Mojo
Moustache Café
Napa Valley Grille
Noah's NY Bagels
Palomino
Sandbag's
Shaherzad
Soleil Westwood
South Street
Sprazzo Cuc. Ital.
Sunnin
Tanino
Tengu

THE SOUTH BAY AND LONG BEACH

Bellflower
Johnny Rebs'

Cerritos
Mimi's Cafe
Olive Garden
Romano's
Todai

Downey
In-N-Out Burger
Mimi's Cafe
Olive Garden

El Segundo
Cozymel's
Daily Grill
Fleming's Prime
McCorm. & Schmick's
P.F. Chang's
Taiko
Thai Dishes

Gardena
Bistro Laramie
El Pollo Inka
Sea Empress
Tsukiji

Hawthorne
El Torito

Hermosa Beach
Blue Pacific
Brewski's
El Pollo Inka
Fritto Misto
Il Boccaccio
Jackson's Village
Martha's 22nd St.
Ragin' Cajun

Lakewood
In-N-Out Burger
Outback Steakhse.
Souplantation

Lawndale
El Pollo Inka

LAX
Daily Grill
El Cholo
Encounter
Jody Maroni's
Ruby's

Lomita
Kamiyama

Long Beach
Alegria
Baja Fresh
Belmont Brew.
BJ's
Christy's
Claim Jumper
El Torito
555 East
Frenchy's Bistro
Green Field Churr.
Inka Grill
In-N-Out Burger
Joe's Crab Shack
Johnny Rebs'
Johnny Rockets
Khoury's
King's Fish Hse.
La Salsa
Lasher's
L'Opera

Location Index

Lucille's
Madison
Mimi's Cafe
Roscoe's Hse.
Shenandoah Cafe
Sir Winston's
Sky Room
Yard House

Manhattan Beach
Back Home/Lahaina
Bora Bora
Cafe Pierre
California Piz. Kit.
Fonz's
Francesca
Houston's
Il Fornaio
Islands
Johnny Rockets
Kamiyama
Koo Koo Roo
LA Food Show
Mama D's
Michi
Noah's NY Bagels
Olive Garden
Reed's
Rock 'N Fish
Thai Dishes
Towne
Uncle Bill's Pancake
Versailles

Palos Verdes Peninsula/Rolling Hills
Marmalade Café
Ruby's
Trio Med. Grill

Redondo Beach
Addi's Tandoor
Bluewater Grill
Buca di Beppo
Chart House
Cheesecake Fact.
Chez Melange
Coyote Cantina
El Torito

Gina Lee's
In-N-Out Burger
Joe's Crab Shack
Kincaid's
Koo Koo Roo
La Brea Bakery
La Salsa
Momoyama
Ruby's
Thai Dishes
Zazou

San Pedro
In-N-Out Burger
Marcello Tusc.
Papadakis Tav.
22nd St. Landing
Whale & Ale

Torrance
Aioli
BCD Tofu Hse.
Benihana
Christine
Claim Jumper
Depot
El Pollo Inka
El Torito Grill
In-N-Out Burger
Islands
Koo Koo Roo
Loft
Lucille's
Mimi's Cafe
Mishima
Misto Caffe
Musha
Olive Garden
O-Nami
Outback Steakhse.
Pat & Oscar's
Romano's
Souplantation

Westchester
Alejo's
Buggy Whip
In-N-Out Burger
Paco's Tacos

THE SAN FERNANDO VALLEY AND BURBANK

Agoura Hills/Oak Park
Hamburger Hamlet
Leila's
Maria's Italian
Padri
Wood Ranch BBQ

Burbank
Arnie Morton's
Baja Fresh
BJ's
California Piz. Kit.
Castaway

Location Index

Chevys
Chili John's
Crocodile Café
Daily Grill
El Torito
Gordon Biersch
India's Tandoori
In-N-Out Burger
Islands
Johnny Rockets
Koo Koo Roo
Market City
Mi Piace
Mo's
Olive Garden
Outback Steakhse.
Picanha Churr.
Poquito Mas
Ribs USA
Smoke House
Tony Roma's

Calabasas
Fins
King's Fish Hse.
Marmalade Café
Mi Piace
Saddle Peak

Camarillo
Tony Roma's
Wood Ranch BBQ

Canoga Park
D'Amore's Pizza
Yang Chow

Chatsworth
Les Sisters
Mimi's Cafe
Olive Garden
Omino Sushi

Encino
Benihana
Buca di Beppo
California Ckn.
California Wok
Cha Cha Cha Encino
Chevys
Chin Chin
D'Amore's Pizza
Delmonico's Lobster
El Torito
Fromin's Rest.
Hirosuke
Islands
Johnny Rockets
Koo Koo Roo

Maria's Italian
Mulberry St. Pizz.
Rosti
Stevie's Creole
Tempo
Tony Roma's
Versailles

Granada Hills/Mission Hills
Odyssey

Moorpark
Wood Ranch BBQ

North Hollywood
Barsac Brasserie
Ca' del Sole
In-N-Out Burger
Poquito Mas

Northridge
Brent's Deli
California Ckn.
Claim Jumper
El Torito
In-N-Out Burger
Mandarin Deli
Maria's Italian
Outback Steakhse.
Romano's
Sharky's Mex. Grill
Souplantation
Wood Ranch BBQ

Santa Clarita
In-N-Out Burger
Mimi's Cafe
Outback Steakhse.
Romano's

Saugus/Newhall
Le Chêne

Sherman Oaks
August Chris
Bamboo Inn
Café Bizou
Cafe '50s
Carnival
Casa Vega
Cheesecake Fact.
D'Amore's Pizza
Fab's Italian
Great Greek
Hamburger Hamlet
In-N-Out Burger
Jinky's
Johnnie's NY Pizz.
Kung Pao

Location Index

La Fondue
La Frite
La Pergola
La Salsa
Le Petit Bistro
Maria's Italian
Marmalade Café
Max Rest.
Mazzarino's
Mel's Drive-In
Mistral
Mr. Cecil's
Noah's NY Bagels
P.F. Chang's
Posto
Prego
Rive Gauche
Señor Fred
Sharky's Mex. Grill
Sisley Ital. Kit.
Stanley's

Studio City
Art's Deli
Asanebo
Baja Fresh
Bistro Gdn./Coldwtr.
Caioti Pizza
California Piz. Kit.
Chin Chin
Daily Grill
Du-par's
Emmanuel
Firefly
Gaucho Grill
Hugo's
Iroha
Katsu-ya
Killer Shrimp
Koo Koo Roo
Kung Pao
La Loggia
La Salsa
Louise's Tratt.
Marrakesh
Mazzarino's
Mexicali
Out Take Cafe
Pinot Bistro
Poquito Mas
Spark Woodfire
Spumante
Sushi Nozawa
Talesai
Tama Sushi
Teru Sushi
Todai

Tournesol
Vitello's
Wine Bistro

Tarzana
El Torito
India's Tandoori
La Finestra
Paul's Cafe
Sharky's Mex. Grill

Thousand Oaks
Cheesecake Fact.
D'Amore's Pizza
Du-par's
El Torito
Johnny Rockets
Outback Steakhse.
Piatti
Romano's
Sisley Ital. Kit.
2087 Amer. Bistro

Toluca Lake
Koo Koo Roo

Universal City
Buca di Beppo
Cafe Tu Tu
Daily Grill
Gladstone's Univ.
Hard Rock Cafe
Jody Maroni's
Miceli's
Roma via Paris
Tony Roma's
Versailles
Wolfgang Pk. Cafe

Valencia
BJ's
Claim Jumper
Hamburger Hamlet
Johnny Rockets
Maria's Italian
Poquito Mas
Salt Creek
Sisley Ital. Kit.
Wood Ranch BBQ

Van Nuys
Billingsley's
Dr. Hogly Wogly's
In-N-Out Burger
Matterhorn Chef
Zankou Ckn.

Westlake Village
Fins
Galletto

Location Index

Mandevilla
Marmalade Café
Rosti
Sharky's Mex. Grill
Tuscany II Rist.

Woodland Hills
Baja Fresh
BJ's
Brandywine
Cheesecake Fact.
El Torito
Gaucho Grill
In-N-Out Burger

Islands
La Frite
Maggiano's
Maria's Italian
Monty's Steak.
Nicola's Kitchen
P.F. Chang's
Ruby's
Seashell
Sharky's Mex. Grill
Todai
Villa Piacere
Wolfgang Pk. Cafe

THE SAN GABRIEL VALLEY AND PASADENA/GLENDALE

Alhambra
Bayou
Cuban Bistro
Diner on Main
In-N-Out Burger
Pho 79
Souplantation
Taste of Manila
Wahib's

Arcadia
BJ's
Carmine's
Derby
In-N-Out Burger
Olive Garden
Outback Steakhse.
Souplantation
Todai
Tony Roma's

Azusa
In-N-Out Burger
Tulipano

City of Industry
Benihana
Claim Jumper
In-N-Out Burger
Mimi's Cafe
Outback Steakhse.
Souplantation
Todai

Claremont
Buca di Beppo

Covina/West Covina
BJ's
Chevys
Green Field Churr.
Hayakawa

In-N-Out Burger
O-Nami
Outback Steakhse.

Eagle Rock
Camilo's
Casa Bianca

Glendale
Blue Pyramid
Carousel
Chevys
Cinnabar
Crocodile Café
Damon's Steak.
Far Niente
Fresco Rist.
Gennaro's Rist.
In-N-Out Burger
Islands
Olive Garden
Panda Inn
Todai
Tony Roma's
Zankou Ckn.

Glendora
El Pollo Inka
In-N-Out Burger

La Cañada Flintridge
Dish
Taylor's Prime

Monrovia
Café Mundial
Caffe Citron
Claim Jumper
Koo Koo Roo
La Parisienne
Mimi's Cafe
Rest. Devon

Location Index

Romano's
Tidal Wave

Montclair
Tony Roma's

Montebello
Astro Burger

Monterey Park
El Tepeyac
Empress Harbor
Lake Spring
Mandarin Deli
NBC Seafood
Ocean Star

Montrose
Bric
Zeke's Smokehse.

Ontario
Chevys

Pasadena
Akbar
All India Café
Arroyo Chop
Baja Fresh
Beckham Grill
Bice
Big Mama's Rib
Bistro 45
Border Grill
Buca di Beppo
Burger Contin.
Cafe Atlantic
Café Bizou
Café Med
Cafe Santorini
California Piz. Kit.
Celestino
Cheesecake Fact.
Crocodile Café
De Lacey's Club
Delmonico's Sea.
Derek's
Dino's Italian
El Cholo
El Torito
Five Sixty-One
Fu-Shing
Gaucho Grill
Gordon Biersch
Greco's
Halie
Hamburger Hamlet
Houston's
Il Fornaio

In-N-Out Burger
Islands
Johnny Rockets
Koo Koo Roo
Louise's Tratt.
Madre's
Maison Akira
Maria's Italian
Marston's
McCorm. & Schmick's
Mi Piace
Monty's Steak.
Noah's NY Bagels
Nonya
Panda Inn
Parkway Grill
P.F. Chang's
Pie 'N Burger
Radhika's
Raymond
Ritz-Carlton Hunt.
Robin's Woodfire
Roscoe's Hse.
Ruby's
Russell's Burgers
Saladang
Scampi
Smitty's Grill
SolyAzul
Souplantation
Sushi Roku
Thai Dishes
Tibet Nepal
Tre Venezie
Twin Palms
Xiomara
Yang Chow
Yujean Kang's
Zankou Ckn.

Pico Rivera
Dal Rae
In-N-Out Burger

Rosemead
In-N-Out Burger
Sea Harbour

San Gabriel
Babita
Golden Deli
Pho 79
Tung Lai Shun

San Marino
Julienne
Trio Rist.
Yoshida

get updates at zagat.com

Location Index

Sierra Madre
Mountain View

South Pasadena
Carmine's
Firefly Bistro
Shiro

Whittier
Magalys
Mimi's Cafe
Olive Garden
Ruby's

ORANGE COUNTY

Aliso Viejo
Baja Fresh
JackShrimp
Opah
Peppino's

Anaheim/Anaheim Hills
Anaheim White
Benihana
Catal Rest.
Catch
Chevys
Hibachi Steak
In-N-Out Burger
Mimi's Cafe
Mr. Stox
Napa Rose
Naples Rist.
Original Pancake Hse.
Ralph Brennan's
Rosine's
Wood Ranch BBQ
Yves' Bistro
Zankou Ckn.

Balboa
Ruby's

Brea
Baja Fresh
California Piz. Kit.
Cedar Creek
Claim Jumper
El Torito Grill
Fitness Pizza
Islands
La Salsa
La Vie en Rose
Lucille's
Outback Steakhse.
Taps

Buena Park
Claim Jumper
In-N-Out Burger
Mrs. Knott's
Outback Steakhse.

Corona Del Mar
Bandera
Bungalow
Five Crowns
Mayur
Oysters
Rothschild's
Ruby's

Costa Mesa
Baja Fresh
Bangkok Four
Cafe Pascal
California Piz. Kit.
Claim Jumper
El Torito Grill
Golden Truffle
Gypsy Den
Habana
Inka Grill
In-N-Out Burger
Koo Koo Roo
La Cave
Lawry's Carvery
Lodge
Maggiano's
Mama Rose
Memphis
Mimi's Cafe
Outback Steakhse.
Pinot Provence
Plums Cafe
Ruby's
Sam Woo's
Scott's Seafood
Side Street
Taco Mesa
Troquet
Turner New Zeal.
Wolfgang Pk. Cafe
Yard House
Yujean Kang's Asian
Z'tejas

Dana Point
Chart House
Gemmell's
Ichibiri

Location Index

Luciana's
Ritz-Carlton Lag. Nig.
Salt Creek
Thai This

Foothill Ranch
In-N-Out Burger
Islands
Natraj
Outback Steakhse.

Fountain Valley
Cafe Plaka
Chevys
Claim Jumper
Islands
Mimi's Cafe

Fullerton
Amazon Churr.
Cellar
Heroes B&G
In-N-Out Burger
Islands
Mulberry St. Rist.
Olde Ship
Old Spag. Factory
Summit House
Table Ten
Tony Roma's

Garden Grove
Five Feet
In-N-Out Burger
Outback Steakhse.
Pho 79

Huntington Beach
Baja Fresh
Californian
Chimayo/Beach
Duke's Mal./Hunt.
Inka Grill
Paolo's Rist.
P.F. Chang's
Prego
Red Pearl Kit.
Ruby's
Sam Woo's
Spark Woodfire
Tony Roma's

Irvine
Baja Fresh
Bistango
Britta's Café
California Piz. Kit.
Chanteclair
Cheesecake Fact.
Chevys
Claim Jumper
Daily Grill
El Cholo
El Torito Grill
Fish Market
Fox Sports Grill
Gulliver's
Houston's
Il Fornaio
In-N-Out Burger
Islands
JackShrimp
Koo Koo Roo
La Salsa
McCorm. & Schmick's
Melting Pot
Mimi's Cafe
Outback Steakhse.
Pei Wei Asian
Ruby's
Ruth's Chris
Sam Woo's
Sensasian
Steelhead Brew. Co.
Taiko Jap.
Thaifoon
Vessia Rist.
Wasa
Wolfgang Pk. Cafe
Yard House

Laguna Beach/
S. Laguna Beach
Cafe Zoolu
Cedar Creek
Claes
Cottage
Dexter's
Dizz's as Is
Five Feet
French 75
Javier's
Las Brisas
Picayo
Royal Thai
Ruby's
Savoury's
Sorrento Grille
Splashes
Studio
Taco Loco
Ti Amo
230 Forest
Woody's/Beach
Zinc Cafe

get updates at zagat.com 305

Location Index

Laguna Hills
Baja Fresh
California Piz. Kit.
Claim Jumper
Gordon Biersch
In-N-Out Burger
Islands
King's Fish Hse.
Natraj
O-Nami
Outback Steakhse.

Laguna Niguel
Baja Fresh
Chevys
In-N-Out Burger
Mimi's Cafe
Peppino's
Savannah Chop
Scott's Seafood

La Habra
Cafe El Cholo
Cat & Custard

Lake Forest
Inka Grill
Mimi's Cafe
Peppino's

Los Alamitos
Original Fish Co.
Tony Roma's

Mission Viejo
California Piz. Kit.
Capriccio
Cheesecake Fact.
Claim Jumper
El Torito Grill
Islands
Peppino's
P.F. Chang's
Ruby's
Taco Mesa
Tortilla Flats

Monarch Beach
Aqua
Mirabeau
Motif

Newport Beach
Abe
Accents
Arches
Aubergine
Basilic
Bayside
Benihana
Bluewater Grill
California Piz. Kit.
Cannery Sea.
Chart House
Cheesecake Fact.
Crab Cooker
Daily Grill
Dolce
El Torito Grill
Fleming's Prime
Gulfstream
JackShrimp
Joe's Crab Shack
La Salsa
Muldoons Irish
Old Spag. Factory
Pascal
Pavilion
Pescadou
P.F. Chang's
Ragin' Cajun
Rist. Mamma Gina
Ritz Rest.
Roy's
Rusty Pelican
Sage
Thaifoon
Tommy Bahama's
Tutto Mare
21 Oceanfront
Villa Nova
Wolfgang Pk. Cafe
Yi Dynasty

Newport Coast
Grill at Pelican Hill

Orange
Cafe Tu Tu
Citrus City
Hobbit
Islands
Jody Maroni's
King's Fish Hse.
Mascarpone's
Peppino's
Taco Mesa
Wolfgang Pk. Cafe

Placentia
Rembrandt's

Rancho Santa Margarita
Opah
Tutto Fresco

San Clemente
BeachFire
Iva Lee's

Location Index

San Juan Capistrano
Cedar Creek
L'Hirondelle
Ramos House

Santa Ana
Antonello
Back Pocket
Baja Fresh
Bluewater Grill
California Piz. Kit.
Claim Jumper
Darya
Gustaf Anders
Gypsy Den
La Salsa
Memphis
Morton's Steak.
Olde Ship
Royal Khyber
Tangata

Seal Beach
Ruby's
Spaghettini
Walt's Wharf

Trabuco Canyon
Trabuco Oaks

Tustin
Black Sheep
California Piz. Kit.
Crab Cooker
Mimi's Cafe
Nieuport 17
Peppino's
Ruby's
Tony Roma's
Zov's Bistro

Westminster
Pho 79
Riviera/Fireside
Seafood Paradise
Thanh My

Yorba Linda
Fitness Pizza
Mimi's Cafe
Original Pancake Hse.
Wild Artichoke

Special Feature Index

SPECIAL FEATURES

For multi-location restaurants, the availability of index features may vary by location.

Breakfast
(See also Hotel Dining)
Art's Deli/SF
Babalu/W
Back on the Bch./W
Barney Greengrass/W
Belmont Brew./SB
Berri's Pizza/W
Blueberry/W
Brent's Deli/SF
Brighton Coffee/W
Broadway Deli/W
Cafe '50s†
Cafe Montana/W
Cafe Tartine/LA
Caffe Latte/LA
Canter's/LA
Clafoutis/LA
Clementine/W
Coral Tree/W
Cora's Coffee/W
Cottage/OC
Cravings/LA
Daily Grill†
Diner on Main/SG
Dish/SG
Doughboys/LA
Duke's Coffee/LA
Factor's Deli/LA
Farm of Bev. Hills†
Flora Kitchen/LA
French Country/W
Fromin's Rest.†
Greenblatt's Deli/LA
Griddle Cafe/LA
Gumbo Pot/LA
Hollywood Hills/LA
Hugo's†
Il Fornaio/W
Jack Sprat's/W
Jan's/LA
Jinky's†
Johnny Rebs'/SB
John O'Groats/W
Julienne/SG
Junior's/W
Kate Mantilini/W
King's Road Cafe/LA
Kokomo Cafe/LA
La Brea Bakery/SB
Langer's Deli/LA
Le Marmiton/W
Le Pain Quot.†
Literati Café/W
Mäni's Bakery†
Marmalade Café†
Marston's/SG
Martha's 22nd St./SB
Maxwell's Cafe/W
Mel's Drive-In†
Mimi's Cafe†
Mi Piace/SG
Mort's Deli/W
Mo's/SF
Nate 'n Al's/W
NBC Seafood/SG
Newsroom Café†
Noah's NY Bagels†
Original Pancake Hse./OC
Original Pantry Bak./LA
Original Pantry Cafe/LA
Pacific Din. Car†
Patrick's Road./W
Pie 'N Burger/SG
Rae's/W
Roll 'n Rye Deli/W
Roscoe's Hse.†
Rose Cafe/W
Ruby's†
17th St. Cafe/W
Side Street/OC
Swingers†
Toast Bakery/LA
Tommy's/LA
Uncle Bill's Pancake/SB
Urth Caffé/LA
Zinc Cafe/OC
Zov's Bistro/OC

Brunch
Accents/OC
Ammo/LA
Amuse Café/W
August Chris/SF
Aunt Kizzy's/W
Babalu/W
Bel-Air Hotel/W
Belvedere/W
Bluewater Grill†
Brass. des Artistes/W
Bravo Cucina/W
Brent's Deli/SF
Brighton Coffee/W

308 subscribe to zagat.com

Special Feature Index

Broadway Deli/W
Burger Contin./SG
Cafe Del Rey/W
Cafe El Cholo/OC
Campanile/LA
Canter's/LA
Cedar Creek/OC
Cheesecake Fact.†
Chez Jay/W
Chez Melange/SB
Clafoutis/LA
Cottage/OC
Cravings/LA
Daily Grill†
Du-par's/LA
El Torito†
El Torito Grill†
Emmanuel/SF
Farm of Bev. Hills†
Four Oaks/W
Gardens/W
Gemmell's/OC
Geoffrey's/W
Getty Ctr./W
Gladstone's Malibu/W
Granita/W
Hal's B&G/W
Hamburger Hamlet†
Il Fornaio†
Inn/Seventh Ray/W
Ivy/LA
Ivy/ Shore/W
Joe's/W
Kate Mantilini/W
Khoury's/SB
King's Fish Hse./SB
La Brea Bakery/SB
Lasher's/SB
Le Petit Four/LA
Lucille's/SB
Mäni's Bakery†
Market City/SF
Marmalade Café/SB
McCorm. & Schmick's†
Mi Piace/SF
Mirabelle/LA
Misto Caffe/SB
Mo's/SF
Mrs. Knott's/OC
Napa Rose/OC
Napa Valley Grille/W
Newsroom Café/W
Ocean Seafood/LA
Odyssey/SF
Off Vine/LA
One Pico/W
Pedals/W

Polo Lounge/W
Ralph Brennan's/OC
Raymond/SG
Real Food Daily/W
Reel Inn/W
Robin's Woodfire/SG
Röckenwagner/W
Roll 'n Rye Deli/W
Rose Cafe/W
Saddle Peak/SF
Salt Creek†
17th St. Cafe/W
Smoke House/SF
Spaghettini/OC
Standard/LA
Thousand Cranes/LA
Twin Palms/SG
Typhoon/W
Whale & Ale/SB

Business Dining
Accents/OC
Ago/LA
Alex/LA
Alto Palato/LA
Arnie Morton's/LA
Arroyo Chop/SG
Barney Greengrass/W
Belvedere/W
Bistango/OC
Bistro 45/SG
Breeze/W
Buffalo Club/W
Buggy Whip/SB
Ca'Brea/LA
Café Bizou/SF
Cafe Del Rey/W
Cafe Pinot/LA
Campanile/LA
Celestino/SG
Celestino Ital./LA
Cellar/OC
Chanteclair/OC
Checkers/LA
Cicada/LA
Dan Tana's/LA
Derek's/SG
Diaghilev/LA
Drago/W
Empress Pavilion/LA
Encore/W
555 East/SB
Fleming's Prime/OC
Gardens/W
Grace/LA
Grill/W
Gustaf Anders/OC

get updates at zagat.com

Special Feature Index

Houston's/OC
Il Fornaio/OC
Il Grano/W
Il Moro/W
Impresario/LA
JAR/LA
Josie Rest./W
Kincaid's/SB
La Cachette/W
L.A. Farm/W
La Finestra/SF
La Parisienne/SG
Madeo/LA
Madison/SB
Mandarin/W
Maple Drive/W
Mastro's Steak./W
McCorm. & Schmick's†
Mélisse/W
Michael's/W
Mistral/SF
Morton's Steak./OC
Mr. Stox/OC
Napa Valley Grille/W
Nick & Stef's/LA
Nieuport 17/OC
Oceanfront/W
One Pico/W
Pacific Din. Car/LA
Palm/LA
Parkway Grill/SG
Patina/LA
Pinot Bistro/SF
Pinot Hollywood/LA
Polo Lounge/W
Prego/OC
Reed's/SB
Reg. Bev. Wilshire/W
Ritz-Carlton Hunt./SG
Ritz Rest./OC
Riviera/Fireside/OC
Ruth's Chris†
Salt Creek/OC
Savannah Chop/OC
Scott's Seafood/OC
Smitty's Grill/SG
Spago/W
Studio/OC
Summit House/OC
Table Ten/OC
Tangata/OC
Taylor's Prime†
Thousand Cranes/LA
Traxx/LA
Tutto Mare/OC
Union/W
Valentino/W

Vert/LA
Vessia Rist./OC
Water Grill/LA
Windows/LA
Xiomara/SG
Yujean Kang's/SG
Zax/W
Zov's Bistro/OC
Zucca/LA

Entertainment

(Call for days and times of performances)

Addi's Tandoor/SB (sitar)
Alegria/SB (Latin)
Anaheim White/OC (piano)
Antonio's/LA (jazz/mariachi)
Arroyo Chop/SG (piano)
Bandera/W (jazz)
Barfly/LA (bands/comedy)
Beckham Grill/SG (guitar)
Bel-Air Hotel/W (piano)
Benihana† (chefs)
Berri's Pizza/SF (varies)
Billingsley's/SF (piano)
Bistango/OC (blues/jazz/Latin)
Bistro Gdn./Coldwtr./SF (piano)
Bob Morris'/W (varies)
Brandywine/SF (guitar)
Brass. des Artistes/W (French)
Buggy Whip/SB (piano)
Burger Contin./SG (belly dancing)
Cafe Del Rey/W (piano)
Cafe des Artistes/LA (DJ)
Cafe El Cholo/OC (mariachi)
Café Mundial/SG (jazz)
Cafe Tu Tu† (varies)
Carlito's Gardel/LA (varies)
Carousel/SG (varies)
Casa Antigua/W (Latin)
Cat & Custard/OC (piano)
Cedar Creek/OC (varies)
Cézanne/W (piano)
Chimayo/Beach/OC (varies)
Cinespace/LA (DJ)
Cuban Bistro/SG (Latin)
Dar Maghreb/LA (belly dancing)
Darya/OC (piano/violin)
Diaghilev/LA (harp/piano)
Duke's Mal./Hunt.† (varies)
El Cholo† (mariachi)
El Pollo Inka† (varies)
Encore/W (jazz/piano)
Feinstein's/LA (theatre)
Fenix/Argyle/LA (DJ/jazz/swing)
Fins/SF (jazz/piano)
French 75/OC (jazz/piano)

310 subscribe to zagat.com

Special Feature Index

Galletto/SF (bands)
Granita/W (varies)
Great Greek/SF (Greek)
Gypsy Den/OC (varies)
Hal's B&G/W (jazz)
House of Blues/LA (varies)
Il Cielo/W (strolling musicians)
Inka Grill/OC (DJ)
Javan/W (piano)
Jimmy's Tavern/W (piano)
Joe's Crab† (dancing waiters)
Koutoubia/W (belly dancing)
La Boca del Conga/LA (salsa)
La Cave/OC (jazz)
Las Brisas/OC (mariachi)
L'Hirondelle/OC (varies)
Lola's/LA (blues)
L'Opera/SB (opera singer)
Luciana's/OC (varies)
Lucille's† (blues)
Lunaria/W (jazz/swing)
Madison/SB (jazz/swing)
Maggiano's† (piano)
Maple Drive/W (jazz)
Marouch/LA (belly dancing)
Marrakesh/SF (belly dancing)
Mastro's/W (piano/vocals)
Matterhorn Chef/SF (accordion)
Memphis/OC (varies)
Miceli's† (singing waiters)
Mirabeau/OC (guitar/jazz)
Monsoon Cafe/W (bands)
Monty's Steak.† (varies)
Moonshadows/W (DJ)
Morels French/LA (jazz)
Moun/Tunis/LA (belly dancing)
Mr. Stox/OC (piano)
Nawab of India/W (Indian)
Olde Ship/OC (jazz/vocals)
One Pico/W (bass/piano)
Padri/SF (varies)
Papadakis Tav./SB (varies)
Parkway Grill/SG (jazz/piano)
Pavilion/OC (piano)
Polo Lounge/W (piano)
Ralph Brennan's/OC (jazz)
Reg. Bev. Wilshire/W (jazz)
Reign/W (jazz)
Ritz-Carlton Hunt./SG (piano)
Ritz Rest./OC (contemporary)
Romano's† (opera)
Saddle Ranch/LA (bull riding)
Salt Creek† (varies)
Shaherzad/W (piano)
Sir Winston's/SB (piano)
Sky Room/SB (jazz/swing)
Smoke House/SF (bands)
Spaghettini/OC (jazz)
Steelhead Brew. Co./OC (guitar)
Stevie's Creole/SF (varies)
Summit House/OC (piano)
Sunset Room/LA (DJ/jazz)
Tam O'Shanter/LA (piano)
Taps/OC (blues/jazz/rock)
Taverna Tony/W (belly dancing)
Tengu/W (DJ)
Tommy Bahama's/OC (bands)
Tournesol/SF (jazz)
21 Oceanfront/OC (jazz)
Twin Palms/SG (jazz)
Union/W (jazz)
Villa Nova/OC (band/piano)
Vitello's/SF (opera/piano)
Wahib's/SG (belly dancing)
Whale & Ale/SB (piano)
White Lotus/LA (DJ)

Garden Dining
Alex/LA
Allegria/W
Alto Palato/LA
Anaheim White/OC
Astro Burger†
Bamboo/W
Bluewater Grill/OC
Bravo Cucina/W
Buffalo Club/W
Bungalow/OC
Café Bizou/SF
Cafe Brasil/W
Cafe des Artistes/LA
Cafe Stella/LA
Celestino/SG
Chez Mimi/W
Encore/W
Fins/SF
Four Oaks/W
French 75/OC
Gardens/W
Geoffrey's/W
Gordon Biersch/OC
Habana/OC
Il Cielo/W
Inn/Seventh Ray/W
Ivy/LA
Kinara Cafe/LA
Knoll's Black Forest/W
Koi/LA
La Boheme/LA
L.A. Farm/W
Lasher's/SB
Le Chêne/SF
Les Deux Cafés/LA
Linq/LA

Special Feature Index

Michael's/W
Moishe's/LA
Mr. Cecil's/SF
Noah's NY Bagels/SG
Off Vine/LA
Pavilion/OC
Raymond/SG
Ritz Rest./OC
Rose Cafe/W
Sage/OC
Savannah Chop/OC
Schatzi on Main/W
Sisley Ital. Kit./SF
Teru Sushi/SF
Ti Amo/OC
Traxx/LA
Tutto Mare/OC
Yamashiro/LA
Zinc Cafe/OC

Historic Places

(Year opened; * building)
1881 Ramos House/OC*
1900 Five Crowns/OC*
1900 Raymond/SG*
1900 Saddle Peak/SF*
1906 Pete's Cafe/LA*
1908 Cole's P.E. Buffet/LA
1908 Philippe/Original/LA
1909 Anaheim White/OC*
1910 Via Veneto/W*
1912 Engine Co. No. 28/LA*
1912 Polo Lounge/W*
1916 Madison/SB*
1917 Cottage/OC*
1919 Musso & Frank/LA
1920 Aubergine/OC*
1920 Cannery Sea./OC
1920 La Paella/LA*
1920 Lasher's/SB*
1920 Old Spag. Factory/OC*
1921 Pacific Din. Car/LA
1922 Arches/OC
1922 Tam O'Shanter/LA
1923 El Cholo/LA
1923 Farfalla Tratt./LA*
1923 Lobster/W
1924 Edendale Grill/LA*
1924 Original Pantry Cafe/LA
1925 Palm/LA*
1926 Greenblatt's Deli/LA
1927 Benihana/W*
1927 Pig 'n' Whistle/LA*
1927 Taix French/LA
1928 Cafe Stella/LA*
1928 Ciao Tratt./LA*

1929 Fenix/Argyle/LA*
1930 Brighton Coffee/W
1931 Canter's/LA
1931 El Coyote/LA
1931 Petrelli's Steakhse./W
1933 Villa Nova/OC
1934 Galley/W
1936 Tom Bergin's/LA
1937 Damon's Steak./SG
1938 Cassell's/LA
1938 Chianti/LA
1938 Du-par's†
1938 Lawry's/W
1938 Paul's Cafe/SF*
1939 Formosa Cafe/LA
1939 Mrs. Knott's/OC
1939 Pink's Chili Dogs/LA
1942 Mr. Cecil's/W*
1945 Nate 'n Al's/W
1946 Chili John's/SF
1946 Monty's Steak./SG
1946 Smoke House/SF
1946 Tommy's/LA
1947 Apple Pan/W
1947 Bel-Air Hotel/W
1947 Langer's Deli/LA
1947 Mazzarino's/SF
1948 Du-par's†
1948 Factor's Deli/LA
1949 Dino's Italian/SG
1949 Miceli's/LA
1950 Hamburger Hamlet†
1950 Neptune's Net/W
1950 Toast Bakery/LA*
1950 Uncle Bill's Pancake/SB
1951 Crab Cooker/OC
1951 Derby/SG

Hotel Dining

Anaheim Marriott Stes.
  Five Feet/OC
Argyle Hotel
  Fenix/Argyle/LA
Avalon Hotel
  Blue on Blue/W
Bel-Air Hotel
  Bel-Air Hotel/W
Beverly Hills Hotel
  Polo Lounge/W
Beverly Hilton Hotel
  Trader Vic's/W
Beverly Laurel Hotel
  Swingers/LA
Beverly Terrace Hotel
  Trattoria Amici/W

312 subscribe to zagat.com

Special Feature Index

Breakers
  Sky Room/SB
Burbank Hilton
  Daily Grill/SF
Casa Del Mar
  Oceanfront/W
Century Plaza Hotel & Spa
  Breeze/W
Four Seasons Hotel
  Gardens/W
  Pavilion/OC
Grafton Hotel
  Balboa/LA
Grand Californian Hotel
  Napa Rose/OC
Hilton Checkers Hotel
  Checkers/LA
Hotel Laguna
  Claes/OC
Hyatt Huntington Beach
  Californian/OC
Le Merigot Hotel
  Cézanne/W
Loews Santa Monica Beach
  Lavande/W
Mondrian Hotel
  Asia de Cuba/LA
Montage Resort & Spa
  Studio/OC
New Otani Hotel
  Thousand Cranes/LA
Omni Los Angeles Hotel
  Noé/LA
Palos Verdes Inn
  Chez Melange/SB
Peninsula Beverly Hills Hotel
  Belvedere/W
Raffles L'Ermitage Hotel
  Jaan/W
Ramada Inn
  Du-par's/LA
Regent Beverly Wilshire
  Reg. Bev. Wilshire/W
Ritz-Carlton Huntington
  Ritz-Carlton Hunt./SG
Ritz-Carlton Laguna Niguel
  Ritz-Carlton Lag. Nig./OC
Shutters on the Beach
  One Pico/W
  Pedals/W
Standard Hotel
  Standard/LA
St. Regis Hotel
  Encore/W
St. Regis Monarch Beach
  Aqua/OC
  Motif/OC
Surf & Sand Hotel
  Splashes/OC
Sutton Place Hotel
  Accents/OC
Thousand Oaks Inn
  Du-par's/SF
Viceroy Hotel
  Whist/W
Westin South Coast Plaza
  Pinot Provence/OC
W Hotel
  Mojo/W
Wilshire Grand Hotel
  Seoul Jung/LA
Wyndham Bel Age Hotel
  Diaghilev/LA

"In" Places

Ago/LA
Alex/LA
Ammo/LA
Angelini Osteria/LA
A.O.C./LA
Asia de Cuba/LA
Aubergine/OC
Authentic Cafe/LA
Balboa/LA
Bandera/OC
Barfly/LA
Bastide/LA
Bombay Cafe/W
Border Grill/W
Brent's Deli/SF
Broadway Deli/W
Buddha's Belly/LA
Ca' del Sole/SF
Café Bizou/SF
Cafe Santorini/SG
Caffe Latte/LA
Campanile/LA
Capo/W
Casa Antigua/W
Chaya Brass./LA
Chaya Venice/W
Chinois/Main/W
Cicada/LA
Ciudad/LA
Cobra Lily/W
Cobras & Matadors/LA
Crustacean/W
Dan Tana's/LA
Edendale Grill/LA
Father's Office/W

Special Feature Index

Formosa Cafe/LA
G. Garvin's/LA
Giorgio Baldi/W
Grace/LA
Grill/W
Gyu-kaku/W
Hama Sushi/W
Hump, The/W
Ivy/LA
Ivy/ Shore/W
James' Beach/W
JAR/LA
Joe's/W
Jones Hollywood/LA
Josie Rest./W
Katana/LA
Katsu-ya/SF
Kincaid's/SB
Koi/LA
Le Petit Four/LA
Linq/LA
Little Door/LA
Lobster/W
Lotería! Grill/LA
Lucques/LA
Madre's/SG
Maple Drive/W
Mastro's Steak./W
Matsuhisa/W
Mélisse/W
Mimosa/LA
Morton's/LA
Nobu Malibu/W
Opah/OC
Oysters/OC
Padri/SF
Paladar/LA
Palm/LA
Parkway Grill/SG
Pig, The/LA
Pinot Bistro/SF
Pinot Hollywood/LA
Pinot Provence/OC
Pizzicotto/W
Polo Lounge/W
Rambutan Thai/LA
Red Pearl Kit./OC
Reign/W
Röckenwagner/W
Rock 'N Fish/SB
Roy's/OC
R-23/LA
Saladang/SG
Shiro/SG
Sona/LA
Sorrento Grille/OC
Standard/LA
Studio/OC
Sushi Nozawa/SF
Sushi Roku†
Taps/OC
Tengu/W
Tommy's/LA
Trattoria Amici/W
230 Forest/OC
Urth Caffé/LA
Versailles†
Vert/LA
Wabi-Sabi/W
Water Grill/LA
White Lotus/LA
Woody's/Beach/OC
Yard House/OC
Zen Grill†
Zinc Cafe/OC

Late Dining

(Weekday closing hour)
Airstream Diner/W (24 hrs.)
Arches/OC (1 AM)
Bar Marmont/LA (1:30 AM)
BCD Tofu Hse.† (24 hrs.)
Belly/LA (1 AM)
Berri's Pizza† (varies)
Bravo Cucina/W (varies)
Canter's/LA (24 hrs.)
Casa Vega/SF (1 AM)
Cheebo/LA (3 AM)
Cobra Lily/W (1:30 AM)
Dan Tana's/LA (1 AM)
Delmonico's Sea./SG (varies)
Dolce Enoteca/LA (2 AM)
Firefly/SF (2 AM)
Formosa Cafe/LA (2 AM)
Fred 62/LA (24 hrs.)
Greenblatt's Deli/LA (1:30 AM)
Hal's B&G/W (2 AM)
Hollywood Canteen/LA (2 AM)
In-N-Out Burger† (1 AM)
Jan's/LA (2 AM)
Johnnie's Pastrami/W (varies)
Jones Hollywood/LA (1:30 AM)
Kate Mantilini/W (varies)
Lamonica's Pizza/W (1 AM)
Linq/LA (1 AM)
Lola's/LA (1:30 AM)
Mel's Drive-In† (varies)
Mexicali/SF (1 AM)
Mirabelle/LA (12:30 AM)
Miyagi's/LA (2 AM)
Original Pantry Cafe/LA (24 hrs.)
Pacific Din. Cart† (varies)
Palms Thai/LA (12 AM)
Pink's Chili Dogs/LA (2 AM)

Special Feature Index

Polo Lounge/W (1 AM)
Roscoe's Hse./LA (varies)
Saddle Ranch/LA (2 AM)
Standard/LA (24 hrs.)
Swingers† (varies)
Thanh My/OC (1 AM)
Tommy's/LA (24 hrs.)
Wokcano/LA (varies)
Yard House/SB (varies)

Noteworthy Newcomers

Amuse Café/W
A.O.C./LA
Avenue/W
Bastide/LA
Buddha's Belly/LA
Cafe Atlantic/SG
Chloe/W
Cobra Lily/W
Dolce Enoteca/LA
Edendale Grill/LA
EM Bistro/LA
Five Feet/OC
Grace/LA
Grill at Pelican Hill/OC
Lawry's Carvery/OC
Lotería! Grill/LA
Menemsha/W
Noé/LA
Opaline/LA
Paladar/LA
Rambutan Thai/LA
Señor Fred/SF
Sona/LA
Spanish Kitchen/LA
Studio/OC
Trio Med. Grill/SB
White Lotus/LA

People-Watching

A.O.C./LA
Asia de Cuba/LA
Balboa/LA
Barfly/LA
Barney Greengrass/W
Blue on Blue/W
Buffalo Club/W
Bungalow/OC
Canal Club/W
Canter's/LA
Chaya Brass./LA
Chaya Venice/W
Chinois/Main/W
Clafoutis/LA
Crustacean/W
Edendale Grill/LA
EM Bistro/LA
Fonz's/SB
Formosa Cafe/LA
Gina Lee's/SB
Grace/LA
Granita/W
Grill/W
Habana/OC
Hump, The/W
Ivy/LA
Jones Hollywood/LA
Katana/LA
Koi/LA
La Boheme/LA
Linq/LA
Little Door/LA
Lola's/LA
Madre's/SG
Maple Drive/W
Memphis/OC
Morton's/LA
Mr. Chow/W
Nate 'n Al's/W
Paladar/LA
Palm/LA
Patina/LA
Pearl Dragon/W
Pig 'n' Whistle/LA
Pinot Hollywood/LA
Red Pearl Kit./OC
Sorrento Grille/OC
Spago/W
Spanish Kitchen/LA
Standard/LA
Sushi Roku†
Wabi-Sabi/W
White Lotus/LA
Woody's/Beach/OC
Yard House/OC
Zinc Cafe/OC

Power Scenes

Ago/LA
Alex/LA
A.O.C./LA
Aubergine/OC
Balboa/LA
Barney Greengrass/W
Bastide/LA
Bel-Air Hotel/W
Belvedere/W
Buffalo Club/W
Checkers/LA
Crustacean/W
Drago/W
Fleming's Prime/OC
Grace/LA
Grill/W
Grill at Pelican Hill/OC

Special Feature Index

Gustaf Anders/OC
Hamasaku/W
La Cachette/W
L.A. Farm/W
Locanda Veneta/LA
Mandarin/W
Maple Drive/W
Matsuhisa/W
Morton's/LA
Morton's Steak./OC
Motif/OC
Mr. Stox/OC
Musso & Frank/LA
Nate 'n Al's/W
Orso/LA
Paladar/LA
Palm/LA
Pascal/OC
Patina/LA
Pavilion/OC
Pinot Bistro/SF
Pinot Hollywood/LA
Pinot Provence/OC
Prego/OC
Ritz-Carlton Lag. Nig./OC
Ritz Rest./OC
Roy's/OC
Ruth's Chris/OC
Sona/LA
Spago/W
Studio/OC
Troquet/OC
Valentino/W
Water Grill/LA
White Lotus/LA

Romantic Places

Alex/LA
Anaheim White/OC
Antonello/OC
Aubergine/OC
Avenue/W
Bastide/LA
Beau Rivage/W
Bel-Air Hotel/W
Belvedere/W
Bistro 45/SG
Black Sheep/OC
Brandywine/SF
Brentwood Rest./W
Buffalo Club/W
Ca'Brea/LA
Cafe Del Rey/W
Cafe des Artistes/LA
Californian/OC
Capo/W
Cat & Custard/OC
Cellar/OC
Cézanne/W
Chanteclair/OC
Checkers/LA
Chez Mimi/W
Chianti/LA
Crustacean/W
Dar Maghreb/LA
Derek's/SG
Diaghilev/LA
EM Bistro/LA
Encore/W
Fenix/Argyle/LA
Four Oaks/W
Francesca/SB
French 75/OC
Gardens/W
Geoffrey's/W
Grace/LA
Grill at Pelican Hill/OC
Gustaf Anders/OC
Hobbit/OC
Il Cielo/W
Inn/Seventh Ray/W
Ivy/LA
Ivy/ Shore/W
Jaan/W
Joe's/W
Josie Rest./W
La Cachette/W
L.A. Farm/W
La Finestra/SF
La Parisienne/SG
Lavande/W
La Vie en Rose/OC
Le Chêne/SF
Linq/LA
Little Door/LA
L'Orangerie/LA
Luciana's/OC
Mélisse/W
Michael's/W
Mimosa/LA
Mirabeau/OC
Mistral/SF
Mr. Stox/OC
Oceanfront/W
One Pico/W
Opaline/LA
Pascal/OC
Patina/LA
Pavilion/OC
Picayo/OC
Pinot Bistro/SF
Pinot Provence/OC
Raymond/SG
Reg. Bev. Wilshire/W

Special Feature Index

Ritz-Carlton Hunt./SG
Ritz-Carlton Lag. Nig./OC
Ritz Rest./OC
Rothschild's/OC
Saddle Peak/SF
Savoury's/OC
Sky Room/SB
Sona/LA
Splashes/OC
Studio/OC
Thousand Cranes/LA
Ti Amo/OC
Trio Rist./SG
21 Oceanfront/OC
Union/W
Valentino/W
Villa Nova/OC
White Lotus/LA
Yamashiro/LA

Singles Scenes

Angeli Caffe/LA
Barfly/LA
Bayside/OC
BeachFire/OC
Beach House/W
Bistro 45/SG
Border Grill/W
Broadway Deli/W
Buddha's Belly/LA
Café Med/SG
Cafe Santorini/SG
Canter's/LA
Casa Antigua/W
Chaya Brass./LA
Chaya Venice/W
Chez Melange/SB
Cobra Lily/W
Edendale Grill/LA
El Coyote/LA
El Dorado/W
Electric Lotus/LA
Engine Co. No. 28/LA
Father's Office/W
Formosa Cafe/LA
Gardens/Glendon/W
Gordon Biersch†
Grace/LA
Gulfstream/OC
Habana/OC
Hal's B&G/W
Hama Sushi/W
Hillmont/LA
Houston's/OC
i Cugini/W
Ivy/ Shore/W
James' Beach/W
Jones Hollywood/LA
Katana/LA
Koi/LA
La Boheme/LA
Las Brisas/OC
Linq/LA
Lobster/W
Lola's/LA
Lunaria/W
Maple Drive/W
Mastro's Steak./W
McCorm. & Schmick's†
Mel's Drive-In/SF
Miyagi's/LA
Mojo/W
Morton's/LA
Nick & Stef's/LA
Ocean Ave./W
Oceanfront/W
Odyssey/SF
O-Nami/OC
Orso/LA
Outlaws B&G/W
Oysters/OC
Palm/LA
Parkway Grill/SG
Pinot Hollywood/LA
Red Pearl Kit./OC
RJ's Rib Joint/W
Rock 'N Fish/SB
Spanish Kitchen/LA
Standard/LA
Stanley's/SF
Steelhead Brew. Co./OC
Sushi Roku†
Swingers/LA
Tengu/W
Teru Sushi/SF
Trader Vic's/W
Tutto Mare/OC
230 Forest/OC
Typhoon/W
Union/W
Urth Caffé/LA
Wabi-Sabi/W
Water Grill/LA
White Lotus/LA
Woody's/Beach/OC
Ye Olde King's/W

Special Occasions

Antonello/OC
Aqua/OC
Arches/OC
Art's Deli/SF
Aubergine/OC
Avenue/W

get updates at zagat.com 317

Special Feature Index

Bastide/LA
Bayside/OC
Belvedere/W
Bistango/OC
Bistro 45/SG
Broadway Deli/W
Bungalow/OC
Ca'Brea/LA
Ca' del Sole/SF
Cafe Del Rey/W
Californian/OC
Cellar/OC
Chanteclair/OC
Chart House†
Checkers/LA
Chinois/Main/W
Cicada/LA
Diaghilev/LA
Dizz's as Is/OC
Drago/W
EM Bistro/LA
Emmanuel/SF
Encore/W
Five Crowns/OC
Fleming's Prime/OC
French 75/OC
Grace/LA
Gustaf Anders/OC
Hobbit/OC
Jaan/W
JAR/LA
Joe's/W
La Boheme/LA
La Cachette/W
Las Brisas/OC
La Vie en Rose/OC
Magic Carpet/LA
Mandarin/W
Mandarin Deli†
Manhattan Wonton/W
Mäni's Bakery/LA
Maple Drive/W
Maria's Italian/SF
Marino/LA
Mastro's Steak./W
Matsuhisa/W
Morton's Steak./OC
Napa Rose/OC
Napa Valley Grille/W
Nieuport 17/OC
One Pico/W
Palm/LA
Pascal/OC
Patina/LA
Pavilion/OC
Pinot Bistro/SF
Pinot Hollywood/LA
Pinot Provence/OC
Riviera/Fireside/OC
R-23/LA
Saddle Peak/SF
Sona/LA
Splashes/OC
Studio/OC
Taiko/W
Ti Amo/OC
Tuscany Il Rist./SF
21 Oceanfront/OC
Union/W
White Lotus/LA
Xiomara/SG
Zax/W

Views

Asia de Cuba/LA
Back on the Bch./W
Belmont Brew./SB
Blue Pacific/SB
Bluewater Grill†
Cafe Del Rey/W
Cafe Pinot/LA
Californian/OC
Cannery Sea./OC
Castaway/SF
Chart House†
Chimayo/Beach/OC
Claes/OC
Clafoutis/LA
D'Amore's Pizza/W
Delmonico's Sea./SG
Dexter's/OC
Duke's Mal./Hunt.†
El Torito†
El Torito Grill/W
Encounter/SB
Fenix/Argyle/LA
Fins/SF
Geoffrey's/W
Getty Ctr./W
Gladstone's Malibu/W
Gray Whale/W
Grill at Pelican Hill/OC
Gypsy Den/OC
Houston's/W
Hump, The/W
Il Boccaccio/SB
Impresario/LA
Ivy/ Shore/W
Las Brisas/OC
Lobster/W
Malibu Seafood/W
Martha's 22nd St./SB
Monsieur Marcel/LA

Special Feature Index

Moonshadows/W
Motif/OC
One Pico/W
Rist. Mamma Gina/OC
Ritz Rest./OC
Rusty Pelican/OC
Sir Winston's/SB
Sky Room/SB
Splashes/OC
Studio/OC
Summit House/OC
Tony P's Dockside/W
Tortilla Flats/OC
21 Oceanfront/OC
22nd St. Landing/SB
Typhoon/W
Windows/LA
Yamashiro/LA

Waterside

Back on the Bch./W
Bayside/OC
Belmont Brew./SB
Bluewater Grill†
Bob Morris'/W
Cafe Del Rey/W
Cannery Sea./OC
Chart House†
Cheesecake Fact.†
Chimayo/Beach/OC
Claes/OC
Duke's Mal./Hunt.†
El Torito†
Geoffrey's/W
Gladstone's Malibu/W
Gray Whale/W
Ivy/ Shore/W
Joe's Crab Shack†
Khoury's/SB
Kincaid's/SB
Las Brisas/OC
Lobster/W
Malibu Seafood/W
Martha's 22nd St./SB
Mirabeau/OC
Moonshadows/W
Motif/OC
Oceanfront/W
One Pico/W
Pedals/W
Rock 'N Fish/SB
Rusty Pelican/OC
Sky Room/SB
Splashes/OC
Tony P's Dockside/W
Tortilla Flats/OC
21 Oceanfront/OC
22nd St. Landing/SB
Villa Nova/OC

Winning Wine Lists

A.O.C./LA
Aqua/OC
Arroyo Chop/SG
Aubergine/OC
Bastide/LA
Bayside/OC
Bel-Air Hotel/W
Bistro 45/SG
Buffalo Club/W
Ca'Brea/LA
Cafe Del Rey/W
Cafe Pinot/LA
Campanile/LA
Celestino Ital./LA
Chaya Brass./LA
Checkers/LA
Chez Melange/SB
Chianti/LA
Chinois/Main/W
Crustacean/W
Drago/W
Encore/W
555 East/SB
Fleming's Prime/OC
Golden Truffle/OC
Grace/LA
Granita/W
Grill/W
Il Grano/W
Il Moro/W
Ivy/LA
JiRaffe/W
King's Fish Hse./SF
Le Chêne/SF
L'Opera/SB
L'Orangerie/LA
Maple Drive/W
Mélisse/W
Michael's/W
Mr. Stox/OC
Napa Rose/OC
Napa Valley Grille/W
Nick & Stef's/LA
Opaline/LA
Oysters/OC
Parkway Grill/SG
Patina/LA
Peppone/W
Pinot Bistro/SF
Pinot Hollywood/LA
Polo Lounge/W
Posto/SF
Primitivo Wine/W

Special Feature Index

Raymond/SG
Reg. Bev. Wilshire/W
Rest. Devon/SG
Ritz-Carlton Lag. Nig./OC
Ritz Rest./OC
Spago/W
Troquet/OC
2087 Amer. Bistro/SF
Valentino/W
Walt's Wharf/OC
Water Grill/LA

Worth a Trip

Anaheim
  Napa Rose/OC
Costa Mesa
  Pinot Provence/OC
  Troquet/OC
Dana Point
  Aqua/OC
  Ritz-Carlton Lag. Nig./OC
Fullerton
  Cellar/OC
Laguna Beach
  Five Feet/OC
  Studio/OC
Long Beach
  555 East/SB
  Frenchy's Bistro/SB
  L'Opera/SB
Malibu
  Beau Rivage/W
  Geoffrey's/W
  Granita/W
  Nobu Malibu/W
  Reel Inn/W
  Taverna Tony/W
  Tra Di Noi/W
Newport Beach
  Abe/OC
  Aubergine/OC
  Pascal/OC
  Pavilion/OC
  Ritz Rest./OC

San Gabriel Valley
  Babita/SG
  Empress Harbor/SG
  Golden Deli/SG
  Hayakawa/SG
  Lake Spring/SG
  NBC Seafood/SG
  Ocean Star/SG
  Rest. Devon/SG
  Tung Lai Shun/SG
Santa Ana
  Antonello/OC
  Gustaf Anders/OC
Santa Monica
  Lobster/W
Saugus
  Le Chêne/SF
South Bay
  Cafe Pierre/SB
  Chez Melange/SB
  Christine/SB
  Fonz's/SB
  Francesca/SB
  Gina Lee's/SB
  Il Boccaccio/SB
  Kincaid's/SB
  Michi/SB
  Papadakis Tav./SB
  Reed's/SB
  Sea Empress/SB
  Tsukiji/SB
Tustin
  Zov's Bistro/OC
West Valley/Conejo Valley
  Leila's/SF
  Mandevilla/SF
  Mi Piace/SF
  Padri/SF
  Saddle Peak/SF
  Tuscany II Rist./SF

Alphabetical Page Index

Restaurant locations are indicated by the following abbreviations: Los Angeles/Hollywood=LA; The Westside=W; The South Bay and Long Beach=SB; The San Fernando Valley and Burbank=SF; The San Gabriel Valley and Pasadena/Glendale=SG; Orange County=OC.

get updates at zagat.com

Alphabetical Page Index

Abbot's Pizza/W 86	Back Home/Lahaina/SB 158
ABC Seafood/LA 22	Back on the Beach/W 89
Abe/OC 236	Back Pocket/OC 237
Accents/OC 236	Baja Fresh 25, 90, 158, 180,
Addi's Tandoor/SB.........158	210, 238
Ago/LA...................22	Balboa/LA.................25
Aioli/SB 158	Ballona Fish Mkt./W 90
Airstream Diner/W 86	Bamboo/W.................90
Akbar................86, 210	Bamboo Inn/SF 180
A La Tarte Bistrot/W 86	Bandera 90, 238
Alegria/SB 158	Bangkok Four/OC 238
Alejo's 86, 158	Barbara's/Brewery/LA 25
Alessi Rist. & Bar/LA.......22	Barefoot B&G/LA 25
Alex/LA...................22	Barfly/LA..................26
Allegria/W.................87	Bar Marmont/LA 26
All India Café 87, 210	Barney Greengrass/W 90
Alto Palato/LA 22	Barney's Hamburger/W 91
Amazon Churras./OC......236	Barsac Brasserie/SF.......181
Ammo/LA.................22	Basilic/OC................238
Amuse Café/W.............87	Basix Cafe/LA 26
Anaheim White Hse./OC....236	Bastide/LA 26
Anarkali/LA................23	Bayou/SG 210
Angeli Caffe/LA 23	Bayside/OC...............238
Angelini Osteria/LA........23	BCD Tofu..............26, 159
Angelique Cafe/LA.........23	BeachFire/OC.............239
Anna's/W..................87	Beach House/W 91
Antica Pizzeria/W 87	Beau Rivage/W 91
Antonello/OC 236	Beckham Grill/SG 210
Antonio's/LA...............23	Bel-Air B&G/W 91
A.O.C./LA..................24	Bel-Air Hotel/W 91
Apple Pan/W...............88	Belly/LA 27
Aqua/OC 237	Belmont Brewing/SB 159
Arches/OC 237	Belvedere, The/W..........92
Arnie Morton's........24, 180	Benihana...92, 159, 181, 211, 239
Arroyo Chop Hse./SG 210	Benny's BBQ/W............92
Art's Deli/SF 180	Berri's Pizza............27, 92
Asahi Ramen/W............88	Bice...................27, 211
Asakuma/W 88	Big Mama's Rib/SG........211
Asanebo/SF 180	Billingsley's............92, 181
Asia de Cuba/LA 24	Bistango/OC 239
Asian Noodles/LA 24	Bistro 45/SG 211
Astro Burger...........24, 210	Bistro Gdn./Coldwtr./SF ...181
Asuka/W..................88	Bistro Laramie/SB 159
Aubergine/OC 237	Bistro 31/W................93
August Chris Cafe/SF 180	Bistro 21/LA 27
Aunt Kizzy's/W.............88	BJ's 93, 159, 181, 211
Authentic Cafe/LA 25	Black Sheep/OC 239
Avenue/W.................89	Bliss/LA...................27
A Votre Sante/W 89	Blueberry/W...............93
Axe/W....................89	Blue on Blue/W............93
Babalu/W 89	Blue Pacific/SB 159
Babita Mex./SG 210	Blue Pyramid/SG.........211

322 subscribe to zagat.com

Alphabetical Page Index

Bluewater Grill 159, 239	Caffe Latte/LA. 30
Bob Morris'/W 93	Caffe Pinguini/W 98
Bombay Bite/W. 94	Caioti Pizza/SF 182
Bombay Cafe/W 94	California Ckn. 30, 98, 183
Bombay Palace/W 94	Californian, The/OC 241
Bora Bora/SB 160	California Piz. Kit. . . 30, 98, 160,
Border Grill 94, 212	183, 213, 241
Bourbon St. 28, 94	California Wok 30, 98, 183
Brandywine/SF. 181	Camilo's/SG. 213
Brass. des Artistes/W 94	Campanile/LA 30
Bravo Cucina/W 95	Canal Club/W 98
Breeze/W. 95	Cannery Seafood/OC. 241
Brent's Deli/SF 182	Canter's/LA 31
Brentwood Rest./W 95	Capo/W 99
Brewski's/SB 160	Capriccio/OC 242
Bric/SG. 212	Carlito's Gardel/LA 31
Brighton Coffee/W. 95	Carmine's/SG 213
Britta's Café/OC 239	Carnival/SF 183
Broadway Deli/W. 95	Carousel 31, 214
Buca di Beppo 96, 160, 182, 212	Casa Antigua Cant./W. 99
Buddha's Belly/LA 28	Casa Bianca/SG. 214
Buffalo Club/W 96	Casablanca/W 99
Buggy Whip/SB 160	Casa Vega/SF 183
Bungalow, The/OC 240	Casbah Cafe/LA 31
Burger Continental/SG. 212	Cassell's/LA. 31
Ca'Brea/LA 28	Castaway/SF. 183
Ca' del Sole/SF 182	Catal Rest./OC. 242
Cadillac Cafe/SF 28	Cat & Custard Cup/OC 242
Café Atlantic/SG 212	Catch, The/OC. 242
Café Bizou 96, 182, 212	Cedar Creek Inn/OC. 242
Cafe Blanc/W 96	Celestino/SG 214
Cafe Brasil/W 96	Celestino Ital./LA 32
Cafe Del Rey/W. 97	Cellar, The/OC 243
Cafe des Artistes/LA 28	Cézanne/W 99
Cafe El Cholo/OC. 240	Cha Cha Cha/LA 32
Cafe '50s 97, 182	Cha Cha Cha Encino/SF. . . . 184
Café Med. 29, 212	Cha Cha Chicken/W. 99
Cafe Misto/W 97	Chameau/LA 32
Cafe Montana/W 97	Chan Dara 32, 100
Café Mundial/SG 213	Chanteclair/OC 243
Cafe Pascal/OC. 240	Chao Krung/LA 32
Cafe Pierre/SB 160	Chart Hse. 100, 160, 243
Cafe Pinot/LA 29	Chaya Brasserie/LA. 33
Cafe Plaka/OC. 240	Chaya Venice/W. 100
Cafe Santorini/SG 213	Checkers/LA 33
Cafe Stella/LA 29	Cheebo/LA. 33
Cafe Sushi/LA 29	Cheesecake Fact. . . . 100, 161, 184,
Cafe Tartine/LA 29	214, 243
Cafe Tu Tu 182, 240	Chevys 184, 214, 243
Cafe Zoolu/OC. 241	Chez Jay/W. 100
Caffe Citron/SG. 213	Chez Melange/SB 161
Caffe Delfini/W 97	

get updates at zagat.com

Alphabetical Page Index

Chez Mimi/W	101	De Mori/W	104
Chianti/LA	33	Depot, The/SB	162
Chianti Cucina/LA	33	Derby, The/SG	216
Chi Dynasty/LA	34	Derek's/SG	216
Chili John's/SF	184	Dexter's/OC	245
Chimayo at Bch./OC	244	Diaghilev/LA	37
Chin Chin	34, 101, 184	Diner on Main/SG	216
Chinois on Main/W	101	Dino's Italian/SG	216
Chloe/W	101	Dish/SG	216
Cholada/W	101	Di Stefano/W	104
Chow Fun/LA	34	Divino/W	104
Christine/SB	161	Dolce/OC	246
Christy's/SB	161	Dolce Enoteca/LA	37
Chung King/W	102	Doughboys/LA	37
Ciao Trattoria/LA	34	Drago/W	105
Cicada/LA	34	Dr. Hogly Wogly's/SF	185
Cinespace/LA	35	Duke's Coffee/LA	38
Cinnabar/SG	214	Duke's Mal./Hunt.	105, 246
Citrus City Grille/OC	244	Du-par's	38, 186
Ciudad/LA	35	Edendale Grill/LA	38
Claes/OC	244	El Cholo	38, 105, 162, 217, 246
Clafoutis/LA	35	El Coyote Cafe/LA	38
Claim Jumper	161, 185, 214, 244	El Dorado/W	105
Clay Pit/W	102	Electric Lotus/LA	39
Clementine/W	102	El Pollo Inka	105, 162, 217
Cobra Lily/W	102	El Tepeyac	39, 217
Cobras & Matadors/LA	35	El Texate/W	106
Cole's P.E. Buffet/LA	35	El Torito	106, 163, 186, 217
Coral Tree Café/W	102	El Torito Grill	106, 163, 246
Cora's Coffee/W	103	EM Bistro/LA	39
Cottage, The/OC	244	Emmanuel/SF	186
Coyote Cantina/SB	162	Empress Harbor/SG	217
Cozymel's/SB	162	Empress Pavilion/LA	39
Crab Cooker/OC	245	Encore/W	106
Cravings/LA	36	Encounter/SB	163
Crazy Fish/W	103	Engine Co. No. 28/LA	39
Crocodile Café	103, 185, 215	Enterprise Fish/W	106
Crustacean/W	103	Eurochow/W	107
Cuban Bistro/SG	215	Fabiolus Café/LA	40
Cynthia's/LA	36	Fab's Italian/SF	186
Daily Grill	36, 103, 162, 185, 245	Factor's Deli/LA	40
Dal Rae/SG	215	Falafel King/W	107
Damon's Steak./SG	215	Farfalla Trattoria/LA	40
D'Amore's	103, 185	Farm of Bev. Hills	40, 107
Dan Tana's/LA	36	Far Niente/SG	217
Da Pasquale/W	104	Fat Fish/LA	40
Dar Maghreb/LA	36	Father's Office/W	107
Darya/OC	245	Feast from East/W	107
De Lacey's/SG	215	Feinstein's/Cinegrill/LA	41
Delmonico's Lobster/SF	185	Fenix/Argyle/LA	41
Delmonico's Seafood	37, 215	Figaro Brasserie/LA	41
Delphi Greek/W	104		

Alphabetical Page Index

Fins/SF	186	Gray Whale/W	111
Firefly/SF	187	Great Greek/SF	188
Firefly Bistro/SG	217	Greco's/SG	219
Fish Market/OC	246	Greenblatt's Deli/LA	44
Fitness Pizza/OC	246	Green Field Churr.	164, 219
Five Crowns/OC	247	Griddle Cafe/LA	44
5 Dudley/W	108	Grill, The/W	111
Five Feet/OC	247	Grill at Pelican Hill/OC	248
555 East/SB	163	Grill on Hollywood/LA	44
Five Sixty-One/SG	218	Guelaguetza/W	111
Flavor of India/LA	41	Guido's/W	111
Fleming's Prime	163, 247	Gulfstream	112, 249
Flora Kitchen/LA	41	Gulliver's/OC	249
Fonz's/SB	163	Gumbo Pot/LA	44
Formosa Cafe/LA	42	Gustaf Anders/OC	249
Four Oaks/W	108	Gypsy Den/OC	249
410 Boyd/LA	42	Gyu-kaku/W	112
Fox Sports Grill/OC	247	Habana/OC	249
Francesca/SB	164	Halie/SG	219
Frankie & Johnnie's	42, 108	Hal's B&G/W	112
Fred 62/LA	42	Hamasaku/W	112
French Country/W	108	Hama Sushi/W	112
French 75/OC	248	Hamburger Hamlet	44, 113, 188, 219
Frenchy's Bistro/SB	164		
Fresco Rist./SG	218	Hard Rock Cafe	45, 188
Fritto Misto	108, 164	Harold & Belle's/LA	45
Fromin's	109, 187	Hayakawa/SG	219
Fu-Shing/SG	218	Heroes B&G/OC	250
Galletto/SF	187	Hibachi Steak/OC	250
Galley, The/W	109	Hide Sushi/W	113
Gardens/W	109	Hillmont/LA	45
Gardens/Glendon/W	109	Hirosuke/SF	188
Gate of India/W	109	Hirozen/LA	45
Gaucho Grill	42, 109, 187, 218	Hobbit, The/OC	250
Gemmell's/OC	248	Hollywood Canteen/LA	45
Genghis Cohen/LA	43	Hollywood Hills/LA	46
Gennaro's Rist./SG	218	Hop Li	46, 113
Geoffrey's/W	110	Hop Woo/W	113
Getty Center/W	110	House, The/LA	46
G. Garvin's/LA	43	House of Blues/LA	46
Gina Lee's Bistro/SB	164	Houston's	113, 164, 219, 250
Giorgio Baldi/W	110	Hugo's	46, 188
Girasole/LA	43	Hump, The/W	113
Gladstone's Malibu/W	110	Hu's Szechwan/W	114
Gladstone's Univ./SF	187	Ichibiri/OC	250
Globe Venice Bch./W	110	i Cugini/W	114
Golden Deli/SG	218	Il Boccaccio/SB	165
Golden Truffle/OC	248	Il Buco/W	114
Gordon Biersch	187, 219, 248	Il Capriccio/LA	47
Grace/LA	43	Il Cielo/W	114
Grand Lux Café/LA	43	Il Fornaio	115, 165, 220, 250
Granita/W	111	Il Forno/W	115

get updates at zagat.com 325

Alphabetical Page Index

Il Grano/W 115
Il Moro/W 115
Il Pastaio/W 115
Impresario/LA 47
India's Oven 47, 116
India's Tandoori ...47, 116, 188
Indo Cafe/W 116
Inka Grill 165, 251
Inn of Seventh Ray/W 116
In-N-Out Burger... 47, 116, 165, 188, 220, 251
Iroha/SF...............189
Islands...116, 165, 189, 220, 251
Ita-Cho/LA..............48
Iva Lee's/OC 251
Ivy, The/LA 48
Ivy at the Shore/W......117
Jaan/W 117
JackShrimp/OC 252
Jackson's Village/SB 165
Jack Sprat's/W.........117
Jacopo's 48, 117
James' Beach/W........117
Jan's/LA 48
Jar/LA 48
Javan/W 118
Javier's/OC 252
Jimmy's Tavern/W 118
Jinky's 118, 189
JiRaffe/W 118
Jitlada/LA 48
Jody Maroni's ...118, 166, 189, 252
Joe's/W 119
Joe's Crab.........166, 252
Johnnie's NY Pizz....49, 119, 189
Johnnie's Pastrami/W......119
Johnny Rebs'/SB 166
Johnny Rockets ... 49, 119, 166, 190, 220
John O'Groats/W.........119
Jones Hollywood/LA........49
Josie Rest./W...........120
JR's BBQ/W 120
JR Seafood/W 120
Juliano's Raw/W 120
Julienne/SG 220
Junior's/W 120
Kabob & Chin. 49, 121
Kamiyama/SB 166
Katana/LA..............49
Kate Mantilini/W 121
Katsu-ya/SF 190

Kay 'n Dave's/W..........121
Khoury's/SB 167
Killer Shrimp.........121, 190
Kinara Cafe/LA...........50
Kincaid's/SB 167
King's Fish.......167, 190, 252
King's Road/LA...........50
Kitchen, The/LA..........50
Knoll's Black Forest/W 121
Koi/LA 50
Kokomo Cafe/LA 50
Koo Koo Roo..... 51, 121, 167, 190, 220, 252
Koutoubia/W 122
Kung Pao 51, 190
La Boca del Conga/LA 51
La Boheme/LA 51
La Bottega 51, 122
La Brea Bakery/SB 167
La Bruschetta Rist./W......122
La Cachette/W..........122
La Cave/OC 253
La Dijonaise/W 122
L.A. Farm/W 123
La Finestra/SF 190
La Fondue/SF 191
LA Food Show/SB 168
La Frite/SF..............191
Lake Spring/SG 221
La Korea/LA.............52
La Loggia/SF............191
La Luna/LA 52
Lamonica's Pizza/W 123
Langer's Deli/LA 52
La Paella/LA.............52
La Parisienne/SG.........221
La Parrilla/LA............52
La Pergola/SF...........191
La Salsa ..53, 123, 168, 191, 253
Las Brisas/OC 253
La Scala/W............123
La Scala Presto/W 123
La Serenata/Garibaldi...53, 124
La Serenata Gourmet/W ...124
Lasher's/SB 168
Lavande/W............124
La Vecchia Cucina/W......124
La Vie en Rose/OC........253
Lawry's Carvery/OC.......253
Lawry's Prime Rib/W......124
Le Chêne/SF 192
Leila's/SF..............192

326 subscribe to zagat.com

Alphabetical Page Index

Le Marmiton/W	124	Marino/LA	57
Le Pain Quot.	53, 125	Mario's Peruvian/LA	58
Le Petit Bistro	53, 125, 192	Marix Tex Mex	58, 128
Le Petit Café/W	125	Market City Caffe/SF	193
Le Petit Four/LA	53	Marmalade Café	128, 169, 193
Le Petit Greek/LA	54	Marouch/LA	58
Le Saigon/W	125	Marrakesh/SF	193
Les Deux Cafés/LA	54	Marston's/SG	222
Les Sisters/SF	192	Martha's 22nd St./SB	170
L'Hirondelle/OC	254	Mascarpone's/OC	255
Lilly's French/W	125	Mastro's Steak./W	128
Linq/LA	54	Matsuhisa/W	128
Literati Café/W	125	Matteo's/W	128
Little Door/LA	54	Matteo's Hoboken/W	129
Lobster, The/W	126	Matterhorn Chef/SF	193
Locanda del Lago/W	126	Max Rest./SF	194
Locanda Veneta/LA	54	Maxwell's Cafe/W	129
Lodge, The/OC	254	Mayur/OC	255
Loft, The/SB	168	Mazzarino's/SF	194
Lola's/LA	55	McCorm. & Schmick's	58, 129, 170, 222, 255
L'Opera/SB	168		
L'Orangerie/LA	55	Mélisse/W	129
Lotería! Grill/LA	55	Mel's Drive-In	58, 194
Louise's	55	Melting Pot/OC	255
Louise's Tratt.	55, 126, 192, 221	Memphis/OC	255
Luciana's/OC	254	Menemsha/W	129
Lucille's Smokehse.	169, 254	Menjin/LA	59
Lucques/LA	55	Mexicali/SF	194
Lunaria/W	126	Mexico City/LA	59
Madame Wu's/LA	56	Miceli's	59, 194
Madeo/LA	56	Michael's/W	129
Madison, The/SB	169	Michelia/LA	59
Madre's/SG	221	Michi/SB	170
Magalys/SG	221	Milky Way/LA	59
Maggiano's	56, 192, 254	Mimi's	60, 170, 194, 222, 255
Magic Carpet/LA	56	Mimosa/LA	60
Maison Akira/SG	221	Mi Piace	195, 222
Mako/W	126	Mirabeau/OC	256
Malibu Seafood/W	127	Mirabelle/LA	60
Mama D's/SB	169	Mi Ranchito/W	130
Mama Rose/OC	254	Mishima	60, 130, 170
Mandarette/LA	57	Misto Caffe/SB	170
Mandarin, The/W	127	Mistral/SF	195
Mandarin Deli	57, 192, 222	Miyagi's/LA	60
Mandevilla/SF	192	Moishe's/LA	60
Manhattan Wonton/W	127	Mojo/W	130
Mäni's Bakery	57, 127	Momoyama/SB	170
Manna/LA	57	Mon Kee's/LA	61
Maple Drive/W	127	Monsieur Marcel/LA	61
Marcello Tuscany/SB	169	Monsoon Cafe/W	130
Marguerite/W	127	Monte Alban/W	130
Maria's	193, 222	Monty's	195, 222

get updates at zagat.com   327

Alphabetical Page Index

Moonshadows/W 131
Morels First Floor/LA........61
Morels French/LA 61
Mori Sushi/W 131
Morton's/LA 61
Morton's Steakhse./OC.....256
Mort's Deli/W 131
Mo's/SF 195
Motif/OC 256
Moun of Tunis/LA...........62
Mountain View/SG 222
Moustache Café 62, 131
Mr. Cecil's 131, 195
Mr. Chow/W 131
Mrs. Knott's/OC 256
Mr. Stox/OC 257
Mulberry St. Pizz.......132, 195
Mulberry St. Rist./OC.......257
Muldoons Irish/OC.........257
Musha 132, 171
Musso & Frank/LA..........62
Nak Won Korean/LA 62
Napa Rose/OC 257
Napa Valley Grille/W......132
Naples Rist./OC 258
Natalee Thai/W 132
Nate 'n Al's/W 132
Natraj/OC 258
Nawab of India/W 133
NBC Seafood/SG 223
Neptune's Net/W 133
Newsroom Café 62, 133
Nick & Stef's/LA...........63
Nicola's Kitchen/SF........196
Nic's/W 133
Nieuport 17/OC............258
Nishimura/LA 63
Nizam/W 133
Noah's Bagels 63, 134, 171,
 196, 223
Nobu Malibu/W 134
Noé/LA 63
Nonya/SG 223
Noura Cafe/LA 63
Nyala Ethiopian/LA 63
Ocean Ave. Seafood/W 134
Oceanfront/W 134
Ocean Seafood/LA 64
Ocean Star/SG 223
Odyssey/SF 196
Off Vine/LA 64
Olde Ship/OC 258
Old Spag. Factory/OC 258
Olive Garden .. 134, 171, 196, 223
Omino Sushi/SF 196
O-Nami 171, 223, 259
One Pico/W 135
Opah/OC 259
Opaline/LA 64
Original Fish Co./OC 259
Original Pancake/OC......259
Original Pantry Bak./LA 64
Original Pantry Cafe/LA 64
Orso/LA 65
Osteria Nonni/LA..........65
Otto's/LA 65
Outback Steak. .. 171, 196, 224, 259
Outlaws B&G/W 135
Out Take Cafe/SF.........196
Oysters/OC 260
Pace/LA 65
Pacific Din. Car 65, 135
Pacifico's/W.............135
Paco's Tacos 135, 171
Padri/SF 197
Paladar/LA 66
Palermo/LA..............66
Palm/LA.................66
Palms Thai/LA 66
Palomino/W 135
Pammolli/W 136
Panda Inn/SG............224
Pane e Vino/LA 66
Paolo's Rist./OC 260
Papa Cristo's/LA 67
Papadakis Tav./SB 172
Parkway Grill/SG 224
Pascal/OC 260
Pastina/W...............136
Pastis/LA................67
Pat & Oscar's/SB.........172
Patina/LA 67
Patinette Cafe/LA 67
Patrick's Roadhse./W 136
Pat's/LA................68
Paul's Cafe/SF 197
Pavilion/OC 260
Pearl Dragon/W..........136
Pedals/W 136
Pei Wei/OC 260
Pentimento Cafe/LA 68
Peppino's/OC 261
Peppone/W 137

328   subscribe to zagat.com

Alphabetical Page Index

Pescadou Bistro/OC	261	Ritz Rest./OC	264
Pete's Cafe/LA	68	Rive Gauche Cafe/SF	199
Petrelli's Steak./W	137	Riviera/Fireside/OC	264
P.F. Chang's	68, 137, 172, 197, 224, 261	RJ's the Rib Joint/W	140
		Robin's Woodfire/SG	225
Philippe the Original/LA	68	Röckenwagner/W	140
Pho Bac Huynh/W	137	Rock 'N Fish/SB	172
Pho Café/LA	68	Roll 'n Rye Deli/W	141
Pho 79	69, 224, 261	Romano's	173, 199, 226
Piatti/SF	197	Roma via Paris/SF	199
Picanha Churr./SF	197	Roscoe's	71, 173, 226
Picayo/OC	261	Rose Cafe/W	141
Piccolo Paradiso/W	137	Rosine's/OC	264
Pie 'N Burger/SG	224	Rosti	141, 199
Pig, The/LA	69	Rothschild's/OC	264
Pig 'n' Whistle/LA	69	Royal Khyber/OC	265
Pink's Chili Dogs/LA	69	Royal Star/W	141
Pinot Bistro/SF	198	Royal Thai/OC	265
Pinot Hollywood/LA	69	Roy's/OC	265
Pinot Provence/OC	262	R-23/LA	71
Pizzicotto/W	138	Ruby's	141, 173, 199, 226, 265
Plums Cafe/OC	262	Russell's Burgers/SG	226
Polo Lounge/W	138	Rusty Pelican/OC	265
Poquito Mas	70, 138, 198	Ruth's Chris	142, 266
Porterhouse Bistro/W	138	Saddle Peak Lodge/SF	199
Posto/SF	198	Saddle Ranch/LA	71
Prado/LA	70	Sage/OC	266
Prego	70, 138, 198, 262	Saladang/SG	226
Primitivo Wine/W	138	Salt Creek	200, 266
Prizzi's Piazza/LA	70	Sam Woo's/OC	266
Radhika's/SG	225	Sandbag's/W	142
Rae's/W	139	San Gennaro Cafe/W	142
Ragin' Cajun	172, 262	Savannah Chop/OC	266
Ralph Brennan's/OC	262	Savoury's/OC	267
Rambutan Thai/LA	70	Sawtelle Kitchen/W	142
Ramos House Cafe/OC	263	Scampi/SG	226
Raymond, The/SG	225	Schatzi on Main/W	142
Real Food Daily	71, 139	Scott's Seafood/OC	267
Rebecca's/W	139	Sea Empress/SB	173
Reddi Chick BBQ/W	139	Seafood Paradise/OC	267
Red Moon Cafe/W	139	Sea Harbour/SG	227
Red Pearl Kitchen/OC	263	Seashell/SF	200
Reed's/SB	172	Señor Fred/SF	200
Reel Inn/W	139	Sensasian/OC	267
Reg. Bev. Wilshire/W	140	Seoul Jung/LA	72
Reign/W	140	17th Street Cafe/W	143
Rembrandt's/OC	263	Shabu Shabu/LA	72
Rest. Devon/SG	225	Shabu 2/W	143
Ribs USA/SF	198	Shack, The/W	143
Rist. Mamma Gina/OC	263	Shaherzad/W	143
Ritz-Carlton Hunt./SG	225	Sharky's	72, 200
Ritz-Carlton Lag. Nig./OC	263	Shenandoah Cafe/SB	173

get updates at zagat.com

Alphabetical Page Index

Shiro/SG	227
Side Street Cafe/OC	267
Sir Winston's/SB	174
Sisley Ital.	143, 200
Sky Room/SB	174
Smitty's Grill/SG	227
Smoke House/SF	201
Sofi/LA	72
Soleil Westwood/W	144
SolyAzul/SG	227
Sona/LA	72
Sonora Cafe/LA	73
Soot Bull Jeep/LA	73
Sorrento Grille/OC	268
Souplantation	73, 144, 174, 201, 227
South Street/W	144
Spaghettini/OC	268
Spago/W	144
Spanish Kitchen/LA	73
Spark Woodfire	201, 268
Splashes/OC	268
Sprazzo Cuc. Ital./W	144
Spumante/SF	201
Standard, The/LA	73
Stanley's/SF	201
Steelhead Brewing/OC	268
Stevie's Creole/SF	201
Stinking Rose/W	145
Studio/OC	269
Summit House/OC	269
Sunnin/W	145
Sunset Room/LA	74
Surya India/LA	74
Sushi Masu/W	145
Sushi Mon/LA	74
Sushi Nozawa/SF	202
Sushi Roku	74, 145, 228
Sushi Sasabune/W	145
Sweet Lady Jane/LA	74
Swingers	75, 145
Table Ten/OC	269
Taco Loco/OC	269
Taco Mesa/OC	270
Taiko	146, 174
Taiko Jap./OC	270
Taix French/LA	75
Takao/W	146
Talesai	75, 146, 202
Tama Sushi/SF	202
Tam O'Shanter Inn/LA	75
Tangata/OC	270
Tanino/W	146
Tantra/LA	75
Taps/OC	270
Taste of Manila/SG	228
Taverna Tony/W	146
Taylor's Prime	76, 228
Tempo/SF	202
Tengu/W	146
Teru Sushi/SF	202
Tesoro Trattoria/LA	76
Thai Dishes	147, 174, 228
Thaifoon/OC	271
Thai This/OC	271
Thanh My/OC	271
Thousand Cranes/LA	76
Ti Amo/OC	271
Tibet Nepal/SG	228
Tidal Wave/SG	228
Tlapazola Grill/W	147
Toast Bakery/LA	76
Todai	76, 174, 202, 228
Tom Bergin's/LA	77
Tommy Bahama's/OC	271
Tommy's/LA	77
Tommy Tang's/LA	77
Tony P's Dockside/W	147
Tony Roma's	147, 203, 229, 272
Torafuku/W	148
Tortilla Flats/OC	272
Toscana/W	148
Tournesol/SF	203
Towne/SB	174
Trabuco Oaks/OC	272
Trader Vic's/W	148
Tra Di Noi/W	148
Trastevere	77, 148
Trattoria Amici/W	148
Traxx/LA	77
Tre Venezie/SG	229
Trio Med. Grill/SB	175
Trio Rist./SG	229
Troquet/OC	272
Tsuji No Hana/W	149
Tsukiji/SB	175
Tuk Tuk Thai/LA	78
Tulipano/SG	229
Tung Lai Shun/SG	229
Turner New Zeal./OC	272
Tuscany II Rist./SF	203
Tutto Fresco/OC	273
Tutto Mare/OC	273
2087 An Amer. Bistro/SF	203

330   subscribe to zagat.com

Alphabetical Page Index

21 Oceanfront/OC 273	Whale & Ale/SB 176
2117/W 149	Whist/W 152
22nd St. Landing/SB 175	White Lotus/LA 80
26 Beach Café/W 149	Wild Artichoke/OC 274
Twin Palms/SG 229	Windows/LA 80
230 Forest/OC 273	Wine Bistro/SF 204
Typhoon/W 149	Wokcano/LA 80
Ubon/LA 78	Wolfgang Puck ... 80, 152, 204, 274
Ulysses Voyage/LA 78	Wood Ranch 80, 204, 275
Uncle Bill's/SB 175	Woody's/Beach/OC 275
Union/W 149	Woo Lae Oak 81, 152
Urth Caffé/LA 78	Xi'an/W 152
Uzbekistan/LA 78	Xiomara/SG 230
U-Zen/W 150	Yabu 81, 152
Valentino/W 150	Yamashiro/LA 81
vermont/LA 79	Yang Chow 81, 205, 230
Versailles 79, 150, 175, 203	Yard House 176, 275
Vert/LA 79	Ye Olde King's Head/W 152
Vessia Ristorante/OC 273	Yi Dynasty/OC 275
Via Veneto/W 150	Yoshida/SG 230
Village Pizzeria/LA 79	Yujean Kang's/SG 230
Villa Nova/OC 274	Yujean Kang's Asian/OC ... 275
Villa Piacere/SF 204	Yves' Bistro/OC 275
Vincenti/W 150	Zankou Ckn .... .81, 205, 231, 276
V.I.P. Harbor/W 151	Zax/W 152
Vessia Ristorante/OC	Zazou/SB 176
Via Veneto/W 150	Zeidler's Café/W 153
Vitello's/SF 204	Zeke's Smokehse./SG 231
Vito/W 151	Zen Grill 82, 153
Vittorio/W 151	Zinc Cafe/OC 276
Wabi-Sabi/W 151	Zita Trattoria/LA 82
Wahib's Mid. East/SG 230	Zov's Bistro/OC 276
Walt's Wharf/OC 274	Z'tejas/OC 276
Warszawa/W 151	Zucca/LA 82
Wasa/OC 274	
Water Grill/LA 79	

get updates at zagat.com

Wine Vintage Chart

This chart is designed to help you select wine to go with your meal. It is based on the same 0 to 30 scale used throughout this *Survey*. The ratings (prepared by our friend **Howard Stravitz**, a professor at the University of South Carolina) reflect both the quality of the vintage and the wine's readiness for present consumption. Thus, if a wine is not fully mature or is over the hill, its rating has been reduced. We do not include 1987, 1991–1993 vintages because they are not especially recommended for most areas.

	'85	'86	'88	'89	'90	'94	'95	'96	'97	'98	'99	'00	'01
WHITES													
French:													
Alsace	24	18	22	28	28	26	25	23	23	25	23	25	26
Burgundy	26	25	17	25	24	15	29	28	25	24	25	22	20
Loire Valley	–	–	–	–	25	23	24	26	24	23	24	25	23
Champagne	28	25	24	26	29	–	26	27	24	24	25	25	–
Sauternes	21	28	29	25	27	–	20	23	27	22	22	22	28
California (Napa, Sonoma, Mendocino):													
Chardonnay	–	–	–	–	–	22	27	23	27	25	25	23	26
Sauvignon Blanc/Semillon	–	–	–	–	–	–	–	–	24	24	25	22	26
REDS													
French:													
Bordeaux	25	26	24	27	29	22	26	25	23	24	23	25	23
Burgundy	23	–	21	25	28	–	26	27	25	22	27	22	20
Rhône	25	19	27	29	29	24	25	23	25	28	26	27	24
Beaujolais	–	–	–	–	–	–	–	–	23	22	25	25	18
California (Napa, Sonoma, Mendocino):													
Cab./Merlot	26	26	–	21	28	29	27	25	28	23	26	23	26
Pinot Noir	–	–	–	–	–	27	24	24	26	25	26	25	27
Zinfandel	–	–	–	–	–	25	22	23	21	22	24	19	24
Italian:													
Tuscany	26	–	24	–	26	22	25	20	28	24	27	26	25
Piedmont	26	–	26	28	29	–	23	26	28	26	25	24	22

So, where are you going *after* dinner?

ZAGATSURVEY

2004

LOS ANGELES NIGHTLIFE

Check out the Zagat Survey Los Angeles Nightlife guide. Over 700 Tinseltown bars, clubs and lounges were rated and reviewed by 2,000+ night-crawling natives – who weren't too tired to tell us the truth.

Available wherever books are sold, at zagat.com or by calling **888-371-5440**.